EDITED BY

ROBERT M. BAIRD
STUART E. ROSENBAUM

THE
DEATH
PENALTY

DEBATING THE MORAL, LEGAL, AND POLITICAL ISSUES

Prometheus Books

59 John Glenn Drive
Amherst, New York 14228–2119

Published 2011 by Prometheus Books

Inquiries should be addressed to
Prometheus Books
59 John Glenn Drive
Amherst, New York 14228–2119
VOICE: 716–691–0133
FAX: 716–691–0137
WWW.PROMETHEUSBOOKS.COM

15 14 13 12 11   5 4 3 2 1

Library of Congress Cataloging-in-Publication Data

The death penalty : debating the moral, legal, and political issues / edited by
Robert M. Baird and Stuart E. Rosenbaum.
    p. cm.
Includes bibliographical references.
ISBN 978-1-59102-760-7 (pbk.)
    1. Capital punishment—Moral and ethical aspects—United States.
2. Capital punishment—Political aspects—United States. 3. Capital
punishment—United States—History. 4. Capital punishment—United States—
Cases. 5. Capital punishment—History. I. Baird, Robert M. II. Rosenbaum,
Stuart E.

KF9227.C2D41175 2010
364.660973—dc22

                                                                2010013073

Printed in the United States of America

CONTENTS

PART THREE: CAPITAL PUNISHMENT AND LETHAL INJECTION

PART FOUR: CAPITAL PUNISHMENT AND THE RAPE OF CHILDREN

PART FIVE: CAPITAL PUNISHMENT AND DNA

PART SIX: CAPITAL PUNISHMENT AND RACISM

INTRODUCTION

In early October 1283, Prince David of Wales was hanged, drawn, and quartered for an attack during the Easter season against the English King Edward. This occasion may have been the first use of this particularly gruesome form of execution, one that was rare but was occasionally employed until it was officially ruled unacceptable in 1870. Edward intended to make an especially vivid example of what would happen to rebels against his authority.

On March 25, 1586, Margaret Clitherow was pressed to death in York for her failure to plead in the charge against her that she had harbored Catholic priests. Margaret was herself a Catholic, though her husband was a Protestant, as were many of her friends; her crime—she probably was guilty of sheltering Catholic priests—was modest, but her Catholic faith was important to her, and she refused to admit or deny the charge. Margaret's death came from her being pressed between large stones, additional stones being dropped on her until she expired. Margaret was a woman well loved by her husband and neighbors, most of whom were Protestant, and she died willingly and faithfully at the age of thirty. Margaret Clitherow became St. Margaret of York in 1970.

The deaths of Prince David of Wales and St. Margaret of York were not exceptional in their cultural times and places. Until almost the twentieth century, the issue of capital punishment was no issue; death was a standard punishment for almost any offense against established authority. Heresy was especially offensive to established author-ities of state and church, and these institutions were seldom distin-guished; wrongdoings of crime or sin or belief naturally called for death as a penalty. The Inquisition was a natural Catholic response to the Protestant Reformation, and it demanded death by burning at the stake for many thousands of heretics who refused to bend to the authority of Catholicism. Joan of Arc is a famous example of death by fire, as are Giordano Bruno and Servetus. And not only did Catholics demand this fiery and particularly gruesome death for nonconformity of belief, but so did Anglicans; Bartholomew Legate's execution by fire in 1612 evidenced the insistence of Anglican authorities on similar sub-mission to their own authority. These sorts of stories are common coin in the history of Western culture until only very recently.

Similar stories appear in equal number and equal degree of offense to contemporary moral sensibilities in the early centuries of the Amer-ican experience. Sixteen-year-old Stephen Clark was hanged for arson in the spring of 1812 in Salem, Massachusetts, in spite of many appeals to the governor on Stephen's behalf for clemency.[1] Heresy was perhaps not so common an occasion for death sentences as it was on the Anglo-European scene, but seventeenth-century America saw witch hunts in Massachusetts that produced their fair share of torture and execution on religious grounds. Still, on the American scene, executions served the purpose primarily of maintaining integrity of community by enforcing conformity to community moral standards. When individ-uals wandered away from those community standards, punishment came quickly, and the death penalty was the most common form in which it came. Individuals were executed for murder, not a common offense, and they were also executed for burglary, forgery, arson, and theft; the death penalty and the threat of it were virtually the only pun-ishment or sanction available for offenses against community stan-dards. There were, in those early American times, no prisons where offenses against community standards might be expiated by "serving time." Those who did not measure up were executed or sometimes banished. (Rhode Island was a haven in those early times for those guilty of heresy against official state religion and saw many refugees, especially from the Massachusetts Bay Colony.)[2]

Historically speaking, nothing is odd or unusual about execution as a penalty for offenses against community standards of behavior or belief. From a contemporary, especially an American, perspective, however, execution is a penalty reserved only for the most grievous crimes against community standards; murder is the most common crime generally thought to require death as an appropriate penalty. And although murder is the most common such crime, a significant amount of opinion holds that execution is the proper response to other offenses; when the House of Representatives in April 2009 passed HR 1913 extending the federal law against hate crimes to include offenses based on sexual orientation, gender, or disability, they narrowly defeated (241–185) a further motion requiring the execution of anybody convicted of committing a hate crime. (There may have been political solidarity involved in getting those 185 votes in favor of the further motion, but the fact that there was a large number of such votes indicates that the death penalty is politically viable in the American context.)

Further indications of the vitality of a strong favorable response to execution as a penalty for certain crimes abound throughout American culture. Here is one sample from a newspaper column by Ted Nugent, written in 2009 while he attended the 135th National Rifle Association meeting in Phoenix, Arizona:

> Good people don't want the rapist to succeed. They want him dead. We don't want our homes invaded. We want invaders dead. We don't like carjackers. We like them dead. We don't like armed robbers. We like them dead. All the evidence tells us that calling 9-1-1 is a joke. For those of us for whom self-defense is no joke, we'll call 9-1-1 after we've defended our families. We'll tell authorities to bring a dustpan and a mop to clean up the dead monster we just shot.[3]

Nugent's attitude toward criminals is not explicitly elicited by a question about the propriety of the death penalty, but it is consonant with the majority opinion expressed in many public opinion polls that do ask how Americans feel about the death penalty.

Since the Supreme Court's *Furman* decision in 1972 banning execution apart from specific procedural constraints on its application, a large majority of Americans have expressed their approval of the death penalty.[4] Americans' reactions to the *Furman* decision, represented by their ever-increasing approval of the death penalty in polling data, may have been rooted in fear or apprehension of the undesirable social conditions they believed might follow the loss of the death penalty. However one accounts for the polling data, Supreme Court justices took note that one could no longer argue that the death penalty ought to be abandoned because it violated evolving standards of decency, as some were inclined to argue prior to the *Furman* decision; in the face of strong majority approval of execution as a penalty, that argument could no longer be made. (A majority of Supreme Court justices had themselves made the "evolving standards of decency" argument in their 5–4 decision in *Kennedy v. Louisiana* that capital punishment for the rape of a child—in this case she was eight—violated the cruel-and-unusual-punishment clause of the Eighth Amendment. The majority decision in that case, as well as the minority response, appears here. We note that the Court in this case was following fairly closely, though clearly extending, its own precedent in the 1977 *Coker v. Georgia* case ruling unconstitutional a capital sentence in another rape of a minor, though in *Coker* the minor involved was a sixteen-year-old.)

But perhaps a nobler, more constructive interpretation can be put on the polling data that indicates wide support of the death penalty. Walter Berns argues elegantly in his essay included here, "The Morality of Anger," that a country's worthiness of its heroes' sacrifices requires that country's willingness to execute the worst of its criminals; to be worthy of the ultimate sacrifice—and most Americans surely do believe this of their own country—a country must be willing to impose the ultimate penalty. This construal of the public opinion data is, if not noble, then at least positive. (And perhaps one might even read Ted Nugent's remarks, quoted above, in this noble or positive way.)

Berns's perspective about capital punishment and variations of it find frequent expression among those who reflect about the propriety of capital punishment. Berns sees something like nobility and respect for oneself and others in the practice of capital punishment, a perspective that appears to conflict decisively with the evolving-standards-of-decency argument against capital punishment. In Berns's view, evolving standards of decency may not evolve beyond the basic respect and regard for human dignity captured in capital punishment statutes; such "evolution" in his view would be in fact devolution, regress rather than progress. This conflict of perspective about the values that express higher regard for human communities is one that has real "bite" in the contemporary world.

In what we tend to think of—in not an especially value-neutral way—as the "first world," the world of the Western democracies, the practice of capital punishment does not exist except in the United States of America. Compare briefly the treatment of two notorious criminals in these Western democracies, Abdel al-Megrahi and Timothy McVeigh.

Al-Megrahi was convicted of bombing the Pan-American flight that crashed in Lockerbie, Scotland, in 1988, leaving 270 dead; he was convicted and sentenced in accord with British law to life imprisonment. In August 2009, al-Megrahi was released on humanitarian grounds so that he could return to Libya and visit with his family during his last days of terminal cancer. McVeigh was the Oklahoma City bomber who, in 1995, set off a huge bomb outside the Alfred Murrah building that killed hundreds of innocent people, including many children at a day care center located in the building. McVeigh, like al-Megrahi, was unrepentant, but unlike al-Megrahi, McVeigh was executed for his crime on June 11, 2001.

This contrast between the treatment of murderers in the United States and their treatment in the United Kingdom may be seen almost daily in news reports in those countries. The same contrast may be seen in comparisons of the contemporary treatment of murderers in the United States and their treatment in other European democracies. Which of these perspectives on the treatment of violent criminals is better? Which represents the more appropriate understanding of decency? Which is more progressive or more "evolved?"

The evolving-standards-of-decency argument has certainly been definitive in some critical Supreme Court decisions, including most prominently perhaps the controversial decision in *Kennedy*. Abolitionists, including prominently the American Civil Liberties Union, believe that capital punishment is a barbaric practice not worthy of a civilized society; they join the Europeans and the British and most of the economically advanced part of the world in condemning capital punishment. Others, following Berns and ignoring what they see as regressive practices in other parts of the economically advanced world, see the integrity of moral communities to require the practice of capital punishment. The controversy—or "battle" if one prefers the imagery of warfare—between these contending parties finds its most acute cultural focus in America in cases brought before the Supreme Court for adjudication. Our Supreme Court justices are not only representatives speaking on behalf of our founding document, the Constitution, but also our moral and social consciences; their opinions are the soil for the growth of that founding document into the legal practices that make possible our daily and common life. What does that document tell us about capital punishment? The quick answer is that it tells us nothing apart from the interpretations of it offered by our Supreme Court justices.

The interpretation of our Constitution as regards the death penalty has a vexed, troubled history. In *Furman* in 1972, the death penalty was held unconstitutional; in *Gregg* in 1976, the death penalty returned as constitutionally acceptable. What made the death penalty unconstitutional during those four years was its violation of the Eighth Amendment as "cruel and unusual." What returned it as constitutionally acceptable was individual state legislation designed to remove its cruel and unusual features as those were identified in *Furman*. What were those features?

Justice Potter Stewart identified the death penalty as cruel and unusual "in the same way that getting struck by lightning is cruel and unusual."[5] What Justice Stewart meant was that as getting struck by lightning is arbitrary and unpredictable, in just the same way getting a sentence of death is likewise arbitrary and unpredictable. On one day in one county a defendant might receive the death penalty for his crime; on another day in the same county, the same, or a similar, defendant might receive life imprisonment instead. When the sentencing data about which defendants in what counties receive or do not receive the death penalty are observed carefully, one finds, according to the majority of justices in *Furman*, no defensible rationale for assigning death to one defendant while not assigning death to another. The justices voting with the majority were deeply troubled by this evident arbitrariness in the application of the death penalty; the justices voting with the minority were not so troubled. In the years between *Furman* and *Gregg*, state legislatures—apparently motivated partly by the reviving popularity of capital punishment—enacted legislation designed to obviate the apparent arbitrariness of application of the death penalty; the favored technique of these legislatures was to remove from juries the discretion to decide which defendants get the death penalty and which do not.

Specific crimes were identified as requiring capital punishment— murder and aggravated rape, for example; this specificity of the required punishment removed arbitrariness by taking away from juries their discretion about what punishment was appropriate in the specific case they were considering. Another legislative technique was to specify "aggravating circumstances" and "mitigating circum- stances" designed to provide explicit guidance for juries' deliberation about whether or not the case before them required application of the death penalty. Since the arbitrariness problem was a result of jury dis- cretion, the legislatures politically inclined to do so set about system- atically removing, or radically constricting, jury discretion. However the various state legislatures managed to restrict jury discretion, their strategies worked. *Gregg* brought capital punishment back with such vigor that never again did justices allege that it violated evolving stan- dards of decency. Legislative action combined with vigorous public support made capital punishment a standard alternative for specific crimes in specific conditions. But the constitutionality of capital pun- ishment itself—executing criminals for their crimes—was not the only constitutional issue about capital punishment; other issues focused on techniques for executing those who were convicted of capital crimes and on the racism that seemed embedded in the practice of executing black defendants at a much higher rate than white defendants.

Hanging was the standard technique of execution for centuries. Because of occasional difficulties with that technique, the advent of electricity made electrocution preferable; because of occasional diffi- culties with electrocution, poison gas became preferable; because of occasional difficulties with administering poison gas, lethal injection became a preferred technique. (This rough account suggests the appearance of too much system and order in the transition among techniques. The executing agencies are states, and the wheels of state government turn slowly and sporadically; Utah, for example, has con- tinued to make use of firing squads to execute capital criminals.)[6]

The dominant idea motivating each change of technique was that of achieving a more humane, painfree technique of execution. Oppo- nents of capital punishment, willing to make use of all available strategies for challenging the constitutionality of the practice, appro-priated the idea that lethal injection—which itself occasionally yielded awkwardly lengthy and evidently painful occasions of dying—violated the Eighth Amendment's prohibition against cruel and unusual punishment. In *Baze v Rees*, this issue about lethal injection came before the Supreme Court, which rendered its judgment in April 2008: Kentucky's technique of lethal injection was indeed constitu-tional and did not violate the Eighth Amendment. The opinions by Chief Justice John Roberts and other justices in *Baze* express their acute awareness that the issue of abolition of capital punishment remains before them as they consider the constitutionality of this par-ticular technique of execution. Part two of this collection focuses on issues rooted in the *Baze* decision.

The justices do not expect the issue of the constitutionality of capital punishment to go away. And indeed the issue arises again and again.

In *Coker* and *Kennedy*, the issue came with respect to the crime of child rape. The Court in those cases held execution for the crime of raping a child to be unconstitutional, to be cruel and unusual. (The *Kennedy* case, mentioned earlier, was a particularly poignant case; if any circumstances might constitutionally justify execution for the crime of rape, the circumstances in *Kennedy* do so.) Part three of this collection focuses on issues that arise out of the *Kennedy* decision.

Another relevant issue about which the Court has rendered defin-itive judgment is racism, which appears to infect decisions by juries to impose capital punishment. In the 1987 *McCleskey* case, the Supreme Court judged it obvious that racist sentencing occurs—convicted black men in Georgia whose victims were white had four times the likelihood of receiving the death penalty as did those whose victims were black. Justice Powell, writing for the majority, acknowledged the gravity of the general statistics indicative of racism but argued that the evidence was "clearly insufficient to support an inference that any of the decision makers in McCleskey's case acted with discriminatory purpose."[7] In Powell's view, McCleskey needed to prove that the jurors who convicted and sentenced *him* were motivated by racist atti-tudes; it was not sufficient that the system yielded racist results. An interesting addendum to this 5–4 decision in *McCleskey* is that Justice Powell expressed after his retirement from the Court regret about his opinion in that case. The last part of this collection focuses on racism in capital punishment sentencing. (We note that the first item in this last part of this collection is from W.E.B. Du Bois's *The Souls of Black Folk* set, like the *McCleskey* case, in Georgia; it captures in full poignancy the racist history of this country.)

Another issue relevant to current practices of capital sentencing and execution is exoneration of convicted defendants by DNA evidence. Juries make mistakes; district attorneys make mistakes; and defendants' counsels make mistakes. Some of these mistakes are identified by investigations carried out after the trials and sentencing decisions that put defendants on death row. The gravity of these mistakes has usually been recognized by jurists and informed observers; the frequency of such mistakes usually has not been recognized. The study by University of Virginia law professor Brandon Garrett, published in 2008 in the *Columbia Law Review*, "Judging Innocence,"[8] impressively documents the frequency of such mistakes. Garrett's study involves the first two hundred postconviction DNA exonerations and shows that such mistakes are more frequent and more difficult to correct than anyone might expect. The risk of our criminal justice system convicting and executing an innocent defendant appears as a result of Garrett's study far more serious than even well-informed observers of that system might anticipate. The selection included here by Colin Starger gives brief account of the significance of the Garrett study. The selections in part five of this collection focus on DNA exoneration.

We note that execution of innocent defendants is not as rare as most of us like to think, and certainly a significant number of innocent Americans are tried and convicted and sentenced, and some of them are executed. One prominent such case is that of Todd Willingham, convicted, sentenced, and executed on February 17, 2004, for the murder by arson of his three children. Evidence available to the Texas Board of Pardons and Paroles before Willingham's execution completely exonerated him; there had been no arson, and Willingham had not been responsible for the death of his three children. The board voted unanimously to deny Willingham's petition. And Texas's Governor Perry refused to grant a thirty-day stay of execution.[9]

A basic values issue remains insufficiently addressed by this collection of materials, and it should continue nagging at contemporary American psyches, especially after a careful reading of the materials included here. That issue is decency—what does decency require of us? According to several justices and also the American Civil Liberties Union, greater decency comes from abandoning capital punishment. The evolving-standards-of-decency argument, explicitly made by the 5–4 majority in *Kennedy*, sees the retreat from state-approved execution of criminals as moral progress. The minority justices in that case, along with Walter Berns (and perhaps Ted Nugent), see decency as requiring our willingness to execute our most vicious criminals; our very integrity as a community they see as threatened by the possibility of our abandoning the ultimate punishment. American execution of Timothy McVeigh is, in that view, a symptom of moral superiority to other Western legal systems that let mass murderers live, as Britain allowed al-Megrahi to live.

Complicating this decency issue is the fact that different religious bodies see it differently. The Catholic Church officially condemns execution of criminals, even of mass murderers. The National Association of Evangelicals supports capital punishment. The people and institutions we think of as morally representative differ about the issue. How may this issue about decency be resolved? Does the historical record provide any clue to how we might think constructively about this issue?

We conclude at least that nobody who holds an opinion about this issue should be comfortable without wide historical knowledge about practices of capital punishment in the Western world and also about relevant practices of capital punishment among non-Western communities. The fact that those practices are very different in geographically distant communities and in different historical periods in the Western world is somehow significant; that fact requires that we be intentional and deliberate in our thinking about what is required of us. Also significant is that, in spite of the best efforts and intentions on the part of everyone involved in prosecuting, defending, convicting, and executing those convicted of capital crimes, mistakes are made. Some innocents are executed, and this fact alone demands that the issue of capital punishment be a matter for continuous consideration and reconsideration. This collection is an effort to participate in ongoing thoughtful reconsideration.

PART ONE

CAPITAL PUNISHMENT

History and Current Status

1

HISTORY OF THE DEATH PENALTY

Death Penalty Information Center

INTRODUCTION

Early Death Penalty Laws

The first established death penalty laws date as far back as the eighteenth century BCE in the Code of King Hammurabi of Babylon, which codified the death penalty for twenty-five different crimes. The death penalty was also part of the fourteenth century BCE's Hittite Code; in the seventh century BCE's Draconian Code of Athens, which made death the only punishment for all crimes; and in the fifth century BCE's Roman Law of the Twelve Tablets. Death sentences were carried out by such means as crucifixion, drowning, beating to death, burning alive, and impalement.

In the tenth century CE, hanging became the usual method of execution in Britain. In the following century, William the Conqueror would not allow persons to be hanged or otherwise executed for any crime, except in times of war. This trend would not last, for in the sixteenth century, under the reign of Henry VIII, as many as 72,000 people are estimated to have been executed. Some common methods of execution at that time were boiling, burning at the stake, hanging, beheading, and drawing and quartering. Executions were carried out for such capital offenses as marrying a Jew, not confessing to a crime, and treason.

The number of capital crimes in Britain continued to rise throughout the next two centuries. By the 1700s, 222 crimes were punishable by death in Britain, including stealing, cutting down a tree, and robbing a rabbit warren. Because of the severity of the death penalty, many juries would not convict defendants if the offense was not serious. This led to reforms of Britain's death penalty. From 1823 to 1837, the death penalty was eliminated for over 100 of the 222 crimes punishable by death.[1]

The Death Penalty in America

Britain influenced America's use of the death penalty more than any other country. When European settlers came to the new world, they brought the practice of capital punishment. The first recorded execution in the new colonies was that of Captain George Kendall in the Jamestown colony of Virginia in 1608. Kendall was executed for being a spy for Spain. In 1612, Virginia Governor Sir Thomas Dale enacted the Divine, Moral and Martial Laws, which provided the death penalty for even minor offenses such as stealing grapes, killing chickens, and trading with Indians.

Laws regarding the death penalty varied from colony to colony. The Massachusetts Bay Colony held its first execution in 1630, even though the Capital Laws of New England did not go into effect until years later. The New York Colony instituted the Duke's Laws of 1665. Under these laws, offenses such as striking one's mother or father, or denying the "true God," were punishable by death.[2]

THE ABOLITIONIST MOVEMENT

Colonial Times

The abolitionist movement finds its roots in the writings of European theorists Montesquieu, Voltaire and Bentham, and English Quakers John Bellers and John Howard. However, it was Cesare Beccaria's 1767 essay, *On Crimes and Punishment,* which had an especially strong impact throughout the world. In the essay, Beccaria theorized that there was no justification for the state's taking of a life. The essay gave abolitionists an authoritative voice and renewed energy, one result of which was the abolition of the death penalty in Austria and Tuscany.[3]

American intellectuals as well were influenced by Beccaria. The first attempted reforms of the death penalty in the United States occurred when Thomas Jefferson introduced a bill to revise Virginia's death penalty laws. The bill proposed that capital punishment be used only for the crimes of murder and treason. It was defeated by only one vote.

Also influenced was Dr. Benjamin Rush, a signer of the Declaration of Independence and founder of the Pennsylvania Prison Society. Rush challenged the belief that the death penalty serves as a deterrent. In fact, Rush was an early believer in the "brutalization effect." He held that having a death penalty actually increased criminal conduct. Rush gained the support of Benjamin Franklin and Philadelphia Attorney General William Bradford. Bradford, who would later become the US Attorney General, led Pennsylvania to become the first state to consider degrees of murder based on culpability. In 1794, Pennsylvania repealed the death penalty for all offenses except first-degree murder.[4]

Nineteenth Century

In the early to mid-nineteenth century, the abolitionist movement gained momentum in the northeast. In the early part of the century, many states reduced the number of their capital crimes and built state penitentiaries. In 1834, Pennsylvania became the first state to move executions away from the public eye and carrying them out in correctional facilities.

In 1846, Michigan became the first state to abolish the death penalty for all crimes except treason. Later, Rhode Island and Wisconsin abolished the death penalty for all crimes. By the end of the century, the world would see the countries of Venezuela, Portugal, Netherlands, Costa Rica, Brazil, and Ecuador follow suit.[5]

Although some US states began abolishing the death penalty, most states held on to capital punishment. Some states made more crimes capital offenses, especially for offenses committed by slaves. In 1838, in an effort to make the death penalty more palatable to the public, some states began passing laws against mandatory death sentencing, instead enacting discretionary death penalty statutes. The 1838 enactment of discretionary death penalty statutes in Tennessee, and later in Alabama, were seen as a great reform. This introduction of sentencing discretion in the capital process was perceived as a victory for abolitionists because prior to the enactment of these statutes, all states mandated the death penalty for anyone convicted of a capital crime, regardless of circumstances. With the exception of a small number of rarely committed crimes in a few jurisdictions, all mandatory capital punishment laws had been abolished by 1963.[6]

During the Civil War, opposition to the death penalty waned, as more attention was given to the antislavery movement. After the war, new developments in the means of executions emerged. The electric chair was introduced at the end of the century. New York built the first electric chair in 1888, and in 1890 executed William Kemmler. Soon, other states adopted this execution method.[7] . . .

Early and Mid-Twentieth Century

Although some states abolished the death penalty in the mid-nineteenth century, it was actually the first half of the twentieth century that marked the beginning of the "Progressive Period" of reform in the United States. From 1907 to 1917, six states completely outlawed the death penalty and three limited it to the rarely committed crimes of treason and first-degree murder of a law enforcement official. However, this reform was short-lived. There was a frenzied atmosphere in the United States, as citizens began to panic about the threat of revolution in the wake of the Russian Revolution. In addition, the United States had just entered World War I and there were intense class conflicts as socialists mounted the first serious challenge to capitalism. As a result, five of the six abolitionist states reinstated their death penalty by 1920.[8]

In 1924, the use of cyanide gas was introduced, as Nevada sought a more humane way of executing its inmates. Gee Jon was the first person executed by lethal gas. The state tried to pump cyanide gas into Jon's cell while he slept, but this proved impossible, and the gas chamber was constructed.[9]

From the 1920s to the 1940s, there was a resurgence in the use of the death penalty. This was due, in part, to the writings of criminologists, who argued that the death penalty was a necessary social measure. In the United States, Americans were suffering through Prohibition and the Great Depression. There were more executions in the 1930s than in any other decade in American history, an average of 167 per year.[10]

In the 1950s, public sentiment began to turn away from capital punishment. Many allied nations either abolished or limited the death penalty, and in the United States, the number of executions dropped dramatically. Whereas there were 1,289 executions in the 1940s, there were 715 in the 1950s, and the number fell even further, to only 191, from 1960 to 1976. In 1966, support for capital punishment reached an all-time low. A Gallup poll showed support for the death penalty at only 42 percent.[11]

CONSTITUTIONALITY OF THE DEATH PENALTY IN AMERICA

Challenging the Death Penalty

The 1960s brought challenges to the fundamental legality of the death penalty. Before then, the Fifth, Eighth, and Fourteenth Amendments were interpreted as permitting the death penalty. However, in the early 1960s, it was suggested that the death penalty was a "cruel and unusual" punishment, and therefore unconstitutional under the Eighth Amendment. In 1958, the Supreme Court had decided in *Trop v. Dulles* (356 U.S. 86) that the Eighth Amendment contained an "evolving standard of decency that marked the progress of a maturing society." Although *Trop* was not a death penalty case, abolitionists applied the Court's logic to executions and maintained that the United States had, in fact, progressed to a point that its "standard of decency" should no longer tolerate the death penalty.[12]

In the late 1960s, the Supreme Court began "fine tuning" the way the death penalty was administered. To this effect, the Court heard two cases in 1968 dealing with the discretion given to the prosecutor and the jury in capital cases. The first case was *U.S. v. Jackson* (390 U.S. 570), where the Supreme Court heard arguments regarding a provision of the federal kidnapping statute requiring that the death penalty be imposed only upon recommendation of a jury. The Court held that this practice was unconstitutional because it encouraged defendants to waive their right to a jury trial to ensure they would not receive a death sentence.

The other 1968 case was *Witherspoon v. Illinois* (391 U.S. 510). In this case, the Supreme Court held that a potential juror's mere reservations about the death penalty were insufficient grounds to prevent that person from serving on the jury in a death penalty case. Jurors could be disqualified only if prosecutors could show that the juror's attitude toward capital punishment would prevent him or her from making an impartial decision about the punishment.

In 1971, the Supreme Court again addressed the problems associated with the role of jurors and their discretion in capital cases. The Court decided *Crampton v. Ohio* and *McGautha v. California* (consolidated under 402 U.S. 183). The defendants argued it was a violation of their Fourteenth Amendment right to due process for jurors to have unrestricted discretion in deciding whether the defendants should live or die, and such discretion resulted in arbitrary and capricious sentencing. *Crampton* also argued that it was unconstitutional to have his guilt and sentence determined in one set of deliberations, as the jurors in his case were instructed that a first-degree murder conviction would result in a death sentence. The Court, however, rejected these claims, thereby approving of unfettered jury discretion and a single proceeding to determine guilt and sentence. The Court stated that guiding capital sentencing discretion was "beyond present human ability."

Suspending the Death Penalty

The issue of arbitrariness of the death penalty was again brought before the Supreme Court in 1972 in *Furman v. Georgia, Jackson v. Georgia*, and *Branch v. Texas* (known collectively as the landmark case *Furman v. Georgia* [408 U.S. 238]). Furman, like McGautha, argued that capital cases resulted in arbitrary and capricious sentencing. *Furman*, however, was a challenge brought under the Eighth Amendment, unlike McGautha, which was a Fourteenth Amendment due process claim. With the *Furman* decision the Supreme Court set the standard that a punishment would be "cruel and unusual" if it was too severe for the crime, if it was arbitrary, if it offended society's sense of justice, or if it was not more effective than a less severe penalty.

In nine separate opinions, and by a vote of 5 to 4, the Court held that Georgia's death penalty statute, which gave the jury complete sentencing discretion, could result in arbitrary sentencing. The Court held that the scheme of punishment under the statute was therefore "cruel and unusual" and violated the Eighth Amendment. Thus, on June 29, 1972, the Supreme Court effectively voided forty death penalty statutes, thereby commuting the sentences of 629 death row inmates around the country and suspending the death penalty because existing statutes were no longer valid.

Reinstating the Death Penalty

Although the separate opinions by Justices Brennan and Marshall stated that the death penalty itself was unconstitutional, the overall holding in *Furman* was that the specific death penalty statutes were unconstitutional. With that holding, the Court essentially opened the door to states to rewrite their death penalty statutes to eliminate the problems cited in *Furman*. Advocates of capital punishment began proposing new statutes that they believed would end arbitrariness in capital sentencing. The states were led by Florida, which rewrote its death penalty statute only five months after *Furman*. Shortly after, thirty-four other states proceeded to enact new death penalty statutes. To address the unconstitutionality of unguided jury discretion, some states removed all of that discretion by mandating capital punishment for those convicted of capital crimes. However, this practice was held unconstitutional by the Supreme Court in *Woodson v. North Carolina* (428 U.S. 280 [1976]).

Other states sought to limit that discretion by providing sentencing guidelines for the judge and jury when deciding whether to impose death. The guidelines allowed for the introduction of aggravating and mitigating factors in determining sentencing. These guided discretion statutes were approved in 1976 by the Supreme Court in *Gregg v. Georgia* (428 U.S. 153), *Jurek v. Texas* (428 U.S. 262), and *Proffitt v. Florida* (428 U.S. 242), collectively referred to as the *Gregg* decision. This landmark decision held that the new death penalty statutes in Florida, Georgia, and Texas were constitutional, thus reinstating the death penalty in those states. The Court also held that the death penalty itself was constitutional under the Eighth Amendment.

In addition to sentencing guidelines, three other procedural reforms were approved by the Court in *Gregg*. The first was bifurcated trials, in which there are separate deliberations for the guilt and penalty phases of the trial. Only after the jury has determined that the defendant is guilty of capital murder does it decide in a second trial whether the defendant should be sentenced to death or given a lesser sentence of prison time. Another reform was the practice of automatic appellate review of convictions and sentence. The final procedural reform from *Gregg* was proportionality review, a practice that helps the state identify and eliminate sentencing disparities. Through this process, the state appellate court can compare the sentence in the case being reviewed with other cases within the state, to see if it is disproportionate.

Because these reforms were accepted by the Supreme Court, some states wishing to reinstate the death penalty included them in their new death penalty statutes. The Court, however, did not require that each of the reforms be present in the new statutes. Therefore, some of the resulting new statutes include variations on the procedural reforms found in *Gregg*.

The ten-year moratorium on executions that had begun with the *Jackson* and *Witherspoon* decisions ended on January 17, 1977, with the execution of Gary Gilmore by firing squad in Utah. Gilmore did not challenge his death sentence. That same year, Oklahoma became the first state to adopt lethal injection as a means of execution, though it would be five more years until Charles Brooks became the first person executed by lethal injection in Texas on December 7, 1982.

LIMITING THE DEATH PENALTY

Creation of International Human Rights Doctrines

In the aftermath of World War II, the United Nations General Assembly adopted the Universal Declaration of Human Rights. This 1948 doctrine proclaimed a "right to life" in an absolute fashion, any limitations being only implicit. Knowing that international abolition of the death penalty was not yet a realistic goal in the years following the Universal Declaration, the United Nations shifted its focus to limiting the scope of the death penalty to protect juveniles, pregnant women, and the elderly.

During the 1950s and 1960s, subsequent international human rights treaties were drafted, including the International Covenant on Civil and Political Rights, the European Convention on Human Rights, and the American Convention on Human Rights. These documents also provided for the right to life, but included the death penalty as an exception that must be accompanied by strict procedural safeguards. Despite this exception, many nations throughout Western Europe stopped using capital punishment, even if they did not, technically, abolish it. As a result, this de facto abolition became the norm in Western Europe by the 1980s.[13] . . .

Limitations within the United States

Despite growing European abolition, the United States retained the death penalty but established limitations on capital punishment.

In 1977, the United States Supreme Court held in *Coker v. Georgia* (433 U.S. 584) that the death penalty is an unconstitutional punishment for the rape of an adult woman when the victim was not killed. Other limits to the death penalty followed in the next decade.

In 1986, the Supreme Court banned the execution of insane persons and required an adversarial process for determining mental competency in *Ford v. Wainwright* (477 U.S. 399). In *Penry v. Lynaugh* (492 U.S. 584 [1989]), the Court held that executing persons with mental retardation was not a violation of the Eighth Amendment. However, in 2002 in *Atkins v. Virginia* (536 U.S. 304), the Court held that a national consensus had evolved against the execution of the mentally retarded and concluded that such a punishment violates the Eighth Amendment's ban on cruel and unusual punishment.

Race became the focus of the criminal justice debate when the Supreme Court held in *Batson v. Kentucky* (476 U.S. 79 [1986]) that a prosecutor who strikes a disproportionate number of citizens of the same race in selecting a jury is required to rebut the inference of discrimination by showing neutral reasons for the strikes.

Race was again in the forefront when the Supreme Court decided the 1987 case, *McCleskey v. Kemp* (481 U.S. 279). McCleskey argued that there was racial discrimination in the application of Georgia's death penalty, by presenting a statistical analysis showing a pattern of racial disparities in death sentences, based on the race of the victim.

The Supreme Court held, however, that racial disparities would not be recognized as a constitutional violation of "equal protection of the law" unless intentional racial discrimination against the defendant could be shown.

In the late 1980s, the Supreme Court decided three cases regarding the constitutionality of executing juvenile offenders. In 1988, in *Thompson v. Oklahoma* (487 U.S. 815), four justices held that the execution of offenders aged fifteen and younger at the time of their crimes was unconstitutional. The fifth vote was Justice O'Connor's concurrence, which restricted *Thompson* only to states without a specific minimum age limit in their death penalty statute. The combined effect of the opinions by the four justices and Justice O'Connor in *Thompson* is that no state without a minimum age in its death penalty statute can execute someone who was under sixteen at the time of the crime.

The following year, the Supreme Court held that the Eighth Amendment does not prohibit the death penalty for crimes committed at age sixteen or seventeen. (*Stanford v. Kentucky*, and *Wilkins v. Missouri* [collectively, 492 U.S. 361]). At present, nineteen states with the death penalty bar the execution of anyone under eighteen at the time of his or her crime.

In 1992, the United States ratified the *International Covenant on Civil and Political Rights*. Article 6(5) of this international human rights doctrine requires that the death penalty not be used on those who committed their crimes when they were below the age of eighteen. However, in doing so . . . the United States reserved the right to execute juvenile offenders. The United States is the only country with an outstanding reservation to this article. International reaction has been highly critical of this reservation, and ten countries have filed formal objections to the US reservation.

In March 2005, in *Roper v. Simmons*, the United States Supreme Court declared the practice of executing defendants whose crimes were committed as juveniles unconstitutional.

ADDITIONAL DEATH PENALTY ISSUES

Innocence

The Supreme Court addressed the constitutionality of executing someone who claimed actual innocence in *Herrera v. Collins* (506 U.S. 390 [1993]). Although the Court left open the possibility that the Constitution bars the execution of someone who conclusively demonstrates that he or she is actually innocent, the Court noted that such cases would be very rare. The Court held that, in the absence of other constitutional violations, new evidence of innocence is no reason for federal courts to order a new trial. The Court also held that an innocent inmate could seek to prevent his execution through the clemency process, which, historically, has been "the 'fail safe' in our justice system." Herrera was not granted clemency and was executed in 1993.

Since *Herrera*, concern regarding the possibility of executing the innocent has grown. Currently, over 115 people in twenty-five states have been released from death row because of innocence since 1973. In November 1998 Northwestern University held the first-ever National Conference on Wrongful Convictions and the Death Penalty, in Chicago, Illinois. The Conference, which drew nationwide attention, brought together thirty of these wrongfully convicted inmates who were exonerated and released from death row. Many of these cases were discovered not as the result of the justice system, but instead as the result of new scientific techniques, investigations by journalism students, and the work of volunteer attorneys. These resources are not available to the typical death row inmate.

In January 2000, after Illinois had released thirteen innocent inmates from death row in the same time that it had executed twelve people, Illinois governor George Ryan declared a moratorium on executions and appointed a blue-ribbon Commission on Capital Punishment to study the issue.

Public Support

Support for the death penalty has fluctuated throughout the century. According to Gallup surveys, in 1936, 61 percent of Americans favored the death penalty for persons convicted of murder. Support reached an all-time low of 42 percent in 1966. Throughout the 1970s and 1980s, the percentage of Americans in favor of the death penalty increased steadily, culminating in an 80 percent approval rating in 1994. A May 2004 Gallup poll found that a growing number of Americans support a sentence of life without parole rather than the death penalty for those convicted of murder. Gallup found that 46 percent of respondents favor life imprisonment over the death penalty, up from 44 percent in May 2003. During that same time frame, support for capital punishment as an alternative fell from 53 percent to 50 percent. The poll also revealed a growing skepticism that the death penalty deters crime, with 62 percent of those polled saying that it is not a deterrent. These percentages are a dramatic shift from the responses given to this same question in 1991, when 51 percent of Americans believed the death penalty deterred crime and only 41 percent believed it did not. Only 55 percent of those polled responded that they believed the death penalty is implemented fairly, down from 60 percent in 2003. When not offered an alternative sentence, 71 percent supported the death penalty and 26 percent opposed. The overall support is about the same as that reported in 2002, but down from the 80 percent support in 1994.[14] . . .

Religion

In the 1970s, the National Association of Evangelicals (NAE), representing more then ten million conservative Christians, forty-seven denominations, and the Moral Majority, were among the Christian groups supporting the death penalty. NAE's successor, the Christian Coalition, also supports the death penalty. Today, Fundamentalist and Pentecostal churches support the death penalty, typically on biblical grounds, specifically citing the Old Testament.[15] The Church of Jesus Christ of Latter-day Saints regards the question as a matter to be decided solely by the process of civil law and thus neither promotes nor opposes capital punishment.

Although traditionally also a supporter of capital punishment, the Roman Catholic Church now opposes the death penalty. In addition, most Protestant denominations, including Baptists, Episcopalians, Lutherans, Methodists, Presbyterians, and the United Church of Christ, oppose the death penalty. During the 1960s, religious activists worked to abolish the death penalty and continue to do so today.

In recent years, and in the wake of an appeal by Pope John Paul II to end the death penalty, religious organizations around the nation issued statements opposing the death penalty. . . .

Women

Women have, historically, not been subject to the death penalty at the same rates as men. From the first woman executed in the United States, Jane Champion, who was hanged in James City, Virginia, in 1632, to the present, women have constituted only about 3 percent of US executions. In fact, only ten women have been executed in the post-*Gregg* era.[16]

RECENT DEVELOPMENTS IN CAPITAL PUNISHMENT

The Federal Death Penalty

In addition to the death penalty laws in many states, the federal government has also employed capital punishment for certain federal offenses, such as murder of a government official, kidnapping resulting in death, running a large-scale drug enterprise, and treason. When the Supreme Court struck down state death penalty statutes in *Furman*, the federal death penalty statutes suffered from the same constitutional infirmities that the state statutes did. As a result, death sentences under the old federal death penalty statutes have not been upheld.

In 1988, a new federal death penalty statute was enacted for murder in the course of a drug-kingpin conspiracy. The statute was modeled on the post-*Gregg* statutes that the Supreme Court has approved. Since its enactment, six people have been sentenced to death for violating this law, though none has been executed.

In 1994, President Clinton signed the Violent Crime Control and Law Enforcement Act that expanded the federal death penalty to some sixty crimes, three of which do not involve murder. The exceptions are espionage, treason, and drug trafficking in large amounts.

Two years later, in response to the Oklahoma City Bombing, President Clinton signed the Anti-Terrorism and Effective Death Penalty Act of 1996. The act, which affects both state and federal prisoners,

restricts review in federal courts by establishing tighter filing dead-
lines, limiting the opportunity for evidentiary hearings, and ordinarily
allowing only a single habeas corpus filing in federal court. Proponents of the death penalty argue that this streamlining will speed up
the death penalty process and significantly reduce its cost, although
others fear that quicker, more limited federal review may increase the
risk of executing innocent defendants.[17]

International Abolition

In the 1980s, the international abolition movement gained momentum and treaties proclaiming abolition were drafted and ratified. Protocol No. 6 to the European Convention on Human Rights and its
successors, the Inter-American Additional Protocol to the American
Convention on Human Rights to Abolish the Death Penalty, and the
United Nation's Second Optional Protocol to the International
Covenant on Civil and Political Rights Aiming at the Abolition of the
Death Penalty were created with the goal of making abolition of the
death penalty an international norm.

Today, the Council of Europe requires new members to undertake
and ratify Protocol No. 6. This has, in effect, led to the abolition of
the death penalty in Eastern Europe. For example, the Ukraine, formerly one of the world's leaders in executions, has now halted the
death penalty and has been admitted to the council. South Africa's
parliament voted to formally abolish the death penalty, which had
earlier been declared unconstitutional by the Constitutional Court. In
addition, Russian President Boris Yeltsin signed a decree commuting
the death sentence for all of the convicts on Russia's death row, in
June 1999.[18] Between 2000 and 2004, seven additional countries
abolished the death penalty for all crimes, and four more abolished
the death penalty for ordinary crimes. . . .

The Death Penalty Today

In April 1999, the United Nations Human Rights Commission passed
the Resolution Supporting Worldwide Moratorium on Executions.
The resolution calls on countries which have not abolished the death
penalty to restrict its use of the death penalty, including not imposing

it on juvenile offenders and limiting the number of offenses for which it can be imposed. Ten countries, including the United States, China, Pakistan, Rwanda, and Sudan, voted against the resolution.[19] Each year since 1997, the United Nations Commission on Human Rights has passed a resolution calling on countries that have not abolished the death penalty to establish a moratorium on executions. In April 2004, the resolution was cosponsored by seventy-six UN member states.[20]

In the United States, numbers of death sentences are steadily declining from three hundred in 1998 to 143 in 2003.

Presently, more than half of the countries in the international community have abolished the death penalty completely, de facto, or for ordinary crimes. However, over seventy-eight countries retain the death penalty, including China, Iran, the United States, and Vietnam, all of which rank among the highest for international executions in 2003.[21]

2

DEATH SENTENCES AND EXECUTIONS IN 2008

Summary Report

Amnesty International

[M]ore people were executed in Asia than in any other part of the world in 2008. China carried out more executions than the rest of the world put together. By contrast, in Europe, only one country continues to use the death penalty: Belarus. . . .

[B]etween January and December 2008, at least 2,390 people were executed in twenty-five countries around the world, with at least 8,864 sentenced to death in fifty-two states.

Amnesty International also reports on countries that handed down death sentences after unfair trials, like Afghanistan, Iran, Iraq, Nigeria, Saudi Arabia, Sudan, and Yemen. The report addresses the discriminatory manner with which the death penalty was often applied in 2008, with a disproportionate number of sentences handed down to the poor, minorities, and members of racial, ethnic, and religious communities, in countries such as Iran, Sudan, Saudi Arabia, and the USA. And the risk of executing the innocent continues, as highlighted by the four inmates released from death row in the USA on grounds of innocence.

Many death row inmates languish in harsh detention conditions and face psychological hardship. For example, in Japan, inmates are typically notified of their hanging only on the morning of their execution, and their families are informed only after the execution has taken place. . . .

Most of the world is moving a step closer to the abolition of the death penalty, with only twenty-five out of the fifty-nine countries that retain the death penalty reported to have actually executed in 2008. But Amnesty International warned that, in spite of this trend, death sentences continue to be handed out in the hundreds all over the world.

Progress was undermined, however, in 2008 by countries like St. Kitts and Nevis, which carried out the first execution in the Americas outside the USA since 2003 and Liberia, where the death penalty was introduced for the crimes of robbery, terrorism, and hijacking.

"The good news is that executions are only carried out by a small number of countries, which shows that we are moving closer to a death-penalty-free world," said Irene Khan. "By contrast, the bad news is that hundreds of people continue to be sentenced to death and suffer in the many countries that have not yet formally abolished the death penalty."

Regional summaries:

- Most of the executions in 2008 were carried out in Asia, where eleven countries continue to practice the death penalty: Afghanistan, Bangladesh, China, Indonesia, Japan, North Korea, Malaysia, Mongolia, Pakistan, Singapore, and Vietnam. China alone accounted for almost three-quarters of the world's executions, carrying out at least 1,718 executions—although the figure is believed to be much higher as statistics on death sentences and executions remain state secrets.
- The Middle East and North Africa was the region with the second-highest number of executions (508). In Iran, stoning and hanging were among the cruel and inhumane methods used with at least 346 people put to death, including eight juvenile offenders. In Saudi Arabia, where execution is usually by public beheading and is, in some cases, followed by crucifixion, at least 102 people were executed.
- In the Americas, only the United States of America consistently executes, with thirty-seven executions carried out in 2008, including more in Texas than in any other state. The release of four men from death row in the USA on grounds of innocence brings to more than 120 the number of such cases released since

1975. The only other country in the Americas to execute in 2008 was St. Kitts and Nevis, the first Caribbean state to carry out an execution since 2003.

- Europe would be a "death-penalty-free zone" if it were not for Belarus, where the death penalty is shrouded in secrecy: execution by a gunshot to the back of the head, with no official information given to relatives about the date of the execution or where the body is buried. The former Soviet country carried out four executions in 2008 and remains the only country in Europe to retain the death penalty.

- Only two officially recorded executions were carried out in Sub-Saharan Africa in 2008, but at least 362 people were sentenced to death. 2008 also saw a regressive development in Liberia, where the death penalty was reintroduced for the crimes of robbery, terrorism, and hijacking.

3

NUMBER OF EXECUTIONS AS OF MAY 20, 2011, BY STATE SINCE 1976

Death Penalty Information Center

Number of Executions as of January 26, 2011, by State Since 1976

Death Penalty Information Center

TOTAL EXECUTIONS SINCE 1976	1,252
EXECUTIONS TO DATE IN 2011	11
EXECUTIONS TO DATE IN 2010	46
EXECUTIONS TO DATE IN 2009	52

EXECUTIONS BY STATE

State	Total Executions	Executions in 2011	Executions in 2010	Executions in 2009
Texas	467	3	17	24
Virginia	108		3	3
Oklahoma	96	2	3	3
Florida	69		1	2
Missouri	68	1		1
Alabama	52	3	5	6
Georgia	48	1	2	3
Ohio	45	4	8	5

State	Total Executions	Executions in 2011	Executions in 2010	Executions in 2009
North Carolina	43			
South Carolina	43	1		2
Louisiana	28		1	
Arkansas	27			
Arizona	25	1	1	
Indiana	20			1
Delaware	14			
California	13			
Mississippi	15	2	3	
Illinois	12			
Nevada	12			
Utah	7		1	
Tennessee	6			2
Maryland	5			
Washington	5		1	
Nebraska	3			
Montana	3			
Pennsylvania	3			
Us Federal Government	3			
Kentucky	3			
Oregon	2			
Colorado	1			
Connecticut	1			
Idaho	1			
New Mexico	1			
South Dakota	1			
Wyoming	1			

PART TWO

CAPITAL PUNISHMENT

Why? Why Not?

4

THE MORALITY OF ANGER

Walter Berns

Until recently, my business did not require me to think about the punishment of criminals in general or the legitimacy and efficacy of capital punishment in particular. In a vague way, I was aware of the disagreement among professionals concerning the purpose of punishment—whether it was intended to deter others, to rehabilitate the criminal, or to pay him back—but like most laymen, I had no particular reason to decide which purpose was right or to what extent they may all have been right. I did know that retribution was held in ill repute among criminologists and jurists—to them, retribution was a fancy name for revenge, and revenge was barbaric—and, of course, I knew that capital punishment had the support only of policemen, prison guards, and some local politicians, the sort of people Arthur Koestler calls "hanghards" (Philadelphia's Mayor Rizzo comes to mind). The intellectual community denounced it as both unnecessary and immoral. It was the phenomenon of Simon Wiesenthal that allowed me to understand why the intellectuals were wrong and why the police, the politicians, and the majority of the voters were right: We punish criminals principally in order to pay them back, and we execute the worst of them out of moral necessity. Anyone who respects Wiesenthal's mission will be driven to the same conclusion.

Of course, not everyone will respect that mission. It will strike the busy man—I mean the sort of man who sees things only in the light cast by a concern for his own interests—as somewhat bizarre. Why should anyone devote his life—more than thirty years of it!—exclusively to the task of hunting down the Nazi war criminals who survived World War II and escaped punishment? Wiesenthal says his conscience forces him "to bring the guilty ones to trial." But why punish them? What do we hope to accomplish now by punishing SS Obersturmbannführer Adolf Eichmann or SS Obersturmbannführer Franz Stangl or someday—who knows?—Reichsleiter Martin Bormann? We surely don't expect to rehabilitate them, and it would be foolish to think that by punishing them we might thereby deter others. The answer, I think, is clear: We want to punish them in order *to pay them back*. We think they must be made to pay for their crimes with their lives, and we think that we, the survivors of the world they violated, may legitimately exact that payment because we, too, are their victims. By punishing them, we demonstrate that there are laws that bind men across generations as well as across (and within) nations, that we are not simply isolated individuals, each pursuing his selfish interests and connected with others by a mere contract to live and let live. To state it simply, Wiesenthal allows us to see that it is right, morally right, to be angry with criminals and to express that anger publicly, officially, and in an appropriate manner, which may require the worst of them to be executed.

Modern civil-libertarian opponents of capital punishment do not understand this. They say that to execute a criminal is to deny his human dignity; they also say that the death penalty is not useful, that nothing useful is accomplished by executing anyone. Being utilitarians, they are essentially selfish men, distrustful of passion, who do not understand the connection between anger and justice, and between anger and human dignity.

Anger is expressed or manifested on those occasions when someone has acted in a manner that is thought to be unjust, and one of its origins is the opinion that men are responsible, and should be held responsible, for what they do. Thus, as Aristotle teaches us, anger is accompanied not only by the pain caused by the one who is the object of anger, but by the pleasure arising from the expectation of inflicting revenge on someone who is thought to deserve it. We can become angry with an inanimate object (the door we run into and then kick in return) only by foolishly attributing responsibility to it, and we cannot do that for long, which is why we do not think of returning later to revenge ourselves on the door. For the same reason, we cannot be more than momentarily angry with any one creature other than man; only a fool and worse would dream of taking revenge on a dog. And, finally, we tend to pity rather than to be angry with men who—because they are insane, for example—are not responsible for their acts. Anger, then, is a very human passion not only because only a human being can be angry, but also because anger acknowledges the humanity of its objects: it holds them accountable for what they do. And in holding particular men responsible, it pays them the respect that is due them as men. Anger recognizes that only men have the capacity to be moral beings and, in so doing, acknowledges the dignity of human beings. Anger is somehow connected with justice, and it is this that modern penology has not understood; it tends, on the whole, to regard anger as a selfish indulgence.

Anger can, of course, be that; and if someone does not become angry with an insult or an injury suffered unjustly, we tend to think he does not think much of himself. But it need not be selfish, not in the sense of being provoked only by an injury suffered by oneself. There were many angry men in America when President Kennedy was killed; one of them—Jack Ruby—took it upon himself to exact the punishment that, if indeed deserved, ought to have been exacted by the law. There were perhaps even angrier men when Martin Luther King Jr. was killed, for King, more than anyone else at the time, embodied a people's quest for justice; the anger—more, the "black rage"—expressed on that occasion was simply a manifestation of the great change that had occurred among black men in America, a change wrought in large part by King and his associates in the civil rights movement: the servility and fear of the past had been replaced by pride and anger, and the treatment that had formerly been accepted as a matter of course or as if it were deserved was now seen for what it was, unjust and unacceptable. King preached love, but the movement he led depended on anger as well as love, and that anger was not despicable, being neither selfish nor unjustified. On the contrary, it was a reflection of what was called solidarity and may more accurately be called a profound caring for others, black for other blacks, white for blacks, and, in the world King was trying to build, American for other Americans. If men are not saddened when someone else suffers, or angry when someone else suffers unjustly, the implication is that they do not care for anyone other than themselves or that they lack some quality that befits a man. When we criticize them for this, we acknowledge that they ought to care for others. If men are not angry when a neighbor suffers at the hands of a criminal, the implication is that their moral faculties have been corrupted, that they are not good citizens.

Criminals are properly the objects of anger, and the perpetrators of terrible crimes—for example, Lee Harvey Oswald and James Earl Ray—are properly the objects of great anger. They have done more than inflict an injury on an isolated individual; they have violated the foundations of trust and friendship, the necessary elements of a moral community, the only community worth living in. A moral community, unlike a hive of bees or a hill of ants, is one whose members are expected freely to obey the laws and, unlike those in a tyranny, are trusted to obey the laws. The criminal has violated that trust, and in so doing has injured not merely his immediate victim but the community as such. He has called into question the very possibility of that community by suggesting that men cannot be trusted to respect freely the property, the person, and the dignity of those with whom they are associated. If, then, men are not angry when someone else is robbed, raped, or murdered, the implication is that no moral community exists, because those men do not care for anyone other than themselves. Anger is an expression of that caring, and society needs men who care for one another, who share their pleasures and their pains, and do so for the sake of the others. It is the passion that can cause us to act for reasons having nothing to do with selfish or mean calculation; indeed, when educated, it can become a generous passion, the passion that protects the community or country by demanding punishment for its enemies. It is the stuff from which heroes are made.

A moral community is not possible without anger and the moral indignation that accompanies it. Thus the most powerful attack on capital punishment was written by a man, Albert Camus, who denied the legitimacy of anger and moral indignation by denying the very possibility of a moral community in our time. The anger expressed in our world, he said, is nothing but hypocrisy. His novel *L'Etranger* (variously translated as *The Stranger* or *The Outsider*) is a brilliant portrayal of what Camus insisted is our world, a world deprived of

God, as he put it. It is a world we would not choose to live in and one that Camus, the hero of the French Resistance, disdained. Nevertheless, the novel is a modern masterpiece, and Meursault, its antihero (for a world without anger can have no heroes), is a murderer.

He is a murderer whose crime is excused, even as his lack of hypocrisy is praised, because the universe, we are told, is "benignly indifferent" to how we live or what we do. Of course, the law is not indifferent; the law punished Meursault, and it threatens to punish us if we do as he did. But Camus the novelist teaches us that the law is simply a collection of arbitrary conceits. The people around Meursault apparently were not indifferent; they expressed dismay at his lack of attachment to his mother and disapprobation of his crime. But Camus the novelist teaches us that other people are hypocrites. They pretend not to know what Camus the opponent of capital punishment tells: namely, that "our civilization has lost the only values that, in a certain way, can justify that penalty . . . [the existence of] a truth or a principle that is superior to man." There is no basis for friendship and no moral law; therefore, no one, not even a murderer, can violate the terms of friendship or break that law; and there is no basis for the anger that we express when someone breaks that law. The only thing we share as men, the only thing that connects us one to another, is a "solidarity against death," and a judgment of capital punishment "upsets" that solidarity. The purpose of human life is to stay alive.

Like Meursault, Macbeth was a murderer, and like L'Etranger, Shakespeare's Macbeth is the story of a murder; but there the similarity ends. As Lincoln said, "Nothing equals Macbeth." He was comparing it with the other Shakespearean plays he knew, the plays he had "gone over perhaps as frequently as any unprofessional reader . . . Lear, Richard Third, Henry the Eighth, Hamlet"; but I think he meant to say more than that none of these equals Macbeth. I think he meant that no other literary work equals it. "It is wonderful," he said. Macbeth is wonderful because, to say nothing more here, it teaches us the awesomeness of the commandment "Thou shalt not kill."

What can a dramatic poet tell us about murder? More, probably, than anyone else, if he is a poet worthy of consideration, and yet nothing that does not inhere in the act itself. In Macbeth Shakespeare shows us murders committed in a political world by a man so driven by ambition to rule that world that he becomes a tyrant. He shows us also the consequences, which were terrible, worse even than Macbeth feared. The cosmos rebelled, turned into chaos by his deeds. He shows a world that was not "benignly indifferent" to what we call crimes and especially to murder, a world constituted by laws divine as well as human, and Macbeth violated the most awful of those laws. Because the world was so constituted, Macbeth suffered the torments of the great and the damned, torments far beyond the "practice" of any physician. He had known glory and had deserved the respect and affection of king, countrymen, army, friends, and wife; and he lost it all. At the end he was reduced to saying that life "is a tale told by an idiot, full of sound and fury, signifying nothing"; yet, in spite of the horrors provoked in us by his acts, he excites no anger in us. We pity him; even so, we understand the anger of his countrymen and the dramatic necessity of his death. *Macbeth* is a play about ambition, murder, tyranny; about horror, anger, vengeance, and perhaps more than any other of Shakespeare's plays, justice. Because of justice, Macbeth has to die, not by his own hand—he will not "play the Roman fool, and die on [his] sword"—but at the hand of the avenging Macduff. The dramatic necessity of his death would appear to rest on its moral necessity. Is that right? Does this play conform to our sense of what a murder means? Lincoln thought it was "wonderful."

Surely Shakespeare's is a truer account of murder than the one provided by Camus, and by truer I mean truer to our moral sense of what a murder is and what the consequences that attend it must be. Shakespeare shows us vengeful men because there is something in the souls of men—then and now—that requires such crimes to be revenged. Can we imagine a world that does not take its revenge on the man who kills Macduff's wife and children? (Can we imagine the play in which Macbeth does not die?) Can we imagine a people that does not hate murderers? (Can we imagine a world where Meursault is an outsider only because he does not *pretend* to be outraged by murder?) Shakespeare's poetry could not have been written out of the moral sense that the death penalty's opponents insist we ought to have. Indeed, the issue of capital punishment can be said to turn on whether Shakespeare's or Camus' is the more telling account of murder.

There is a sense in which punishment may be likened to dramatic poetry. Dramatic poetry depicts men's actions because men are revealed in, or make themselves known through, their actions; and the essence of a human action, according to Aristotle, consists in its being virtuous or vicious. Only a ruler or a contender for rule can act with the freedom and on a scale that allows the virtuousness or viciousness of human deeds to be fully displayed. Macbeth was such a man, and in his fall, brought about by his own acts, and in the consequent suffering he endured, is revealed the meaning of morality. In *Macbeth* the majesty of the moral law is demonstrated to us; as I said, it teaches us the awesomeness of the commandment "Thou shalt not kill." In a similar fashion, the punishments imposed by the legal order remind us of the reign of the moral order; not only do they remind us of it, but by enforcing its prescriptions, they enhance the dignity of the legal order in the eyes of moral men, in the eyes of those decent citizens who cry out "for gods who will avenge injustice." That is especially important in a self-governing community, a community that gives laws to itself.

If the laws were understood to be divinely inspired or, in the extreme case, divinely given, they would enjoy all the dignity that the opinions of men can grant and all the dignity they require to ensure their being obeyed by most of the men living under them. Like Duncan in the opinion of Macduff, the laws would be "the Lord's anointed" and would be obeyed even as Macduff obeyed the laws of the Scottish kingdom. Only a Macbeth would challenge them, and only a Meursault would ignore them. But the laws of the United States are not of this description; in fact, among the proposed amendments that became the Bill of Rights was one declaring, not that all power comes from God, but rather "that all power is originally vested in, and consequently derives from the people"; and this proposal was dropped only because it was thought to be redundant: the Constitution's preamble said essentially the same thing, and what we know as the Tenth Amendment reiterated it. So Madison proposed to make the Constitution venerable in the minds of the people, and Lincoln, in an early speech, went so far as to say that a "political religion" should be made of it. They did not doubt that the Constitution and the laws made pursuant to it would be supported by "enlightened reason," but fearing that enlightened reason would be in short supply, they sought to augment it. The laws of the United States would be obeyed by some men because they could hear and understand "the voice of enlightened reason," and by other men because they would regard the laws with that "veneration which time bestows on everything."

Supreme Court Justices have occasionally complained of our habit of making "constitutionality synonymous with wisdom." But the extent to which the Constitution is venerated and its authority accepted depends on the compatibility of its rules with our moral sensibilities; despite its venerable character, the Constitution is not the only source of these moral sensibilities.

There was even a period, before slavery was abolished by the Thirteenth Amendment, when the Constitution was regarded by some very moral men as an abomination: Garrison called it "a covenant with death and an agreement with Hell," and there were honorable men holding important political offices and judicial appointments who refused to enforce the Fugitive Slave Law even though its constitutionality had been affirmed. In time this opinion spread far beyond the ranks of the original abolitionists until those who held it composed a constitutional majority of the people, and slavery was abolished.

But Lincoln knew that more than amendments were required to make the Constitution once more worthy of the veneration of moral men. That is why, in the Gettysburg Address, he made the principle of the Constitution an inheritance from "our fathers." That it should be so esteemed is especially important in a self-governing nation that gives laws to itself, because it is only a short step from the principle that the laws are merely a product of one's own will to the opinion that the only consideration that informs the law is self-interest; and this opinion is only one remove from lawlessness. A nation of simple self-interested men will soon enough perish from the earth.

It was not an accident that Lincoln spoke as he did at Gettysburg or that he chose as the occasion for his words the dedication of a cemetery built on a portion of the most significant battlefield of the Civil War. Two and a half years earlier, in his First Inaugural Address, he had said that Americans, north and south, were not and must not be enemies, but friends. Passion had strained but must not be allowed to break the bonds of affection that tied them one to another. He closed by saying this: "The mystic chords of memory, stretching from every battlefield, and patriot grave, to every living heart and hearthstone, all over this broad land, will yet swell the chorus of the Union, when again touched, as surely they will be, by the better angels of our nature." The chords of memory that would swell the chorus of the Union could be touched, even by a man of Lincoln's stature, only on the most solemn occasions, and in the life of a nation no occasion is more solemn than the burial of the patriots who have died defending it on the field of battle. War is surely an evil, but as Hegel said, it is not an "absolute evil." It exacts the supreme sacrifice, but precisely because of that it can call forth such sublime rhetoric as Lincoln's. His words at Gettysburg serve to remind Americans in particular of what Hegel said people in general needed to know, and could be made to know by means of war and the sacrifices demanded of them in wars: namely, that their country is something more than a "civil society" the purpose of which is simply the protection of individual and selfish interests.

Capital punishment, like Shakespeare's dramatic and Lincoln's political poetry (and it is surely that, and was understood by him to be that), serves to remind us of the majesty of the moral order that is embodied in our law, and of the terrible consequences of its breach. The law must not be understood to be merely a statute that we enact or repeal at our will, and obey or disobey at our convenience—especially not the criminal law. Wherever law is regarded as merely statutory, men will soon enough disobey it and will learn how to do so without any inconvenience to themselves. The criminal law must possess a dignity far beyond that possessed by mere statutory enactment or utilitarian and self-interested calculations. The most powerful means we have to give it that dignity is to authorize it to impose the ultimate penalty. The criminal law must be made awful, by which I mean inspiring, or commanding "profound respect or reverential fear." It must remind us of the moral order by which alone we can live as human beings, and in America, now that the Supreme Court has outlawed banishment, the only punishment that can do this is capital punishment.

The founder of modern criminology, the eighteenth-century Italian Cesare Beccaria, opposed both banishment and capital punishment because he understood that both were inconsistent with the principle of self-interest, and self-interest was the basis of the political order he favored. If a man's first or only duty is to himself, of course he will prefer his money to his country; he will also prefer his money to his brother. In fact, he will prefer his brother's money to his brother, and a people of this description, or a country that understands itself in this Beccarian manner, can put the mark of Cain on no one. For the same reason, such a country can have no legitimate reason to execute its criminals, or, indeed, to punish them in any manner. What would be accomplished by punishment in such a place? Punishment arises out of the demand for justice, and justice is demanded by angry, morally indignant men; its purpose is to satisfy that moral indignation and thereby promote the law-abidingness that, it is assumed, accompanies it. But the principle of self-interest denies the moral basis of that indignation.

Not only will a country based solely on self-interest have no legitimate reason to punish; it may have no need to punish. It may be able to solve what we call the crime problem by substituting a law of contracts for a law of crimes. According to Beccaria's social contract, men agree to yield their natural freedom to the "sovereign" in exchange for his promise to keep the peace. As it becomes more difficult for the sovereign to fulfill his part of the contract, there is a demand that he be made to pay for his nonperformance. From this comes compensation or insurance schemes embodied in statutes whereby the sovereign (or state), being unable to keep the peace by punishing criminals, agrees to compensate its contractual partners for injuries suffered at the hands of criminals, injuries the police are unable to prevent. The insurance policy takes the place of law enforcement and the *posse comitatus*, and John Wayne and Gary Cooper give way to Mutual of Omaha. There is no anger in this kind of law, and none (or no reason for any) in the society. The principle can be carried further still. If we ignore the victim (and nothing we do can restore his life anyway), there would appear to be no reason why—the worth of a man being his price, as Beccaria's teacher, Thomas Hobbes, put it—coverage should not be extended to the losses incurred in a murder. If we ignore the victim's sensibilities (and what are they but absurd vanities?), there would appear to be no reason why—the worth of a woman being *her* price—coverage should not be extended to the losses incurred in a rape. Other examples will no doubt suggest themselves.

This might appear to be an almost perfect solution to what we persist in calling the crime problem, achieved without risking the terrible things sometimes done by an angry people. A people that is not angry with criminals will not be able to deter crime, but a people fully covered by insurance has no need to deter crime: they will be insured against all the losses they can, in principle, suffer. What is now called crime can be expected to increase in volume, of course, and this will cause an increase in the premiums paid, directly or in the form of taxes. But it will no longer be necessary to apprehend, try, and punish criminals, which now costs Americans more than $1.5 billion a month (and is increasing at an annual rate of about 15 percent), and one can buy a lot of insurance for $1.5 billion. There is this difficulty, as Rousseau put it: To exclude anger from the human community is to concentrate all the passions in a "self-interest of the meanest sort," and such a place would not be fit for human habitation.

When, in 1976, the Supreme Court declared death to be a constitutional penalty, it decided that the United States was not that sort of country; most of us, I think, can appreciate that judgment. We want to live among people who do not value their possessions more than their citizenship, who do not think exclusively or even primarily of their own rights, people whom we can depend on even as they exercise their rights, and whom we can trust, which is to say, people who, even in the absence of a policeman, will not assault our bodies or steal our possessions, and might even come to our assistance when we need it, and who stand ready, when the occasion demands it, to risk their lives in defense of their country. If we are of the opinion that the United States may rightly ask of its citizens this awful sacrifice, then we are also of the opinion that it may rightly impose the most awful penalty; if it may rightly honor its heroes, it may rightly execute the worst of its criminals. By doing so, it will remind its citizens that it is a country worthy of heroes.

5

EXECUTION IS INHERENTLY INHUMANE, UNFAIRLY APPLIED, AND INEFFECTIVE IN DETERRING CRIME

Mahua Das

According to Amnesty International's briefing for the European Union and India Summit on September 7, 2005, 120 countries have abolished the death penalty in law or practice. Some of the countries that have repealed it for all crimes are Australia, Canada, South Africa, Venezuela, New Zealand, Mauritius, and the twenty-five countries of the European Union. India is among seventy-six countries that retain the death penalty. Amnesty International's annual report on official judicial execution states that in 2004 there were 3,797 executions in twenty-five countries. The People's Republic of China was the most prolific executioner of the world, carrying out more than thirty-four hundred executions. This was followed by Iran (159), Vietnam (64), the United States (59), and Saudi Arabia (35).

Methods of execution in the modern era include hanging, stoning, beheading, shooting, electrocution, and, more recently, lethal injection. Many countries retain hanging as the standard mode, notably India, Pakistan, Malaysia, Japan, Singapore, and Egypt. Some nations use firing squads, either exclusively or for certain classes of crime or criminal. For instance, in Egypt and India, military personnel are shot, while civilians are hanged. Six countries stone condemned criminals to death. Beheading is used in Congo, in the United Arab Emirates, and in Saudi Arabia, where thirty-five men and one woman were publicly beheaded in 2004. Five countries use lethal injection. It is the most popular mode in the United States, accounting for fifty-eight of fifty-nine executions in 2004.

The death penalty can be found in human society as far back as history can reveal. It is present in India's ancient scriptural epics, the *Ramayana* and *Mahabharata,* as well as in the laws of ancient Egypt. The earliest written version is the eighteenth-century-BCE code of King Hammurabi of Babylon. Numerous crimes in these ancient codes called for death. In the seventh century BCE, the Draconian Code of Athens made every crime punishable by death—hence the term draconian, meaning extremely harsh. Every ancient religion endorsed capital punishment, with at least the exception of Jainism and Buddhism, though rulers of both religions were known to have executed criminals.

Today there is a vigorous international debate over the death penalty. On one side are the "abolitionists," who want to eliminate it; on the other are the "retentionists," who want to keep it. Abolitionists, of which I am one, focus on the issues of morality, effectiveness, and fairness in application. Retentionists assert that deterrence and retribution justify the continued use of capital punishment across the world. In my opinion, their position is fraught with the dangers of undermining the cherished values and principles of a civilized society. It would be worthwhile to delve deeper and assess the ground realities, beginning with the most common rationale for the death penalty, that it deters others from committing crime.

Evaluating the deterrence rationale: There is a lack of convincing evidence to indicate that the death penalty deters crime more effectively than other punishments. A study conducted for the United Nations concludes, "It is not prudent to accept the hypothesis that capital punishment deters murder to a marginally greater extent than does the threat and application of the supposedly lesser punishment of life imprisonment." Statistics show that countries without the death penalty have a lower murder rate than those with it. For example, the murder rates in Germany, Britain, Italy, France, the Netherlands, and Sweden are less than two per one hundred thousand people per year, whereas the rate in the United States is 6.3. In Canada, the murder rate has fallen 23 percent since the death penalty was abolished in 1976. The Canadian statistic supports the contention that abolishing the death penalty can lower the homicide rate rather than increase it.

The US experience is instructive. In 1972, the Supreme Court banned the death penalty. Five years later, the court reinstated it, with certain conditions. Many states thereupon reintroduced the death penalty on the rationale that it deters violent crime. However, there is no conclusive statistical evidence that states with the death penalty have lower rates of homicide than those without it. One US-based nonprofit organization, the Death Penalty Information Center, claims that states without the death penalty have lower murder rates than states where executions take place. But this statistic, even if true, would not take into account the unique demographics of various states, such as a lower poverty rate, which could account for the lower murder rate.

Why would the death penalty not decrease the murder rate? W. T. McGrath wrote in his 1956 book *Should Canada Abolish the Gallows and the Lash?*:

> Murderers might be classified arbitrarily into three groups—the insane killer, the person who strikes in a moment of blind fury, and the deliberate killer who murders for gain. Which of these three will be deterred by the possible consequences of his crime? Obviously not the insane killer who is living in a world of his own. Surely not the impulsive killer who is in the grip of a passion he cannot control. Surely not the deliberate killer, who has based his decision to kill on considerations of profit and loss; life in prison would make it an unprofitable transaction indeed. He does not expect to be caught.

Logic reasons that rational people will be deterred from murder because of the existence of the death penalty, but since most murders are unplanned, a logical analysis is not feasible.

China is the world's record executioner, imposing the death penalty for sixty-eight crimes, including murder, rape, drug trafficking, pimping, habitual theft, reselling of VAT receipts (a form of tax evasion), stealing or dealing in national treasures or cultural relics, publishing pornography, selling counterfeit money, and economic offenses such as graft, speculation and profiteering. Even killing a panda, the national animal, is a capital offense.

China considers information regarding the death penalty a state secret, and a realistic estimate of the judicial carnage is not divulged by the communist regime. Amnesty International is the only organization that systematically monitors and records executions and death sentences in China. Its annual death-penalty log revealed that China sentenced at least 3,152 people to death and executed more than 1,876 during 1997. These figures represent a drop from 1996, at the peak of the "Strike Hard" anticrime campaign, but are comparable to figures for the previous three years. Amnesty International stated, "1996 was an exceptionally high year for executions, and 1997 just marks a return to the level before then." It concluded that the sharp increase in the number of executions in 1996 did not in any way deter crime rates.

In spite of the profusion of executions, the crime rate in China has shown an increase in recent years. Violent crimes, such as murder and robbery, and crimes associated with gangs abroad, such as trafficking in narcotics, smuggling of gold and relics, and counterfeiting of currency and credit cards, have multiplied. In 1997, the Special Rapporteur for the United Nations on extrajudicial, summary, and arbitrary executions stated, "The death penalty is not an appropriate tool to fight the growing crime rate in China."

Rather than deterring crime, there is evidence that capital punishment actually increases the murder rate. The most dramatic is from a study done by Bowers and Pierce in New York State, examining the period between 1907 and 1963, when the state carried out more executions than any other state. It was revealed that there were, on average, two additional homicides above the normal rate in the month after an execution. They surmised that this periodic rise in homicides might be due to a "brutalizing" effect of executions, similar to the effect of other violent events, like publicized suicides, mass murders, and assassinations. One researcher concluded there to be a penchant of persons with criminal tendencies to commit a crime with the intent of getting executed. Playwright George Bernard Shaw observed, "Murder and capital punishment are not opposites that cancel one another, but similars that breed their kind." In a poll conducted by the *Journal of Criminal Law and Criminology*, more than 80 percent of professional criminologists interviewed were of the opinion that capital punishment does not lower murder rates.

The abolitionist view: In addition to contending that the death penalty does not, in fact, reduce the crime rate, those opposed to it cite several other ethical and practical issues. There is, for example, the fallibility of the judicial system. Death penalty trials are prone to errors, and the possibility of sending an innocent man to the gallows is always lurking in the background. Forensic DNA evidence was a boon to prosecutors in trying and convicting criminals. But at the same time, DNA evidence has in the last thirty years proven 107 people innocent of the crime for which they were sent to death row in the United States. Several of the India-based saints interviewed for this article complained that the justice system in India is highly corrupt, and one can bribe one's way out of even murder charges.

Then there are the astounding costs of death penalty cases, at least as prosecuted in Western countries. According to a study of North Carolina State, a murder case costs us $2.16 million more with a death penalty than with a sentence of life imprisonment. This includes all the expenses from trial through appeals and execution compared to incarceration for forty years. It is estimated that the death penalty costs the US justice system an extra one billion dollars a year.

Though the constitution of each nation guarantees equality before the law, several studies reveal that discrimination and procedural unfairness in death-penalty cases are epidemic. Ethnic and religious minorities, the unprivileged, the disempowered poor, and the less educated are more likely to be convicted and sentenced to death. Studies in the United States reveal that 95 percent of death-row inmates are classified poor, and a disproportionate number are from minority groups. For example, in Texas, of the four hundred people on death row in 2006, 31 percent were white, 41 percent black, 27 percent Hispanic, and 1 percent "other." The state's population [at that time was] 50 percent white, 12 percent black, and 34 percent Hispanic.

Abolitionists hold that the death penalty is a violation of human rights and an outrage to the intrinsic worth and sacredness of human life. The Universal Declaration of Human Rights directs, "No one shall be subjected to torture or to cruel, inhuman, or degrading treatment or punishment"—though neither the Declaration nor the subsequent binding covenants based upon it actually forbid the death penalty in every circumstance (e.g., treason in time of war). Not only is the death penalty a human rights violation, but the biased manner in which it is applied is a clear violation of the dignity of persons. It is time we strive to transcend the gruesome history of capital punishment and face the daunting challenge of providing basic human rights to all, irrespective of social or economic status and class distinctions. The European Union strongly considers the death penalty a "denial of human dignity" and is of the opinion "that the abolition of the death penalty contributes to the progressive development of human rights." The basic human rights philosophy is universal, based on human values and a spiritual essence that is common to all religions. Hinduism emphasizes that "All humanity is one family" and urges us to treat every member of the family with due respect and dignity. The theory of uncompromising human dignity echoes in the splendid expression of Ramakrishna Paramahansa, "Each soul is potentially divine."

Conclusion: Crime changes its contours with the passage of time, and the evolution of the culture from which it emerges. As society progresses rapidly, the concept of criminality and punishment also undergoes a change. The arbitrariness of a particular punishment is further highlighted when measured in terms of evolving standards of human decency. We should not allow the burden of our past to weigh us down. We must make an earnest attempt to recognize that we need to infuse fresh laws, ideals, and beliefs to replace an obsolete mode of punishment that is not worthy of a humane society. The Hindu lawgiver Manu said that laws would change with the maturity of the human race. . . .

Before we decide to unflinchingly extinguish the flame of another human life, it would further the cause of mankind if we strive to ignite the sleeping embers of our minds and humanize the penal system by remembering that "every saint has a past and every sinner a future." Imprisonment for life without the possibility of parole is a befitting alternative to capital punishment. Italian criminologist Cesare Beccaria's essay "Crimes and Punishments," published in 1764, still holds contemporary relevance. He believed that while the death penalty is successful in shocking people momentarily, it does not leave a lasting impact on people's mind: "The death of a criminal is a terrible but momentary spectacle and therefore a less efficacious method of deterring others than the continued example of a man deprived of his liberty."

Former United Nations secretary-general Kofi Annan has aptly enunciated his view of the future of capital punishment around the world: "The forfeiture of life is too absolute, too irreversible, for one human being to inflict it on another, even when backed by legal process. And I believe that future generations, throughout the world, will come to agree." Mahatma Gandhi was firmly against the death penalty: "I cannot in all conscience agree to anyone being sent to the gallows. God alone can take life because He alone gives it." And let us end with the words of the Rig Veda 10.137.1: "Ye enlightened men, uplift once more the fallen and forlorn, lowly and forlorn; ye illustrious men, raise him who has sinned and degraded himself, restore him to life again."

6

TRIAL BY FIRE

Did Texas Execute an Innocent Man?

David Grann

I

The fire moved quickly through the house, a one-story wood-frame structure in a working-class neighborhood of Corsicana, in northeast Texas. Flames spread along the walls, bursting through doorways, blistering paint and tiles and furniture. Smoke pressed against the ceiling, then banked downward, seeping into each room and through crevices in the windows, staining the morning sky.

Buffie Barbee, who was eleven years old and lived two houses down, was playing in her backyard when she smelled the smoke. She ran inside and told her mother, Diane, and they hurried up the street; that's when they saw the smoldering house and Cameron Todd Willingham standing on the front porch, wearing only a pair of jeans, his chest blackened with soot, his hair and eyelids singed. He was screaming, "My babies are burning up!" His children—Karmon and Kameron, who were one-year-old twin girls, and two-year-old Amber—were trapped inside.

Willingham told the Barbees to call the fire department, and while Diane raced down the street to get help he found a stick and broke the children's bedroom window. Fire lashed through the hole. He broke another window; flames burst through it, too, and he retreated into the yard, kneeling in front of the house. A neighbor later told police that Willingham intermittently cried, "My babies!" then fell silent, as if he had "blocked the fire out of his mind."

Diane Barbee, returning to the scene, could feel intense heat radiating off the house. Moments later, the five windows of the children's room exploded and flames "blew out," as Barbee put it. Within minutes, the first firemen had arrived, and Willingham approached them, shouting that his children were in their bedroom, where the flames were thickest. A fireman sent word over his radio for rescue teams to "step on it."

More men showed up, uncoiling hoses and aiming water at the blaze. One fireman, who had an air tank strapped to his back and a mask covering his face, slipped through a window but was hit by water from a hose and had to retreat. He then charged through the front door, into a swirl of smoke and fire. Heading down the main corridor, he reached the kitchen, where he saw a refrigerator blocking the back door.

Todd Willingham, looking on, appeared to grow more hysterical, and a police chaplain named George Monaghan led him to the back of a fire truck and tried to calm him down. Willingham explained that his wife, Stacy, had gone out earlier that morning, and that he had been jolted from sleep by Amber screaming, "Daddy! Daddy!" "My little girl was trying to wake me up and tell me about the fire," he said, adding, "I couldn't get my babies out."

While he was talking, a fireman emerged from the house, cradling Amber. As she was given CPR, Willingham, who was twenty-three years old and powerfully built, ran to see her, then suddenly headed toward the babies' room. Monaghan and another man restrained him. "We had to wrestle with him and then handcuff him, for his and our protection," Monaghan later told police. "I received a black eye." One of the first firemen at the scene told investigators that, at an earlier point, he had also held Willingham back. "Based on what I saw on how the fire was burning, it would have been crazy for anyone to try and go into the house," he said.

Willingham was taken to a hospital, where he was told that Amber—who had actually been found in the master bedroom—had died of smoke inhalation. Kameron and Karmon had been lying on the floor of the children's bedroom, their bodies severely burned. According to the medical examiner, they, too, died from smoke inhalation.

News of the tragedy, which took place on December 23, 1991, spread through Corsicana. A small city fifty-five miles northeast of Waco, it had once been the center of Texas's first oil boom, but many of the wells had since dried up, and more than a quarter of the city's twenty thousand inhabitants had fallen into poverty. Several stores along the main street were shuttered, giving the place the feel of an abandoned outpost.

Willingham and his wife, who was twenty-two years old, had virtually no money. Stacy worked in her brother's bar, called Some Other Place, and Willingham, an unemployed auto mechanic, had been caring for the kids. The community took up a collection to help the Willinghams pay for funeral arrangements.

Fire investigators, meanwhile, tried to determine the cause of the blaze. (Willingham gave authorities permission to search the house: "I know we might not ever know all the answers, but I'd just like to know why my babies were taken from me.") Douglas Fogg, who was then the assistant fire chief in Corsicana, conducted the initial inspection. He was tall, with a crew cut, and his voice was raspy from years of inhaling smoke from fires and cigarettes. He had grown up in Corsicana and, after graduating from high school, in 1963, he had joined the navy, serving as a medic in Vietnam, where he was wounded on four occasions. He was awarded a Purple Heart each time. After he returned from Vietnam, he became a firefighter, and by the time of the Willingham blaze he had been battling fire—or what he calls "the beast"—for more than twenty years, and had become a certified arson investigator. "You learn that fire talks to you," he told me.

He was soon joined on the case by one of the state's leading arson sleuths, a deputy fire marshal named Manuel Vasquez, who has since died. Short, with a paunch, Vasquez had investigated more than twelve hundred fires. Arson investigators have always been considered a special breed of detective. In the 1991 movie *Backdraft*, a heroic arson investigator says of fire, "It breathes, it eats, and it hates. The only way to beat it is to think like it. To know that this flame will spread this way across the door and up across the ceiling." Vasquez, who had previously worked in Army intelligence, had several maxims of his own. One was "Fire does not destroy evidence—it creates it." Another was "The fire tells the story. I am just the interpreter." He cultivated a Sherlock Holmes–like aura of invincibility. Once, he was asked under oath whether he had ever been mistaken in a case. "If I have, sir, I don't know," he responded. "It's never been pointed out."

Vasquez and Fogg visited the Willinghams' house four days after the blaze. Following protocol, they moved from the least burned areas toward the most damaged ones. "It is a systematic method," Vasquez later testified, adding, "I'm just collecting information. . . . I have not made any determination. I don't have any preconceived idea."

The men slowly toured the perimeter of the house, taking notes and photographs, like archeologists mapping out a ruin. Upon opening the back door, Vasquez observed that there was just enough space to squeeze past the refrigerator blocking the exit. The air smelled of burned rubber and melted wires; a damp ash covered the ground, sticking to their boots. In the kitchen, Vasquez and Fogg discerned only smoke and heat damage—a sign that the fire had not originated there—and so they pushed deeper into the nine-hundred-and-seventy-five-square-foot building. A central corridor led past a utility room and the master bedroom, then past a small living room, on the left, and the children's bedroom, on the right, ending at the front door, which opened onto the porch. Vasquez tried to take in everything, a process that he compared to entering one's mother-in-law's house for the first time: "I have the same curiosity."

In the utility room, he noticed on the wall pictures of skulls and what he later described as an image of "the Grim Reaper." Then he turned into the master bedroom, where Amber's body had been found. Most of the damage there was also from smoke and heat, suggesting that the fire had started farther down the hallway, and he headed that way, stepping over debris and ducking under insulation and wiring that hung down from the exposed ceiling.

As he and Fogg removed some of the clutter, they noticed deep charring along the base of the walls. Because gases become buoyant when heated, flames ordinarily burn upward. But Vasquez and Fogg observed that the fire had burned extremely low down, and that there were peculiar char patterns on the floor, shaped like puddles.

Vasquez's mood darkened. He followed the "burn trailer"—the path etched by the fire—which led from the hallway into the children's bedroom. Sunlight filtering through the broken windows illuminated more of the irregularly shaped char patterns. A flammable or combustible liquid doused on a floor will cause a fire to concentrate in these kinds of pockets, which is why investigators refer to them as "pour patterns" or "puddle configurations."

The fire had burned through layers of carpeting and tile and ply-wood flooring. Moreover, the metal springs under the children's beds had turned white—a sign that intense heat had radiated beneath them. Seeing that the floor had some of the deepest burns, Vasquez deduced that it had been hotter than the ceiling, which, given that heat rises, was, in his words, "not normal."

Fogg examined a piece of glass from one of the broken windows. It contained a spiderweb-like pattern—what fire investigators call "crazed glass." Forensic textbooks had long described the effect as a key indicator that a fire had burned "fast and hot," meaning that it had been fuelled by a liquid accelerant, causing the glass to fracture.

The men looked again at what appeared to be a distinct burn trailer through the house: it went from the children's bedroom into the corridor, then turned sharply to the right and proceeded out the front door. To the investigators' surprise, even the wood under the door's aluminum threshold was charred. On the concrete floor of the porch, just outside the front door, Vasquez and Fogg noticed another unusual thing: brown stains, which, they reported, were consistent with the presence of an accelerant.

The men scanned the walls for soot marks that resembled a V. When an object catches on fire, it creates such a pattern, as heat and smoke radiate outward; the bottom of the V can therefore point to where a fire began. In the Willingham house, there was a distinct V in the main corridor. Examining it and other burn patterns, Vasquez identified three places where fire had originated: in the hallway, in the children's bedroom, and at the front door. Vasquez later testified that multiple origins pointed to one conclusion: the fire was "intentionally set by human hands."

By now, both investigators had a clear vision of what had happened. Someone had poured liquid accelerant throughout the children's room, even under their beds, then poured some more along the adjoining hallway and out the front door, creating a "fire barrier" that prevented anyone from escaping; similarly, a prosecutor later suggested, the refrigerator in the kitchen had been moved to block the back-door exit. The house, in short, had been deliberately transformed into a death trap.

The investigators collected samples of burned materials from the house and sent them to a laboratory that could detect the presence of a liquid accelerant. The lab's chemist reported that one of the samples contained evidence of "mineral spirits," a substance that is often found in charcoal-lighter fluid. The sample had been taken by the threshold of the front door.

The fire was now considered a triple homicide, and Todd Willingham—the only person, besides the victims, known to have been in the house at the time of the blaze—became the prime suspect.

Police and fire investigators canvassed the neighborhood, interviewing witnesses. Several, like Father Monaghan, initially portrayed Willingham as devastated by the fire. Yet, over time, an increasing number of witnesses offered damning statements. Diane Barbee said that she had not seen Willingham try to enter the house until after the authorities arrived, as if he were putting on a show. And when the children's room exploded with flames, she added, he seemed more preoccupied with his car, which he moved down the driveway. Another neighbor reported that when Willingham cried out for his babies he "did not appear to be excited or concerned." Even Father Monaghan wrote in a statement that, upon further reflection, "things were not as they seemed. I had the feeling that [Willingham] was in complete control."

The police began to piece together a disturbing profile of Willingham. Born in Ardmore, Oklahoma, in 1968, he had been abandoned by his mother when he was a baby. His father, Gene, who had divorced his mother, eventually raised him with his stepmother, Eugenia. Gene, a former US Marine, worked in a salvage yard, and the family lived in a cramped house; at night, they could hear freight trains rattling past on a nearby track. Willingham, who had what the family called the "classic Willingham look"—a handsome face, thick black hair, and dark eyes—struggled in school, and as a teenager began to sniff paint. When he was seventeen, Oklahoma's Department of Human Services evaluated him, and reported, "He likes 'girls,' music, fast cars, sharp trucks, swimming, and hunting, in that order." Willingham dropped out of high school, and over time was arrested for, among other things, driving under the influence, stealing a bicycle, and shoplifting.

In 1988, he met Stacy, a senior in high school, who also came from a troubled background: when she was four years old, her step-father had strangled her mother to death during a fight. Stacy and Willingham had a turbulent relationship. Willingham, who was unfaithful, drank too much Jack Daniel's and sometimes hit Stacy—even when she was pregnant. A neighbor said that he once heard Willingham yell at her, "Get up, bitch, and I'll hit you again."

On December 31, the authorities brought Willingham in for questioning. Fogg and Vasquez were present for the interrogation, along with Jimmie Hensley, a police officer who was working his first arson case. Willingham said that Stacy had left the house around 9 AM to pick up a Christmas present for the kids, at the Salvation Army. "After she got out of the driveway, I heard the twins cry, so I got up and gave them a bottle," he said. The children's room had a safety gate across the doorway, which Amber could climb over but not the twins, and he and Stacy often let the twins nap on the floor after they drank their bottles. Amber was still in bed, Willingham said, so he went back into his room to sleep. "The next thing I remember is hearing 'Daddy, Daddy,'" he recalled. "The house was already full of smoke." He said that he got up, felt around the floor for a pair of pants, and put them on. He could no longer hear his daughter's voice ("I heard that last 'Daddy, Daddy' and never heard her again"), and he hollered, "Oh, God—Amber, get out of the house! Get out of the house!'"

He never sensed that Amber was in his room, he said. Perhaps she had already passed out by the time he stood up, or perhaps she came in after he left, through a second doorway, from the living room. He said that he went down the corridor and tried to reach the children's bedroom. In the hallway, he said, "you couldn't see nothing but black." The air smelled the way it had when their microwave had blown up, three weeks earlier—like "wire and stuff like that." He could hear sockets and light switches popping, and he crouched down, almost crawling. When he made it to the children's bedroom, he said, he stood and his hair caught on fire. "Oh, God, I never felt anything that hot before," he said of the heat radiating out of the room.

After he patted out the fire on his hair, he said, he got down on the ground and groped in the dark. "I thought I found one of them once," he said, "but it was a doll." He couldn't bear the heat any longer. "I felt myself passing out," he said. Finally, he stumbled down the corridor and out the front door, trying to catch his breath. He saw

Diane Barbee and yelled for her to call the fire department. After she left, he insisted, he tried without success to get back inside.

The investigators asked him if he had any idea how the fire had started. He said that he wasn't sure, though it must have originated in the children's room, since that was where he first saw flames; they were glowing like "bright lights." He and Stacy used three space heaters to keep the house warm, and one of them was in the children's room. "I taught Amber not to play with it," he said, adding that she got "whuppings every once in a while for messing with it." He said that he didn't know if the heater, which had an internal flame, was turned on. (Vasquez later testified that when he had checked the heater, four days after the fire, it was in the "Off" position.) Willingham speculated that the fire might have been started by something electrical: he had heard all that popping and crackling.

When pressed whether someone might have a motive to hurt his family, he said that he couldn't think of anyone that "cold-blooded." He said of his children, "I just don't understand why anybody would take them, you know? We had three of the most pretty babies anybody could have ever asked for." He went on: "Me and Stacy's been together for four years, but off and on we get into a fight and split up for a while, and I think those babies is what brought us so close together . . . neither one of us . . . could live without them kids." Thinking of Amber, he said, "To tell you the honest-to-God's truth, I wish she hadn't woke me up."

During the interrogation, Vasquez let Fogg take the lead. Finally, Vasquez turned to Willingham and asked a seemingly random question: had he put on shoes before he fled the house?

"No, sir," Willingham replied.

A map of the house was on a table between the men, and Vasquez pointed to it. "You walked out this way?" he said.

Willingham said yes.

Vasquez was now convinced that Willingham had killed his children. If the floor had been soaked with a liquid accelerant and the fire had burned low, as the evidence suggested, Willingham could not have run out of the house the way he had described without badly burning his feet. A medical report indicated that his feet had been unscathed.

Willingham insisted that, when he left the house, the fire was still around the top of the walls and not on the floor. "I didn't have to jump through any flames," he said. Vasquez believed that this was impossible, and that Willingham had lit the fire as he was retreating—first, torching the children's room, then the hallway, and then, from the porch, the front door. Vasquez later said of Willingham, "He told me a story of pure fabrication. . . . He just talked and he talked and all he did was lie."

Still, there was no clear motive. The children had life-insurance policies, but they amounted to only fifteen thousand dollars, and Stacy's grandfather, who had paid for them, was listed as the primary beneficiary. Stacy told investigators that even though Willingham hit her he had never abused the children—"Our kids were spoiled rotten," she said—and she did not believe that Willingham could have killed them.

Ultimately, the authorities concluded that Willingham was a man without a conscience whose serial crimes had climaxed, almost inexorably, in murder. John Jackson, who was then the assistant district attorney in Corsicana, was assigned to prosecute Willingham's case. He later told the *Dallas Morning News* that he considered Willingham to be "an utterly sociopathic individual" who deemed his children "an impediment to his lifestyle." Or, as the local district attorney, Pat Batchelor, put it, "The children were interfering with his beer drinking and dart throwing."

On the night of January 8, 1992, two weeks after the fire, Willingham was riding in a car with Stacy when SWAT teams surrounded them, forcing them to the side of the road. "They pulled guns out like we had just robbed ten banks," Stacy later recalled. "All we heard was 'click, click.' . . . Then they arrested him."

Willingham was charged with murder. Because there were multiple victims, he was eligible for the death penalty under Texas law. Unlike many other prosecutors in the state, Jackson, who had ambitions of becoming a judge, was personally opposed to capital punishment. "I don't think it's effective in deterring criminals," he told me. "I just don't think it works." He also considered it wasteful: because of the expense of litigation and the appeals process, it costs, on average, $2.3 million to execute a prisoner in Texas—about three times the cost of incarcerating someone for forty years. Plus, Jackson said, "What's the recourse if you make a mistake?" Yet his boss, Batchelor, believed that, as he once put it, "certain people who commit bad enough crimes give up the right to live," and Jackson came to agree that the heinous nature of the crime in the Willingham case—"one of the worst in terms of body count" that he had ever tried—mandated death.

Willingham couldn't afford to hire lawyers and was assigned two by the state: David Martin, a former state trooper, and Robert Dunn, a local defense attorney who represented everyone from alleged murderers to spouses in divorce cases—a "Jack-of-all-trades," as he calls himself. ("In a small town, you can't say, 'I'm a so-and-so lawyer,' because you'll starve to death," he told me.)

Not long after Willingham's arrest, authorities received a message from a prison inmate named Johnny Webb, who was in the same jail as Willingham. Webb alleged that Willingham had confessed to him that he took "some kind of lighter fluid, squirting [it] around the walls and the floor, and set a fire." The case against Willingham was considered airtight.

Even so, several of Stacy's relatives—who, unlike her, believed that Willingham was guilty—told Jackson that they preferred to avoid the anguish of a trial. And so, shortly before jury selection, Jackson approached Willingham's attorneys with an extraordinary offer: if their client pleaded guilty, the state would give him a life sentence. "I was really happy when I thought we might have a deal to avoid the death penalty," Jackson recalls.

Willingham's lawyers were equally pleased. They had little doubt that he had committed the murders and that, if the case went before a jury, he would be found guilty and, subsequently, executed. "Everyone thinks defense lawyers must believe their clients are innocent, but that's seldom true," Martin told me. "Most of the time, they're guilty as sin." He added of Willingham, "All the evidence showed that he was one hundred percent guilty. He poured accelerant all over the house and put lighter fluid under the kids' beds." It was, he said, "a classic arson case": there were "puddle patterns all over the place—no disputing those."

Martin and Dunn advised Willingham that he should accept the offer, but he refused. The lawyers asked his father and stepmother to speak to him. According to Eugenia, Martin showed them photographs of the burned children and said, "Look what your son did. You got to talk him into pleading, or he's going to be executed."

His parents went to see their son in jail. Though his father did not believe that he should plead guilty if he were innocent, his stepmother beseeched him to take the deal. "I just wanted to keep my boy alive," she told me.

Willingham was implacable. "I ain't gonna plead to something I didn't do, especially killing my own kids," he said. It was his final decision. Martin says, "I thought it was nuts at the time—and I think it's nuts now."

Willingham's refusal to accept the deal confirmed the view of the prosecution, and even that of his defense lawyers, that he was an unrepentant killer.

In August 1992, the trial commenced in the old stone courthouse in downtown Corsicana. Jackson and a team of prosecutors summoned a procession of witnesses, including Johnny Webb and the Barbees. The crux of the state's case, though, remained the scientific evidence gathered by Vasquez and Fogg. On the stand, Vasquez detailed what he called more than "twenty indicators" of arson.

"Do you have an opinion as to who started the fire?" one of the prosecutors asked.

"Yes, sir," Vasquez said. "Mr. Willingham."

The prosecutor asked Vasquez what he thought Willingham's intent was in lighting the fire. "To kill the little girls," he said.

The defense had tried to find a fire expert to counter Vasquez and Fogg's testimony, but the one they contacted concurred with the prosecution. Ultimately, the defense presented only one witness to the jury: the Willinghams' babysitter, who said she could not believe that Willingham could have killed his children. (Dunn told me that Willingham had wanted to testify, but Martin and Dunn thought that he would make a bad witness.) The trial ended after two days.

During his closing arguments, Jackson said that the puddle configurations and pour patterns were Willingham's inadvertent "confession," burned into the floor. Showing a Bible that had been salvaged from the fire, Jackson paraphrased the words of Jesus from the Gospel of Matthew: "Whomsoever shall harm one of my children, it's better for a millstone to be hung around his neck and for him to be cast in the sea."

The jury was out for barely an hour before returning with a unanimous guilty verdict. As Vasquez put it, "The fire does not lie."

II

When Elizabeth Gilbert approached the prison guard, on a spring day in 1999, and said Cameron Todd Willingham's name, she was uncertain about what she was doing. A forty-seven-year-old French teacher and playwright from Houston, Gilbert was divorced with two children. She had never visited a prison before. Several weeks earlier, a friend, who worked at an organization that opposed the death penalty, had encouraged her to volunteer as a pen pal for an inmate on death row, and Gilbert had offered her name and address. Not long after, a short letter, written with unsteady penmanship, arrived from Willingham. "If you wish to write back, I would be honored to correspond with you," he said. He also asked if she might visit him. Perhaps out of a writer's curiosity, or perhaps because she didn't feel quite herself (she had just been upset by news that her ex-husband was dying of cancer), she agreed. Now she was standing in front of the decrepit penitentiary in Huntsville, Texas—a place that inmates referred to as "the death pit."

She filed past a razor-wire fence, a series of floodlights, and a checkpoint, where she was patted down, until she entered a small chamber. Only a few feet in front of her was a man convicted of multiple infanticide. He was wearing a white jumpsuit with "DR"—for death row—printed on the back, in large black letters. He had a tattoo of a serpent and a skull on his left biceps. He stood nearly six feet tall and was muscular, though his legs had atrophied after years of confinement.

A Plexiglas window separated Willingham from her; still, Gilbert, who had short brown hair and a bookish manner, stared at him uneasily. Willingham had once fought another prisoner who called him a "baby killer," and since he had been incarcerated, seven years earlier, he had committed a series of disciplinary infractions that had periodically landed him in the segregation unit, which was known as "the dungeon."

Willingham greeted her politely. He seemed grateful that she had come. After his conviction, Stacy had campaigned for his release. She wrote to Ann Richards, then the governor of Texas, saying, "I know him in ways that no one else does when it comes to our children. Therefore, I believe that there is no way he could have possibly committed this crime." But within a year Stacy had filed for divorce, and Willingham had few visitors except for his parents, who drove from Oklahoma to see him once a month. "I really have no one outside my parents to remind me that I am a human being, not the animal the state professes I am," he told Gilbert at one point.

He didn't want to talk about death row. "Hell, I live here," he later wrote her. "When I have a visit, I want to escape from here." He asked her questions about her teaching and art. He expressed fear that, as a playwright, she might find him a "one-dimensional character," and apologized for lacking social graces; he now had trouble separating the mores in prison from those of the outside world.

When Gilbert asked him if he wanted something to eat or drink from the vending machines, he declined. "I hope I did not offend you by not accepting any snacks," he later wrote her. "I didn't want you to feel I was there just for something like that."

She had been warned that prisoners often tried to con visitors. He appeared to realize this, subsequently telling her, "I am just a simple man. Nothing else. And to most other people a convicted killer looking for someone to manipulate."

Their visit lasted for two hours, and afterward they continued to correspond. She was struck by his letters, which seemed introspective and were not at all what she had expected. "I am a very honest person with my feelings," he wrote her. "I will not bullshit you on how I feel or what I think." He said that he used to be stoic, like his father. But, he added, "losing my three daughters . . . my home, wife and my life, you tend to wake up a little. I have learned to open myself."

She agreed to visit him again, and when she returned, several weeks later, he was visibly moved. "Here I am this person who nobody on the outside is ever going to know as a human, who has lost so much, but still trying to hold on," he wrote her afterward. "But you came back! I don't think you will ever know of what importance that visit was in my existence."

They kept exchanging letters, and she began asking him about the fire. He insisted that he was innocent and that, if someone had poured accelerant through the house and lit it, then the killer remained free. Gilbert wasn't naïve—she assumed that he was guilty. She did not mind giving him solace, but she was not there to absolve him.

Still, she had become curious about the case, and one day that fall she drove down to the courthouse in Corsicana to review the trial records. Many people in the community remembered the tragedy, and a clerk expressed bewilderment that anyone would be interested in a man who had burned his children alive.

Gilbert took the files and sat down at a small table. As she examined the eyewitness accounts, she noticed several contradictions. Diane Barbee had reported that, before the authorities arrived at the fire, Willingham never tried to get back into the house—yet she had been absent for some time while calling the fire department. Meanwhile, her daughter Buffie had reported witnessing Willingham on the porch breaking a window, in an apparent effort to reach his children. And the firemen and police on the scene had described Willingham frantically trying to get into the house.

The witnesses' testimony also grew more damning after authorities had concluded, in the beginning of January 1992, that Willingham was likely guilty of murder. In Diane Barbee's initial statement to authorities, she had portrayed Willingham as "hysterical," and described the front of the house exploding. But on January 4, after arson investigators began suspecting Willingham of murder, Barbee suggested that he could have gone back inside to rescue his children, for at the outset she had seen only "smoke coming from out of the front of the house"—smoke that was not "real thick."

An even starker shift occurred with Father Monaghan's testimony. In his first statement, he had depicted Willingham as a devastated father who had to be repeatedly restrained from risking his life. Yet, as investigators were preparing to arrest Willingham, he concluded that Willingham had been *too* emotional ("He seemed to have the type of distress that a woman who had given birth would have upon seeing her children die"); and he expressed a "gut feeling" that Willingham had "something to do with the setting of the fire."

Dozens of studies have shown that witnesses' memories of events often change when they are supplied with new contextual information. Itiel Dror, a cognitive psychologist who has done extensive research on eyewitness and expert testimony in criminal investigations, told me, "The mind is not a passive machine. Once you believe in something—once you expect something—it changes the way you perceive information and the way your memory recalls it."

After Gilbert's visit to the courthouse, she kept wondering about

Willingham's motive, and she pressed him on the matter. In response, he wrote, of the death of his children, "I do not talk about it much anymore and it is still a very powerfully emotional pain inside my being." He admitted that he had been a "sorry-ass husband" who had hit Stacy—something he deeply regretted. But he said that he had loved his children and would never have hurt them. Fatherhood, he said, had changed him; he stopped being a hoodlum and "settled down" and "became a man." Nearly three months before the fire, he and Stacy, who had never married, wed at a small ceremony in his hometown of Ardmore. He said that the prosecution had seized upon incidents from his past and from the day of the fire to create a portrait of a "demon," as Jackson, the prosecutor, referred to him. For instance, Willingham said, he had moved the car during the fire simply because he didn't want it to explode by the house, further threatening the children.

Gilbert was unsure what to make of his story, and she began to approach people who were involved in the case, asking them questions. "My friends thought I was crazy," Gilbert recalls. "I'd never done anything like this in my life."

One morning, when Willingham's parents came to visit him, Gilbert arranged to see them first, at a coffee shop near the prison. Gene, who was in his seventies, had the Willingham look, though his black hair had gray streaks and his dark eyes were magnified by glasses. Eugenia, who was in her fifties, with silvery hair, was as sweet and talkative as her husband was stern and reserved. The drive from Oklahoma to Texas took six hours, and they had woken at three in the morning; because they could not afford a motel, they would have to return home later that day. "I feel like a real burden to them," Willingham had written Gilbert.

As Gene and Eugenia sipped coffee, they told Gilbert how grateful they were that someone had finally taken an interest in Todd's case. Gene said that his son, though he had flaws, was no killer.

The evening before the fire, Eugenia said, she had spoken on the phone with Todd. She and Gene were planning on visiting two days later, on Christmas Eve, and Todd told her that he and Stacy and the kids had just picked up family photographs. "He said, 'We got your pictures for Christmas,'" she recalled. "He put Amber on the phone, and she was tattling on one of the twins. Todd didn't seem upset. If something was bothering him, I would have known."

Gene and Eugenia got up to go: they didn't want to miss any of the four hours that were allotted for the visit with their son. Before they left, Gene said, "You'll let us know if you find anything, won't you?"

Over the next few weeks, Gilbert continued to track down sources. Many of them, including the Barbees, remained convinced that Willingham was guilty, but several of his friends and relatives had doubts. So did some people in law enforcement. Willingham's former probation officer in Oklahoma, Polly Goodin, recently told me that Willingham had never demonstrated bizarre or sociopathic behavior. "He was probably one of my favorite kids," she said. Even a former judge named Bebe Bridges—who had often stood, as she put it, on the "opposite side" of Willingham in the legal system, and who had sent him to jail for stealing—told me that she could not imagine him killing his children. "He was polite, and he seemed to care," she said. "His convictions had been for dumb-kid stuff. Even the things stolen weren't significant." Several months before the fire, Willingham tracked Goodin down at her office, and proudly showed her photographs of Stacy and the kids. "He wanted Bebe and me to know he'd been doing good," Goodin recalled.

Eventually, Gilbert returned to Corsicana to interview Stacy, who had agreed to meet at the bed-and-breakfast where Gilbert was staying. Stacy was slightly plump, with pale, round cheeks and feathered dark-blond hair; her bangs were held in place by gel, and her face was heavily made up. According to a tape recording of the conversation, Stacy said that nothing unusual had happened in the days before the fire. She and Willingham had not fought, and were preparing for the holiday. Though Vasquez, the arson expert, had recalled finding the space heater off, Stacy was sure that, at least on the day of the incident —a cool winter morning—it had been on. "I remember turning it down," she recalled. "I always thought, 'Gosh, could Amber have put something in there?'" Stacy added that, more than once, she had caught Amber "putting things too close to it."

Willingham had often not treated her well, she recalled, and after his incarceration she had left him for a man who did. But she didn't think that her former husband should be on death row. "I don't think he did it," she said, crying.

Though only the babysitter had appeared as a witness for the defense during the main trial, several family members, including Stacy, testified during the penalty phase, asking the jury to spare Willingham's life. When Stacy was on the stand, Jackson grilled her about the "significance" of Willingham's "very large tattoo of a skull, encircled by some kind of a serpent."

"It's just a tattoo," Stacy responded.

"He just likes skulls and snakes. Is that what you're saying?"

"No. He just had—he got a tattoo on him."

The prosecution cited such evidence in asserting that Willingham fit the profile of a sociopath, and brought forth two medical experts to confirm the theory. Neither had met Willingham. One of them was Tim Gregory, a psychologist with a master's degree in marriage and family issues, who had previously gone goose hunting with Jackson, and had not published any research in the field of sociopathic behavior. His practice was devoted to family counseling.

At one point, Jackson showed Gregory Exhibit No. 60—a photograph of an Iron Maiden poster that had hung in Willingham's house—and asked the psychologist to interpret it. "This one is a picture of a skull, with a fist being punched through the skull," Gregory said; the image displayed "violence" and "death." Gregory looked at photographs of other music posters owned by Willingham. "There's a hooded skull, with wings and a hatchet," Gregory continued. "And all of these are in fire, depicting—it reminds me of something like Hell. And there's a picture—a Led Zeppelin picture of a falling angel. . . . I see there's an association many times with cultive-type of activities. A focus on death, dying. Many times individuals that have a lot of this type of art have interest in satanic-type activities."

The other medical expert was James P. Grigson, a forensic psychiatrist. He testified so often for the prosecution in capital-punishment cases that he had become known as Dr. Death. (A Texas appellate judge once wrote that when Grigson appeared on the stand the defendant might as well "commence writing out his last will and testament.") Grigson suggested that Willingham was an "extremely severe sociopath," and that "no pill" or treatment could help him. Grigson had previously used nearly the same words in helping to secure a death sentence against Randall Dale Adams, who had been convicted of murdering a police officer, in 1977. After Adams, who had no prior criminal record, spent a dozen years on death row—and once came within seventy-two hours of being executed—new evidence emerged that absolved him, and he was released. In 1995, three years after Willingham's trial, Grigson was expelled from the American Psychiatric Association for violating ethics. The association stated that Grigson had repeatedly arrived at a "psychiatric diagnosis without first having examined the individuals in question, and for indicating, while testifying in court as an expert witness, that he could predict with 100-per-cent certainty that the individuals would engage in future violent acts."

After speaking to Stacy, Gilbert had one more person she wanted to interview: the jailhouse informant Johnny Webb, who was incarcerated in Iowa Park, Texas. She wrote to Webb, who said that she could see him, and they met in the prison visiting room. A man in his late twenties, he had pallid skin and a closely shaved head; his eyes were jumpy, and his entire body seemed to tremble. A reporter who once met him described him to me as "nervous as a cat around rocking chairs." Webb had begun taking drugs when he was nine years old, and had been convicted of, among other things, car theft, selling marijuana, forgery, and robbery.

As Gilbert chatted with him, she thought that he seemed paranoid. During Willingham's trial, Webb disclosed that he had been given a diagnosis of "post-traumatic stress disorder" after he was sexually assaulted in prison, in 1988, and that he often suffered from "mental impairment." Under cross-examination, Webb testified that he had no recollection of a robbery that he had pleaded guilty to only months earlier.

Webb repeated for her what he had said in court: he had passed by Willingham's cell, and as they spoke through a food slot Willingham broke down and told him that he intentionally set the house on fire. Gilbert was dubious. It was hard to believe that Willingham, who had otherwise insisted on his innocence, had suddenly confessed to an inmate he barely knew. The conversation had purportedly taken place by a speaker system that allowed any of the guards to listen—an unlikely spot for an inmate to reveal a secret. What's more, Webb alleged that Willingham had told him that Stacy had hurt one of the kids, and that the fire was set to cover up the crime. The autopsies, however, had revealed no bruises or signs of trauma on the children's bodies.

Jailhouse informants, many of whom are seeking reduced time or special privileges, are notoriously unreliable. According to a 2004 study by the Center on Wrongful Convictions, at Northwestern University Law School, lying police and jailhouse informants are the leading cause of wrongful convictions in capital cases in the United States. At the time that Webb came forward against Willingham, he was facing charges of robbery and forgery. During Willingham's trial, another inmate planned to testify that he had overheard Webb saying to another prisoner that he was hoping to "get time cut," but the testimony was ruled inadmissible, because it was hearsay. Webb, who pleaded guilty to the robbery and forgery charges, received a sentence of fifteen years. Jackson, the prosecutor, told me that he generally considered Webb "an unreliable kind of guy," but added, "I saw no real motive for him to make a statement like this if it wasn't true. We didn't cut him any slack." In 1997, five years after Willingham's trial, Jackson urged the Texas Board of Pardons and Paroles to grant Webb parole. "I asked them to cut him loose early," Jackson told me. The reason, Jackson said, was that Webb had been targeted by the Aryan Brotherhood. The board granted Webb parole, but within months of his release he was caught with cocaine and returned to prison.

In March 2000, several months after Gilbert's visit, Webb unexpectedly sent Jackson a Motion to Recant Testimony, declaring, "Mr. Willingham is innocent of all charges." But Willingham's lawyer was not informed of this development, and soon afterward Webb, without explanation, recanted his recantation. When I recently asked Webb, who was released from prison two years ago, about the turnabout and why Willingham would have confessed to a virtual stranger, he said that he knew only what "the dude told me." After I pressed him, he said, "It's very possible I misunderstood what he said." Since the trial, Webb has been given an additional diagnosis, bipolar disorder. "Being locked up in that little cell makes you kind of crazy," he said. "My memory is in bits and pieces. I was on a lot of medication at the time. Everyone knew that." He paused, then said, "The statute of limitations has run out on perjury, hasn't it?"

Aside from the scientific evidence of arson, the case against Willingham did not stand up to scrutiny. Jackson, the prosecutor, said of Webb's testimony, "You can take it or leave it." Even the refrigerator's placement by the back door of the house turned out to be innocuous;

there were two refrigerators in the cramped kitchen, and one of them was by the back door. Jimmie Hensley, the police detective, and Douglas Fogg, the assistant fire chief, both of whom investigated the fire, told me recently that they had never believed that the fridge was part of the arson plot. "It didn't have nothing to do with the fire," Fogg said.

After months of investigating the case, Gilbert found that her faith in the prosecution was shaken. As she told me, "What if Todd really was innocent?"

III

In the summer of 1660, an Englishman named William Harrison vanished on a walk, near the village of Charingworth, in Gloucestershire. His bloodstained hat was soon discovered on the side of a local road. Police interrogated Harrison's servant, John Perry, and eventually Perry gave a statement that his mother and his brother had killed Harrison for money. Perry, his mother, and his brother were hanged.

Two years later, Harrison reappeared. He insisted, fancifully, that he had been abducted by a band of criminals and sold into slavery. Whatever happened, one thing was indisputable: he had not been murdered by the Perrys.

The fear that an innocent person might be executed has long haunted jurors and lawyers and judges. During America's Colonial period, dozens of crimes were punishable by death, including horse thievery, blasphemy, "man-stealing," and highway robbery. After independence, the number of crimes eligible for the death penalty was gradually reduced, but doubts persisted over whether legal procedures were sufficient to prevent an innocent person from being executed. In 1868, John Stuart Mill made one of the most eloquent defenses of capital punishment, arguing that executing a murderer did not display a wanton disregard for life but, rather, proof of its value. "We show, on the contrary, most emphatically our regard for it by the adoption of a rule that he who violates that right in another forfeits it for himself," he said. For Mill, there was one counterargument that carried weight—"that if by an error of justice an innocent person is put to death, the mistake can never be corrected."

The modern legal system, with its lengthy appeals process and clemency boards, was widely assumed to protect the kind of "error of justice" that Mill feared. In 2000, while George W. Bush was governor of Texas, he said, "I know there are some in the country who don't care for the death penalty, but . . . we've adequately answered innocence or guilt." His top policy adviser on issues of criminal justice emphasized that there is "super due process to make sure that no innocent defendants are executed."

In recent years, though, questions have mounted over whether the system is fail-safe. Since 1976, more than a hundred and thirty people on death row have been exonerated. DNA testing, which was developed in the eighties, saved seventeen of them, but the technique can be used only in rare instances. Barry Scheck, a cofounder of the Innocence Project, which has used DNA testing to exonerate prisoners, estimates that about 80 percent of felonies do not involve biological evidence.

In 2000, after thirteen people on death row in Illinois were exonerated, George Ryan, who was then governor of the state, suspended the death penalty. Though he had been a longtime advocate of capital punishment, he declared that he could no longer support a system that has "come so close to the ultimate nightmare—the state's taking of innocent life." Former Supreme Court Justice Sandra Day O'Connor has said that the "execution of a legally and factually innocent person would be a constitutionally intolerable event."

Such a case has become a kind of grisly Holy Grail among opponents of capital punishment. In his 2002 book, *The Death Penalty*, Stuart Banner observes, "The prospect of killing an innocent person seemed to be the one thing that could cause people to rethink their support for capital punishment. Some who were not troubled by statistical arguments against the death penalty—claims about deterrence or racial disparities—were deeply troubled that such an extreme injustice might occur in an individual case." Opponents of the death penalty have pointed to several questionable cases. In 1993, Ruben Cantu was executed in Texas for fatally shooting a man during a robbery. Years later, a second victim, who survived the shooting, told the *Houston Chronicle* that he had been pressured by police to identify Cantu as the gunman, even though he believed Cantu to be innocent. Sam Millsap, the district attorney in the case, who had once supported capital punishment ("I'm no wild-eyed, pointy-headed liberal"), said that he was disturbed by the thought that he had made a mistake.

In 1995, Larry Griffin was put to death in Missouri, for a drive-by shooting of a drug dealer. The case rested largely on the eyewitness testimony of a career criminal named Robert Fitzgerald, who had been an informant for prosecutors before and was in the witness-protection program. Fitzgerald maintained that he happened to be at the scene because his car had broken down. After Griffin's execution, a probe sponsored by the NAACP's Legal Defense and Educational Fund revealed that a man who had been wounded during the incident insisted that Griffin was not the shooter. Moreover, the first police officer at the scene disputed that Fitzgerald had witnessed the crime.

These cases, however, stopped short of offering irrefutable proof that a "legally and factually innocent person" was executed. In 2005, a St. Louis prosecutor, Jennifer Joyce, launched an investigation of the Griffin case, upon being presented with what she called "compelling" evidence of Griffin's potential innocence. After two years of reviewing the evidence, and interviewing a new eyewitness, Joyce said that she and her team were convinced that the "right person was convicted."

Supreme Court Justice Antonin Scalia, in 2006, voted with a majority to uphold the death penalty in a Kansas case. In his opinion, Scalia declared that, in the modern judicial system, there has not been "a single case—not one—in which it is clear that a person was executed for a crime he did not commit. If such an event had occurred in recent years, we would not have to hunt for it; the innocent's name would be shouted from the rooftops."

"My problems are simple," Willingham wrote Gilbert in September 1999. "Try to keep them from killing me at all costs. End of story."

During his first years on death row, Willingham had pleaded with his lawyer, David Martin, to rescue him. "You can't imagine what it's like to be here, with people I have no business even being around," he wrote.

For a while, Willingham shared a cell with Ricky Lee Green, a serial killer, who castrated and fatally stabbed his victims, including a sixteen-year-old boy. (Green was executed in 1997.) Another of Willingham's cellmates, who had an IQ below seventy and the emotional development of an eight-year-old, was raped by an inmate. "You remember me telling you I had a new celly?" Willingham wrote in a letter to his parents. "The little retarded boy. . . . There was this guy here on the wing who is a shit sorry coward (who is the same one I got into it with a little over a month ago). Well, he raped [my cell-mate] in the 3 row shower week before last." Willingham said that he couldn't believe that someone would "rape a boy who cannot even defend himself. Pretty damn low."

Because Willingham was known as a "baby killer," he was a target of attacks. "Prison is a rough place, and with a case like mine they never give you the benefit of a doubt," he wrote his parents. After he tried to fight one prisoner who threatened him, Willingham told a friend that if he hadn't stood up for himself several inmates would have "beaten me up or raped or"—his thought trailed off.

Over the years, Willingham's letters home became increasingly despairing. "This is a hard place, and it makes a person hard inside," he wrote. "I told myself that was one thing I did not want and that was for this place to make me bitter, but it is hard." He went on, "They have [executed] at least one person every month I have been here. It is senseless and brutal. . . . You see, we are not living in here, we are only existing." In 1996, he wrote, "I just been trying to figure out why after having a wife and 3 beautiful children that I loved my life has to end like this. And sometimes it just seems like it is not worth it all. . . . In the 3½ years I been here I have never felt that my life was as worthless and desolate as it is now." Since the fire, he wrote, he had the sense that his life was slowly being erased. He obsessively looked at photographs of his children and Stacy, which he stored in his cell. "So long ago, so far away," he wrote in a poem. "Was everything truly there?"

Inmates on death row are housed in a prison within a prison, where there are no attempts at rehabilitation, and no educational or training programs. In 1999, after seven prisoners tried to escape from Huntsville, Willingham and four hundred and fifty-nine other inmates on death row were moved to a more secure facility, in Livingston, Texas. Willingham was held in isolation in a sixty-square-foot cell, twenty-three hours a day. He tried to distract himself by drawing— "amateur stuff," as he put it—and writing poems. In a poem about his children, he wrote, "There is nothing more beautiful than you on this earth." When Gilbert once suggested some possible revisions to his poems, he explained that he wrote them simply as expressions, however crude, of his feelings. "So to me to cut them up and try to improve on them just for creative-writing purposes would be to destroy what I was doing to start with," he said.

Despite his efforts to occupy his thoughts, he wrote in his diary that his mind "deteriorates each passing day." He stopped working out and gained weight. He questioned his faith: "No God who cared about his creation would abandon the innocent." He seemed not to care if another inmate attacked him. "A person who is already dead inside does not fear death," he wrote.

One by one, the people he knew in prison were escorted into the execution chamber. There was Clifton Russell Jr., who, at the age of eighteen, stabbed and beat a man to death and who said, in his last statement, "I thank my Father, God in Heaven, for the grace he has granted me—I am ready." There was Jeffery Dean Motley, who kidnapped and fatally shot a woman, and who declared, in his final words, "I love you, Mom. Good-bye." And there was John Fearance, who murdered his neighbor, and who turned to God in his last moments and said, "I hope He will forgive me for what I done."

Willingham had grown close to some of his prison mates, even though he knew that they were guilty of brutal crimes. In March 2000, Willingham's friend Ponchai Wilkerson—a twenty-eight-year-old who had shot and killed a clerk during a jewelry heist—was executed. Afterward, Willingham wrote in his diary that he felt "an emptiness that has not been touched since my children were taken from me." A year later, another friend who was about to be executed—"one of the few real people I have met here not caught up in the bravado of prison"—asked Willingham to make him a final drawing. "Man, I never thought drawing a simple Rose could be so emotionally hard," Willingham wrote. "The hard part is knowing that this will be the last thing I can do for him."

Another inmate, Ernest Ray Willis, had a case that was freakishly similar to Willingham's. In 1987, Willis had been convicted of setting a fire, in West Texas, that killed two women. Willis told investigators that he had been sleeping on a friend's living-room couch and woke up to a house full of smoke. He said that he tried to rouse one of the women, who was sleeping in another room, but the flames and smoke drove him back, and he ran out the front door before the house exploded with flames. Witnesses maintained that Willis had acted suspiciously; he moved his car out of the yard, and didn't show "any emotion," as one volunteer firefighter put it. Authorities also wondered how Willis could have escaped the house without burning his bare feet. Fire investigators found pour patterns, puddle configurations, and other signs of arson. The authorities could discern no motive for the crime, but concluded that Willis, who had no previous record of violence, was a sociopath—a "demon," as the prosecutor put it. Willis was charged with capital murder and sentenced to death.

Willis had eventually obtained what Willingham called, enviously, a "bad-ass lawyer." James Blank, a noted patent attorney in New York, was assigned Willis's case as part of his firm's pro-bono work. Convinced that Willis was innocent, Blank devoted more than a dozen years to the case, and his firm spent millions, on fire consultants, private investigators, forensic experts, and the like. Willingham, meanwhile, relied on David Martin, his court-appointed lawyer, and one of Martin's colleagues to handle his appeals. Willingham often told his parents, "You don't know what it's like to have lawyers who won't even believe you're innocent." Like many inmates on death row, Willingham eventually filed a claim of inadequate legal representation. (When I recently asked Martin about his representation of Willingham, he said, "There were no grounds for reversal, and the verdict was absolutely the right one." He said of the case, "Shit, it's incredible that anyone's even thinking about it.")

Willingham tried to study the law himself, reading books such as "Tact in Court, or How Lawyers Win: Containing Sketches of Cases Won by Skill, Wit, Art, Tact, Courage and Eloquence." Still, he confessed to a friend, "The law is so complicated it is hard for me to understand." In 1996, he obtained a new court-appointed lawyer, Walter Reaves, who told me that he was appalled by the quality of Willingham's defense at trial and on appeal. Reaves prepared for him a state writ of habeas corpus, known as a Great Writ. In the byzantine appeals process of death-penalty cases, which frequently takes more than ten years, the writ is the most critical stage: a prisoner can introduce new evidence detailing such things as perjured testimony, unreliable medical experts, and bogus scientific findings. Yet most indigent inmates, like Willingham, who constitute the bulk of those on death row, lack the resources to track down new witnesses or dig up fresh evidence. They must depend on court-appointed lawyers, many of whom are "unqualified, irresponsible, or overburdened," as a study by the Texas Defender Service, a nonprofit organization, put it. In 2000, a *Dallas Morning News* investigation revealed that roughly a quarter of the inmates condemned to death in Texas were represented by court-appointed attorneys who had, at some point in their careers, been "reprimanded, placed on probation, suspended or banned from practicing law by the State Bar." Although Reaves was more competent, he had few resources to reinvestigate the case, and his writ introduced no new exculpatory evidence: nothing further about Webb, or the reliability of the eyewitness testimony, or the credibility of the medical experts. It focused primarily on procedural questions, such as whether the trial court erred in its instructions to the jury.

The Texas Court of Criminal Appeals was known for upholding convictions even when overwhelming exculpatory evidence came to light. In 1997, DNA testing proved that sperm collected from a rape victim did not match Roy Criner, who had been sentenced to ninety-nine years for the crime. Two lower courts recommended that the verdict be overturned, but the Court of Criminal Appeals upheld it, arguing that Criner might have worn a condom or might not have ejaculated. Sharon Keller, who is now the presiding judge on the court, stated in a majority opinion, "The new evidence does not establish innocence." In 2000, George W. Bush pardoned Criner. (Keller was recently charged with judicial misconduct, for refusing to keep open past five o'clock a clerk's office in order to allow a last-minute petition from a man who was executed later that night.)

On October 31, 1997, the Court of Criminal Appeals denied Willingham's writ. After Willingham filed another writ of habeas corpus, this time in federal court, he was granted a temporary stay. In a poem, Willingham wrote, "One more chance, one more strike / Another bullet dodged, another date escaped."

Willingham was entering his final stage of appeals. As his anxieties mounted, he increasingly relied upon Gilbert to investigate his case and for emotional support. "She may never know what a change she brought into my life," he wrote in his diary. "For the first time in many years she gave me a purpose, something to look forward to."

As their friendship deepened, he asked her to promise him that she would never disappear without explanation. "I already have that in my life," he told her.

Together, they pored over clues and testimony. Gilbert says that she would send Reaves leads to follow up, but although he was sympathetic, nothing seemed to come of them. In 2002, a federal district court of appeals denied Willingham's writ without even a hearing. "Now I start the last leg of my journey," Willingham wrote to Gilbert. "Got to get things in order."

He appealed to the US Supreme Court, but in December 2003, he was notified that it had declined to hear his case. He soon received a court order announcing that "the Director of the Department of Criminal Justice at Huntsville, Texas, acting by and through the executioner designated by said Director . . . is hereby DIRECTED and COMMANDED, at some hour after 6:00 p.m. on the 17th day of February, 2004, at the Department of Criminal Justice in Huntsville, Texas, to carry out this sentence of death by intravenous injection of a substance or substances in a lethal quantity sufficient to cause the death of said Cameron Todd Willingham."

Willingham wrote a letter to his parents. "Are you sitting down?" he asked, before breaking the news. "I love you both so much," he said.

His only remaining recourse was to appeal to the governor of Texas, Rick Perry, a Republican, for clemency. The process, considered the last gatekeeper to the executioner, has been called by the US Supreme Court "the 'fail safe' in our criminal justice system."

IV

One day in January 2004, Dr. Gerald Hurst, an acclaimed scientist and fire investigator, received a file describing all the evidence of arson gathered in Willingham's case. Gilbert had come across Hurst's name and, along with one of Willingham's relatives, had contacted him, seeking his help. After their pleas, Hurst had agreed to look at the case pro bono, and Reaves, Willingham's lawyer, had sent him the relevant documents, in the hope that there were grounds for clemency.

Hurst opened the file in the basement of his house in Austin, which served as a laboratory and an office, and was cluttered with microscopes and diagrams of half-finished experiments. Hurst was nearly six and half feet tall, though his stooped shoulders made him seem considerably shorter, and he had a gaunt face that was partly shrouded by long gray hair. He was wearing his customary outfit: black shoes, black socks, a black T-shirt, and loose-fitting black pants supported by black suspenders. In his mouth was a wad of chewing tobacco.

A child prodigy who was raised by a sharecropper during the Great Depression, Hurst used to prowl junkyards, collecting magnets and copper wires in order to build radios and other contraptions. In the early sixties, he received a PhD in chemistry from Cambridge University, where he started to experiment with fluorine and other explosive chemicals, and once detonated his lab. Later, he worked as the chief scientist on secret weapons programs for several American companies, designing rockets and deadly fire bombs—or what he calls "god-awful things." He helped patent what has been described, with only slight exaggeration, as "the world's most powerful nonnuclear explosive": an Astrolite bomb. He experimented with toxins so lethal that a fraction of a drop would rot human flesh, and in his laboratory he often had to wear a pressurized moon suit; despite such precautions, exposure to chemicals likely caused his liver to fail, and in 1994 he required a transplant. Working on what he calls "the dark side of arson," he retrofitted napalm bombs with Astrolite, and developed ways for covert operatives in Vietnam to create bombs from local materials, such as chicken manure and sugar. He also perfected a method for making an exploding T-shirt by nitrating its fibers.

His conscience eventually began pricking him. "One day, you wonder, 'What the hell am I doing?'" he recalls. He left the defense industry and went on to invent the Mylar balloon, an improved version of Liquid Paper, and Kinepak, a kind of explosive that reduces the risk of accidental detonation. Because of his extraordinary knowledge of fire and explosives, companies in civil litigation frequently sought his help in determining the cause of a blaze. By the nineties, Hurst had begun devoting significant time to criminal-arson cases, and, as he was exposed to the methods of local and state fire investigators, he was shocked by what he saw.

Many arson investigators, it turned out, had only a high-school education. In most states, in order to be certified, investigators had to take a forty-hour course on fire investigation, and pass a written exam. Often, the bulk of an investigator's training came on the job, learning from "old-timers" in the field, who passed down a body of wisdom about the telltale signs of arson, even though a study in 1977 warned that there was nothing in "the scientific literature to substantiate their validity."

In 1992, the National Fire Protection Association, which promotes fire prevention and safety, published its first scientifically based guidelines to arson investigation. Still, many arson investigators believed that what they did was more an art than a science—a blend of experience and intuition. In 1997, the International Association of Arson Investigators filed a legal brief arguing that arson sleuths should not be bound by a 1993 Supreme Court decision requiring experts who testified at trials to adhere to the scientific method. What arson sleuths did, the brief claimed, was "less scientific." By 2000, after the courts had rejected such claims, arson investigators increasingly recognized the scientific method, but there remained great variance in the field, with many practitioners still relying on the unverified techniques that had been used for generations. "People investigated fire largely with a flat-earth approach," Hurst told me. "It looks like arson—therefore, it's arson." He went on, "My view is you have to have a scientific basis. Otherwise, it's no different than witch-hunting."

In 1998, Hurst investigated the case of a woman from North Carolina named Terri Hinson, who was charged with setting a fire that killed her seventeen-month-old son, and faced the death penalty. Hurst ran a series of experiments re-creating the conditions of the fire, which suggested that it had not been arson, as the investigators had claimed; rather, it had started accidentally, from a faulty electrical wire in the attic. Because of this research, Hinson was freed. John Lentini, a fire expert and the author of a leading scientific textbook on arson, describes Hurst as "brilliant." A Texas prosecutor once told the *Chicago Tribune*, of Hurst, "If he says it was an arson fire, then it was. If he says it wasn't, then it wasn't."

Hurst's patents yielded considerable royalties, and he could afford to work pro bono on an arson case for months, even years. But he received the files on Willingham's case only a few weeks before Willingham was scheduled to be executed. As Hurst looked through the case records, a statement by Manuel Vasquez, the state deputy fire marshal, jumped out at him. Vasquez had testified that, of the roughly twelve hundred to fifteen hundred fires he had investigated, "most all of them" were arson. This was an oddly high estimate; the Texas State

Fire Marshals Office typically found arson in only fifty per cent of its cases.

Hurst was also struck by Vasquez's claim that the Willingham blaze had "burned fast and hot" because of a liquid accelerant. The notion that a flammable or combustible liquid caused flames to reach higher temperatures had been repeated in court by arson sleuths for decades. Yet the theory was nonsense: experiments have proved that wood and gasoline-fuelled fires burn at essentially the same temperature.

Vasquez and Fogg had cited as proof of arson the fact that the front door's aluminum threshold had melted. "The only thing that can cause that to react is an accelerant," Vasquez said. Hurst was incredulous. A natural-wood fire can reach temperatures as high as two thousand degrees Fahrenheit—far hotter than the melting point for aluminum alloys, which ranges from a thousand to twelve hundred degrees. And, like many other investigators, Vasquez and Fogg mistakenly assumed that wood charring beneath the aluminum threshold was evidence that, as Vasquez put it, "a liquid accelerant flowed underneath and burned." Hurst had conducted myriad experiments showing that such charring was caused simply by the aluminum conducting so much heat. In fact, when liquid accelerant is poured under a threshold a fire will extinguish, because of a lack of oxygen. (Other scientists had reached the same conclusion.) "Liquid accelerants can no more burn under an aluminum threshold than can grease burn in a skillet even with a loose-fitting lid," Hurst declared in his report on the Willingham case.

Hurst then examined Fogg and Vasquez's claim that the "brown stains" on Willingham's front porch were evidence of "liquid accelerant," which had not had time to soak into the concrete. Hurst had previously performed a test in his garage, in which he poured charcoal-lighter fluid on the concrete floor, and lit it. When the fire went out, there were no brown stains, only smudges of soot. Hurst had run the same experiment many times, with different kinds of liquid accelerants, and the result was always the same. Brown stains were common in fires; they were usually composed of rust or gunk from charred debris that had mixed with water from fire hoses.

Another crucial piece of evidence implicating Willingham was the "crazed glass" that Vasquez had attributed to the rapid heating from a fire fuelled with liquid accelerant. Yet, in November of 1991, a team of fire investigators had inspected fifty houses in the hills of Oakland, California, which had been ravaged by brush fires. In a dozen houses, the investigators discovered crazed glass, even though a liquid accelerant had not been used. Most of these houses were on the outskirts of the blaze, where firefighters had shot streams of water; as the investigators later wrote in a published study, they theorized that the fracturing had been induced by rapid cooling, rather than by sudden heating—thermal shock had caused the glass to contract so quickly that it settled disjointedly. The investigators then tested this hypothesis in a laboratory. When they heated glass, nothing happened. But each time they applied water to the heated glass the intricate patterns appeared. Hurst had seen the same phenomenon when he had blowtorched and cooled glass during his research at Cambridge. In his report, Hurst wrote that Vasquez and Fogg's notion of crazed glass was no more than an "old wives' tale."

Hurst then confronted some of the most devastating arson evidence against Willingham: the burn trailer, the pour patterns and puddle configurations, the V-shape and other burn marks indicating that the fire had multiple points of origin, the burning underneath the children's beds. There was also the positive test for mineral spirits by the front door, and Willingham's seemingly implausible story that he had run out of the house without burning his bare feet.

As Hurst read through more of the files, he noticed that Willingham and his neighbors had described the windows in the front of the house suddenly exploding and flames roaring forth. It was then that Hurst thought of the legendary Lime Street Fire, one of the most pivotal in the history of arson investigation.

On the evening of October 15, 1990, a thirty-five-year-old man named Gerald Wayne Lewis was found standing in front of his house on Lime Street, in Jacksonville, Florida, holding his three-year-old son. His two-story wood-frame home was engulfed in flames. By the time the fire had been extinguished, six people were dead, including Lewis's wife. Lewis said that he had rescued his son but was unable to get to the others, who were upstairs.

When fire investigators examined the scene, they found the classic signs of arson: low burns along the walls and floors, pour patterns and puddle configurations, and a burn trailer running from the living room into the hallway. Lewis claimed that the fire had started accidentally, on a couch in the living room—his son had been playing with matches. But a V-shaped pattern by one of the doors suggested that the fire had originated elsewhere. Some witnesses told authorities that Lewis seemed too calm during the fire and had never tried to get help. According to the *Los Angeles Times*, Lewis had previously been arrested for abusing his wife, who had taken out a restraining order against him. After a chemist said that he had detected the presence of gasoline on Lewis's clothing and shoes, a report by the sheriff's office concluded, "The fire was started as a result of a petroleum product being poured on the front porch, foyer, living room, stairwell and second floor bedroom." Lewis was arrested and charged with six counts of murder. He faced the death penalty.

Subsequent tests, however, revealed that the laboratory identification of gasoline was wrong. Moreover, a local news television camera had captured Lewis in a clearly agitated state at the scene of the fire, and investigators discovered that at one point he had jumped in front of a moving car, asking the driver to call the fire department.

Seeking to bolster their theory of the crime, prosecutors turned to John Lentini, the fire expert, and John DeHaan, another leading investigator and textbook author. Despite some of the weaknesses of the case, Lentini told me that, given the classic burn patterns and puddle configurations in the house, he was sure that Lewis had set the fire: "I was prepared to testify and send this guy to Old Sparky"—the electric chair.

To discover the truth, the investigators, with the backing of the prosecution, decided to conduct an elaborate experiment and re-create the fire scene. Local officials gave the investigators permission to use a condemned house next to Lewis's home, which was about to be torn down. The two houses were virtually identical, and the investigators refurbished the condemned one with the same kind of carpeting, curtains, and furniture that had been in Lewis's home. The scientists also wired the building with heat and gas sensors that could withstand fire. The cost of the experiment came to twenty thousand dollars. Without using liquid accelerant, Lentini and DeHaan set the couch in the living room on fire, expecting that the experiment would demonstrate that Lewis's version of events was implausible.

The investigators watched as the fire quickly consumed the couch, sending upward a plume of smoke that hit the ceiling and spread outward, creating a thick layer of hot gases overhead—an efficient radiator of heat. Within three minutes, this cloud, absorbing more gases from the fire below, was banking down the walls and filling the living room. As the cloud approached the floor, its temperature rose, in some areas, to more than eleven hundred degrees Fahrenheit. Suddenly, the entire room exploded in flames, as the radiant heat ignited every piece of furniture, every curtain, every possible fuel source, even the carpeting. The windows shattered.

The fire had reached what is called "flashover"—the point at which radiant heat causes a fire in a room to become a room on fire. Arson investigators knew about the concept of flashover, but it was widely believed to take much longer to occur, especially without a liquid accelerant. From a single fuel source—a couch—the room had reached flashover in four and a half minutes.

Because all the furniture in the living room had ignited, the blaze went from a fuel-controlled fire to a ventilation-controlled fire—or what scientists call "post-flashover." During post-flashover, the path of the fire depends on new sources of oxygen, from an open door or window. One of the fire investigators, who had been standing by an open door in the living room, escaped moments before the oxygen-starved fire roared out of the room into the hallway—a fireball that caused the corridor to go quickly into flashover as well, propelling the fire out the front door and onto the porch.

After the fire was extinguished, the investigators inspected the hallway and living room. On the floor were irregularly shaped burn patterns that perfectly resembled pour patterns and puddle configurations. It turned out that these classic signs of arson can also appear on their own, after flashover. With the naked eye, it is impossible to distinguish between the pour patterns and puddle configurations caused by an accelerant and those caused naturally by post-flashover. The only reliable way to tell the difference is to take samples from the burn patterns and test them in a laboratory for the presence of flammable or combustible liquids.

During the Lime Street experiment, other things happened that were supposed to occur only in a fire fuelled by liquid accelerant: charring along the base of the walls and doorways, and burning under furniture. There was also a V-shaped pattern by the living-room doorway, far from where the fire had started on the couch. In a small fire, a V-shaped burn mark may pinpoint where a fire began, but during post-flashover these patterns can occur repeatedly, when various objects ignite.

One of the investigators muttered that they had just helped prove the defense's case. Given the reasonable doubt raised by the experiment, the charges against Lewis were soon dropped. The Lime Street experiment had demolished prevailing notions about fire behavior. Subsequent tests by scientists showed that, during post-flashover, burning under beds and furniture was common, entire doors were consumed, and aluminum thresholds melted.

John Lentini says of the Lime Street Fire, "This was my epiphany. I almost sent a man to die based on theories that were a load of crap."

Hurst next examined a floor plan of Willingham's house that Vasquez had drawn, which delineated all the purported pour patterns and puddle configurations. Because the windows had blown out of the children's room, Hurst knew that the fire had reached flashover. With his finger, Hurst traced along Vasquez's diagram the burn trailer that had gone from the children's room, turned right in the hallway, and headed out the front door. John Jackson, the prosecutor, had told me that the path was so "bizarre" that it had to have been caused by a liquid accelerant. But Hurst concluded that it was a natural product of the dynamics of fire during post-flashover. Willingham had fled out the front door, and the fire simply followed the ventilation path, toward the opening. Similarly, when Willingham had broken the windows in the children's room, flames had shot outward.

Hurst recalled that Vasquez and Fogg had considered it impossible for Willingham to have run down the burning hallway without scorching his bare feet. But if the pour patterns and puddle configurations were a result of a flashover, Hurst reasoned, then they were consonant with Willingham's explanation of events. When Willingham exited his bedroom, the hallway was not yet on fire; the flames were contained within the children's bedroom, where, along the ceiling, he saw the "bright lights." Just as the investigator safely stood by the door in the Lime Street experiment seconds before flashover, Willingham could have stood close to the children's room without being harmed. (Prior to the Lime Street case, fire investigators had generally assumed that carbon monoxide diffuses quickly through a house during a fire. In fact, up until flashover, levels of carbon monoxide can be remarkably low beneath and outside the thermal cloud.) By the time the Corsicana fire achieved flashover, Willingham had already fled outside and was in the front yard.

Vasquez had made a videotape of the fire scene, and Hurst looked at the footage of the burn trailer. Even after repeated viewings, he could not detect three points of origin, as Vasquez had. (Fogg recently told me that he also saw a continuous trailer and disagreed with Vasquez, but added that nobody from the prosecution or the defense ever asked him on the stand about his opinion on the subject.)

After Hurst had reviewed Fogg and Vasquez's list of more than twenty arson indicators, he believed that only one had any potential validity: the positive test for mineral spirits by the threshold of the front door. But why had the fire investigators obtained a positive reading only in that location? According to Fogg and Vasquez's theory of the crime, Willingham had poured accelerant throughout the children's bedroom and down the hallway. Officials had tested extensively in these areas—including where all the pour patterns and puddle configurations were—and turned up nothing. Jackson told me that he "never did understand why they weren't able to recover" positive tests in these parts.

Hurst found it hard to imagine Willingham pouring accelerant on the front porch, where neighbors could have seen him. Scanning the files for clues, Hurst noticed a photograph of the porch taken before the fire, which had been entered into evidence. Sitting on the tiny porch was a charcoal grill. The porch was where the family barbecued. Court testimony from witnesses confirmed that there had been a grill, along with a container of lighter fluid, and that both had burned when the fire roared onto the porch during post-flashover. By the time Vasquez inspected the house, the grill had been removed from the porch, during cleanup. Though he cited the container of lighter fluid in his report, he made no mention of the grill. At the trial, he insisted that he had never been told of the grill's earlier placement. Other authorities were aware of the grill but did not see its relevance. Hurst, however, was convinced that he had solved the mystery: when firefighters had blasted the porch with water, they had likely spread charcoal-lighter fluid from the melted container.

Without having visited the fire scene, Hurst says, it was impossible to pinpoint the cause of the blaze. But, based on the evidence, he had little doubt that it was an accidental fire—one caused most likely by the space heater or faulty electrical wiring. It explained why there had never been a motive for the crime. Hurst concluded that there was no evidence of arson, and that a man who had already lost his three children and spent twelve years in jail was about to be executed based on "junk science." Hurst wrote his report in such a rush that he didn't pause to fix the typos.

V

"I am a realist and I will not live a fantasy," Willingham once told Gilbert about the prospect of proving his innocence. But in February 2004, he began to have hope. Hurst's findings had helped to exonerate more than ten people. Hurst even reviewed the scientific evidence against Willingham's friend Ernest Willis, who had been on death row for the strikingly similar arson charge. Hurst says, "It was like I was looking at the same case. Just change the names." In his report on the Willis case, Hurst concluded that not "a single item of physical evidence . . . supports a finding of arson." A second fire expert hired by Ori White, the new district attorney in Willis's district, concurred. After seventeen years on death row, Willis was set free. "I don't turn killers loose," White said at the time. "If Willis was guilty, I'd be retrying him right now. And I'd use Hurst as my witness. He's a brilliant scientist." White noted how close the system had come to murdering an innocent man. "He did not get executed, and I thank God for that," he said.

On February 13, four days before Willingham was scheduled to be executed, he got a call from Reaves, his attorney. Reaves told him that the fifteen members of the Board of Pardons and Paroles, which reviews an application for clemency and had been sent Hurst's report, had made their decision.

"What is it?" Willingham asked.

"I'm sorry," Reaves said. "They denied your petition."

The vote was unanimous. Reaves could not offer an explanation: the board deliberates in secret, and its members are not bound by any specific criteria. The board members did not even have to review Willingham's materials, and usually don't debate a case in person; rather, they cast their votes by fax—a process that has become known as "death by fax." Between 1976 and 2004, when Willingham filed his petition, the state of Texas had approved only one application for clemency from a prisoner on death row. A Texas appellate judge has called the clemency system "a legal fiction." Reaves said of the board members, "They never asked me to attend a hearing or answer any questions."

The Innocence Project obtained, through the Freedom of Information Act, all the records from the governor's office and the board pertaining to Hurst's report. "The documents show that they received the report, but neither office has any record of anyone acknowledging it, taking note of its significance, responding to it, or calling any attention to it within the government," Barry Scheck said. "The only reasonable conclusion is that the governor's office and the Board of Pardons and Paroles ignored scientific evidence."

LaFayette Collins, who was a member of the board at the time, told me of the process, "You don't vote guilt or innocence. You don't retry the trial. You just make sure everything is in order and there are no glaring errors." He noted that although the rules allowed for a hearing to consider important new evidence, "in my time there had never been one called." When I asked him why Hurst's report didn't constitute evidence of "glaring errors," he said, "We get all kinds of reports, but we don't have the mechanisms to vet them." Alvin Shaw, another board member at the time, said that the case didn't "ring a bell," adding, angrily, "Why would I want to talk about it?" Hurst calls the board's actions "unconscionable."

Though Reaves told Willingham that there was still a chance that Governor Perry might grant a thirty-day stay, Willingham began to prepare his last will and testament. He had earlier written Stacy a letter apologizing for not being a better husband and thanking her for everything she had given him, especially their three daughters. "I still know Amber's voice, her smile, her cool Dude saying and how she said: I wanna hold you! Still feel the touch of Karmon and Kameron's hands on my face." He said that he hoped that "some day, somehow the truth will be known and my name cleared."

He asked Stacy if his tombstone could be erected next to their children's graves. Stacy, who had for so long expressed belief in Willingham's innocence, had recently taken her first look at the original court records and arson findings. Unaware of Hurst's report, she had determined that Willingham was guilty. She denied him his wish, later telling a reporter, "He took my kids away from me."

Gilbert felt as if she had failed Willingham. Even before his pleas for clemency were denied, she told him that all she could give him was her friendship. He told her that it was enough "to be a part of your life in some small way so that in my passing I can know I was at last able to have felt the heart of another who might remember me when I'm gone." He added, "There is nothing to forgive you for." He told her that he would need her to be present at his execution, to help him cope with "my fears, thoughts, and feelings."

On February 17, the day he was set to die, Willingham's parents and several relatives gathered in the prison visiting room. Plexiglas still separated Willingham from them. "I wish I could touch and hold both of you," Willingham had written to them earlier. "I always hugged Mom but I never hugged Pop much."

As Willingham looked at the group, he kept asking where Gilbert was. Gilbert had recently been driving home from a store when another car ran a red light and smashed into her. Willingham used to tell her to stay in her kitchen for a day, without leaving, to comprehend what it was like to be confined in prison, but she had always found an excuse not to do it. Now she was paralyzed from the neck down.

While she was in an intensive-care unit, she had tried to get a message to Willingham, but apparently failed. Gilbert's daughter later read her a letter that Willingham had sent her, telling her how much he had grown to love her. He had written a poem: "Do you want to see beauty—like you have never seen? / Then close your eyes, and open your mind, and come along with me."

Gilbert, who spent years in physical rehabilitation, gradually regaining motion in her arms and upper body, says, "All that time, I thought I was saving Willingham, and I realized then that he was saving me, giving me the strength to get through this. I know I will one day walk again, and I know it is because Willingham showed me the kind of courage it takes to survive."

Willingham had requested a final meal, and at 4 PM on the seventeenth he was served it: three barbecued pork ribs, two orders of onion rings, fried okra, three beef enchiladas with cheese, and two slices of lemon cream pie. He received word that Governor Perry had refused to grant him a stay. (A spokesperson for Perry says, "The Governor made his decision based on the facts of the case.") Willingham's mother and father began to cry. "Don't be sad, Momma," Willingham said. "In fifty-five minutes, I'm a free man. I'm going home to see my kids." Earlier, he had confessed to his parents that there was one thing about the day of the fire he had lied about. He said that he had never actually crawled into the children's room. "I just didn't want people to think I was a coward," he said. Hurst told me, "People who have never been in a fire don't understand why those who survive often can't rescue the victims. They have no concept of what a fire is like."

The warden told Willingham that it was time. Willingham, refusing to assist the process, lay down; he was carried into a chamber eight feet wide and ten feet long. The walls were painted green, and in the center of the room, where an electric chair used to be, was a sheeted gurney. Several guards strapped Willingham down with leather belts, snapping buckles across his arms and legs and chest. A medical team then inserted intravenous tubes into his arms. Each official had a separate role in the process, so that no one person felt responsible for taking a life.

Willingham had asked that his parents and family not be present in the gallery during this process, but as he looked out he could see Stacy watching. The warden pushed a remote control, and sodium thiopental, a barbiturate, was pumped into Willingham's body. Then came a second drug, pancuronium bromide, which paralyzes the diaphragm, making it impossible to breathe. Finally, a third drug, potassium chloride, filled his veins, until his heart stopped, at 6:20 PM. On his death certificate, the cause was listed as "Homicide."

After his death, his parents were allowed to touch his face for the first time in more than a decade. Later, at Willingham's request, they cremated his body and secretly spread some of his ashes over his children's graves. He had told his parents, "Please don't ever stop fighting to vindicate me."

In December 2004, questions about the scientific evidence in the Willingham case began to surface. Maurice Possley and Steve Mills, of the *Chicago Tribune*, had published an investigative series on flaws in forensic science; upon learning of Hurst's report, Possley and Mills asked three fire experts, including John Lentini, to examine the original investigation. The experts concurred with Hurst's report. Nearly two years later, the Innocence Project commissioned Lentini and three other top fire investigators to conduct an independent review of the arson evidence in the Willingham case. The panel concluded that "each and every one" of the indicators of arson had been "scientifically proven to be invalid."

In 2005, Texas established a government commission to investigate allegations of error and misconduct by forensic scientists. The first cases that are being reviewed by the commission are those of Willingham and Willis. In mid-August, the noted fire scientist Craig Beyler, who was hired by the commission, completed his investigation. In a scathing report, he concluded that investigators in the Willingham case had no scientific basis for claiming that the fire was arson, ignored evidence that contradicted their theory, had no comprehension of flashover and fire dynamics, relied on discredited folklore, and failed to eliminate potential accidental or alternative causes of the fire. He said that Vasquez's approach seemed to deny "rational reasoning" and was more "characteristic of mystics or psychics." What's more, Beyler determined that the investigation violated, as he put it to me, "not only the standards of today but even of the time period." The commission is reviewing his findings, and plans to release its own report next year. [As of January 2011 this investigation is ongoing.] Some legal scholars believe that the commission may narrowly assess the reliability of the scientific evidence. There is a chance, however, that Texas could become the first state to acknowledge officially that, since the advent of the modern judicial system, it had carried out the "execution of a legally and factually innocent person."

Just before Willingham received the lethal injection, he was asked if he had any last words. He said, "The only statement I want to make is that I am an innocent man convicted of a crime I did not commit. I have been persecuted for twelve years for something I did not do. From God's dust I came and to dust I will return, so the Earth shall become my throne."

PART THREE

CAPITAL PUNISHMENT AND LETHAL INJECTION

7

A GUILTY MAN
[AND THE HISTORY OF
LETHAL INJECTION]

Vince Beiser

Bill Wiseman: "I always think about my role, whenever I hear about a capital case being tried. It's always with me, like an old wound."

Wiseman . . . [thirty-three] years ago, as a young state legislator, . . . wrote the bill that made Oklahoma the first jurisdiction in the world to adopt lethal injection as a means of execution . . . [now the method of choice for executions throughout the United States].

Wiseman pushed the concept into law in an effort to expiate his shame for having voted to restore the death penalty in Oklahoma, despite his deep moral opposition to it. By introducing lethal injections, [Wiseman, who died in a plane crash in 2007,] had hoped to at least make executions more humane. . . . [He came to believe that he] helped make them more common, by making it easier for squeamish judges and juries to hand down the ultimate punishment. "In a sense," . . . [he once said], "I bear the responsibility for those deaths." . . .

Wiseman was steeped in religious thinking during his childhood in Philadelphia. His father and grandfather were both ministers, and his mother taught at the Quaker school Wiseman attended, where he imbibed their tenets of compassion and nonviolence. "My father is my huge hero . . . but the Quakers had as much to do with my moral formation as my parents." As a kid, he was convinced he would become a reverend himself. . . .

[Eventually, however,] he eschewed the seminary for North Carolina's Davidson College, where he majored in philosophy. He followed with a master's in literature from the University of Tulsa, Oklahoma, and went on to begin a PhD in American literature, but he soon lost interest. Dropping out to go live in the North Carolina sticks, he spent a while writing fiction and poetry, doing construction work, and "drinking a lot of corn liquor." Eventually he returned to Oklahoma and started his own highway-building contracting business in the Tulsa area. That job brought him in touch with local politicians, and their jobs looked good to him. "I thought I could be very competent as a legislator. Second, I liked the idea that it gave me an identity. I've always lived in the shadow of my father . . . and it would be a chance to take all these ideas I have on ethics and moral behavior and social justice and do something about them." In 1974, he successfully ran as a Republican for the state Assembly.

Wiseman absolutely loved being a lawmaker. . . . "I must admit, [he once said] that staying in office became my top priority. . . . I had an identity, a mission, all kinds of recognition. Anything that would threaten that would strike dark, hidden terror."

The threat turned out to be his own principles. The US Supreme Court struck down capital punishment in 1972 but in 1976 opened the door for states to bring it back, provided they amend their laws to make it less arbitrary. Oklahoma legislators wasted no time introducing a bill to do just that.

Wiseman hated the idea. On a practical level, he didn't believe state-sponsored executions deterred others from killing, and morally he simply opposed taking human life. But he knew his conservative constituents would never forgive him if he voted his conscience. He even ran an informal telephone poll to make sure. "It was, like, eighty percent in favor, and the rest not sure . . . no one was opposed."

Searching for a way out, Wiseman asked his father what he thought, hoping the respected minister would assure him that capital punishment was morally impermissible. To his dismay, his father said that in some circumstances it was acceptable. "That took away my theological cover to vote against it," Wiseman said. "I was left on my own, as was right, to see if I had any moral gumption. And I didn't."

So in July of 1976, Wiseman found himself sitting under the stained-glass skylights of the Oklahoma House of Representatives chamber, pushing the green button to vote yes. That put him safely amid the majority: The final tally was 93–5. "I just felt sick. I was actually executing people," he said. "I knew it was wrong, and I should have voted against it. But I didn't."

In an effort to salve his conscience while the bill was being debated, Wiseman latched on to another legislator's amendments to soften some of its provisions. They all failed, but one particularly intrigued him: a vaguely worded provision calling for the electric chair to be replaced with some more humane method of execution.

How, though, to kill a person painlessly? Wiseman first asked the Oklahoma Medical Association for help, but the doctors refused to get involved, lest they violate their Hippocratic oath to do no harm. Wiseman kept asking around until one day he got a call from Jay Chapman, the state medical examiner. Chapman had previously worked in Colorado overseeing that state's electric chair executions. In an essay he wrote for the *Christian Century* magazine, Wiseman recounted what Chapman told him about electrocutions: "When the lever is pulled, the body twists and shudders violently, cooks and sizzles obscenely, and emits horrible noises from the nose, mouth and anus. . . . Chapman said it was the ghastliest mode of death he could have conjured, short of slow torture, and that no sane person who witnessed it could possibly oppose its replacement by a less violent means of execution."

Chapman had an alternative. Sitting in Wiseman's little wood-paneled office in the Capitol, he dictated the following lines, which Wiseman jotted down on a yellow legal pad: "An intravenous saline drip shall be started in the prisoner's arm, into which shall be introduced a lethal injection consisting of an ultra-short-acting barbiturate in combination with a chemical paralytic." The barbiturate would put the condemned person to sleep, and then the paralytic would stop his heart and lungs. No struggle, no stench, no pain—just a quick, merciful snuffing out of life.

Wiseman drafted a bill around Chapman's simple sentence and got it moving through the legislature. A few hard-line legislators complained that such an easy death was too kind a punishment; others raised concerns that the new technology might not pass constitutional muster, but most responded favorably—particularly after Wiseman distributed grisly color photos of men killed by Colorado's electric chair. While the bill was still in the works, Wiseman attended a lecture by a prominent British criminologist at which someone in the audience asked the speaker what he thought of the idea of lethal injection. The criminologist declared it "a notion worthy of Nuremberg." Around the same time, a reporter friend suggested that such an easy, clean-looking way to kill would likely only lead to more executions. "It hadn't occurred to me," says Wiseman. "But he was right."

Wiseman's conscience stirred uneasily, but momentum carried the day. His bill passed by a wide margin and became law on May 10, 1977. Texas enacted an almost identical measure, modeled on Wiseman's, the very next day.

Wiseman didn't realize it, but he was only the latest in a series of reformers who have introduced new technologies to make killing kinder. The idealists of the French Revolution developed the swift certainty of the guillotine as an improvement over messy medieval methods like being torn apart by wild horses. Well-intentioned reformers in the United States promoted the electric chair, and later the gas chamber, to replace hanging.

Wiseman's contribution to this dubious progress was utilized by Texas in 1982, where Charlie Brooks Jr. became the first person put to death by lethal injection. Liberal pundits and the ACLU were appalled, but it did seem to work as promised. A pleased Texas judge declared that "1983 will bring some more [executions] . . . and this humane way will make it more palatable." . . . [Now lethal injection is the primary method of execution in all states that permit executions.] . . .

[*Editor's note:* On May 12, 2005, George James Miller Jr. was executed by lethal injection in Oklahoma. Vince Beiser describes his witness of the execution.]

Miller's crime, the capstone of a long history of violence, was a horrific one. He was convicted of murdering an Oklahoma City motel clerk by stabbing him with a knife and a pair of hedge shears, battering him with a paint can, and then pouring muriatic acid down his throat. After years of failed appeals, his death was scheduled for . . . May 12.

Executions have grown so common in Oklahoma that I was one of only three journalists who showed up at the century-old state penitentiary outside McAlester to cover it. A half hour before Miller was to die, a grand total of three death-penalty opponents were standing a glum vigil outside the prison's massive, whitewashed brick walls.

At 6 PM (killing time was moved up from midnight a few years ago, to make things easier on prison staff and witnesses), we were escorted through the prison's double gates, down a gleamingly clean concrete corridor, and into a narrow, brightly lit room. Facing a set of four windows, Miller's teary but composed mother, a few other relatives, and a handful of prison officials occupied a couple of rows of folding metal chairs.

On the other side of the windows lay Miller, bald-headed, mustached, and wearing a blue smock. Most of the straps holding him to the gurney were covered by a white sheet pulled up to his chest. He leaned up, smiled, and nodded at his family before lying back down, closing his eyes, and uttering his last words: "I love you."

Over the course of the next eight minutes, Miller was executed. There was almost no visible sign that anything at all was happening to him. An intravenous tube had been inserted into his arm before the witnesses arrived. It led through a hole in the wall behind Miller's head. Hidden by the wall, technicians fed a dose of sodium thiopental into the tube to put him to sleep; then vecuronium bromide, to paralyze his muscles; and finally potassium chloride, to stop his heart [the protocol that had been recommended by Chapman and politically advanced by Wiseman]. Miller exhaled wetly a couple of times as the first drug began working. A few minutes later, his jaws and lips quivered slightly. Then his eyes opened just a slit, and stayed that way while a prison medical examiner checked him with a stethoscope and pronounced him dead.

It was deeply disturbing to see the process of dying reduced to such spartan mechanics, with no ceremony, no last rites, nothing but an efficiently administered end to life. But it did look about as painless as such a thing can be.

That absence of pain and drama, says Richard Dieter, executive director of the Washington, DC–based Death Penalty Information Center, has made lethal injection a huge boon to capital-punishment advocates. "I don't think the public today would stand for sixty electrocutions a year," says Dieter. "By now lethal injection is essentially the only method used. It's more palatable to guards, to juries, and to legislators. I think it has resulted in more executions than would otherwise have been the case."

[Now] . . . activists and lawyers around the country have begun calling into question whether the process is really as painless as it looks. Most states use drug combinations and dosages similar to those used in Oklahoma. But considering that these drugs are usually administered by untrained prison officials rather than medical personnel, and are given to convicts whose veins may be damaged from drug use and who are likely to be understandably agitated, it's possible that some condemned people might not get enough anesthetic to actually put them to sleep—leaving them conscious but, paralyzed by the second drug, incapable of screaming or convulsing as their hearts are squeezed to a stop.

Death-penalty opponents have raised this argument before [and increasingly from the vantage point of 2011—*Eds.*] . . . evidence [has] emerged to back them up. Autopsies of inmates executed in Kentucky, South Carolina, and North Carolina have found concentrations of anesthetic that could have left the condemned conscious as their lives were taken. In April [2005], the British medical journal the *Lancet* published a study that analyzed toxicology reports of forty-nine executed inmates in four states; it concluded that forty-three of them showed levels of anesthetic lower than that required for surgery, and twenty-one "had concentrations consistent with awareness." If an inmate were indeed conscious when the potassium chloride hit his veins, a Columbia University anesthesiology professor testified at a recent hearing in Connecticut, it would cause a searing pain similar "to that of boiling oil or branding with a red-hot iron." . . .

Oklahoma, however, has taken no pause. A spokesman for the Department of Corrections brushes aside such concerns, saying simply, "We believe the amount of anesthetic we use is sufficient."

The day after Miller's execution, Wiseman, dressed in a blue turtleneck and khakis, led early-morning prayers for a handful of worshippers at a little nondenominational chapel on the University of Central Oklahoma campus. The readings included Psalm 102: "For the Lord looked down from his holy place on high; from the heavens he beheld the earth; that he might hear the groan of the captive and set free those condemned to die." . . .

8

BAZE-D AND CONFUSED

What's the Deal with Lethal Injection? A Debate

Alison J. Nathan and Douglas A. Berman

LETHAL INJECTION'S KNOWN UNKNOWNS: OPENING STATEMENT

Alison J. Nathan

The United States Supreme Court has recently heard oral argument in the case of *Baze v. Rees*, a constitutional challenge to the lethal injection procedures that Kentucky uses to execute death-row inmates. Kentucky's lethal injection formula is the same employed by almost every death penalty state in the country. As a result, the day after the Court granted certiorari in *Baze*, I argued that because the Supreme Court is considering the standard by which such challenges must be judged, for the sake of even-handed and deliberative justice, all lethal injection executions across the nation should be stayed pending the Court's decision in *Baze*. . . .

One execution did go forward in Texas on the same day that *Baze* was granted, apparently as a result of the refusal by the chief justice of the Texas Court of Criminal Appeals to allow the twenty-minute late filing of the condemned man's stay request. Since that time, however, every scheduled execution (nineteen as of the time of this writing) has been temporarily stayed by the Supreme Court, lower federal courts, state courts, or governors. This national pausing of the machinery of death has garnered significant press attention and some controversy, even leading a few commentators to suggest that lethal injection challenges are, at base, nothing more than a death-row delay tactic. This is a significant error. How states execute convicted defendants is an issue that implicates important aspects of governmental transparency and democratic reform and should be a serious concern both to those who support the death penalty and those who oppose it. What we know about how states and the federal government currently execute people in the United States is deeply troubling—troubling enough that the Supreme Court has involved itself in the controversy. But the real danger of lethal injection as currently practiced lies in what we do not know. A number of historical and structural factors have coalesced to shroud the administration of lethal injection in secrecy. These factors have entrenched, rather than cured, a needlessly cruel practice. This lack of transparency must change, and it is the existence of constitutional judicial review that will ensure that it does.

One thing we know for sure about lethal injection is its macabre history. As shown by the research of one of the leading experts in this field, Professor Deborah Denno of Fordham University School of Law, lethal injection as pervasively practiced in the United States today is the result of a historical accident, not scientifically informed deliberation. The genesis of today's method of lethal injection can be traced to 1976, the year the Supreme Court decided *Gregg v. Georgia* (1976), and ended the nine-year execution hiatus that had begun in the period leading up to the 1972 case of *Furman v. Georgia* (1972). After almost a decade without an execution, intense public scrutiny accompanied the preparations for the post-*Gregg* executions. In this context, and in order to help maintain public support for the death penalty, some state legislators scrambled to find a more humane substitute to the viscerally brutal and painful electric chair or gas chamber, the two methods that previously had gained national dominance but were facing increasing public scrutiny and criticism. Legislators in Oklahoma moved first.

Seeking guidance on how to carry out a potentially more humane execution, two Oklahoma state senators turned to the state's chief medical examiner, Dr. A. Jay Chapman. Although Dr. Chapman conceded that he lacked relevant training or expertise—stating at the time that he "'was an expert in dead bodies but not an expert in getting them that way,'"[1] he conjured up a procedure that would become the basis for lethal injection protocols nationwide. The Oklahoma legislators did not receive input from experts, did not conduct or commission any studies, and failed to consider the foreseeable administrative difficulties and dangers of Dr. Chapman's proposed procedure. Nevertheless, in 1977, Oklahoma's legislature adopted Dr. Chapman's method and delegated important details—what specific drugs to use, what dosage to administer, who would administer the drugs and how—to unqualified prison officials who made administrative decisions free from public scrutiny and oversight. After further consultation between Dr. Chapman and state prison officials, Oklahoma became the first state to adopt a three-drug lethal injection protocol—a short-acting anesthetic, a paralyzing agent, and a heart-stopping drug—as its preferred method of execution. Texas followed immediately afterwards, becoming the first state to actually carry out a lethal injection execution, which it did in 1982, using the three-drug protocol.

Despite the inadequate origins of Oklahoma's lethal injection protocol, a ripple effect soon occurred. State after state followed Oklahoma's lead, uncritically borrowing its new three-drug formula and delegating important details to state prison officials who lacked pertinent experience and knowledge. By 2002, thirty-seven states had switched to lethal injection, with all but one state employing Dr. Chapman's original three-drug formula. Yet *none* of these states engaged in any additional medical or scientific study of the method they were adopting. Historical accident (or what sociologists would call a "cascade to mistaken consensus") explains far better than science or medicine the current ubiquity of the three-drug protocol.

We also know, as a result of information just beginning to emerge, that there have been seriously flawed lethal injection executions. For example, in May 2007, an Ohio inmate named Christopher Newton appeared to be suffocating alive during parts of an execution that lasted almost two hours. Newton's botched execution came one year after a similarly controversial execution in Ohio that lasted approximately ninety minutes and caused the state to reexamine its execution procedures. This execution was sufficiently gruesome that the brother of the victim, who witnessed the execution, has gone on record condemning the lethal injection process as unnecessarily cruel. As another example, it took the state of Florida thirty-four minutes to execute

Angel Diaz in 2006. During that time Diaz was flailing, gasping for air, grimacing, and struggling to breathe. A post-execution investigation concluded that Diaz was likely not properly anesthetized during the execution. According to the Florida Supreme Court, the execution "raised legitimate concerns about the adequacy of Florida's lethal injection procedures and the ability of the [Department of Corrections] to implement them."[2] Given the incidences of error-prone and flawed executions, it is unsurprising that the three-drug protocol is forbidden for use in animal euthanasia by most states.

The public also is beginning to learn that unqualified individuals are providing guidance and participating in executions, creating circumstances ripe for error. In addition to relying on Dr. Chapman's admittedly inexpert opinions, many states received guidance in administering lethal injection from Fred Leuchter, who was a leading figure in the execution equipment "business" of electric chairs and gas chambers. Despite Mr. Leuchter's dearth of experience with lethal injection, states relied on his advice for years before they learned, during the course of his providing testimony about gas chambers in support of a holocaust denier, that he had lied about his scientific qualifications and educational background, for which he was subsequently prosecuted. Yet Mr. Leuchter's "lethal injection machine" played a role in further entrenching the three-drug protocol nationwide.

Similarly, recent lethal injection litigation in Missouri exposed that the doctor involved in that state's lethal injection executions, known as "Dr. Doe" because his identity was steadfastly guarded by Missouri, was the subject of more than twenty malpractice suits and suffers from a form of dyslexia that affects his ability to prepare the drug combinations properly. As a result of this information, a federal judge in Missouri banned his participation in future executions.[3] Despite this, the *Los Angeles Times* recently reported that the very same doctor has continued to assist the federal government in preparing lethal injection executions of federal inmates. There is also evidence emerging of ill-trained executioners in California, including one who smuggled illegal drugs into the prison. And in Kentucky, the execution protocol allowed improperly trained executioners to insert catheters into an inmate's neck despite a doctor's refusal to do so. Even Dr. Chapman now agrees that the wrong drugs are being used and that states should be compelled to use expert personnel rather than the "complete idiots . . . [w]hich we seem to have."[4]

Arguably more alarming than what we know of the current practice of lethal injection is what we do not know. Several aspects of the history of lethal injection have caused a continued repression of public knowledge and scrutiny of the procedure and its implementation. First, public scrutiny of the three-drug protocol has been stifled because, in copying Oklahoma, state after state has adopted the unnecessary paralytic agent as its second drug. The nature of this drug is to *mask* the realities of the execution from meaningful public scrutiny. A paralyzed inmate suffering pain during the execution will be physically unable to express his suffering. As a result, witnesses, including members of the media who report executions to the public, see only a sanitized version. Unaware of the painful suffering endured by inmates, the public has assumed wrongly that states always execute inmates in a humane and painless manner.

Second, by copying Oklahoma's vague lethal injection protocol, states also have followed Oklahoma in delegating critical implementation decisions to department of corrections personnel. The procedures these personnel develop are often exempt from state administrative law notice-and-comment requirements or have been treated as exempt by prison personnel. As a result, prison officials' critical lethal injection implementation decisions—what specific drugs to use, what dosage amounts, and how to administer the drugs—have remained hidden from public scrutiny.

Third, states have frustrated attempts to evaluate lethal injection protocols and procedures by tenaciously guarding the information as secret and nonpublic. In addition to refusing to release information about the qualifications and training of executioners, states also conceal execution procedures by limiting witnesses' ability to view portions of the execution process and by refusing to release postexecution autopsy information. The public, therefore, is precluded from learning of flawed procedures, incompetent administration, and execution errors.

Taken together, lethal injection's peculiar history, attendant secrecy, and protocol involving the use of the pain-masking paralytic drug have produced—and continue to produce—a failure of democratic reform. In the past, public scrutiny of cruel punishment practices led to legislative changes. For example, in the early- to mid-twentieth century, nearly every state sought to introduce a more humane method of execution when the public learned of the actual horrors of the electric chair, and deemed electrocution to be too barbaric and open to a high risk of pain and error relative to other available options. The same was true for hanging before electrocution and the gas chamber. In contrast, the factors described here have led to systematic and continued repression of public information related to lethal injection's actual procedures and administration, undermining a similar process of public deliberation and democratic reform. As a result, a needlessly risky and unnecessarily cruel method has become entrenched. This is true despite readily available alternatives such as the method veterinarians typically use to euthanize animals: a massive overdose of a single drug barbiturate. Veterinarians favor this approach because it does not carry a significant risk of pain even if unforeseen errors in the implementation process occur.

In this context of nontransparency, it is distinctly the role and responsibility of the judiciary, led by the Supreme Court, to scrutinize the practice of lethal injection and its history, as well as to see through the ill-informed and reflexive state decision making that has perpetuated an execution method that needlessly risks severe and unnecessary pain.

THE BLISS OF IGNORANCE AND THE PERFECTION PROBLEM—A REBUTTAL

Douglas A. Berman

Professor Nathan's opening statement provides an effective account of why the Supreme Court has now finally come to examine the constitutionality of modern execution procedures. As she spotlights, the development and administration of lethal injection protocols have been haphazard and sloppy, and state internal reviews of protocols have mostly been nonexistent or perfunctory. Jurisdictions that utilize the death penalty generally have not fulfilled their moral and constitutional obligations to ensure that unreasonable execution methods are not utilized. I thus agree with Professor Nathan that, in light of the failings of other branches, "it is distinctly the role and responsibility of the judiciary, led by the Supreme Court, to scrutinize" prevailing lethal injection protocols.

But Professor Nathan's essay fails to examine the reasons *why* so many states have tended to repress "public information related to lethal injection's actual procedures and administration" and the deeper death penalty dilemmas that in part account for the absence of a "process of public deliberation and democratic reform" concerning prevailing protocols. Specifically, Professor Nathan does not grapple with three critical practical and political realities that surround the modern administration of capital punishment: (1) a perfect death penalty system is practically impossible for fallible humans to create and maintain; (2) few persons actively involved with or concerned about modern death penalty systems are genuinely interested in making these systems more perfect; and (3) the vast majority of democratic lawmakers and the public in general is blissfully ignorant of the modern death penalty's imperfections. These critical practical and political realities infect all legal and social debates over capital punishment, and they significantly impede effective tinkering with the machinery of death. Though each of these realities justifies a lengthy law review article, here I will briefly unpack them with an emphasis on how they impact the lethal injection debate.

1. *Fallibility.* In the words of renowned pop philosopher Hannah Montana, "Nobody's perfect." Indeed, the reality of human error is often stressed by death penalty opponents who contend that even the smallest risks of wrongful executions justify the abolition of capital punishment. In the wake of death-row exonerations, the fallibility argument resonates with many, but this argument is largely inconsistent with how we assess other governmental functions. The well-known and unavoidable risk of human error does not keep governments from engaging in many life-and-death activities—ranging from waging war to regulating drug safety to running a public transit system—if the public and lawmakers view the benefits of these activities to be worth the risks. Of course, governments generally aspire to reduce the risks of human error as much as possible, but nobody argues that city buses should stop running when one driver negligently causes a fatal crash.

In the context of lethal injection protocols, the reality of human fallibility means that there will always be at least some risk of error and unnecessary pain in any state killing process. Of course, the selection of execution methods and execution personnel can greatly impact the magnitude of these risks: hangings conducted by untrained government officials—the execution norm throughout most of American history—surely will create greater risks of error and unnecessary pain than lethal injections conducted by trained medical personnel.

As Professor Nathan notes, over the last century, governments have generally aspired to adopt more humane methods of execution, apparently recognizing that they should try to minimize the risk of error and unnecessary pain in administering the death penalty. Problematically, as Professor Nathan stresses, a "cascade to mistaken consensus" has led nearly all capital jurisdictions to adopt an imperfect three-drug lethal injection protocol. Yet there is little doubt that the prevailing protocol is still a significant improvement over other execution methods; defendants are not clamoring for a return of the hangman's noose or the electric chair, and capital jurisdictions are not seriously considering building new gas chambers or assembling firing squads. The formal terms of the modern debate over lethal injection protocols concern whether states, after having adopted an improved, but still flawed execution method, should now have to make their protocols even more perfect. But, as explained below, few persons actively involved with, or seriously concerned about, modern death penalty systems are genuinely interested in trying to make these systems more perfect.

2. *Modern Disinterest in an Even More Perfect System*. For nearly all death-row defendants, their lawyers, and opponents of capital punishment, the only perfect death penalty system is one that has been abolished. Though death penalty opponents regularly chronicle flaws in capital punishment's administration, rarely do they seriously advocate realistic legislative reforms that would enable modern death penalty systems to operate more efficiently and regularly. Notably, death penalty opponents spotlight tales of wrongful convictions and botched executions primarily to boost their advocacy for the elimination of capital punishment altogether. Indeed, sophisticated abolitionists realize that a death penalty system made truly more perfect is a death penalty system more likely to garner broad public support and increase the number of state executions of convicted murderers.

For nearly all prosecutors and supporters of capital punishment, existing death penalty systems are already, in a sense, too perfect because they readily enable defendants and their advocates to delay or avoid the ultimate sanction. With decades often elapsing between a capital verdict and even the setting of an execution date, proponents of capital punishment are understandably far more concerned about repeated appeals and extensive delays than they are troubled by the occasional anecdote of a wrongful conviction or a botched execution of a gruesome murderer. Moreover, sophisticated proponents of capital punishment realize that serious efforts to perfect a death penalty system will provide defense lawyers and abolitionists with new opportunities to impede the progress of any murderer toward a state's death chamber.

Outside the context of lethal injection debates, there is ample evidence that few advocates are genuinely interested in making the administration of capital punishment more perfect. A few years ago, then-Massachusetts governor Mitt Romney assembled a blue-ribbon panel of experts to devise a death penalty system for his state that he deemed "as foolproof as humanly possible." Tellingly, his proposed more perfect system received virtually no support in Massachusetts: it was attacked on numerous grounds by both death penalty proponents and opponents. Moreover, the astute procedural and substantive reforms suggested by Romney's blue-ribbon panel—like those of many other groups of lawyers urging capital improvements—have found few serious advocates and have had virtually no traction in modern legislative debates in those jurisdictions still in the business of state killing.

The pragmatic disinterest in death penalty perfection largely accounts for why states have tended, in Professor Nathan's words, to repress "public information related to lethal injection's actual procedures and administration." State officials believe, quite justifiably, that any information-sharing good deed will be punished through new rounds of litigation brought by death-row defendants and death penalty opponents. State officials believe, quite justifiably, that most everyone complaining about lethal injection protocols will not start endorsing capital punishment if and when the state successfully develops a more perfect execution method. And, perhaps even more importantly, state officials believe, also justifiably, that very few persons are genuinely concerned about relatively minor imperfections in the administration of the death penalty.

3. *Ignorance Is Bliss.* For the vast majority of the public and law-

makers, the death penalty is a highly symbolic and inconsequential aspect of governmental work. Even in the few active death penalty states, capital cases are a tiny component of massive state criminal justice systems and an even more minuscule part of state governments' broader activities. Practically speaking, the average citizen is impacted far more by street cleaning schedules and school lunch menus than by the day-to-day administration of the death penalty. Moreover, the average citizen assumes—correctly—that most prosecutors and judges generally aspire to reduce the most extreme risks of error in the operation of the death penalty. Politically speaking, the average lawmaker recognizes that voters will care about her basic position on the death penalty, but she also realizes that the symbolism of her position is far more important than any specifics.

These practical and political realities mean that the vast majority of lawmakers and members of the public are blissfully ignorant concerning the modern death penalty's imperfections. Indeed, only the most engaged activists even try to keep up with the copious research about the modern operation of the death penalty, and often lawmakers will resist efforts to commission official studies of the death penalty's administration. Of course, neither the general public nor lawmakers favor a deeply flawed death penalty system, and profound evidence of wrongful convictions or botched executions will often prompt executive officials and legislators to begin a serious program of reform. But when identified problems appear to be minor imperfections and not gross injustices, most people remain more interested in the death penalty as an idea than as a practice. Indeed, by paying little attention to the death penalty in practice, the public and their elected representatives can hold onto the blissfully ignorant belief that our existing death penalty systems are as perfect as possible.

In the context of lethal injection protocols, the reality of blissful ignorance is reflected in the fact that few are advocating for perfect transparency. In our modern technological era, greater transparency concerning lethal injection protocols could be easily achieved by having all jurisdictions digitally record all executions. But, to my knowledge, nobody has even seriously suggested videotaping all executions. (It is notable, and telling, that thanks to a sneaky cell phone and YouTube, more Americans have seen the execution of Saddam Hussein than any of the 1,099 modern executions in the United States.)

These broader realities have an intriguing resonance now that the lethal injection debates have finally reached the Supreme Court in *Baze*. Notably, the Supreme Court's modern death penalty jurisprudence seems to be driven, in fits and starts, by the goal of creating an ever more perfect death penalty system through persistent tinkering with the machinery of death. And, unlike the public and lawmakers, the justices cannot remain blissfully ignorant to the historical, medical, and legal issues surrounding lethal injection protocols and their imperfections. I am not sure what this will mean for the Court's forthcoming work in *Baze*, but the points stressed above must be considered in understanding the likely reactions of the public and the likely responses of government officials after *Baze*—no matter what the justices say.

CLOSING STATEMENT BY NATHAN

On several key points related to *Baze v. Rees*, Professor Berman and I agree. Importantly, we appear to agree that state lethal injection protocols have been developed and administered in constitutionally problematic ways, that the ubiquity of the current lethal injection process is the result of a cascade to mistaken consensus, that there has been a significant lack of transparency surrounding the process by which states execute death row inmates, and that, as a result of these flaws, the Court in *Baze* must carefully scrutinize lethal injection protocols and procedures to ensure that they pass constitutional muster.

Beyond these points, Professor Berman reasonably takes my opening to task for failing to grapple with "*why* so many states have tended to repress 'public information related to lethal injection's actual procedures and administration.'" In attempting to answer that question himself, Professor Berman places the lethal injection debate within the context of "three critical practical and political realities that surround the modern administration of capital punishment." And he concludes that these realities "infect all legal and social debates over capital punishment, and they significantly impede effective tinkering with the machinery of death." Although I concur with much of what Professor Berman argues in laying out his three political and practical realities—factors that result generally from the often polarized and overly symbolic debate about the death penalty in the

United States—I do not agree that his observations fully answer the question of why states refuse to allow so much information about lethal injection procedures and protocols into the public record. More important, his observations concerning the lack of transparency and robust public debate are not merely descriptive, as he suggests. Rather, these factors require that the judiciary, including the Supreme Court, vigorously scrutinize whether the *realities* of lethal injection procedures satisfy constitutional demands.

Professor Berman's first noted practical reality is that any system operated by human beings, including the administration of the death penalty, is fallible. In the lethal injection context, this means that "there will always be at least some risk of error and unnecessary pain in any state killing process." This is unquestionably true, as the plaintiffs in *Baze* themselves acknowledge by advocating for a constitutional standard that upholds a method of execution unless it "creates a *significant* and *avoidable* risk that an inmate will suffer *severe* pain." Accordingly, it is not dispositive, or even legally relevant, that lethal injection is an improvement over previously entrenched execution methods such as hanging, electrocution, and lethal gas. Nor do I agree with Professor Berman that the "modern debate over lethal injection protocols concerns whether states, after adopting an improved, but still flawed execution method, should now have to make their protocols even more perfect." Considering the fundamental constitutional right in issue, seeking reasonable improvements in light of existing technologies and information is not the same as a disingenuous and unending search for an impossible-to-achieve "perfection." An analogy to voting technology is helpful. Surely electronic voting machines offer some improvement over previous voting technology (no more dangling chads, for example). Nevertheless, in light of the constitutional right at stake, voting rights advocates are justified in seeking a paper trail requirement for electronic voting, even if the new technology is an improvement and even if a paper trail still does not make electronic voting a perfect system.

Professor Berman's response to my voting machine analogy might well be that it fails because of his second political reality factor, what he calls "pragmatic disinterest in death penalty perfection." Perhaps he would contend that unlike the voting technology context, in which there are people genuinely concerned with assuring that every legitimate vote is counted, advocates on both sides of the death penalty debate have no interest in genuinely improving the capital punishment system. In the lethal injection context (as well as other areas of the death penalty debate beyond the scope of this exchange), I do not entirely agree. There are death penalty proponents—or at least those who firmly believe that the death penalty is and should remain constitutional—who would argue genuinely that states can and should execute defendants in a way that reasonably guards against the severe imposition of pain. There are also certainly death penalty proponents who realize that the best way to safeguard public support for the death penalty is through the adoption of execution methods that are—or at least appear to be—as humane as reasonably possible. To borrow from Professor Berman's terminology, these individuals could be deemed "sophisticated [death penalty] proponents." The use in every lethal injection state of the otherwise unnecessary paralytic agent, which can make potentially painful executions look like peaceful slumber, may well benefit the "sophisticated [death penalty] proponent[']s" cause.

I also disagree with Professor Berman that all who challenge the administration of lethal injection seek only delay and are, at heart, entirely disinterested in genuine improvement of the execution process. I gather these are Professor Berman's "unsophisticated" abolitionists. It is because of their efforts, Professor Berman contends, that states repress public information related to lethal injection because "[s]tate officials believe, quite justifiably, that any information-sharing good deed will be punished through new rounds of litigation." Professor Berman's cynical view overlooks that death penalty lawyers have an ethical obligation to challenge unconstitutional conduct by the government. This obligation may include attempting to ensure that their clients are executed in a manner consistent with the Eighth Amendment. The lawyers, of course, also have an ethical obligation not to bring frivolous or vexatious litigation. Several years ago, challenges to lethal injection were perceived by many as just that. However, given the reaction of lower court judges to the evidence of maladministration and incompetence finally surfacing in these lawsuits, such legal efforts appear vindicated. More important, I am unconvinced that the lack of transparency results from states simply seeking to hasten executions. If the underlying information could readily withstand judicial scrutiny, states would be well advised to provide information without the delay that has impeded judicial review of the merits of lethal injection procedures.

This previous point relates to Professor Berman's final practical and political reality factor: blissful ignorance. He argues that the modern death penalty debate largely occurs at the symbolic level, with little interest in a deeper understanding of the death penalty in its actual practice. I agree with this important observation but see this failure of informed public debate as precisely the value of the current lethal injection litigation. Contrary to the impression Professor Berman leaves, transparency advocates have made serious attempts to bring greater public access to executions through photographing or video recording, but courts have consistently rejected the efforts. For example, in *Rice v. Kempker* (8th Cir. 2004), the Eighth Circuit upheld a ban on the video recording of executions; the Fifth Circuit refused to recognize a First Amendment right to film executions in *Garrett v. Estelle* (5th Cir. 1977); and a district court in Indiana denied a request to broadcast the execution of Oklahoma City bomber Timothy McVeigh in *Entertainment Network, Inc. v. Lappin* (S.D. Ind. 2001). Lethal injection litigation, and in particular such transparency-related efforts, has the potential to dramatically change the national debate. Transparency places stark reality, rather than symbolism, at the center of public consciousness and discourse concerning state-sponsored executions.

What then is the answer to Professor Berman's question of why states refuse to release information to the public about how they execute people? One answer is surely that defending the secrecy of lethal injection procedures is easier for the states than defending the Rube Goldberg machine that is the pervasive three-drug protocol administered by the states. The claim of protecting the identity of executioners for "personal safety" reasons, for example, is easier than defending the employment of dyslexic doctors with multiple malpractice suits against them who have been banned from engaging in executions in other jurisdictions. Similarly, arguing that states do not need to disclose the drugs or dosage amounts used in the execution process because doing so would be detrimental to "national security" is easier than justifying the use of a paralytic drug that serves no purpose other than to hide pain that would result from improper anesthetization.

Another potential explanation for the states' insistence on secrecy relates to a doctrinal argument that some states have used to defend their current lethal injection procedures. These states note that in the death penalty context the Supreme Court has required "deference . . . to the decisions of the state legislatures under our federal system" (*Gregg v. Georgia* [1976]). But the deference rule rests on the assumption that states have carried out at least a minimal level of investigation into a procedure that eliminates the serious danger of unnecessary and cruel pain. As the history of lethal injection demonstrates, the states never engaged in any such investigation. By refusing to release information about lethal injection protocols and procedures, states have largely been able to avoid having to justify their problematic decision making.

Furthermore, the repression of the details of lethal injection procedures allows these states to hide behind the seeming consensus of a majority of death penalty states, all of whom authorize execution pursuant to similar lethal injection processes. A consensus argument won the day when, in 2002, the Supreme Court held in *Atkins v. Virginia* (2002) that the Eighth Amendment prohibits states from executing a person with mental retardation. Similarly, in 2005, the Supreme Court held the execution of juvenile offenders unconstitutional in *Roper v. Simmons* (2005). The Supreme Court reached its conclusions in *Atkins* and *Roper*, at least in part, by tallying the number of states that prohibited the execution of the mentally retarded and juvenile offenders and deciding that because more than a majority of states rejected the practices, those practices conflicted with contemporary standards and, therefore, were unconstitutional under the Eighth Amendment.

But the standard Eighth Amendment consensus analysis is premised upon transparency and public knowledge of a penological practice from which a consensus for or against the practice can develop. As I argued in my opening, in the lethal injection context, the systemic failings of transparency disrupt this process. Moreover, the lack of transparency obstructs the proper framing or level of generality of a consensus analysis. At one level, it can be argued—as twenty states and the United States have argued in an amicus brief filed in *Baze*—that lethal injection, and even the three-drug protocol, is accepted by a majority of states as the preferred method of execution.

But the legal challenges to lethal injection, including the one the Supreme Court has heard in *Baze*, are not challenges to lethal injection in the abstract. Rather, they are challenges to the specific protocols and procedures that states use to administer lethal injection. The point of these challenges is that although states have chosen lethal injection as a supposedly more humane alternative, and have adopted a drug protocol that is meant to anesthetize an inmate prior to the injection of painful drugs, the implementation of the protocol *in practice* lends itself to a substantial risk that inmates will be improperly anesthetized, will suffer excruciating pain, but will be paralyzed and thus unable to make known their conscious suffering.

Thus, in *Baze*, the petitioners correctly contend that to the extent a "consensus" analysis is relevant in the method-of-execution context, there is in fact a consensus in favor of execution by anesthetized death and the actual procedures challenged in *Baze* cannot stand because they lie outside this consensus. In other words, the constitutional failure of the current three-drug lethal injection protocol and its implementation is that while it *appears* to produce an anesthetized death, there exists an unnecessary risk that it in fact does not. Given the uninformed and nontransparent public debate that Professor Berman has identified, it is the role of the Supreme Court to probe the troubling realities of lethal injection and to ensure that even seemingly humane procedures actually satisfy the Constitution's demands.

CLOSING STATEMENT BY BERMAN

I am pleased to conclude this debate by noting yet again that Professor Nathan and I agree more than we disagree. In particular, like Professor Nathan, I believe that the "significant lack of transparency surrounding the process by which states execute death row inmates" now demands that courts "vigorously scrutinize whether the *realities* of lethal injection procedures satisfy constitutional demands." Nevertheless, as Professor Nathan correctly surmises, I still have a "cynical view" of the lethal injection litigation principally because, to my knowledge, defendants have never offered to drop their Eighth Amendment claims if states adopt a particular preferred execution protocol. Professor Nathan is justified in complaining that states haven't been more forthcoming about lethal injection realities. But states are justified in complaining that defendants and defense attorneys haven't been more forthcoming about execution protocols they would consider constitutionally unassailable.

Professor Nathan asserts that "it is not dispositive, or even legally relevant, that lethal injection is an improvement over previously entrenched execution methods such as hanging, electrocution, and lethal gas." But, even though the humane evolution of state execution methods may not be of great legal significance as the justices consider the constitutional claims in *Baze*, this evolution (1) reveals that states have been genuinely willing to improve their execution methods, and (2) explains why states genuinely fear that defense attorneys, in Professor Nathan's words, "seek only delay and are, at heart, entirely disinterested in genuine improvement of the execution process." In this context, Professor Nathan's voting technology analogy is telling. In the litigation over voting technologies, advocates make clear that they principally desire a paper trail to accompany electronic voting methods. But, in the litigation over execution technologies, advocates often obscure that they principally desire the elimination of all execution methods.

Importantly, I do not question either the judgment or ethics of defense lawyers challenging lethal injection protocols; indeed, when I have defended persons on death row, I have felt a professional obligation to raise any and every nonfrivolous argument that might delay or prevent my client's execution. But the fact that defense attorneys have an ethical responsibility to try to delay or prevent executions contributes to the "bunker mentality" that state officials have tended to adopt in response to evidence about flaws in their lethal injection protocols.

I emphasize these realities neither to justify nor excuse many states' troubling responses to the mounting evidence of problems in the administration of the traditional three-drug lethal injection protocol. Rather, my goal is to spotlight the litigation "realpolitik" that will necessarily attend, and may perhaps significantly inform, the justices' consideration of the arguments in *Baze*. Indeed, those justices who have previously expressed concerns about extended death row litigation will surely be cognizant of the fact that nearly *two decades* have transpired since the *Baze* defendants committed the brutal murders that landed them on death row. And, though technically Kentucky's execution protocol is all that is at stake in *Baze*, the justices know that their ruling in this case will greatly influence whether executions across the country are few or frequent in the months and years ahead.

I close by stressing the litigation "realpolitik" because it helps explain not only why the Supreme Court has long avoided challenges to execution methods, but also the real reason *Baze* presents difficulties for the justices. The justices surely realize that, no matter how much or how little they decide to tinker with the machinery of death in *Baze*, the broader practical and political realities that surround the modern administration of capital punishment ensure that the machinations of death will persist.

9

BAZE V. REES, SUPREME COURT OF THE UNITED STATES, APRIL 16, 2008[1]

Chief Justice John Roberts

SUPREME COURT OF THE UNITED STATES

Ralph Baze and Thomas C. Bowling, Petitioners

v.

John D. Rees, Commissioner, Kentucky Department of Corrections, et al.

April 16, 2008

Chief Justice John Roberts announced the judgment of the Court and delivered an opinion, in which Justice Anthony Kennedy and Justice Samuel Alito joined.

Like thirty-five other states and the federal government, Kentucky has chosen to impose capital punishment for certain crimes. As is true with respect to each of these states and the federal government, Kentucky has altered its method of execution over time to more humane means of carrying out the sentence. That progress has led to the use of lethal injection by every jurisdiction that imposes the death penalty.

Petitioners in this case—each convicted of double homicide—acknowledge that the lethal injection procedure, if applied as intended, will result in a humane death. They nevertheless contend that the lethal injection protocol is unconstitutional under the Eighth Amendment's ban on "cruel and unusual punishments," because of the risk that the protocol's terms might not be properly followed, resulting in significant pain. They propose an alternative protocol, one that they concede has not been adopted by any state and has never been tried.

The trial court held extensive hearings and entered detailed Findings of Fact and Conclusions of Law. It recognized that "[t]here are no methods of legal execution that are satisfactory to those who oppose the death penalty on moral, religious, or societal grounds," but concluded that Kentucky's procedure "complies with the constitutional requirements against cruel and unusual punishment." The state supreme court affirmed. We too agree that petitioners have not carried their burden of showing that the risk of pain from maladministration of a concededly humane lethal injection protocol, and the failure to adopt untried and untested alternatives, constitute cruel and unusual punishment. The judgment below is affirmed.

I

A

By the middle of the nineteenth century, "hanging was the 'nearly universal form of execution' in the United States." In 1888, following the recommendation of a commission empanelled by the Governor to find "the most humane and practical method known to modern science of carrying into effect the sentence of death," New York became the first state to authorize electrocution as a form of capital punishment. By 1915, eleven other states had followed suit, motivated by the "well-grounded belief that electrocution is less painful and more humane than hanging."

Electrocution remained the predominant mode of execution for nearly a century, although several methods, including hanging, firing squad, and lethal gas were in use at one time. Following the nine-year hiatus in executions that ended with our decision in *Gregg v. Georgia*, (1976), however, state legislatures began responding to public calls to reexamine electrocution as a means of assuring a humane death. In 1977, legislators in Oklahoma, after consulting with the head of the anesthesiology department at the University of Oklahoma College of

Medicine, introduced the first bill proposing lethal injection as the state's method of execution. A total of thirty-six states have now adopted lethal injection as the exclusive or primary means of implementing the death penalty, making it by far the most prevalent method of execution in the United States. It is also the method used by the federal government.

Of these thirty-six states, at least thirty (including Kentucky) use the same combination of three drugs in their lethal injection protocols. The first drug, sodium thiopental (also known as Pentathol), is a fast-acting barbiturate sedative that induces a deep, comalike unconsciousness when given in the amounts used for lethal injection. The second drug, pancuronium bromide (also known as Pavulon), is a paralytic agent that inhibits all muscular-skeletal movements and, by paralyzing the diaphragm, stops respiration. Potassium chloride, the third drug, interferes with the electrical signals that stimulate the contractions of the heart, inducing cardiac arrest. The proper administration of the first drug ensures that the prisoner does not experience any pain associated with the paralysis and cardiac arrest caused by the second and third drugs.

B

Kentucky replaced electrocution with lethal injection in 1998. The Kentucky statute does not specify the drugs or categories of drugs to be used during an execution, instead mandating that "every death sentence shall be executed by continuous intravenous injection of a substance or combination of substances sufficient to cause death" (Ky. Rev. Stat. Ann. §431.220[1][a]). Prisoners sentenced before 1998 have the option of electing either electrocution or lethal injection, but lethal injection is the default if—as is the case with petitioners—the prisoner refuses to make a choice at least twenty days before the scheduled execution. If a court invalidates Kentucky's lethal injection method, Kentucky law provides that the method of execution will revert to electrocution.

Shortly after the adoption of lethal injection, officials working for the Kentucky Department of Corrections set about developing a written protocol to comply with the requirements of §431.220(1)(a). Kentucky's protocol called for the injection of 2 grams of sodium

thiopental, 50 milligrams of pancuronium bromide, and 240 milliequivalents of potassium chloride. In 2004, as a result of this litigation, the department chose to increase the amount of sodium
thiopental from 2 grams to 3 grams. Between injections, members of
the execution team flush the intravenous (IV) lines with 25 milligrams
of saline to prevent clogging of the lines by precipitates that may form
when residual sodium thiopental comes into contact with pancuronium bromide. The protocol reserves responsibility for inserting the
IV catheters to qualified personnel having at least one year of professional experience. Currently, Kentucky uses a certified phlebotomist
and an emergency medical technician (EMT) to perform the venipunctures necessary for the catheters. They have up to one hour to establish both primary and secondary peripheral intravenous sites in the
arm, hand, leg, or foot of the inmate. Other personnel are responsible
for mixing the solutions containing the three drugs and loading them
into syringes.

Kentucky's execution facilities consist of the execution chamber, a
control room separated by a one-way window, and a witness room.
The warden and deputy warden remain in the execution chamber
with the prisoner, who is strapped to a gurney. The execution team
administers the drugs remotely from the control room through five
feet of IV tubing. If, as determined by the warden and deputy warden
through visual inspection, the prisoner is not unconscious within sixty
seconds following the delivery of the sodium thiopental to the primary IV site, a new three-gram dose of thiopental is administered to
the secondary site before injecting the pancuronium and potassium
chloride. In addition to assuring that the first dose of thiopental is successfully administered, the warden and deputy warden also watch for
any problems with the IV catheters and tubing.

A physician is present to assist in any effort to revive the prisoner
in the event of a last-minute stay of execution. By statute, however,
the physician is prohibited from participating in the "conduct of an
execution," except to certify the cause of death. An electrocardiogram
(EKG) verifies the death of the prisoner. Only one Kentucky prisoner,
Eddie Lee Harper, has been executed since the Commonwealth
adopted lethal injection. There were no reported problems at Harper's
execution.

C

Petitioners Ralph Baze and Thomas C. Bowling were each convicted of two counts of capital murder and sentenced to death. The Kentucky Supreme Court upheld their convictions and sentences on direct appeal.

After exhausting their state and federal collateral remedies, Baze and Bowling sued three state officials in the Franklin Circuit Court for the Commonwealth of Kentucky, seeking to have Kentucky's lethal injection protocol declared unconstitutional. After a seven-day bench trial during which the trial court received the testimony of approximately twenty witnesses, including numerous experts, the court upheld the protocol, finding there to be minimal risk of various claims of improper administration of the protocol. On appeal, the Kentucky Supreme Court stated that a method of execution violates the Eighth Amendment when it "creates a substantial risk of wanton and unnecessary infliction of pain, torture or lingering death." Applying that standard, the court affirmed.

We granted certiorari to determine whether Kentucky's lethal injection protocol satisfies the Eighth Amendment. We hold that it does.

II

The Eighth Amendment to the Constitution, applicable to the states through the Due Process Clause of the Fourteenth Amendment, provides that "[e]xcessive bail shall not be required, nor excessive fines imposed, nor cruel and unusual punishments inflicted." We begin with the principle, settled by *Gregg*, that capital punishment is constitutional. It necessarily follows that there must be a means of carrying it out. Some risk of pain is inherent in any method of execution—no matter how humane—if only from the prospect of error in following the required procedure. It is clear, then, that the Constitution does not demand the avoidance of all risk of pain in carrying out executions.

Petitioners do not claim that it does. Rather, they contend that the Eighth Amendment prohibits procedures that create an "unnecessary risk" of pain. Specifically, they argue that courts must evaluate "(a) the severity of pain risked, (b) the likelihood of that pain occurring, and (c) the extent to which alternative means are feasible, either by modifying existing execution procedures or adopting alternative procedures." Petitioners envision that the quantum of risk necessary to make out an Eighth Amendment claim will vary according to the severity of the pain and the availability of alternatives, but that the risk must be "significant" to trigger Eighth Amendment scrutiny.

Kentucky responds that this "unnecessary risk" standard is tantamount to a requirement that states adopt the "least risk" alternative in carrying out an execution, a standard the Commonwealth contends will cast recurring constitutional doubt on any procedure adopted by the states. Instead, Kentucky urges the Court to approve the "substantial risk" test used by the courts below.

A

This Court has never invalidated a state's chosen procedure for carrying out a sentence of death as the infliction of cruel and unusual punishment. In *Wilkerson v. Utah* (1879), we upheld a sentence to death by firing squad imposed by a territorial court, rejecting the argument that such a sentence constituted cruel and unusual punishment. We noted there the difficulty of "defin[ing] with exactness the extent of the constitutional provision which provides that cruel and unusual punishments shall not be inflicted." Rather than undertake such an effort, the *Wilkerson* Court simply noted that "it is safe to affirm that punishments of torture . . . and all others in the same line of unnecessary cruelty, are forbidden" by the Eighth Amendment. By way of example, the Court cited cases from England in which "terror, pain, or disgrace were sometimes superadded" to the sentence, such as where the condemned was "emboweled alive, beheaded, and quartered," or instances of "public dissection in murder, and burning alive." In contrast, we observed that the firing squad was routinely used as a method of execution for military officers. What each of the forbidden punishments had in common was the deliberate infliction of pain for the sake of pain—"superadd[ing]" pain to the death sentence through torture and the like.

We carried these principles further in *In re Kemmler* (1890). There we rejected an opportunity to incorporate the Eighth Amendment against the states in a challenge to the first execution by electrocution, to be carried out by the state of New York. In passing over that question, however, we observed that "[p]unishments are cruel when they involve torture or a lingering death; but the punishment of death is not cruel within the meaning of that word as used in the Constitution. It implies there something inhuman and barbarous, something more than the mere extinguishment of life." We noted that the New York statute adopting electrocution as a method of execution "was passed in the effort to devise a more humane method of reaching the result."

B

Petitioners do not claim that lethal injection or the proper administration of the particular protocol adopted by Kentucky by themselves constitute the cruel or wanton infliction of pain. Quite the contrary, they concede that "if performed properly," an execution carried out under Kentucky's procedures would be "humane and constitutional." That is because, as counsel for petitioners admitted at oral argument, proper administration of the first drug, sodium thiopental, eliminates any meaningful risk that a prisoner would experience pain from the subsequent injections of pancuronium and potassium chloride.

Instead, petitioners claim that there is a significant risk that the procedures will *not* be properly followed—in particular, that the sodium thiopental will not be properly administered to achieve its intended effect—resulting in severe pain when the other chemicals are administered. Our cases recognize that subjecting individuals to a risk of future harm—not simply actually inflicting pain—can qualify as cruel and unusual punishment. To establish that such exposure violates the Eighth Amendment, however, the conditions presenting the risk must be "*sure or very likely* to cause serious illness and needless suffering," and give rise to "sufficiently *imminent* dangers" *Helling v. McKinney* (1993) (emphasis added). We have explained that to prevail on such a claim there must be a "substantial risk of serious harm," an "objectively intolerable risk of harm" that prevents prison officials from pleading that they were "subjectively blameless for purposes of the Eighth Amendment" *Farmer v. Brennan* (1994).

Simply because an execution method may result in pain, either by accident or as an inescapable consequence of death, does not establish the sort of "objectively intolerable risk of harm" that qualifies as cruel and unusual. In *Louisiana ex rel. Francis v. Resweber* (1947), a plurality of the Court upheld a second attempt at executing a prisoner by electrocution after a mechanical malfunction had interfered with the first attempt. The principal opinion noted that "[a]ccidents happen for which no man is to blame," and concluded that such "an accident, with no suggestion of malevolence," did not give rise to an Eighth Amendment violation.

As Justice Frankfurter noted in a separate opinion based on the Due Process Clause, however, "a hypothetical situation" involving "a series of abortive attempts at electrocution" would present a different case. In terms of our present Eighth Amendment analysis, such a situation—unlike an "innocent misadventure"—would demonstrate an "objectively intolerable risk of harm" that officials may not ignore. In other words, an isolated mishap alone does not give rise to an Eighth Amendment violation, precisely because such an event, while regrettable, does not suggest cruelty, or that the procedure at issue gives rise to a "substantial risk of serious harm."

C

Much of petitioners' case rests on the contention that they have identified a significant risk of harm that can be eliminated by adopting alternative procedures, such as a one-drug protocol that dispenses with the use of pancuronium and potassium chloride, and additional monitoring by trained personnel to ensure that the first dose of sodium thiopental has been adequately delivered. Given what our cases have said about the nature of the risk of harm that is actionable under the Eighth Amendment, a condemned prisoner cannot successfully challenge a state's method of execution merely by showing a slightly or marginally safer alternative.

Permitting an Eighth Amendment violation to be established on such a showing would threaten to transform courts into boards of inquiry charged with determining "best practices" for executions, with each ruling supplanted by another round of litigation touting a new and improved methodology. Such an approach finds no support in our cases, would embroil the courts in ongoing scientific controversies beyond their expertise, and would substantially intrude on the role of state legislatures in implementing their execution procedures—a role that by all accounts the states have fulfilled with an earnest desire to provide for a progressively more humane manner of death. Accordingly, we reject petitioners' proposed "unnecessary risk" standard, as well as the dissent's "untoward" risk variation.

Instead, the proffered alternatives must effectively address a "substantial risk of serious harm." To qualify, the alternative procedure must be feasible, readily implemented, and in fact significantly reduce a substantial risk of severe pain. If a state refuses to adopt such an alternative in the face of these documented advantages, without a legitimate penological justification for adhering to its current method of execution, then a state's refusal to change its method can be viewed as "cruel and unusual" under the Eighth Amendment.

III

In applying these standards to the facts of this case, we note at the outset that it is difficult to regard a practice as "objectively intolerable" when it is in fact widely tolerated. Thirty-six states that sanction capital punishment have adopted lethal injection as the preferred method of execution. The federal government uses lethal injection as well. This broad consensus goes not just to the method of execution, but also to the specific three-drug combination used by Kentucky. Thirty states, as well as the federal government, use a series of sodium thiopental, pancuronium bromide, and potassium chloride, in varying amounts. No state uses or has ever used the alternative one-drug protocol belatedly urged by petitioners. This consensus is probative but not conclusive with respect to that aspect of the alternatives proposed by petitioners.

In order to meet their "heavy burden" of showing that Kentucky's procedure is "cruelly inhumane," petitioners point to numerous aspects of the protocol that they contend create opportunities for error. Their claim hinges on the improper administration of the first drug, sodium thiopental. It is uncontested that, failing a proper dose of sodium thiopental that would render the prisoner unconscious, there is a substantial, constitutionally unacceptable risk of suffocation from the administration of pancuronium bromide and pain from the injection of potassium chloride. We agree with the state trial court and state supreme court, however, that petitioners have not shown that the risk of an inadequate dose of the first drug is substantial. And we reject the argument that the Eighth Amendment requires Kentucky to adopt the untested alternative procedures petitioners have identified.

A

Petitioners contend that there is a risk of improper administration of thiopental because the doses are difficult to mix into solution form and load into syringes; because the protocol fails to establish a rate of injection, which could lead to a failure of the IV; because it is possible that the IV catheters will infiltrate into surrounding tissue, causing an inadequate dose to be delivered to the vein; because of inadequate facilities and training; and because Kentucky has no reliable means of monitoring the anesthetic depth of the prisoner after the sodium thiopental has been administered.

As for the risk that the sodium thiopental would be improperly prepared, petitioners contend that Kentucky employs untrained personnel who are unqualified to calculate and mix an adequate dose, especially in light of the omission of volume and concentration amounts from the written protocol. The state trial court, however, specifically found that "[i]f the manufacturers' instructions for reconstitution of Sodium Thiopental are followed . . . there would be minimal risk of improper mixing, despite converse testimony that a layperson would have difficulty performing this task." We cannot say that this finding is clearly erroneous, particularly when that finding is substantiated by expert testimony describing the task of reconstituting powder sodium thiopental into solution form as "[n]ot difficult at all. . . . You take a liquid, you inject it into a vial with the powder, then you shake it up until the powder dissolves, and you're done. The instructions are on the package insert."

Likewise, the asserted problems related to the IV lines do not establish a sufficiently substantial risk of harm to meet the requirements of the Eighth Amendment. Kentucky has put in place several important safeguards to ensure that an adequate dose of sodium thiopental is delivered to the condemned prisoner. The most significant of these is the written protocol's requirement that members of the

IV team must have at least one year of professional experience as a certified medical assistant, phlebotomist, EMT, paramedic, or military corpsman. Kentucky currently uses a phlebotomist and an EMT, personnel who have daily experience establishing IV catheters for inmates in Kentucky's prison population. Moreover, these IV team members, along with the rest of the execution team, participate in at least ten practice sessions per year. These sessions, required by the written protocol, encompass a complete walk-through of the execution procedures, including the siting of IV catheters into volunteers. In addition, the protocol calls for the IV team to establish both primary and backup lines and to prepare two sets of the lethal injection drugs before the execution commences. These redundant measures ensure that if an insufficient dose of sodium thiopental is initially administered through the primary line, an additional dose can be given through the backup line before the last two drugs are injected.

The IV team has one hour to establish both the primary and backup IVs, a length of time the trial court found to be "not excessive but rather necessary," contrary to petitioners' claim that using an IV inserted after any "more than ten or fifteen minutes of unsuccessful attempts is dangerous because the IV is almost certain to be unreliable." And, in any event, merely because the protocol gives the IV team one hour to establish intravenous access does not mean that team members are required to spend the entire hour in a futile attempt to do so. The qualifications of the IV team also substantially reduce the risk of IV infiltration.

In addition, the presence of the warden and deputy warden in the execution chamber with the prisoner allows them to watch for signs of IV problems, including infiltration. Three of the Commonwealth's medical experts testified that identifying signs of infiltration would be "very obvious," even to the average person, because of the swelling that would result. Kentucky's protocol specifically requires the warden to redirect the flow of chemicals to the backup IV site if the prisoner does not lose consciousness within sixty seconds. In light of these safeguards, we cannot say that the risks identified by petitioners are so substantial or imminent as to amount to an Eighth Amendment violation.

B

Nor does Kentucky's failure to adopt petitioners' proposed alternatives demonstrate that the Commonwealth's execution procedure is cruel and unusual.

First, petitioners contend that Kentucky could switch from a three-drug protocol to a one-drug protocol by using a single dose of sodium thiopental or other barbiturate. That alternative was not proposed to the state courts below.[2] As a result, we are left without any findings on the effectiveness of petitioners' barbiturate-only protocol, despite scattered references in the trial testimony to the sole use of sodium thiopental or pentobarbital as a preferred method of execution.

In any event, the Commonwealth's continued use of the three-drug protocol cannot be viewed as posing an "objectively intolerable risk" when no other state has adopted the one-drug method and petitioners proffered no study showing that it is an equally effective manner of imposing a death sentence. Indeed, the state of Tennessee, after reviewing its execution procedures, rejected a proposal to adopt a one-drug protocol using sodium thiopental. The state concluded that the one-drug alternative would take longer than the three-drug method and that the "required dosage of sodium thiopental would be less predictable and more variable when it is used as the sole mechanism for producing death. . . ." We need not endorse the accuracy of those conclusions to note simply that the comparative efficacy of a one-drug method of execution is not so well established that Kentucky's failure to adopt it constitutes a violation of the Eighth Amendment.

Petitioners also contend that Kentucky should omit the second drug, pancuronium bromide, because it serves no therapeutic purpose while suppressing muscle movements that could reveal an inadequate administration of the first drug. The state trial court, however, specifically found that pancuronium serves two purposes. First, it prevents involuntary physical movements during unconsciousness that may accompany the injection of potassium chloride. The Commonwealth has an interest in preserving the dignity of the procedure, especially where convulsions or seizures could be misperceived as signs of consciousness or distress. Second, pancuronium stops respiration, hastening death. Kentucky's decision to include the drug does not offend the Eighth Amendment.

Petitioners' barbiturate-only protocol, they contend, is not untested; it is used routinely by veterinarians in putting animals to sleep. Moreover, twenty-three states, including Kentucky, bar veterinarians from using a neuromuscular paralytic agent like pancuronium bromide, either expressly or, like Kentucky, by specifically directing the use of a drug like sodium pentobarbital. If pancuronium is too cruel for animals, the argument goes, then it must be too cruel for the condemned inmate. Whatever rhetorical force the argument carries, it overlooks the states' legitimate interest in providing for a quick, certain death. In the Netherlands, for example, where physician-assisted euthanasia is permitted, the Royal Dutch Society for the Advancement of Pharmacy recommends the use of a muscle relaxant (such as pancuronium dibromide) in addition to thiopental in order to prevent a prolonged, undignified death. That concern may be less compelling in the veterinary context, and in any event other methods approved by veterinarians—such as stunning the animal or severing its spinal cord—make clear that veterinary practice for animals is not an appropriate guide to humane practices for humans.

Petitioners also fault the Kentucky protocol for lacking a systematic mechanism for monitoring the "anesthetic depth" of the prisoner. Under petitioners' scheme, qualified personnel would employ monitoring equipment, such as a Bispectral Index (BIS) monitor, blood pressure cuff, or EKG to verify that a prisoner has achieved sufficient unconsciousness before injecting the final two drugs. The visual inspection performed by the warden and deputy warden, they maintain, is an inadequate substitute for the more sophisticated procedures they envision.

At the outset, it is important to reemphasize that a proper dose of thiopental obviates the concern that a prisoner will not be sufficiently sedated. All the experts who testified at trial agreed on this point. The risks of failing to adopt additional monitoring procedures are thus even more "remote" and attenuated than the risks posed by the alleged inadequacies of Kentucky's procedures designed to ensure the delivery of thiopental.

But more than this, Kentucky's expert testified that a blood pressure cuff would have no utility in assessing the level of the prisoner's unconsciousness following the introduction of sodium thiopental, which depresses circulation. Furthermore, the medical community has yet to endorse the use of a BIS monitor, which measures brain function, as an indication of anesthetic awareness. The asserted need for a professional anesthesiologist to interpret the BIS monitor readings is nothing more than an argument against the entire procedure, given that both Kentucky law and the American Society of Anesthesiologists' own ethical guidelines prohibit anesthesiologists from participating in capital punishment. Nor is it pertinent that the use of a blood pressure cuff and EKG is "the standard of care in surgery requiring anesthesia," as the dissent points out. Petitioners have not shown that these supplementary procedures, drawn from a different context, are necessary to avoid a substantial risk of suffering.

The dissent believes that rough-and-ready tests for checking consciousness—calling the inmate's name, brushing his eyelashes, or presenting him with strong, noxious odors—could materially decrease the risk of administering the second and third drugs before the sodium thiopental has taken effect. Again, the risk at issue is already attenuated, given the steps Kentucky has taken to ensure the proper administration of the first drug. Moreover, the scenario the dissent posits involves a level of unconsciousness allegedly sufficient to avoid detection of improper administration of the anesthesia under Kentucky's procedure, but not sufficient to prevent pain. There is no indication that the basic tests the dissent advocates can make such fine distinctions. If these tests are effective only in determining whether the sodium thiopental has entered the inmate's bloodstream, the record confirms that the visual inspection of the IV site under Kentucky's procedure achieves that objective.

The dissent would continue the stay of these executions (and presumably the many others held in abeyance pending decision in this case) and send the case back to the lower courts to determine whether such added measures redress an "untoward" risk of pain. But an inmate cannot succeed on an Eighth Amendment claim simply by showing one more step the state could take as a failsafe for other, independently adequate measures. This approach would serve no meaningful purpose and would frustrate the state's legitimate interest in carrying out a sentence of death in a timely manner.

Justice Stevens suggests that our opinion leaves the disposition of other cases uncertain, but the standard we set forth here resolves more challenges than he acknowledges. A stay of execution may not be granted on grounds such as those asserted here unless the condemned prisoner establishes that the state's lethal injection protocol creates a demonstrated risk of severe pain. He must show that the risk is substantial when compared to the known and available alternatives. A state with a lethal injection protocol substantially similar to the protocol we uphold today would not create a risk that meets this standard.

※※※

Reasonable people of good faith disagree on the morality and efficacy of capital punishment, and for many who oppose it, no method of execution would ever be acceptable. But as Justice Frankfurter stressed in *Resweber*, "[o]ne must be on guard against finding in personal disapproval a reflection of more or less prevailing condemnation." This Court has ruled that capital punishment is not prohibited under our Constitution, and that the states may enact laws specifying that sanction. "[T]he power of a State to pass laws means little if the State cannot enforce them." State efforts to implement capital punishment must certainly comply with the Eighth Amendment, but what that Amendment prohibits is wanton exposure to "objectively intolerable risk," not simply the possibility of pain.

Kentucky has adopted a method of execution believed to be the most humane available, one it shares with thirty-five other states. Petitioners agree that, if administered as intended, that procedure will result in a painless death. The risks of maladministration they have suggested—such as improper mixing of chemicals and improper setting of IVs by trained and experienced personnel—cannot remotely be characterized as "objectively intolerable." Kentucky's decision to adhere to its protocol despite these asserted risks, while adopting safeguards to protect against them, cannot be viewed as probative of the wanton infliction of pain under the Eighth Amendment. Finally, the alternative that petitioners belatedly propose has problems of its own, and has never been tried by a single state.

Throughout our history, whenever a method of execution has been challenged in this Court as cruel and unusual, the Court has rejected the challenge. Our society has nonetheless steadily moved to more humane methods of carrying out capital punishment. The firing squad, hanging, the electric chair, and the gas chamber have each, in turn, given way to more humane methods, culminating in today's consensus on lethal injection. The broad framework of the Eighth Amendment has accommodated this progress toward more humane methods of execution, and our approval of a particular method in the past has not precluded legislatures from taking the steps they deem appropriate, in light of new developments, to ensure humane capital punishment. There is no reason to suppose that today's decision will be any different.

The judgment . . . concluding that Kentucky's procedure is consistent with the Eighth Amendment is, accordingly, affirmed.

It is so ordered.

10

BAZE V. REES[1]

Justice Ruth Ginsburg, Dissenting; Justice David Souter, Joining

April 16, 2008

It is undisputed that the second and third drugs used in Kentucky's three-drug lethal injection protocol, pancuronium bromide and potassium chloride would cause a conscious inmate to suffer excruciating pain. Pancuronium bromide paralyzes the lung muscles and results in slow asphyxiation. Potassium chloride causes burning and intense pain as it circulates throughout the body. Use of pancuronium bromide and potassium chloride on a conscious inmate, the plurality recognizes, would be "constitutionally unacceptable."

The constitutionality of Kentucky's protocol therefore turns on whether inmates are adequately anesthetized by the first drug in the protocol, sodium thiopental. Kentucky's system is constitutional, the plurality states, because "petitioners have not shown that the risk of an inadequate dose of the first drug is substantial." I would not dispose of the case so swiftly given the character of the risk at stake. Kentucky's protocol lacks basic safeguards used by other states to confirm that an inmate is unconscious before injection of the second and third drugs. I would vacate and remand with instructions to consider whether Kentucky's omission of those safeguards poses an untoward, readily avoidable risk of inflicting severe and unnecessary pain.

I

The Court has considered the constitutionality of a specific method of execution on only three prior occasions. Those cases, and other decisions cited by the parties and amici, provide little guidance on the standard that should govern petitioners' challenge to Kentucky's lethal injection protocol.

In *Wilkerson v. Utah* (1879), the Court held that death by firing squad did not rank among the "cruel and unusual punishments" banned by the Eighth Amendment. In so ruling, the Court did not endeavor "to define with exactness the extent of the constitutional provision which provides that cruel and unusual punishments shall not be inflicted." But it was "safe to affirm," the Court stated, that "punishments of torture . . . and all others in the same line of unnecessary cruelty, are forbidden."

Next, in *In re Kemmler* (1890), death by electrocution was the assailed method of execution. The Court reiterated that the Eighth Amendment prohibits "torture" and "lingering death." The word "cruel," the Court further observed, "implies . . . something inhuman . . . something more than the mere extinguishment of life." Those statements, however, were made en passant. *Kemmler*'s actual holding was that the Eighth Amendment does not apply to the states, a proposition we have since repudiated, see, for example, *Robinson v. California* (1962).

Finally, in *Louisiana ex rel. Francis v. Resweber* (1947), the Court rejected Eighth and Fourteenth Amendment challenges to a reelectrocution following an earlier attempt that failed to cause death. The plurality opinion in that case first stated: "The traditional humanity of modern Anglo-American law forbids the infliction of unnecessary pain in the execution of the death sentence." But the very next sentence varied the formulation; it referred to the "[p]rohibition against the wanton infliction of pain."

No clear standard for determining the constitutionality of a method of execution emerges from these decisions. Moreover, the age of the opinions limits their utility as an aid to resolution of the present controversy. The Eighth Amendment, we have held, "'must draw its meaning from the evolving standards of decency that mark the progress of a maturing society.'" *Wilkerson* was decided 129 years ago, *Kemmler* 118 years ago, and *Resweber* 61 years ago. Whatever little light our prior method-of-execution cases might shed is thus dimmed by the passage of time.

Further phrases and tests can be drawn from more recent decisions, for example, *Gregg v. Georgia* (1976). Speaking of capital punishment in the abstract, the lead opinion said that the Eighth Amendment prohibits "the unnecessary and wanton infliction of pain"; the same opinion also cautioned that a death sentence cannot "be imposed under sentencing procedures that creat[e] a substantial risk that it would be inflicted in an arbitrary and capricious manner."

Relying on *Gregg* and our earlier decisions, the Kentucky Supreme Court stated that an execution procedure violates the Eighth Amendment if it "creates a substantial risk of wanton and unnecessary infliction of pain, torture or lingering death." Petitioners respond that courts should consider "(a) the severity of pain risked, (b) the likelihood of that pain occurring, *and* (c) the extent to which alternative means are feasible" Brief for Petitioners 38 (emphasis added). The plurality settles somewhere in between, requiring a "substantial risk of serious harm" and considering whether a "feasible, readily implemented" alternative can "significantly reduce" that risk.

I agree with petitioners and the plurality that the degree of risk, magnitude of pain, and availability of alternatives must be considered. I part ways with the plurality, however, to the extent its "substantial risk" test sets a fixed threshold for the first factor. The three factors are interrelated; a strong showing on one reduces the importance of the others.

Lethal injection as a mode of execution can be expected, in most instances, to result in painless death. Rare though errors may be, the consequences of a mistake about the condemned inmate's consciousness are horrendous and effectively undetectable after injection of the second drug. Given the opposing tugs of the degree of risk and magnitude of pain, the critical question here, as I see it, is whether a feasible alternative exists. Proof of "a slightly or marginally safer alternative" is, as the plurality notes, insufficient. But if readily available measures can materially increase the likelihood that the protocol will cause no pain, a state fails to adhere to contemporary standards of decency if it declines to employ those measures.

II

Kentucky's legislature adopted lethal injection as a method of execution in 1998. Lawmakers left the development of the lethal injection protocol to officials in the Department of Corrections. Those officials, the trial court found, were "given the task without the benefit of scientific aid or policy oversight." "Kentucky's protocol," that court observed, "was copied from other states and accepted without challenge." Kentucky "did not conduct any independent scientific or medical studies or consult any medical professionals concerning the drugs and dosage amounts to be injected into the condemned." Instead, the trial court noted, Kentucky followed the path taken in other states that "simply fell in line" behind the three-drug protocol first developed by Oklahoma in 1977.

Kentucky's protocol begins with a careful measure: Only medical professionals may perform the venipunctures and establish intravenous (IV) access. Members of the IV team must have at least one year's experience as a certified medical assistant, phlebotomist, emergency medical technician (EMT), paramedic, or military corpsman. Kentucky's IV team currently has two members: a phlebotomist with eight years' experience and an EMT with twenty years' experience. Both members practice siting catheters at ten lethal injection training sessions held annually.

Other than using qualified and trained personnel to establish IV access, however, Kentucky does little to ensure that the inmate receives an effective dose of sodium thiopental. After siting the catheters, the IV team leaves the execution chamber. From that point forward, only the warden and deputy warden remain with the inmate. Neither the warden nor the deputy warden has any medical training.

The warden relies on visual observation to determine whether the inmate "appears" unconscious. In Kentucky's only previous execution by lethal injection, the warden's position allowed him to see the inmate best from the waist down, with only a peripheral view of the inmate's face. No other check for consciousness occurs before injection of pancuronium bromide. Kentucky's protocol does not include an automatic pause in the "rapid flow" of the drugs, or any of the most basic tests to determine whether the sodium thiopental has worked. No one calls the inmate's name, shakes him, brushes his eyelashes to test for a reflex, or applies a noxious stimulus to gauge his response.

Nor does Kentucky monitor the effectiveness of the sodium thiopental using readily available equipment, even though the inmate is already connected to an electrocardiogram (EKG). A drop in blood pressure or heart rate after injection of sodium thiopental would not prove that the inmate is unconscious, but would signal that the drug has entered the inmate's bloodstream. Kentucky's own expert testified that the sodium thiopental should "cause the inmate's blood pressure to become very, very low," and that a precipitous drop in blood pressure would "confirm" that the drug was having its expected effect. Use of a blood pressure cuff and EKG, the record shows, is the standard of care in surgery requiring anesthesia.

A consciousness check supplementing the warden's visual observation before injection of the second drug is easily implemented and can reduce a risk of dreadful pain. Pancuronium bromide is a powerful paralytic that prevents all voluntary muscle movement. Once it is injected, further monitoring of the inmate's consciousness becomes impractical without sophisticated equipment and training. Even if the inmate were conscious and in excruciating pain, there would be no visible indication.[2]

Recognizing the importance of a window between the first and second drugs, other states have adopted safeguards not contained in Kentucky's protocol. Florida pauses between injection of the first and second drugs so the warden can "determine, after consultation, that the inmate is indeed unconscious." The warden does so by touching the inmate's eyelashes, calling his name, and shaking him. If the inmate's consciousness remains in doubt in Florida, "the medical team members will come out from the chemical room and consult in the assessment of the inmate." During the entire execution, the person who inserted the IV line monitors the IV access point and the inmate's face on closed circuit television.

In Missouri, "medical personnel must examine the prisoner physically to confirm that he is unconscious using standard clinical techniques and must inspect the catheter site again." "The second and third chemicals are injected only after confirmation that the prisoner is unconscious and after a period of at least three minutes has elapsed from the first injection of thiopental."

In California, a member of the IV team brushes the inmate's eyelashes, speaks to him, and shakes him at the halfway point and, again, at the completion of the sodium thiopental injection.

In Alabama, a member of the execution team "begin[s] by saying the condemned inmate's name. If there is no response, the team member will gently stroke the condemned inmate's eyelashes. If there is no response, the team member will then pinch the condemned inmate's arm."

In Indiana, officials inspect the injection site after administration of sodium thiopental, say the inmate's name, touch him, and use ammonia tablets to test his response to a noxious nasal stimulus.

These checks provide a degree of assurance—missing from Kentucky's protocol—that the first drug has been properly administered. They are simple and essentially costless to employ, yet work to lower the risk that the inmate will be subjected to the agony of conscious suffocation caused by pancuronium bromide and the searing pain caused by potassium chloride. The record contains no explanation why Kentucky does not take any of these elementary measures.

The risk that an error administering sodium thiopental would go undetected is minimal, Kentucky urges, because if the drug was mistakenly injected into the inmate's tissue, not a vein, he "would be awake and screaming." That argument ignores aspects of Kentucky's protocol that render passive reliance on obvious signs of consciousness, such as screaming, inadequate to determine whether the inmate is experiencing pain.

First, Kentucky's use of pancuronium bromide to paralyze the inmate means he will not be able to scream after the second drug is injected, no matter how much pain he is experiencing. Kentucky's argument, therefore, appears to rest on the assertion that sodium thiopental is itself painful when injected into tissue rather than a vein. The trial court made no finding on that point, and Kentucky cites no supporting evidence from executions in which it is known that sodium thiopental was injected into the inmate's soft tissue.

Second, the inmate may receive enough sodium thiopental to mask the most obvious signs of consciousness without receiving a dose sufficient to achieve a surgical plane of anesthesia. If the drug is injected too quickly, the increase in blood pressure can cause the inmate's veins to burst after a small amount of sodium thiopental has been administered. Kentucky's protocol does not specify the rate at which sodium thiopental should be injected. The executioner, who does not have any medical training, pushes the drug "by feel" through five feet of tubing.[3] In practice sessions, unlike in an actual execution, there is no resistance on the catheter; thus the executioner's training may lead him to push the drugs too fast.

"The easiest and most obvious way to ensure that an inmate is unconscious during an execution," petitioners argued to the Kentucky Supreme Court, "is to check for consciousness prior to injecting pancuronium [bromide]." See also (Complaint) (alleging Kentucky's protocol does not "require the execution team to determine that the condemned inmate is unconscious prior to administering the second and third chemicals"). The court did not address petitioners' argument. I would therefore remand with instructions to consider whether the failure to include readily available safeguards to confirm that the inmate is unconscious after injection of sodium thiopental, in combination with the other elements of Kentucky's protocol, creates an untoward, readily avoidable risk of inflicting severe and unnecessary pain.

11

BAZE V. REES[1]

Justice John Paul Stevens, Concurring

April 16, 2008

When we granted certiorari in this case, I assumed that our decision would bring the debate about lethal injection as a method of execution to a close. It now seems clear that it will not. The question whether a similar three-drug protocol may be used in other states remains open, and may well be answered differently in a future case on the basis of a more complete record. Instead of ending the controversy, I am now convinced that this case will generate debate not only about the constitutionality of the three-drug protocol, and specifically about the justification for the use of the paralytic agent, pancuronium bromide, but also about the justification for the death penalty itself. . . .

[Section I Omitted]

SECTION II

The thoughtful opinions written by the chief justice and by Justice Ginsburg have persuaded me that current decisions by state legislatures, by the Congress of the United States, and by this Court to retain the death penalty as a part of our law are the product of habit and inattention rather than an acceptable deliberative process that weighs the costs and risks of administering that penalty against its identifiable benefits, and rest in part on a faulty assumption about the retributive force of the death penalty.

In *Gregg v. Georgia* (1976), we explained that unless a criminal sanction serves a legitimate penological function, it constitutes "gratuitous infliction of suffering" in violation of the Eighth Amendment. We then identified three societal purposes for death as a sanction: incapacitation, deterrence, and retribution. In the past three decades, however, each of these rationales has been called into question.

While incapacitation may have been a legitimate rationale in 1976, the recent rise in statutes providing for life imprisonment without the possibility of parole demonstrates that incapacitation is neither a necessary nor a sufficient justification for the death penalty. Moreover, a recent poll indicates that support for the death penalty drops significantly when life without the possibility of parole is presented as an alternative option. And the available sociological evidence suggests that juries are less likely to impose the death penalty when life without parole is available as a sentence.

The legitimacy of deterrence as an acceptable justification for the death penalty is also questionable, at best. Despite thirty years of empirical research in the area, there remains no reliable statistical evidence that capital punishment in fact deters potential offenders. In the absence of such evidence, deterrence cannot serve as a sufficient penological justification for this uniquely severe and irrevocable punishment.

We are left, then, with retribution as the primary rationale for imposing the death penalty. And indeed, it is the retribution rationale that animates much of the remaining enthusiasm for the death penalty.[2] As Lord Justice Denning argued in 1950, "some crimes are so outrageous that society insists on adequate punishment, because the wrong-doer deserves it, irrespective of whether it is a deterrent or not." Our Eighth Amendment jurisprudence has narrowed the class of offenders eligible for the death penalty to include only those who have committed outrageous crimes defined by specific aggravating factors. It is the cruel treatment of victims that provides the most persuasive arguments for prosecutors seeking the death penalty. A natural response to such heinous crimes is a thirst for vengeance.

At the same time, however, as the thoughtful opinions by the chief justice and Justice Ginsburg make pellucidly clear, our society has moved away from public and painful retribution towards ever more humane forms of punishment. State-sanctioned killing is therefore becoming more and more anachronistic. In an attempt to bring executions in line with our evolving standards of decency, we have adopted increasingly less painful methods of execution, and then declared previous methods barbaric and archaic. But by requiring that an execution be relatively painless, we necessarily protect the inmate from enduring any punishment that is comparable to the suffering inflicted on his victim.[3] This trend, while appropriate and required by the Eighth Amendment's prohibition on cruel and unusual punishment, actually undermines the very premise on which public approval of the retribution rationale is based.

Full recognition of the diminishing force of the principal rationales for retaining the death penalty should lead this Court and legislatures to reexamine the question recently posed by Professor Salinas, a former Texas prosecutor and judge.[4] The time for a dispassionate, impartial comparison of the enormous costs that death penalty litigation imposes on society with the benefits that it produces has surely arrived.

III

"[A] penalty may be cruel and unusual because it is excessive and serves no valid legislative purpose." ("The entire thrust of the Eighth Amendment is, in short, against 'that which is excessive.'") Our cases holding that certain sanctions are "excessive," and therefore prohibited by the Eighth Amendment, have relied heavily on "objective criteria," such as legislative enactments. In our recent decision in *Atkins v. Virginia* (2002), holding that death is an excessive sanction for a mentally retarded defendant, we also relied heavily on opinions written by Justice White holding that the death penalty is an excessive punishment for the crime of raping a sixteen-year-old woman, *Coker v. Georgia* (1977), and for a murderer who did not intend to kill, *Enmund v. Florida* (1982). In those opinions we acknowledged that "objective evidence, though of great importance, did not 'wholly determine' the controversy, 'for the Constitution contemplates that in the end our own judgment will be brought to bear on the question of the acceptability of the death penalty under the Eighth Amendment.'"

Justice White was exercising his own judgment in 1972 when he provided the decisive vote in *Furman*, the case that led to a nation-wide reexamination of the death penalty. His conclusion that death amounted to "cruel and unusual punishment in the constitutional sense" as well as the "dictionary sense," rested on both an uncontroversial legal premise and on a factual premise that he admittedly could not "prove" on the basis of objective criteria. As a matter of law, he correctly stated that the "needless extinction of life with only marginal contributions to any discernible social or public purposes . . . would be patently excessive" and violative of the Eighth Amendment. As a matter of fact, he stated, "like my Brethren, I must arrive at judgment; and I can do no more than state a conclusion based on 10 years of almost daily exposure to the facts and circumstances of hundreds and hundreds of federal and state criminal cases involving crimes for which death is the authorized penalty." I agree with Justice White that there are occasions when a Member of this Court has a duty to make judgments on the basis of data that falls short of absolute proof.

Our decisions in 1976 upholding the constitutionality of the death penalty relied heavily on our belief that adequate procedures were in place that would avoid the danger of discriminatory application identified by Justice Douglas's opinion in *Furman*, of arbitrary application identified by Justice Stewart, and of excessiveness identified by Justices Brennan and Marshall. In subsequent years, a number of our decisions relied on the premise that "death is different" from every other form of punishment to justify rules minimizing the risk of error in capital cases. Ironically, however, more recent cases have endorsed procedures that provide fewer protections to capital defendants than to ordinary offenders.

Of special concern to me are rules that deprive the defendant of a trial by jurors representing a fair cross-section of the community. Litigation involving both challenges for cause and peremptory challenges has persuaded me that the process of obtaining a "death qualified jury" is really a procedure that has the purpose and effect of obtaining a jury that is biased in favor of conviction. The prosecutorial concern that death verdicts would rarely be returned by twelve randomly selected jurors should be viewed as objective evidence supporting the conclusion that the penalty is excessive.

Another serious concern is that the risk of error in capital cases may be greater than in other cases because the facts are often so disturbing that the interest in making sure the crime does not go unpunished may overcome residual doubt concerning the identity of the offender. Our former emphasis on the importance of ensuring that decisions in death cases be adequately supported by reason rather than emotion, has been undercut by more recent decisions placing a thumb on the prosecutor's side of the scales. Thus, in *Kansas v. Marsh* (2006), the Court upheld a state statute that requires imposition of the death penalty when the jury finds that the aggravating and mitigating factors are in equipoise. And in *Payne v. Tennessee* (1991), the Court overruled earlier cases and held that "victim impact" evidence relating to the personal characteristics of the victim and the emotional impact of the crime on the victim's family is admissible despite the fact that it sheds no light on the question of guilt or innocence or on the moral culpability of the defendant, and thus serves no purpose other than to encourage jurors to make life or death decisions on the basis of emotion rather than reason.

A third significant concern is the risk of discriminatory application of the death penalty. While that risk has been dramatically reduced, the Court has allowed it to continue to play an unacceptable role in capital cases. Thus, in *McCleskey v. Kemp* (1987), the Court upheld a death sentence despite the "strong probability that [the defendant's] sentencing jury . . . was influenced by the fact that [he was] black and his victim was white."

Finally, given the real risk of error in this class of cases, the irrevocable nature of the consequences is of decisive importance to me. Whether or not any innocent defendants have actually been executed, abundant evidence accumulated in recent years has resulted in the exoneration of an unacceptable number of defendants found guilty of capital offenses. The risk of executing innocent defendants can be entirely eliminated by treating any penalty more severe than life imprisonment without the possibility of parole as constitutionally excessive.

In sum, just as Justice White ultimately based his conclusion in *Furman* on his extensive exposure to countless cases for which death is

the authorized penalty, I have relied on my own experience in reaching
the conclusion that the imposition of the death penalty represents "the
pointless and needless extinction of life with only marginal contributions to any discernible social or public purposes. A penalty with such
negligible returns to the State [is] patently excessive and cruel and
unusual punishment violative of the Eighth Amendment."

IV

The conclusion that I have reached with regard to the constitutionality of the death penalty itself makes my decision in this case particularly difficult. It does not, however, justify a refusal to respect precedents that remain a part of our law. This Court has held that the death
penalty is constitutional, and has established a framework for evaluating the constitutionality of particular methods of execution. Under
those precedents, whether as interpreted by the Chief Justice or Justice Ginsburg, I am persuaded that the evidence adduced by petitioners fails to prove that Kentucky's lethal injection protocol violates
the Eighth Amendment. Accordingly, I join the Court's judgment.

12

BAZE V. REES[1]

Justice Antonin Scalia, Concurring;
Justice Clarence Thomas, Joining

April 16, 2008

I join the opinion of Justice Thomas concurring in the judgment. I write separately to provide what I think is needed response to Justice Stevens's separate opinion.

I

Justice Stevens concludes as follows: "[T]he imposition of the death penalty represents the pointless and needless extinction of life with only marginal contributions to any discernible social or public purposes. A penalty with such negligible returns to the State [is] patently excessive and cruel and unusual punishment violative of the Eighth Amendment."

This conclusion is insupportable as an interpretation of the Constitution, which generally leaves it to democratically elected legislatures rather than courts to decide what makes significant contribution to social or public purposes. Besides that more general proposition, the very text of the document recognizes that the death penalty is a permissible legislative choice. The Fifth Amendment expressly requires a presentment or indictment of a grand jury to hold a person to answer for "a capital, or otherwise infamous crime," and prohibits deprivation of "life" without due process of law. The same Congress that proposed the Eighth Amendment also enacted the act of April 30, 1790, which made several offenses punishable by death. Writing in 1976, Professor Hugo Bedau—no friend of the death penalty himself—observed that "[u]ntil fifteen years ago, save for a few mavericks, no one gave any credence to the possibility of ending the death penalty by judicial interpretation of constitutional law." There is simply no legal authority for the proposition that the imposition of death as a criminal penalty is unconstitutional other than the opinions in *Furman v. Georgia* (1972), which established a nationwide moratorium on capital punishment that Justice Stevens had a hand in ending four years later in *Gregg*.

II

What prompts Justice Stevens to repudiate his prior view and to adopt the astounding position that a criminal sanction expressly mentioned in the Constitution violates the Constitution? His analysis begins with what he believes to be the "uncontroversial legal premise" that the "'extinction of life with only marginal contributions to any discernible social or public purposes . . . would be patently excessive' and violative of the Eighth Amendment." Even if that were uncontroversial in the abstract (and it is certainly not what occurs to me as the meaning of "cruel and unusual punishments"), it is assuredly controversial (indeed, flat-out wrong) as applied to a mode of punishment that is explicitly sanctioned by the Constitution. As to that, *the people* have determined whether there is adequate contribution to social or public purposes, and it is no business of unelected judges to set that judgment aside. But even if we grant Justice Stevens his "uncontroversial premise," his application of that premise to the current practice of capital punishment does not meet the "heavy burden [that] rests on those who would attack the judgment of the representatives of the people." That is to say, Justice Stevens's policy analysis of the constitutionality of capital punishment fails on its own terms.

According to Justice Stevens, the death penalty promotes none of the purposes of criminal punishment because it neither prevents more crimes than alternative measures nor serves a retributive purpose. He argues that "the recent rise in statutes providing for life imprisonment without the possibility of parole" means that states have a ready alternative to the death penalty. Moreover, "[d]espite 30 years of empirical research in the area, there remains no reliable statistical evidence that capital punishment in fact deters potential offenders." Taking the points together, Justice Stevens concludes that the availability of alternatives, and what he describes as the unavailability of "reliable statistical evidence," renders capital punishment unconstitutional. In his view, the benefits of capital punishment—as compared to other forms of punishment such as life imprisonment—are outweighed by the costs.

These conclusions are not supported by the available data. Justice Stevens's analysis barely acknowledges the "significant body of recent evidence that capital punishment may well have a deterrent effect, possibly a quite powerful one."[2] According to a "leading national study," "each execution prevents some eighteen murders, on average. . . . If the current evidence is even roughly correct . . . then a refusal to impose capital punishment will effectively condemn numerous innocent people to death."

Of course, it may well be that the empirical studies establishing that the death penalty has a powerful deterrent effect are incorrect, and some scholars have disputed its deterrent value. But that is not the point. It is simply not our place to choose one set of responsible empirical studies over another in interpreting the Constitution. Nor is it our place to demand that state legislatures support their criminal sanctions with foolproof empirical studies, rather than commonsense predictions about human behavior. "The value of capital punishment as a deterrent of crime is a complex factual issue the resolution of which properly rests with the legislatures, which can evaluate the results of statistical studies in terms of their own local conditions and with a flexibility of approach that is not available to the courts." Were Justice Stevens's current view the constitutional test, even his own preferred criminal sanction—life imprisonment without the possibility of parole—may fail constitutional scrutiny, because it is entirely unclear that enough empirical evidence supports that sanction as compared to alternatives such as life with the possibility of parole.

But even if Justice Stevens's assertion about the deterrent value of the death penalty were correct, the death penalty would yet be constitutional (as he concedes) if it served the appropriate purpose of ret-ribution. I would think it difficult indeed to prove that a criminal sanction fails to serve a retributive purpose—a judgment that strikes me as inherently subjective and insusceptible of judicial review. Justice Stevens, however, concludes that, because the Eighth Amendment "protect[s] the inmate from enduring any punishment that is compa-rable to the suffering inflicted on his victim," capital punishment serves no retributive purpose at all. The infliction of any pain, according to Justice Stevens, violates the Eighth Amendment's prohi-bition against cruel and unusual punishments, but so too does the imposition of capital punishment *without pain* because a criminal penalty lacks a retributive purpose unless it inflicts pain commensu-rate with the pain that the criminal has caused. In other words, if a punishment is not retributive enough, it is not retributive at all. To state this proposition is to refute it, as Justice Stevens once under-stood. "[T]he decision that capital punishment may be the appro-priate sanction in extreme cases is an expression of the community's belief that certain crimes are themselves so grievous an affront to humanity that the only adequate response may be the penalty of death" *Gregg* (joint opinion of Justices Stewart, Powell, and Stevens).

Justice Stevens's final refuge in his cost-benefit analysis is a familiar one: There is a risk that an innocent person might be con-victed and sentenced to death—though not a risk that Justice Stevens can quantify, because he lacks a single example of a person executed for a crime he did not commit in the current American system. His analysis of this risk is thus a series of sweeping condemnations that, if taken seriously, would prevent any punishment under any criminal justice system. According to him, "[t]he prosecutorial concern that death verdicts would rarely be returned by 12 randomly selected jurors should be viewed as objective evidence supporting the conclu-sion that the penalty is excessive." But prosecutors undoubtedly have a similar concern that *any* unanimous conviction would rarely be returned by twelve randomly selected jurors. That is why they, like defense counsel, are permitted to use the challenges for cause and peremptory challenges that Justice Stevens finds so troubling, in order to arrive at a jury that both sides believe will be more likely to do jus-tice in a particular case. Justice Stevens's concern that prosecutors will be inclined to challenge jurors who will not find a person guilty supports not his conclusion, but the separate (and equally erroneous) conclusion that peremptory challenges and challenges for cause are unconstitutional. According to Justice Stevens, "the risk of error in capital cases may be greater than in other cases because the facts are often so disturbing that the interest in making sure the crime does not go unpunished may overcome residual doubt concerning the identity of the offender." That rationale, however, supports not Justice Stevens's conclusion that the death penalty is unconstitutional, but the more sweeping proposition that any conviction in a case in which facts are disturbing is suspect—including, of course, convictions resulting in life without parole in those states that do not have capital punishment. The same is true of Justice Stevens's claim that there is a risk of "discriminatory application of the death penalty." The same could be said of any criminal penalty, including life without parole; there is no proof that in this regard the death penalty is distinctive.

But of all Justice Stevens's criticisms of the death penalty, the hardest to take is his bemoaning of "the enormous costs that death penalty litigation imposes on society," including the "burden on the courts and the lack of finality for victim's families." Those costs, those burdens, and that lack of finality are in large measure the creation of Justice Stevens and other justices opposed to the death penalty, who have "encumber[ed] [it] . . . with unwarranted restrictions neither contained in the text of the Constitution nor reflected in two centuries of practice under it"—the product of their policy views "not shared by the vast majority of the American people."

III

But actually none of this really matters. As Justice Stevens explains, "objective evidence, though of great importance, [does] not wholly determine the controversy, for the Constitution contemplates that in the end *our own judgment will be brought to bear on the question of the acceptability of the death penalty under the Eighth Amendment. . . .* I have relied *on my own experience* in reaching the conclusion that the imposition of the death penalty" is unconstitutional (emphasis added).

Purer expression cannot be found of the principle of rule by judicial fiat. In the face of Justice Stevens's experience, the experience of all others is, it appears, of little consequence. The experience of the state legislatures and the Congress—who retain the death penalty as a form of punishment—is dismissed as "the product of habit and inattention rather than an acceptable deliberative process." The experience of social scientists whose studies indicate that the death penalty deters crime is relegated to a footnote. The experience of fellow citizens who support the death penalty is described, with only the most thinly veiled condemnation, as stemming from a "thirst for vengeance." It is Justice Stevens's experience that reigns over all.

❋❋❋

I take no position on the desirability of the death penalty, except to say that its value is eminently debatable and the subject of deeply, indeed passionately, held views—which means, to me, that it is preeminently not a matter to be resolved here. And especially not when it is explicitly permitted by the Constitution.

13

BAZE v. REES[1]

Justice Stephen Breyer, Concurring

April 16, 2008

Assuming the lawfulness of the death penalty itself, petitioners argue that Kentucky's method of execution, lethal injection, nonetheless constitutes a constitutionally forbidden, "cruel and unusual punishmen[t]." In respect to *how* a court should review such a claim, I agree with Justice Ginsburg. She highlights the relevant question, whether the method creates an untoward, readily avoidable risk of inflicting severe and unnecessary suffering. I agree that the relevant factors—the "degree of risk," the "magnitude of pain," and the "availability of alternatives"—are interrelated and each must be considered. At the same time, I believe that the legal merits of the kind of claim presented must inevitably turn not so much upon the wording of an intermediate standard of review as upon facts and evidence. And I cannot find, either in the record in this case or in the literature on the subject, sufficient evidence that Kentucky's execution method poses the "significant and unnecessary risk of inflicting severe pain" that petitioners assert.

In respect to the literature, I have examined the periodical article that seems first to have brought widespread legal attention to the claim that lethal injection might bring about unnecessary suffering. The article ["Inadequate Anesthesia in Lethal Injection for Execution"], by Dr. Leonidas G. Koniaris, Teresa A. Zimmers (of the University of Miami School of Medicine), and others, appeared in the April 16, 2005, issue of the *Lancet*, an eminent, peer-reviewed medical journal (hereinafter *Lancet* Study). The authors examined "autopsy toxicology results from 49 executions in Arizona, Georgia, North Carolina, and South Carolina." The study noted that lethal injection usually consists of sequential administration of a barbiturate (sodium thiopental), followed by injection of a paralyzing agent (pancuronium bromide) and a heart-attack-inducing drug (potassium chloride). The study focused on the effectiveness of the first drug in anaesthetizing the inmate. It noted that the four states used 2 grams of thiopental. (Kentucky follows a similar system but currently uses 3 grams of sodium thiopental.) Although the sodium thiopental dose (of, say, 2 grams) was several times the dose used in ordinary surgical operations, the authors found that the level of barbiturate present in the bloodstream several hours (or more) after death was *lower* than the level one might expect to find during an operation. With certain qualifications, they state that "21 (43%)" of the examined instances "had [thiopental] concentrations consistent with consciousness"—a fact that should create considerable concern given the related likelihood of unexpressed suffering. The authors suggest that, among other things, inadequate training may help explain the results.

The *Lancet* Study, however, may be seriously flawed. In its September 24, 2005, issue, the *Lancet* published three responses. The first, by one of the initial referees, Jonathan I. Groner of Children's Hospital, Columbus, Ohio, claimed that a low level of thiopental in the bloodstream does not necessarily mean that an inadequate dose was given, for, under circumstances likely common to lethal injections, thiopental can simply diffuse from the bloodstream into surrounding tissues. And a long pause between death and measurement means that this kind of diffusion likely occurred. For this reason and others, Groner, who said he had initially "expressed strong support for the article," had become "concerned" that its key finding "may be erroneous because of lack of equipoise in the study."

The second correspondents—Mark J. S. Heath, Donald R. Stanski, and Derrick J. Pounder, respectively of the Department of Anesthesiology, Columbia University; of Stanford University School of Medicine; and the University of Dundee, United Kingdom—

concluded that "Koniaris and colleagues do not present scientifically convincing data to justify their conclusion that so large a proportion of inmates have experienced awareness during lethal injection." These researchers noted that because the blood samples were taken "several hours to days after" the inmates' deaths, the postmortem concentrations of thiopental—a lipophilic drug that diffuses from blood into tissue—could not be relied on as accurate indicators for concentrations in the blood stream during life.

The third correspondents, Robyn S. Weisman, Jeffrey N. Bernstein, and Richard S. Weisman, of the University of Miami, School of Medicine, and Florida Poison Information Center, said that "[p]ostmortem drug concentrations are extremely difficult to interpret and there is substantial variability in results depending on timing, anatomical origin of the specimen, and physical and chemical properties of the drug." They believed that the original finding "requires further assessment."

The authors of the original study replied, defending the accuracy of their findings. Yet neither the petition for certiorari nor any of the briefs filed in this Court (including seven amici curiae briefs supporting the petitioners) make any mention of the *Lancet* Study, which was published during petitioners' trial. In light of that fact, and the responses to the original study, a judge, nonexpert in these matters, cannot give the *Lancet* Study significant weight.

The literature also contains a detailed article on the subject, which appeared in 2002 in the *Ohio State Law Journal*. The author, Professor Deborah W. Denno, examined executions by lethal injection in the thirty-six states where thiopental is used.[2] In table 9, the author lists thirty-one "Botched Lethal Injection Executions" in the time from our decision in *Gregg v. Georgia* (1976) through 2001. Of these, nineteen involved a problem of locating a suitable vein to administer the chemicals. Eleven of the remaining twelve apparently involved strong, readily apparent physical reactions. One, taking place in Illinois in 1990, is described as involving "some indication that, while appearing calm on the outside due to the paralyzing drugs, [the inmate] suffered excruciating pain." The author adds that "[t]here were reports of faulty equipment and inexperienced personnel." This article, about which Professor Denno testified at petitioners' trial and on which petitioners rely in this Court, may well provide cause for concern about the administration of the lethal injection. But it cannot materially aid the petitioners here. That is because, as far as the record here reveals, and as the Kentucky courts found, Kentucky's use of trained phlebotomists and the presence of observers should prevent the kind of "botched" executions that Denno's table 9 documents.

The literature also casts a shadow of uncertainty upon the ready availability of some of the alternatives to lethal execution methods. Petitioners argued to the trial court, for example, that Kentucky should eliminate the use of a paralytic agent, such as pancuronium bromide, which could, by preventing any outcry, mask suffering an inmate might be experiencing because of inadequate administration of the anesthetic. And they point out that use of pancuronium bromide to euthanize animals is contrary to veterinary standards. In the Netherlands, however, the use of pancuronium bromide is recommended for purposes of lawful assisted suicide. Why, one might ask, if the use of pancuronium bromide is undesirable, would those in the Netherlands, interested in practices designed to bring about a humane death, recommend the use of that, or similar, drugs? Petitioners pointed out that in the Netherlands, physicians trained in anesthesiology are involved in assisted suicide, while that is not the case in Kentucky. While important, that difference does not resolve the apparently conflicting views about the inherent propriety or impropriety of use of this drug to extinguish human life humanely.

Similarly, petitioners argue for better trained personnel. But it is clear that both the American Medical Association (AMA) and the American Nursing Association (ANA) have rules of ethics that strongly oppose their members' participation in executions. And these facts suggest that finding better trained personnel may be more difficult than might, at first blush, appear.

Nor can I find in the record in this case any stronger evidence in petitioners' favor than the literature itself provides of an untoward, readily avoidable risk of severe pain. Indeed, Justice Ginsburg has accepted what I believe is petitioners' strongest claim, namely, Kentucky should require more thorough testing as to unconsciousness. In respect to this matter, however, I must agree with the plurality and Justice Stevens. The record provides too little reason to believe that such measures, if adopted in Kentucky, would make a significant difference.

The upshot is that I cannot find, either in the record or in the readily available literature that I have seen, sufficient grounds to believe that Kentucky's method of lethal injection creates a significant risk of unnecessary suffering. The death penalty itself, of course, brings with it serious risks: for example, risks of executing the wrong person; risks that unwarranted animus (in respect, e.g., to the race of victims), may play a role; risks that those convicted will find themselves on death row for many years, perhaps decades, to come. These risks in part explain why that penalty is so controversial. But the lawfulness of the death penalty is not before us. And petitioners' proof and evidence, while giving rise to legitimate concern, do not show that Kentucky's method of applying the death penalty amounts to "cruel and unusual punishmen[t]."

For these reasons, I concur in the judgment.

14

BAZE V. REES[1]

Justice Clarence Thomas, Concurring; Justice Antonin Scalia, Joining

April 16, 2008

Although I agree that petitioners have failed to establish that Kentucky's lethal injection protocol violates the Eighth Amendment, I write separately because I cannot subscribe to the plurality opinion's formulation of the governing standard. As I understand it, that opinion would hold that a method of execution violates the Eighth Amendment if it poses a substantial risk of severe pain that could be significantly reduced by adopting readily available alternative procedures. This standard—along with petitioners' proposed "unnecessary risk" standard and the dissent's "untoward risk" standard—finds no support in the original understanding of the Cruel and Unusual Punishments Clause or in our previous method-of-execution cases; casts constitutional doubt on long-accepted methods of execution; and injects the Court into matters it has no institutional capacity to resolve. Because, in my view, a method of execution violates the Eighth Amendment only if it is deliberately designed to inflict pain, I concur only in the judgment.

[Sections I, II, and III omitted.]

SECTION IV

... It is not a little ironic—and telling—that lethal injection, hailed just a few years ago as *the* humane alternative in light of which every other method of execution was deemed an unconstitutional relic of the past, is the subject of today's challenge. It appears the Constitution is "evolving" even faster than I suspected. And it is obvious that, for some who oppose capital punishment on policy grounds, the only acceptable end point of the evolution is for this Court, in an exercise of raw judicial power unsupported by the text or history of the Constitution, or even by a contemporary moral consensus, to strike down the death penalty as cruel and unusual in all circumstances. In the meantime, though, the next best option for those seeking to abolish the death penalty is to embroil the states in never-ending litigation concerning the adequacy of their execution procedures. But far from putting an end to abusive litigation in this area, and thereby vindicating in some small measure the states' "significant interest in meting out a sentence of death in a timely fashion," today's decision is sure to engender more litigation. At what point does a risk become "substantial"? Which alternative procedures are "feasible" and "readily implemented"? When is a reduction in risk "significant"? What penological justifications are "legitimate"? Such are the questions the lower courts will have to grapple with in the wake of today's decision. Needless to say, we have left the states with nothing resembling a bright-line rule.

Which brings me to yet a further problem with comparative-risk standards: They require courts to resolve medical and scientific controversies that are largely beyond judicial ken. Little need be said here, other than to refer to the various opinions filed by my colleagues today. Under the competing risk standards advanced by the plurality opinion and the dissent, for example, the difference between a lethal injection procedure that satisfies the Eighth Amendment and one that does not may well come down to one's judgment with respect to something as hairsplitting as whether an eyelash stroke is necessary to ensure that the inmate is unconscious, or whether instead other measures have already provided sufficient assurance of unconsciousness. We have neither the authority nor the expertise to micromanage the states' administration of the death penalty in this manner. There is simply no reason to believe that "unelected" judges without scientific, medical, or penological training are any better suited to resolve the delicate issues surrounding the administration of the death penalty than are state administrative personnel specifically charged with the task.

In short, I reject as both unprecedented and unworkable any standard that would require the courts to weigh the relative advantages and disadvantages of different methods of execution or of different procedures for implementing a given method of execution. To the extent that there is any comparative element to the inquiry, it should be limited to whether the challenged method inherently inflicts significantly more pain than traditional modes of execution such as hanging and the firing squad.

SECTION V

Judged under the proper standard, this is an easy case. It is undisputed that Kentucky adopted its lethal injection protocol in an effort to make capital punishment more humane, not to add elements of terror, pain, or disgrace to the death penalty. And it is undisputed that, if administered properly, Kentucky's lethal injection protocol will result in a swift and painless death. As the Sixth Circuit observed in rejecting a similar challenge to Tennessee's lethal injection protocol, we "do not have a situation where the State has any intent (or anything approaching intent) to inflict unnecessary pain; the complaint is that the State's *pain-avoidance procedure* may fail because the executioners may make a mistake in implementing it." But "[t]he risk of negligence in implementing a death-penalty procedure . . . does not establish a cognizable Eighth Amendment claim." Because Kentucky's lethal injection protocol is designed to eliminate pain rather than to inflict it, petitioners' challenge must fail. I accordingly concur in the Court's judgment affirming the decision. . . .

PART FOUR

CAPITAL PUNISHMENT
AND THE RAPE OF CHILDREN

15

KENNEDY V. LOUISIANA, SUPREME COURT OF THE UNITED STATES, JUNE 25, 2008

Justice Anthony Kennedy

PATRICK KENNEDY, PETITIONER v. LOUISIANA[1]
SUPREME COURT OF THE UNITED STATES
JUSTICE KENNEDY delivered the opinion of the Court.
June 25, 2008

The national government and, beyond it, the separate states are bound by the proscriptive mandates of the Eighth Amendment to the Constitution of the United States, and all persons within those respective jurisdictions may invoke its protection. Patrick Kennedy, the petitioner here, seeks to set aside his death sentence under the Eighth Amendment. He was charged by the respondent, the state of Louisiana, with the aggravated rape of his then-eight-year-old stepdaughter. After a jury trial petitioner was convicted and sentenced to death under a state statute authorizing capital punishment for the rape of a child under twelve years of age. This case presents the question whether the Constitution bars respondent from imposing the death penalty for the rape of a child where the crime did not result, and was not intended to result, in death of the victim. We hold the Eighth Amendment prohibits the death penalty for this offense. The Louisiana statute is unconstitutional.

I

Petitioner's crime was one that cannot be recounted in these pages in a way sufficient to capture in full the hurt and horror inflicted on his victim or to convey the revulsion society, and the jury that represents it, sought to express by sentencing petitioner to death. At 9:18 a.m. on March 2, 1998, petitioner called 911 to report that his step-daughter, referred to here as L. H., had been raped. He told the 911 operator that L. H. had been in the garage while he readied his son for school. Upon hearing loud screaming, petitioner said, he ran out-side and found L. H. in the side yard. Two neighborhood boys, peti-tioner told the operator, had dragged L. H. from the garage to the yard, pushed her down, and raped her. Petitioner claimed he saw one of the boys riding away on a blue ten-speed bicycle.

When police arrived at petitioner's home between 9:20 and 9:30 a.m., they found L. H. on her bed, wearing a T-shirt and wrapped in a bloody blanket. She was bleeding profusely from the vaginal area. Petitioner told police he had carried her from the yard to the bathtub and then to the bed. Consistent with this explanation, police found a thin line of blood drops in the garage on the way to the house and then up the stairs. Once in the bedroom, petitioner had used a basin of water and a cloth to wipe blood from the victim. This later pre-vented medical personnel from collecting a reliable DNA sample.

L. H. was transported to the Children's Hospital. An expert in pediatric forensic medicine testified that L. H.'s injuries were the most severe he had seen from a sexual assault in his four years of practice. A laceration to the left wall of the vagina had separated her cervix from the back of her vagina, causing her rectum to protrude into the vaginal structure. Her entire perineum was torn from the posterior fourchette to the anus. The injuries required emergency surgery.

At the scene of the crime, at the hospital, and in the first weeks that followed, both L. H. and petitioner maintained in their accounts to investigators that L. H. had been raped by two neighborhood boys. One of L. H.'s doctors testified at trial that L. H. told all hospital per-sonnel the same version of the rape, although she reportedly told one family member that petitioner raped her. L. H. was interviewed sev-eral days after the rape by a psychologist. The interview was video-taped, lasted three hours over two days, and was introduced into evi-

dence at trial. On the tape one can see that L. H. had difficulty discussing the subject of the rape. She spoke haltingly and with long
pauses and frequent movement. Early in the interview, L. H.
expressed reservations about the questions being asked: "I'm going to
tell the same story. They just want me to change it. . . . They want me
to say my Dad did it. . . . I don't want to say it. . . . I tell them the
same, same story."

She told the psychologist that she had been playing in the garage
when a boy came over and asked her about Girl Scout cookies she
was selling; and that the boy "pulled [her by the legs to] the backyard," where he placed his hand over her mouth, "pulled down [her]
shorts," and raped her.

Eight days after the crime, and despite L. H.'s insistence that petitioner was not the offender, petitioner was arrested for the rape. The
state's investigation had drawn the accuracy of petitioner and L. H.'s
story into question. Though the defense at trial proffered alternative
explanations, the case for the prosecution, credited by the jury, was
based upon the following evidence: An inspection of the side yard
immediately after the assault was inconsistent with a rape having
occurred there, the grass having been found mostly undisturbed but for
a small patch of coagulated blood. Petitioner said that one of the perpetrators fled the crime scene on a blue ten-speed bicycle but gave
inconsistent descriptions of the bicycle's features, such as its handlebars.
Investigators found a bicycle matching petitioner and L. H.'s description in tall grass behind a nearby apartment, and petitioner identified it
as the bicycle one of the perpetrators was riding. Yet its tires were flat,
it did not have gears, and it was covered in spider webs. In addition
police found blood on the underside of L. H.'s mattress. This convinced
them the rape took place in her bedroom, not outside the house.

Police also found that petitioner made two telephone calls on the
morning of the rape. Sometime before 6:15 a.m., petitioner called his
employer and left a message that he was unavailable to work that day.
Petitioner called back between 6:30 and 7:30 a.m. to ask a colleague
how to get blood out of a white carpet because his daughter had "'just
become a young lady.'" At 7:37 a.m., petitioner called B & B Carpet
Cleaning and requested urgent assistance in removing bloodstains
from a carpet. Petitioner did not call 911 until about an hour and a
half later.

182 PART FOUR: THE RAPE OF CHILDREN

About a month after petitioner's arrest, L. H. was removed from the custody of her mother, who had maintained until that point that petitioner was not involved in the rape. On June 22, 1998, L. H. was returned home and told her mother for the first time that petitioner had raped her. And on December 16, 1999, about twenty-one months after the rape, L. H. recorded her accusation in a videotaped interview with the Child Advocacy Center.

The state charged petitioner with aggravated rape of a child and sought the death penalty under La. Statute. At all times relevant to petitioner's case, the statute provided:

A. Aggravated rape is a rape committed . . . where the anal or vaginal sexual intercourse is deemed to be without lawful consent of the victim because it is committed under any one or more of the following circumstances:

.   .   .   .   .

(4) When the victim is under the age of twelve years. Lack of knowledge of the victim's age shall not be a defense.

.   .   .   .   .

D. Whoever commits the crime of aggravated rape shall be punished by life imprisonment at hard labor without benefit of parole, probation, or suspension of sentence.

(1) However, if the victim was under the age of twelve years, as provided by Paragraph A (4) of this Section:

(a) And if the district attorney seeks a capital verdict, the offender shall be punished by death or life imprisonment at hard labor without benefit of parole, probation, or suspension of sentence, in accordance with the determination of the jury.

(Since petitioner was convicted and sentenced, the statute has been amended to include oral intercourse within the definition of aggravated rape and to increase the age of the victim from 12 to 13.)

Aggravating circumstances are set forth in La. Code. In pertinent part and at all times relevant to petitioner's case, the provision stated:

A. The following shall be considered aggravating circumstances:

(1) The offender was engaged in the perpetration or attempted perpetration of aggravated rape, forcible rape, aggravated kidnapping, second degree kidnapping, aggravated burglary, aggravated arson, aggravated escape, assault by drive-by shooting, armed robbery, first degree robbery, or simple robbery.

.   .   .   .   .   .

(10) The victim was under the age of twelve years or sixty-five years of age or older.

The trial began in August 2003. L. H. was then thirteen years old. She testified that she "'woke up one morning and Patrick was on top of [her].'" She remembered petitioner bringing her "[a] cup of orange juice and pills chopped up in it" after the rape and overhearing him on the telephone saying she had become a "young lady." L. H. acknowledged that she had accused two neighborhood boys but testified petitioner told her to say this and that it was untrue.

The jury having found petitioner guilty of aggravated rape, the penalty phase ensued. The state presented the testimony of S. L., who is the cousin and goddaughter of petitioner's ex-wife. S. L. testified that petitioner sexually abused her three times when she was eight years old and that the last time involved sexual intercourse. She did not tell anyone until two years later and did not pursue legal action.

The jury unanimously determined that petitioner should be sentenced to death. The Supreme Court of Louisiana affirmed. The court rejected petitioner's reliance on *Coker v. Georgia* (1977), noting that, while *Coker* bars the use of the death penalty as punishment for the rape of an adult woman, it left open the question which, if any, other nonhomicide crimes can be punished by death consistent with the Eighth Amendment. Because "children are a class that need special protection," the state court reasoned, the rape of a child is unique in terms of the harm it inflicts upon the victim and our society.

The court acknowledged that petitioner would be the first person executed for committing child rape since La. Stat. Ann. §14:42 was amended in 1995 and that Louisiana is in the minority of jurisdictions that authorize the death penalty for the crime of child rape. But following the approach of *Roper v. Simmons* (2005) and *Atkins v. Virginia* (2002), it found significant not the "numerical counting of which states . . . stand for or against a particular capital prosecution," but "the direction of change." Since 1993, the court explained, four more states—Oklahoma, South Carolina, Montana, and Georgia—had capitalized the crime of child rape and at least eight states had authorized capital punishment for other nonhomicide crimes. By its count, fourteen of the then-thirty-eight states permitting capital punishment, plus the Federal Government, allowed the death penalty for nonhomicide crimes and five allowed the death penalty for the crime of child rape.

The state court next asked whether "child rapists rank among the worst offenders." It noted the severity of the crime; that the execution of child rapists would serve the goals of deterrence and retribution; and that, unlike in *Atkins* and *Roper*, there were no characteristics of petitioner that tended to mitigate his moral culpability. It concluded: "[S]hort of first-degree murder, we can think of no other non-homicide crime more deserving [of capital punishment]."

On this reasoning the Supreme Court of Louisiana rejected peti-tioner's argument that the death penalty for the rape of a child under twelve years is disproportionate and upheld the constitutionality of the statute. Chief Justice Calogero dissented. *Coker* and *Eberheart v. Georgia* (1977), in his view, "set out a bright-line and easily adminis-tered rule" that the Eighth Amendment precludes capital punishment for any offense that does not involve the death of the victim.

We granted certiorari.

II

The Eighth Amendment, applicable to the states through the Four-teenth Amendment, provides that "[e]xcessive bail shall not be required, nor excessive fines imposed, nor cruel and unusual punish-ments inflicted." The Amendment proscribes "all excessive punish-ments, as well as cruel and unusual punishments that may or may not be excessive." The Court explained in *Atkins*, and *Roper*, that the Eighth Amendment's protection against excessive or cruel and unusual punishments flows from the basic "precept of justice that punishment for [a] crime should be graduated and proportioned to [the] offense." Whether this requirement has been fulfilled is deter-mined not by the standards that prevailed when the Eighth Amend-ment was adopted in 1791 but by the norms that "currently prevail." The Amendment "draw[s] its meaning from the evolving standards of decency that mark the progress of a maturing society." This is because "[t]he standard of extreme cruelty is not merely descriptive, but nec-essarily embodies a moral judgment. The standard itself remains the same, but its applicability must change as the basic mores of society change."

Evolving standards of decency must embrace and express respect for the dignity of the person, and the punishment of criminals must conform to that rule. As we shall discuss, punishment is justified under one or more of three principal rationales: rehabilitation, deterrence, and retribution. It is the last of these, retribution, that most often can contradict the law's own ends. This is of particular concern when the Court interprets the meaning of the Eighth Amendment in capital cases. When the law punishes by death, it risks its own sudden descent into brutality, transgressing the constitutional commitment to decency and restraint.

For these reasons we have explained that capital punishment must "be limited to those offenders who commit 'a narrow category of the most serious crimes' and whose extreme culpability makes them 'the most deserving of execution.'" Though the death penalty is not invariably unconstitutional, the Court insists upon confining the instances in which the punishment can be imposed.

Applying this principle, we held in *Roper* and *Atkins* that the execution of juveniles and mentally retarded persons are punishments violative of the Eighth Amendment because the offender had a diminished personal responsibility for the crime. The Court further has held that the death penalty can be disproportionate to the crime itself where the crime did not result, or was not intended to result, in death of the victim. In *Coker*, for instance, the Court held it would be unconstitutional to execute an offender who had raped an adult woman. See also *Eberheart* (holding unconstitutional in light of *Coker* a sentence of death for the kidnapping and rape of an adult woman). And in *Enmund v. Florida* (1982), the Court overturned the capital sentence of a defendant who aided and abetted a robbery during which a murder was committed but did not himself kill, attempt to kill, or intend that a killing would take place. On the other hand, in *Tison v. Arizona* (1987), the Court allowed the defendants' death sentences to stand where they did not themselves kill the victims but their involvement in the events leading up to the murders was active, recklessly indifferent, and substantial.

In these cases the Court has been guided by "objective indicia of society's standards, as expressed in legislative enactments and state practice with respect to executions." The inquiry does not end there, however. Consensus is not dispositive. Whether the death penalty is disproportionate to the crime committed depends as well upon the standards elaborated by controlling precedents and by the Court's own understanding and interpretation of the Eighth Amendment's text, history, meaning, and purpose.

Based both on consensus and our own independent judgment, our holding is that a death sentence for one who raped but did not kill a child, and who did not intend to assist another in killing the child, is unconstitutional under the Eighth and Fourteenth Amendments.

III

A

The existence of objective indicia of consensus against making a crime punishable by death was a relevant concern in *Roper*, *Atkins*, *Coker*, and *Enmund*, and we follow the approach of those cases here. The history of the death penalty for the crime of rape is an instructive beginning point.

In 1925, eighteen states, the District of Columbia, and the Federal Government had statutes that authorized the death penalty for the rape of a child or an adult. Between 1930 and 1964, 455 people were executed for those crimes. To our knowledge the last individual executed for the rape of a child was Ronald Wolfe in 1964.

In 1972, *Furman* invalidated most of the state statutes authorizing the death penalty for the crime of rape; and in *Furman*'s aftermath only six states reenacted their capital rape provisions. Three states—Georgia, North Carolina, and Louisiana—did so with respect to all rape offenses. Three states—Florida, Mississippi, and Tennessee—did so with respect only to child rape. All six statutes were later invalidated under state or federal law.

Louisiana reintroduced the death penalty for rape of a child in 1995. Under the current statute, any anal, vaginal, or oral intercourse with a child under the age of thirteen constitutes aggravated rape and is punishable by death. Mistake of age is not a defense, so the statute imposes strict liability in this regard. Five states have since followed

Louisiana's lead: Georgia, Montana, Oklahoma, South Carolina, and Texas. Four of these states' statutes are more narrow than Louisiana's in that only offenders with a previous rape conviction are death eligible. Georgia's statute makes child rape a capital offense only when aggravating circumstances are present, including but not limited to a prior conviction.

By contrast, forty-four states have not made child rape a capital offense. As for federal law, Congress in the Federal Death Penalty Act of 1994 expanded the number of federal crimes for which the death penalty is a permissible sentence, including certain nonhomicide offenses; but it did not do the same for child rape or abuse. Under 18 U. S. C. §2245, an offender is death eligible only when the sexual abuse or exploitation results in the victim's death.

Petitioner claims the death penalty for child rape is not authorized in Georgia, pointing to a 1979 decision [*Presnell v. State*] in which the Supreme Court of Georgia stated that "[s]tatutory rape is not a capital crime in Georgia." But it appears Presnell was referring to the separate crime of statutory rape, which is not a capital offense in Georgia. The state's current capital rape statute, by contrast, is explicit that the rape of "[a] female who is less than ten years of age" is punishable "by death." Based on a recent statement by the Supreme Court of Georgia it must be assumed that this law is still in force: "Neither the United States Supreme Court, nor this Court, has yet addressed whether the death penalty is unconstitutionally disproportionate for the crime of raping a child" *State v. Velazquez* (2008).

Respondent would include Florida among those states that permit the death penalty for child rape. The state statute does authorize, by its terms, the death penalty for "sexual battery upon . . . a person less than 12 years of age." In 1981, however, the Supreme Court of Florida held the death penalty for child sexual assault to be unconstitutional. It acknowledged that *Coker* addressed only the constitutionality of the death penalty for rape of an adult woman, but held that "[t]he reasoning of the justices in *Coker* . . . compels [the conclusion] that a sentence of death is grossly disproportionate and excessive punishment for the crime of sexual assault and is therefore forbidden by the Eighth Amendment as cruel and unusual punishment." . . .

Definitive resolution of state-law issues is for the states' own courts, and there may be disagreement over the statistics. It is further true that some states, including states that have addressed the issue in just the last few years, have made child rape a capital offense. The summary recited here, however, does allow us to make certain comparisons with the data cited in the *Atkins*, *Roper*, and *Enmund* cases.

When *Atkins* was decided in 2002, thirty states, including twelve noncapital jurisdictions, prohibited the death penalty for mentally retarded offenders; twenty permitted it. When *Roper* was decided in 2005, the numbers disclosed a similar division among the states: thirty states prohibited the death penalty for juveniles, eighteen of which permitted the death penalty for other offenders; and twenty states authorized it. Both in *Atkins* and in *Roper*, we noted that the practice of executing mentally retarded and juvenile offenders was infrequent. Only five states had executed an offender known to have an IQ below 70 between 1989 and 2002, and only three states had executed a juvenile offender between 1995 and 2005.

The statistics in *Enmund* bear an even greater similarity to the instant case. There eight jurisdictions had authorized imposition of the death penalty solely for participation in a robbery during which an accomplice committed murder, and six defendants between 1954 and 1982 had been sentenced to death for felony murder where the defendant did not personally commit the homicidal assault. These facts, the Court concluded, "weigh[ed] on the side of rejecting capital punishment for the crime."

The evidence of a national consensus with respect to the death penalty for child rapists, as with respect to juveniles, mentally retarded offenders, and vicarious felony murderers, shows divided opinion but, on balance, an opinion against it. Thirty-seven jurisdictions—thirty-six states plus the federal government—have the death penalty. As mentioned above, only six of those jurisdictions authorize the death penalty for rape of a child. Though our review of national consensus is not confined to tallying the number of states with applicable death penalty legislation, it is of significance that, in forty-five jurisdictions, petitioner could not be executed for child rape of any kind. That number surpasses the thirty states in *Atkins* and *Roper* and the forty-two states in *Enmund* that prohibited the death penalty under the circumstances those cases considered.

B

At least one difference between this case and our Eighth Amendment proportionality precedents must be addressed. Respondent and its amici suggest that some states have an "erroneous understanding of this Court's Eighth Amendment jurisprudence" (Brief for Missouri Governor Matt Blunt et al. as Amici Curiae 10). They submit that the general propositions set out in *Coker*, contrasting murder and rape, have been interpreted in too expansive a way, leading some state legislatures to conclude that *Coker* applies to child rape when in fact its reasoning does not, or ought not, apply to that specific crime.

This argument seems logical at first, but in the end it is unsound. In *Coker*, a four-member plurality of the Court, plus Justice Brennan and Justice Marshall in concurrence, held that a sentence of death for the rape of a sixteen-year-old woman, who was a minor under Georgia law, yet was characterized by the Court as an adult, was disproportionate and excessive under the Eighth Amendment. (The Court did not explain why the sixteen-year-old victim qualified as an adult, but it may be of some significance that she was married, had a home of her own, and had given birth to a son three weeks prior to the rape.)

The plurality noted that only one state had a valid statute authorizing the death penalty for adult rape and that "in the vast majority of cases, at least 9 out of 10, juries ha[d] not imposed the death sentence." ("Of the 16 States in which rape had been a capital offense, only three provided the death penalty for rape of an adult woman in their revised statutes—Georgia, North Carolina, and Louisiana. In the latter two States, the death penalty was mandatory for those found guilty, and those laws were invalidated by *Woodson* and *Roberts*.") This "history and . . . objective evidence of the country's present judgment concerning the acceptability of death as a penalty for rape of an adult woman" confirmed the Court's independent judgment that punishing adult rape by death was not proportional:

> Rape is without doubt deserving of serious punishment; but in terms of moral depravity and of the injury to the person and to the public, it does not compare with murder, which does involve the unjustified taking of human life. Although it may be accompanied by another

crime, rape by definition does not include the death of . . . another person. The murderer kills; the rapist, if no more than that, does not. . . . We have the abiding conviction that the death penalty, which "is unique in its severity and irrevocability," is an excessive penalty for the rapist who, as such, does not take human life.

Confined to this passage, Coker's analysis of the Eighth Amendment is susceptible of a reading that would prohibit making child rape a capital offense. In context, however, Coker's holding was narrower than some of its language read in isolation. The Coker plurality framed the question as whether, "with respect to rape of an adult woman," the death penalty is disproportionate punishment. And it repeated the phrase "an adult woman" or "an adult female" in discussing the act of rape or the victim of rape eight times in its opinion. The distinction between adult and child rape was not merely rhetorical; it was central to the Court's reasoning. The opinion does not speak to the constitutionality of the death penalty for child rape, an issue not then before the Court. In discussing the legislative background, for example, the Court noted: "Florida, Mississippi, and Tennessee also authorized the death penalty in some rape cases, but only where the victim was a child and the rapist an adult. The Tennessee statute has since been invalidated because the death sentence was mandatory. The upshot is that Georgia is the sole jurisdiction in the United States at the present time that authorizes a sentence of death when the rape victim is an adult woman, and only two other jurisdictions provide capital punishment when the victim is a child. . . . [This] obviously weighs very heavily on the side of rejecting capital punishment as a suitable penalty for raping an adult woman."

Still, respondent contends, it is possible that state legislatures have understood Coker to state a broad rule that covers the situation of the minor victim as well. We see little evidence of this. Respondent cites no reliable data to indicate that state legislatures have read Coker to bar capital punishment for child rape and, for this reason, have been deterred from passing applicable death penalty legislation. In the absence of evidence from those states where legislation has been proposed but not enacted we refuse to speculate about the motivations and concerns of particular state legislators.

The position of the state courts, furthermore, to which state legislators look for guidance on these matters, indicates that *Coker* has not blocked the emergence of legislative consensus. The state courts that have confronted the precise question before us have been uniform in concluding that *Coker* did not address the constitutionality of the death penalty for the crime of child rape. . . .

We conclude on the basis of this review that there is no clear indication that state legislatures have misinterpreted *Coker* to hold that the death penalty for child rape is unconstitutional. The small number of states that have enacted this penalty, then, is relevant to determining whether there is a consensus against capital punishment for this crime.

C

Respondent insists that the six states where child rape is a capital offense, along with the states that have proposed but not yet enacted applicable death penalty legislation, reflect a consistent direction of change in support of the death penalty for child rape. Consistent change might counterbalance an otherwise weak demonstration of consensus. See *Atkins* ("It is not so much the number of these States that is significant, but the consistency of the direction of change"); *Roper* ("Impressive in *Atkins* was the rate of abolition of the death penalty for the mentally retarded"). But whatever the significance of consistent change where it is cited to show emerging support for expanding the scope of the death penalty, no showing of consistent change has been made in this case.

Respondent and its amici identify five states where, in their view, legislation authorizing capital punishment for child rape is pending. It is not our practice, nor is it sound, to find contemporary norms based upon state legislation that has been proposed but not yet enacted. There are compelling reasons not to do so here. Since the briefs were submitted by the parties, legislation in two of the five states [Colorado and Mississippi] has failed. In Tennessee, the house bills were rejected almost a year ago, and the senate bills appear to have died in committee. In Alabama, the recent legislation is similar to a bill that failed in 2007. And in Missouri, the 2008 legislative session has ended, tabling the pending legislation.

Aside from pending legislation, it is true that in the last thirteen years there has been change toward making child rape a capital offense. This is evidenced by six new death penalty statutes, three enacted in the last two years. But this showing is not as significant as the data in *Atkins*, where eighteen states between 1986 and 2001 had enacted legislation prohibiting the execution of mentally retarded persons. Respondent argues the instant case is like *Roper* because, there, only five states had shifted their positions between 1989 and 2005, one fewer state than here. But in *Roper*, we emphasized that, though the pace of abolition was not as great as in *Atkins*, it was counterbalanced by the total number of states that had recognized the impropriety of executing juvenile offenders. When we decided *Stanford v. Kentucky* (1989), twelve death penalty states already prohibited the execution of any juvenile under eighteen, and fifteen prohibited the execution of any juvenile under seventeen. Here, the total number of states to have made child rape a capital offense after *Furman* is six. This is not an indication of a trend or change in direction comparable to the one supported by data in *Roper*. The evidence here bears a closer resemblance to the evidence of state activity in *Enmund*, where we found a national consensus against the death penalty for vicarious felony murder despite eight jurisdictions having authorized the practice.

D

There are measures of consensus other than legislation. Statistics about the number of executions may inform the consideration whether capital punishment for the crime of child rape is regarded as unacceptable in our society. These statistics confirm our determination from our review of state statutes that there is a social consensus against the death penalty for the crime of child rape.

Nine states—Florida, Georgia, Louisiana, Mississippi, Montana, Oklahoma, South Carolina, Tennessee, and Texas—have permitted capital punishment for adult or child rape for some length of time between the Court's 1972 decision in *Furman* and today. Yet no individual has been executed for the rape of an adult or child since 1964, and no execution for any other nonhomicide offense has been conducted since 1963.

Louisiana is the only state since 1964 that has sentenced an individual to death for the crime of child rape; and petitioner and Richard

Davis, who was convicted and sentenced to death for the aggravated rape of a five-year-old child by a Louisiana jury in December 2007, are the only two individuals now on death row in the United States for a nonhomicide offense.

After reviewing the authorities informed by contemporary norms, including the history of the death penalty for this and other non-homicide crimes, current state statutes and new enactments, and the number of executions since 1964, we conclude there is a national consensus against capital punishment for the crime of child rape.

IV

A

As we have said in other Eighth Amendment cases, objective evidence of contemporary values as it relates to punishment for child rape is entitled to great weight, but it does not end our inquiry. "[T]he Constitution contemplates that in the end our own judgment will be brought to bear on the question of the acceptability of the death penalty under the Eighth Amendment." *Coker* (plurality opinion); see also *Roper* [and] *Enmund* ("[I]t is for us ultimately to judge whether the Eighth Amendment permits imposition of the death penalty"). We turn, then, to the resolution of the question before us, which is informed by our precedents and our own understanding of the Constitution and the rights it secures.

It must be acknowledged that there are moral grounds to question a rule barring capital punishment for a crime against an individual that did not result in death. These facts illustrate the point. Here the victim's fright, the sense of betrayal, and the nature of her injuries caused more prolonged physical and mental suffering than, say, a sudden killing by an unseen assassin. The attack was not just on her but on her childhood. For this reason, we should be most reluctant to rely upon the language of the plurality in *Coker*, which posited that, for the victim of rape, "life may not be nearly so happy as it was" but it is not beyond repair. Rape has a permanent psychological, emotional, and sometimes physical impact on the child. We cannot dismiss the years of long anguish that must be endured by the victim of child rape.

It does not follow, though, that capital punishment is a proportionate penalty for the crime. The constitutional prohibition against excessive or cruel and unusual punishments mandates that the state's power to punish "be exercised within the limits of civilized standards." Evolving standards of decency that mark the progress of a maturing society counsel us to be most hesitant before interpreting the Eighth Amendment to allow the extension of the death penalty, a hesitation that has special force where no life was taken in the commission of the crime. It is an established principle that decency, in its essence, presumes respect for the individual and thus moderation or restraint in the application of capital punishment.

To date the Court has sought to define and implement this principle, for the most part, in cases involving capital murder. One approach has been to insist upon general rules that ensure consistency in determining who receives a death sentence. See *California v. Brown* (1987) ("[D]eath penalty statutes [must] be structured so as to prevent the penalty from being administered in an arbitrary and unpredictable fashion.") At the same time the Court has insisted, to ensure restraint and moderation in use of capital punishment, on judging the "character and record of the individual offender and the circumstances of the particular offense as a constitutionally indispensable part of the process of inflicting the penalty of death."

The tension between general rules and case-specific circumstances has produced results not all together satisfactory. This has led some Members of the Court to say we should cease efforts to resolve the tension and simply allow legislatures, prosecutors, courts, and juries greater latitude. For others the failure to limit these same imprecisions by stricter enforcement of narrowing rules has raised doubts concerning the constitutionality of capital punishment itself.

Our response to this case law, which is still in search of a unifying principle, has been to insist upon confining the instances in which capital punishment may be imposed. See *Gregg* (because "death as a punishment is unique in its severity and irrevocability," capital punishment must be reserved for those crimes that are "so grievous an affront to humanity that the only adequate response may be the penalty of death"); see also *Roper* (the Eighth Amendment requires that "the death penalty is reserved for a narrow category of crimes and offenders").

Our concern here is limited to crimes against individual persons. We do not address, for example, crimes defining and punishing treason, espionage, terrorism, and drug kingpin activity, which are offenses against the state. As it relates to crimes against individuals, though, the death penalty should not be expanded to instances where the victim's life was not taken. We said in *Coker* of adult rape:

"We do not discount the seriousness of rape as a crime. It is highly reprehensible, both in a moral sense and in its almost total contempt for the personal integrity and autonomy of the female victim. . . . Short of homicide, it is the 'ultimate violation of self.' . . . [But] [t]he murderer kills; the rapist, if no more than that, does not. . . . We have the abiding conviction that the death penalty, which 'is unique in its severity and irrevocability,' is an excessive penalty for the rapist who, as such, does not take human life."

The same distinction between homicide and other serious violent offenses against the individual informed the Court's analysis in *Enmund*, where the Court held that the death penalty for the crime of vicarious felony murder is disproportionate to the offense. The Court repeated there the fundamental, moral distinction between a "murderer" and a "robber," noting that while "robbery is a serious crime deserving serious punishment," it is not like death in its "severity and irrevocability."

Consistent with evolving standards of decency and the teachings of our precedents we conclude that, in determining whether the death penalty is excessive, there is a distinction between intentional first-degree murder on the one hand and nonhomicide crimes against individual persons, even including child rape, on the other. The latter crimes may be devastating in their harm, as here, but "in terms of moral depravity and of the injury to the person and to the public," they cannot be compared to murder in their "severity and irrevocability."

In reaching our conclusion we find significant the number of executions that would be allowed under respondent's approach. The crime of child rape, considering its reported incidents, occurs more often than first-degree murder. Approximately 5,702 incidents of vaginal, anal, or oral rape of a child under the age of twelve were reported nationwide in 2005; this is almost twice the total incidents of intentional murder for victims of all ages (3,405) reported during the same period. Although we have no reliable statistics on convictions for child rape, we can surmise that, each year, there are hundreds, or more, of these convictions just in jurisdictions that permit capital punishment. But under respondent's approach, the thirty-six states that permit the death penalty could sentence to death all persons convicted of raping a child less than twelve years of age. This could not be reconciled with our evolving standards of decency and the necessity to constrain the use of the death penalty.

It might be said that narrowing aggravators could be used in this context, as with murder offenses, to ensure the death penalty's restrained application. We find it difficult to identify standards that would guide the decision maker so the penalty is reserved for the most severe cases of child rape and yet not imposed in an arbitrary way. Even were we to forbid, say, the execution of first-time child rapists, or require as an aggravating factor a finding that the perpetrator's instant rape offense involved multiple victims, the jury still must balance, in its discretion, those aggravating factors against mitigating circumstances. In this context, which involves a crime that in many cases will overwhelm a decent person's judgment, we have no confidence that the imposition of the death penalty would not be so arbitrary as to be "freakis[h]." We cannot sanction this result when the harm to the victim, though grave, cannot be quantified in the same way as death of the victim.

It is not a solution simply to apply to this context the aggravating factors developed for capital murder. The Court has said that a state may carry out its obligation to ensure individualized sentencing in capital murder cases by adopting sentencing processes that rely upon the jury to exercise wide discretion so long as there are narrowing factors that have some "common-sense core of meaning . . . that criminal juries should be capable of understanding." The Court, accordingly, has upheld the constitutionality of aggravating factors ranging from whether the defendant was a "cold-blooded, pitiless slayer," to whether the "perpetrator inflict[ed] mental anguish or physical abuse before the victim's death," to whether the defendant "would commit criminal acts of violence that would constitute a continuing threat to society." All of these standards have the potential to result in some inconsistency of application.

As noted above, the resulting imprecision and the tension between evaluating the individual circumstances and consistency of treatment have been tolerated where the victim dies. It should not be introduced into our justice system, though, where death has not occurred.

Our concerns are all the more pronounced where, as here, the death penalty for this crime has been most infrequent. We have developed a foundational jurisprudence in the case of capital murder to guide the states and juries in imposing the death penalty. Starting with *Gregg*, we have spent more than thirty-two years articulating limiting factors that channel the jury's discretion to avoid the death penalty's arbitrary imposition in the case of capital murder. Though that practice remains sound, beginning the same process for crimes for which no one has been executed in more than forty years would require experimentation in an area where a failed experiment would result in the execution of individuals undeserving of the death penalty. Evolving standards of decency are difficult to reconcile with a regime that seeks to expand the death penalty to an area where standards to confine its use are indefinite and obscure.

B

Our decision is consistent with the justifications offered for the death penalty. *Gregg* instructs that capital punishment is excessive when it is grossly out of proportion to the crime or it does not fulfill the two distinct social purposes served by the death penalty: retribution and deterrence of capital crimes.

As in *Coker*, here it cannot be said with any certainty that the death penalty for child rape serves no deterrent or retributive function. This argument does not overcome other objections, however. The incongruity between the crime of child rape and the harshness of the death penalty poses risks of over punishment and counsels against a constitutional ruling that the death penalty can be expanded to include this offense.

The goal of retribution, which reflects society's and the victim's interests in seeing that the offender is repaid for the hurt he caused, does not justify the harshness of the death penalty here. In measuring retribution, as well as other objectives of criminal law, it is appropriate to distinguish between a particularly depraved murder that merits death as a form of retribution and the crime of child rape.

There is an additional reason for our conclusion that imposing the death penalty for child rape would not further retributive purposes. In considering whether retribution is served, among other factors we have looked to whether capital punishment "has the potential . . . to allow the community as a whole, including the surviving family and friends of the victim, to affirm its own judgment that the culpability of the prisoner is so serious that the ultimate penalty must be sought and imposed."

It is not at all evident that the child rape victim's hurt is lessened when the law permits the death of the perpetrator. Capital cases require a long-term commitment by those who testify for the prosecution, especially when guilt and sentencing determinations are in multiple proceedings. In cases like this the key testimony is not just from the family but from the victim herself. During formative years of her adolescence, made all the more daunting for having to come to terms with the brutality of her experience, L. H. was required to discuss the case at length with law enforcement personnel. In a public trial she was required to recount once more all the details of the crime to a jury as the state pursued the death of her stepfather. And in the end the state made L. H. a central figure in its decision to seek the death penalty, telling the jury in closing statements: "[L. H.] is asking you, asking you to set up a time and place when he dies."

Society's desire to inflict the death penalty for child rape by enlisting the child victim to assist it over the course of years in asking for capital punishment forces a moral choice on the child, who is not of mature age to make that choice. The way the death penalty here involves the child victim in its enforcement can compromise a decent legal system; and this is but a subset of fundamental difficulties capital punishment can cause in the administration and enforcement of laws proscribing child rape.

There are, moreover, serious systemic concerns in prosecuting the crime of child rape that are relevant to the constitutionality of making it a capital offense. The problem of unreliable, induced, and even imagined child testimony means there is a "special risk of wrongful execution" in some child rape cases. This undermines, at least to some degree, the meaningful contribution of the death penalty to legitimate goals of punishment. Studies conclude that children are highly susceptible to suggestive questioning techniques like repetition, guided imagery, and selective reinforcement.

Similar criticisms pertain to other cases involving child witnesses; but child rape cases present heightened concerns because the central narrative and account of the crime often comes from the child herself. She and the accused are, in most instances, the only ones present when the crime was committed. And the question in a capital case is not just the fact of the crime, including, say, proof of rape as distinct from abuse short of rape, but details bearing upon brutality in its commission. These matters are subject to fabrication or exaggeration, or both. Although capital punishment does bring retribution, and the legislature here has chosen to use it for this end, its judgment must be weighed, in deciding the constitutional question, against the special risks of unreliable testimony with respect to this crime.

With respect to deterrence, if the death penalty adds to the risk of nonreporting, that, too, diminishes the penalty's objectives. Underreporting is a common problem with respect to child sexual abuse. Although we know little about what differentiates those who report from those who do not report, one of the most commonly cited reasons for nondisclosure is fear of negative consequences for the perpetrator, a concern that has special force where the abuser is a family member. The experience of the amici who work with child victims indicates that, when the punishment is death, both the victim and the victim's family members may be more likely to shield the perpetrator from discovery, thus increasing underreporting. As a result, punishment by death may not result in more deterrence or more effective enforcement.

In addition, by in effect making the punishment for child rape and murder equivalent, a state that punishes child rape by death may remove a strong incentive for the rapist not to kill the victim. Assuming the offender behaves in a rational way, as one must to justify the penalty on grounds of deterrence, the penalty in some respects gives less protection, not more, to the victim, who is often the sole witness to the crime. It might be argued that, even if the death penalty results in a marginal increase in the incentive to kill, this is counterbalanced by a marginally increased deterrent to commit the crime at all. Whatever balance the legislature strikes, however, uncertainty on the point makes the argument for the penalty less compelling than for homicide crimes.

Each of these propositions, standing alone, might not establish the unconstitutionality of the death penalty for the crime of child rape.

Taken in sum, however, they demonstrate the serious negative consequences of making child rape a capital offense. These considerations lead us to conclude, in our independent judgment, that the death penalty is not a proportional punishment for the rape of a child.

V

Our determination that there is a consensus against the death penalty for child rape raises the question whether the Court's own institutional position and its holding will have the effect of blocking further or later consensus in favor of the penalty from developing. The Court, it will be argued, by the act of addressing the constitutionality of the death penalty, intrudes upon the consensus-making process. By imposing a negative restraint, the argument runs, the Court makes it more difficult for consensus to change or emerge. The Court, according to the criticism, itself becomes enmeshed in the process, part judge and part the maker of that which it judges.

These concerns overlook the meaning and full substance of the established proposition that the Eighth Amendment is defined by "the evolving standards of decency that mark the progress of a maturing society." Confirmed by repeated, consistent rulings of this Court, this principle requires that use of the death penalty be restrained. The rule of evolving standards of decency with specific marks on the way to full progress and mature judgment means that resort to the penalty must be reserved for the worst of crimes and limited in its instances of application. In most cases justice is not better served by terminating the life of the perpetrator rather than confining him and preserving the possibility that he and the system will find ways to allow him to understand the enormity of his offense. Difficulties in administering the penalty to ensure against its arbitrary and capricious application require adherence to a rule reserving its use, at this stage of evolving standards and in cases of crimes against individuals, for crimes that take the life of the victim.

The judgment of the Supreme Court of Louisiana upholding the capital sentence is reversed. This case is remanded for further proceedings not inconsistent with this opinion.

It is so ordered.

16

KENNEDY V. LOUISIANA

Justice Samuel Alito, Dissenting

PATRICK KENNEDY, PETITIONER v. LOUISIANA[1]
SUPREME COURT OF THE UNITED STATES
JUSTICE ALITO DISSENTING
Joined by CHIEF JUSTICE, JUSTICE SCALIA, and JUSTICE THOMAS
June 25, 2008

The Court today holds that the Eighth Amendment categorically prohibits the imposition of the death penalty for the crime of raping a child. This is so, according to the Court, no matter how young the child, no matter how many times the child is raped, no matter how many children the perpetrator rapes, no matter how sadistic the crime, no matter how much physical or psychological trauma is inflicted, and no matter how heinous the perpetrator's prior criminal record may be. The Court provides two reasons for this sweeping conclusion: First, the Court claims to have identified "a national consensus" that the death penalty is never acceptable for the rape of a child; second, the Court concludes, based on its "independent judgment," that imposing the death penalty for child rape is inconsistent with "'the evolving standards of decency that mark the progress of a maturing society.'" Because neither of these justifications is sound, I respectfully dissent.

I

A

I turn first to the Court's claim that there is "a national consensus" that it is never acceptable to impose the death penalty for the rape of a child. The Eighth Amendment's requirements, the Court writes, are "determined not by the standards that prevailed" when the Amendment was adopted but "by the norms that 'currently prevail.'" In assessing current norms, the Court relies primarily on the fact that only six of the fifty states now have statutes that permit the death penalty for this offense. But this statistic is a highly unreliable indicator of the views of state lawmakers and their constituents. As I will explain, dicta in this Court's decision in *Coker v. Georgia* (1977) have stunted legislative consideration of the question whether the death penalty for the targeted offense of raping a young child is consistent with prevailing standards of decency. The *Coker* dicta gave state legislators and others good reason to fear that any law permitting the imposition of the death penalty for this crime would meet precisely the fate that has now befallen the Louisiana statute that is currently before us, and this threat strongly discouraged state legislators—regardless of their own values and those of their constituents—from supporting the enactment of such legislation.

As the Court correctly concludes, the holding in *Coker* was that the Eighth Amendment prohibits the death penalty for the rape of an "adult woman," and thus *Coker* does not control our decision here. But the reasoning of the justices in the majority had broader implications.

Two Members of the *Coker* majority, Justices Brennan and Marshall, took the position that the death penalty is always unconstitutional. Four other justices, who joined the controlling plurality opinion, suggested that the Georgia capital rape statute was unconstitutional for the simple reason that the impact of a rape, no matter how heinous, is not grievous enough to justify capital punishment. In the words of the plurality: "Life is over for the victim of the murderer; for the rape victim, life may not be nearly so happy as it was, but it is not over and normally is not beyond repair." The plurality summarized its position as follows: "We have the abiding conviction that the death penalty . . . is an excessive penalty for the rapist who, as such, does not take human life."

The implications of the *Coker* plurality opinion were plain. Justice Powell, who concurred in the judgment overturning the death sentence in the case at hand, did not join the plurality opinion because he understood it to draw "a bright line between murder and all rapes—regardless of the degree of brutality of the rape or the effect upon the victim." If Justice Powell read *Coker* that way, it was reasonable for state legislatures to do the same.

Understandably, state courts have frequently read *Coker* in precisely this way. The Court is correct that state courts have generally understood the limited scope of the *holding* in *Coker,* but lower courts and legislators also take into account—and I presume that this Court wishes them to continue to take into account—the Court's dicta. And that is just what happened in the wake of *Coker.* Four years after *Coker,* when Florida's capital child rape statute was challenged, the Florida Supreme Court, while correctly noting that this Court had not *held* that the Eighth Amendment bars the death penalty for child rape, concluded that "[t]he reasoning of the justices in *Coker v. Georgia* compels us to hold that a sentence of death is grossly disproportionate and excessive punishment for the crime of sexual assault and is therefore forbidden by the Eighth Amendment as cruel and unusual punishment."

Numerous other state courts have interpreted the *Coker* dicta similarly. . . . For the past three decades, these interpretations have posed a very high hurdle for state legislatures considering the passage of new laws permitting the death penalty for the rape of a child. The enactment and implementation of any new state death penalty statute—and particularly a new type of statute such as one that specifically targets the rape of young children—imposes many costs. There is the burden of drafting an innovative law that must take into account this Court's exceedingly complex Eighth Amendment jurisprudence. Securing passage of controversial legislation may interfere in a variety of ways with the enactment of other bills on the legislative agenda. Once the statute is enacted, there is the burden of training and coordinating the efforts of those who must implement the new law. Capital prosecutions are qualitatively more difficult than noncapital prosecutions and impose special emotional burdens on all

204 PART FOUR: THE RAPE OF CHILDREN

involved. When a capital sentence is imposed under the new law, there is the burden of keeping the prisoner on death row and the lengthy and costly project of defending the constitutionality of the statute on appeal and in collateral proceedings. And if the law is eventually overturned, there is the burden of new proceedings on remand. Moreover, conscientious state lawmakers, whatever their personal views about the morality of imposing the death penalty for child rape, may defer to this Court's dicta, either because they respect our authority and expertise in interpreting the Constitution or merely because they do not relish the prospect of being held to have violated the Constitution and contravened prevailing "standards of decency." Accordingly, the *Coker* dicta gave state legislators a strong incentive not to push for the enactment of new capital child-rape laws even though these legislators and their constituents may have believed that the laws would be appropriate and desirable.

B

The Court expresses doubt that the *Coker* dicta had this effect, but the skepticism is unwarranted. It would be quite remarkable if state legislators were not influenced by the considerations noted above. And although state legislatures typically do not create legislative materials like those produced by Congress, there is evidence that proposals to permit the imposition of the death penalty for child rape were opposed on the ground that enactment would be futile and costly.

In Oklahoma, the opposition to the state's capital child-rape statute argued that *Coker* had already ruled the death penalty unconstitutional as applied to cases of rape. . . . Likewise, opponents of South Carolina's capital child-rape law contended that the statute would waste state resources because it would undoubtedly be held unconstitutional. Representative Fletcher Smith of the South Carolina House of Representatives forecast that the bill would not meet constitutional standards because "death isn't involved." In Texas, opponents of that state's capital child-rape law argued that *Coker*'s reasoning doomed the proposal.

C

Because of the effect of the *Coker* dicta, the Court is plainly wrong in comparing the situation here to that in *Atkins* or *Roper v. Simmons*. *Atkins* concerned the constitutionality of imposing the death penalty on a mentally retarded defendant. Thirteen years earlier, in *Penry v. Lynaugh*, the Court had held that this was permitted by the Eighth Amendment, and therefore, during the time between *Penry* and *Atkins*, state legislators had reason to believe that this Court would follow its prior precedent and uphold statutes allowing such punishment.

The situation in *Roper* was similar. *Roper* concerned a challenge to the constitutionality of imposing the death penalty on a defendant who had not reached the age of eighteen at the time of the crime. Sixteen years earlier in *Stanford v. Kentucky*, the Court had rejected a similar challenge, and therefore state lawmakers had cause to believe that laws allowing such punishment would be sustained.

When state lawmakers believe that their decision will prevail on the question whether to permit the death penalty for a particular crime or class of offender, the legislators' resolution of the issue can be interpreted as an expression of their own judgment, informed by whatever weight they attach to the values of their constituents. But when state legislators think that the enactment of a new death penalty law is likely to be futile, inaction cannot reasonably be interpreted as an expression of their understanding of prevailing societal values. In that atmosphere, legislative inaction is more likely to evidence acquiescence.

D

If anything can be inferred from state legislative developments, the message is very different from the one that the Court perceives. In just the past few years, despite the shadow cast by the *Coker* dicta, five states have enacted targeted capital child-rape laws. If, as the Court seems to think, our society is "[e]volving" toward ever higher "standards of decency," these enactments might represent the beginning of a new evolutionary line.

Such a development would not be out of step with changes in our society's thinking since *Coker* was decided. During that time, reported instances of child abuse have increased dramatically; and there are many indications of growing alarm about the sexual abuse of children. In 1994, Congress enacted the Jacob Wetterling Crimes against Children and Sexually Violent Offender Registration Program, which requires states receiving certain federal funds to establish registration systems for convicted sex offenders and to notify the public about persons convicted of the sexual abuse of minors. All fifty states have now enacted such statutes. In addition, at least twenty-one states and the District of Columbia now have statutes permitting the involuntary commitment of sexual predators,[2] and at least twelve states have enacted residency restrictions for sex offenders.

Seeking to counter the significance of the new capital child-rape laws enacted during the past two years, the Court points out that in recent months efforts to enact similar laws in five other states have stalled. These developments, however, all took place after our decision to grant certiorari in this case, which gave state legislators reason to delay the enactment of new legislation until the constitutionality of such laws was clarified. And there is no evidence of which I am aware that these legislative initiatives failed because the proposed laws were viewed as inconsistent with our society's standards of decency.

On the contrary, the available evidence suggests otherwise. For example, in Colorado, the Senate Appropriations Committee in April voted 6 to 4 against Senate Bill 195, reportedly because it "would have cost about $616,000 next year for trials, appeals, public defenders, and prison costs." Likewise, in Tennessee, the capital child-rape bill was withdrawn in committee "because of the high associated costs." The bill's sponsor stated that "[b]e-cause of the state's budget situation, we thought to withdraw that bill. . . . We'll revisit it next year to see if we can reduce the cost of the fiscal note." Thus, the failure to enact capital child-rape laws cannot be viewed as evidence of a moral consensus against such punishment.

E

Aside from its misleading tally of current state laws, the Court points to two additional "objective indicia" of a "national consensus," but these arguments are patent makeweights. The Court notes that Congress has not enacted a law permitting the death penalty for the rape of a child, but due to the territorial limits of the relevant federal statutes, very few rape cases, not to mention child-rape cases, are prosecuted in federal court. Congress's failure to enact a death penalty statute for this tiny set of cases is hardly evidence of Congress's assessment of our society's values.

Finally, the Court argues that statistics about the number of executions in rape cases support its perception of a "national consensus," but here too the statistics do not support the Court's position. The Court notes that the last execution for the rape of a child occurred in 1964 but the Court fails to mention that litigation regarding the constitutionality of the death penalty brought executions to a halt across the board in the late 1960s. In 1965 and 1966, there were a total of eight executions for all offenses, and from 1968 until 1977, the year when *Coker* was decided, there were no executions for any crimes. The Court also fails to mention that in Louisiana, since the state law was amended in 1995 to make child rape a capital offense, prosecutors have asked juries to return death verdicts in four cases. In two of those cases, Louisiana juries imposed the death penalty. This 50 percent record is hardly evidence that juries share the Court's view that the death penalty for the rape of a young child is unacceptable under even the most aggravated circumstances.[3]

F

In light of the points discussed above, I believe that the "objective indicia" of our society's "evolving standards of decency" can be fairly summarized as follows. Neither Congress nor juries have done anything that can plausibly be interpreted as evidencing the "national consensus" that the Court perceives. State legislatures, for more than thirty years, have operated under the ominous shadow of the *Coker* dicta and thus have not been free to express their own understanding of our society's standards of decency. And in the months following our grant of certiorari in this case, state legislatures have had an additional reason to pause. Yet despite the inhibiting legal atmosphere that has prevailed since 1977, six states have recently enacted new, targeted child-rape laws.

I do not suggest that six new state laws necessarily establish a "national consensus" or even that they are sure evidence of an ineluctable trend. In terms of the Court's metaphor of moral evolution, these enactments might have turned out to be an evolutionary dead end. But they might also have been the beginning of a strong new evolutionary line. We will never know, because the Court today snuffs out the line in its incipient stage.

II

A

The Court is willing to block the potential emergence of a national consensus in favor of permitting the death penalty for child rape because, in the end, what matters is the Court's "own judgment" regarding "the acceptability of the death penalty." Although the Court has much to say on this issue, most of the Court's discussion is not pertinent to the Eighth Amendment question at hand. And once all of the Court's irrelevant arguments are put aside, it is apparent that the Court has provided no coherent explanation for today's decision.

In the next section of this opinion, I will attempt to weed out the arguments that are not germane to the Eighth Amendment inquiry, and in the final section, I will address what remains.

B

A major theme of the Court's opinion is that permitting the death penalty in child-rape cases is not in the best interests of the victims of these crimes and society at large. In this vein, the Court suggests that it is more painful for child-rape victims to testify when the prosecution is seeking the death penalty. The Court also argues that "a State that punishes child rape by death may remove a strong incentive for the rapist not to kill the victim," and may discourage the reporting of child rape.

These policy arguments, whatever their merits, are simply not pertinent to the question whether the death penalty is "cruel and unusual" punishment. The Eighth Amendment protects the right of an accused. It does not authorize this Court to strike down federal or state criminal laws on the ground that they are not in the best interests of crime victims or the broader society. The Court's policy arguments concern matters that legislators should—and presumably do—take into account in deciding whether to enact a capital child-rape statute, but these arguments are irrelevant to the question that is before us in this case. Our cases [*Atkins v. Virginia* (2002) and *Gregg v. Georgia* (1976)] have cautioned against using "'the aegis of the Cruel and Unusual Punishment Clause' to cut off the normal democratic processes," but the Court forgets that warning here.

The Court also contends that laws permitting the death penalty for the rape of a child create serious procedural problems. Specifically, the Court maintains that it is not feasible to channel the exercise of sentencing discretion in child-rape cases, and that the unreliability of the testimony of child victims creates a danger that innocent defendants will be convicted and executed. Neither of these contentions provides a basis for striking down all capital child-rape laws no matter how carefully and narrowly they are crafted.

The Court's argument regarding the structuring of sentencing discretion is hard to comprehend. The Court finds it "difficult to identify standards that would guide the decision maker so the penalty is reserved for the most severe cases of child rape and yet not imposed in an arbitrary way." Even assuming that the age of a child is not alone a sufficient factor for limiting sentencing discretion, the Court need only examine the child-rape laws recently enacted in Texas, Oklahoma, Montana, and South Carolina, all of which use a concrete factor to limit quite drastically the number of cases in which the death penalty may be imposed. In those states, a defendant convicted of the rape of a child may be sentenced to death only if the defendant has a prior conviction for a specified felony sex offense. Moreover, it takes little imagination to envision other limiting factors that a state could use to structure sentencing discretion in child rape cases. Some of these might be: whether the victim was kidnapped, whether the defendant inflicted severe physical injury on the victim, whether the victim was raped multiple times, whether the rapes occurred over a specified extended period, and whether there were multiple victims.

The Court refers to limiting standards that are "indefinite and obscure," but there is nothing indefinite or obscure about any of the above-listed aggravating factors. Indeed, they are far more definite and clear-cut than aggravating factors that we have found to be adequate in murder cases. For these reasons, concerns about limiting sentencing discretion provide no support for the Court's blanket condemnation of all capital child-rape statutes.

That sweeping holding is also not justified by the Court's concerns about the reliability of the testimony of child victims. First, the Eighth Amendment provides a poor vehicle for addressing problems regarding the admissibility or reliability of evidence, and problems presented by the testimony of child victims are not unique to capital cases. Second, concerns about the reliability of the testimony of child witnesses are not present in every child-rape case. In the case before us, for example, there was undisputed medical evidence that the victim was brutally raped, as well as strong independent evidence that petitioner was the perpetrator. Third, if the Court's evidentiary concerns have Eighth Amendment relevance, they could be addressed by allowing the death penalty in only those child-rape cases in which the independent evidence is sufficient to prove all the elements needed for conviction and imposition of a death sentence. There is precedent for requiring special corroboration in certain criminal cases. For example, some jurisdictions do not allow a conviction based on the uncorroborated testimony of an accomplice. A state wishing to permit the death penalty in child-rape cases could impose an analogous corroboration requirement.

C

After all the arguments noted above are put aside, what is left? What remaining grounds does the Court provide to justify its independent judgment that the death penalty for child rape is categorically unacceptable? I see two.

I

The first is the proposition that we should be "most hesitant before interpreting the Eighth Amendment to allow the *extension* of the death penalty." But holding that the Eighth Amendment does not categorically prohibit the death penalty for the rape of a young child would not "extend" or "expand" the death penalty. Laws enacted by the state legislatures are presumptively constitutional, and until today, this Court has not held that capital child rape laws are unconstitutional. Consequently, upholding the constitutionality of such a law would not "extend" or "expand" the death penalty; rather, it would confirm the status of presumptive constitutionality that such laws have enjoyed up to this point. And in any event, this Court has previously made it clear that "[t]he Eighth Amendment is not a ratchet, whereby a temporary consensus on leniency for a particular crime fixes a permanent constitutional maximum, disabling States from giving effect to altered beliefs and responding to changed social conditions."

2

The Court's final—and, it appears, principal—justification for its holding is that murder, the only crime for which defendants have been executed since this Court's 1976 death penalty decisions, is unique in its moral depravity and in the severity of the injury that it inflicts on the victim and the public. But the Court makes little attempt to defend these conclusions.

With respect to the question of moral depravity, is it really true that every person who is convicted of capital murder and sentenced to death is more morally depraved than every child rapist? Consider the following two cases. In the first, a defendant robs a convenience store and watches as his accomplice shoots the store owner. The defendant acts recklessly, but was not the triggerman and did not intend the killing. In the second case, a previously convicted child rapist kidnaps, repeatedly rapes, and tortures multiple child victims. Is it clear that the first defendant is more morally depraved than the second?

The Court's decision here stands in stark contrast to *Atkins* and *Roper*, in which the Court concluded that characteristics of the affected defendants—mental retardation in *Atkins* and youth in *Roper*—diminished their culpability. Nor is this case comparable to *Enmund v. Florida* (1982), in which the Court held that the Eighth Amendment prohibits the death penalty where the defendant participated in a robbery during which a murder was committed but did not personally intend for lethal force to be used. I have no doubt that, under the prevailing standards of our society, robbery, the crime that the petitioner in *Enmund* intended to commit, does not evidence the

212   PART FOUR: THE RAPE OF CHILDREN

same degree of moral depravity as the brutal rape of a young child. Indeed, I have little doubt that, in the eyes of ordinary Americans, the very worst child rapists—predators who seek out and inflict serious physical and emotional injury on defenseless young children—are the epitome of moral depravity.

With respect to the question of the harm caused by the rape of a child in relation to the harm caused by murder, it is certainly true that the loss of human life represents a unique harm, but that does not explain why other grievous harms are insufficient to permit a death sentence. And the Court does not take the position that no harm other than the loss of life is sufficient. The Court takes pains to limit its holding to "crimes against individual persons" and to exclude "offenses against the State," a category that the Court stretches—without explanation—to include "drug kingpin activity." But the Court makes no effort to explain why the harm caused by such crimes is necessarily greater than the harm caused by the rape of young children. This is puzzling in light of the Court's acknowledgment that "[r]ape has a permanent psychological, emotional, and sometimes physical impact on the child." As the Court aptly recognizes, "[w]e cannot dismiss the years of long anguish that must be endured by the victim of child rape."

The rape of any victim inflicts great injury, and "[s]ome victims are so grievously injured physically or psychologically that life is beyond repair," *Coker* (opinion of Justice Powell). "The immaturity and vulnerability of a child, both physically and psychologically, adds a devastating dimension to rape that is not present when an adult is raped."[4] . . . Long-term studies show that sexual abuse is "grossly intrusive in the lives of children and is harmful to their normal psychological, emotional and sexual development in ways which no just or humane society can tolerate."[5]

It has been estimated that as many as 40 percent of seven- to thirteen-year-old sexual assault victims are considered "seriously disturbed." Psychological problems include sudden school failure, unprovoked crying, dissociation, depression, insomnia, sleep disturbances, nightmares, feelings of guilt and inferiority, and self-destructive behavior, including an increased incidence of suicide.

The deep problems that afflict child-rape victims often become society's problems as well. Commentators have noted correlations between childhood sexual abuse and later problems such as substance abuse, dangerous sexual behaviors or dysfunction, inability to relate to others on an interpersonal level, and psychiatric illness. Victims of child rape are nearly five times more likely than nonvictims to be arrested for sex crimes and nearly thirty times more likely to be arrested for prostitution.

The harm that is caused to the victims and to society at large by the worst child rapists is grave. It is the judgment of the Louisiana lawmakers and those in an increasing number of other states that these harms justify the death penalty. The Court provides no cogent explanation why this legislative judgment should be overridden. Conclusory references to "decency," "moderation," "restraint," "full progress," and "moral judgment" are not enough.

III

In summary, the Court holds that the Eighth Amendment categorically rules out the death penalty in even the most extreme cases of child rape even though: (1) This holding is not supported by the original meaning of the Eighth Amendment; (2) neither *Coker* nor any other prior precedent commands this result; (3) there are no reliable "objective indicia" of a "national consensus" in support of the Court's position; (4) sustaining the constitutionality of the state law before us would not "extend" or "expand" the death penalty; (5) this Court has previously rejected the proposition that the Eighth Amendment is a one-way ratchet that prohibits legislatures from adopting new capital punishment statutes to meet new problems; (6) the worst child rapists exhibit the epitome of moral depravity; and (7) child rape inflicts grievous injury on victims and on society in general.

The party attacking the constitutionality of a state statute bears the "heavy burden" of establishing that the law is unconstitutional. That burden has not been discharged here, and I would therefore affirm the decision of the Louisiana Supreme Court.

17

THE SUPREME COURT IS WRONG ON THE DEATH PENALTY

Laurence H. Tribe

It's not often that the US Supreme Court is asked by a state and the federal government to reconsider a case it has just handed down because it missed key evidence.

But that is what is happening now in *Kennedy v. Louisiana*.[1] In that case, the Court ruled in late June that Louisiana could not execute someone convicted of violently raping a child. Dividing along familiar 5–4 lines, the Court held, speaking through Justice Anthony Kennedy, that the death penalty must be reserved for killers and traitors. To apply it to others, including the most reprehensible violators of young children, would constitute a "cruel and unusual punishment" violating the Constitution's Eighth Amendment.

Emphasizing the evolving character of what constitutes an "unusual" if not an unduly "cruel" punishment, the court rested its condemnation of executing the rapists of children largely on what it described as a trend away from the use of death to punish such crimes both here and abroad.

But there was a problem with the Court's understanding of the basic facts. It failed to take into account—because nobody involved in the case had noticed—that in 2006 no less an authority than Congress, in the National Defense Authorization Act, had prescribed capital punishment as a penalty available for the rape of a child by someone in the military.

Defenders of the court's decision in *Kennedy v. Louisiana* would have it ignore that embarrassing wrinkle by treating the military as a parallel universe that simply does not intersect civilian justice on the plane of constitutional principle. But a court searching for universal principles of justice in the name of the Eighth Amendment would be hard-pressed to accept that view of the military/civilian distinction. Particularly when the Court's division tracks the usual liberal/conservative divide, its credibility depends on both candor and correctness when it comes to the factual predicates of its rulings.

Whatever one's view of the death penalty—and I have long expressed misgivings on both its wisdom and its constitutionality—it's important that the inequities and inequalities in its administration be minimized. Commitment to that principle, not a rush to the center, lay behind Barack Obama's disagreement with the Court's ruling in this case even before the 2006 federal death penalty provision came to public attention.

Many who applauded the Court's original ruling did so not on the basis of the Court's (now evidently faulty) trend-spotting rationale but, rather, on the premise that any way of containing the spread of capital punishment—such as by confining its use to murderers and traitors—is a good idea. But even those who harbor serious doubts about capital punishment should feel duty-bound to oppose carve-outs from its reach that denigrate certain classes of victims, or that arbitrarily override democratic determinations that such victims deserve maximum protection.

If a legislature were to exempt the killers of gay men or lesbians from capital punishment, even dedicated death penalty opponents should cry foul in the Constitution's name. So, too, should they cry foul when the judiciary holds the torturers or violent rapists of young children to be constitutionally exempt from the death penalty imposed by a legislature judicially permitted to apply that penalty to cop killers and murderers for hire. In doing so, the court is imposing a dubious limit on the ability of a representative government to enforce its own, entirely plausible, sense of which crimes deserve the most severe punishment.

To be sure, holding the line at murder and treason gives the judiciary a bright line that blurs once one says a legislature may include other offenses in its catalogue of what it deems the most heinous of all crimes. But the same may be said of virtually any bright line. Placing ease of judicial administration above respect for democracy and for principles of equal justice under law is inexcusable.

The Eighth Amendment's cruel and unusual punishment clause should not be construed in a manner that puts it on a collision course with the Fourteenth Amendment's equal protection clause. The Supreme Court would do well to take that overriding consideration into account as it decides whether to revisit its seriously misinformed as well as morally misguided ruling.

18

THE DEATH PENALTY

Unwise for Child Rape

Vivian Berger

On January 4, the US Supreme Court granted Patrick Kennedy's petition to review his capital sentence for raping his eight-year-old stepdaughter, *Kennedy v. Louisiana*, No. 07-343. One of only two people on death row for a nonhomicidal offense (the other is also in Louisiana), he claims that the Eighth Amendment forbids the ultimate penalty to be imposed on the perpetrator of a violent crime in which the victim does not die. As a matter of constitutional law, he has a very strong position. But even if the court rejects his challenge, legislators should spurn calls to expand a punishment that is plainly counterproductive in this setting—not to mention, declining here and moribund in the rest of the world.

Precedent is on Kennedy's side. In *Coker v. Georgia* (433 U.S. 584 [1977]), Justice Byron R. White, writing for four members of the court, found death to be an excessive sentence for a defendant who raped a sixteen-year-old at knifepoint after tying up her husband, and then abducted her from her home. In his decision (rendered a holding by Justice William J. Brennan Jr.'s and Justice Thurgood Marshall's usual separate statements that capital punishment always violates the Constitution), he conceded the crime's gravity, yet concluded that the death penalty, "unique in its severity and irrevocability," is disproportionate for "the rapist who, as such, does not take human life."

The respondent seeks to limit *Coker* on the ground, relied on by the Louisiana Supreme Court, that the plurality several times mentioned the victim's status as an "adult woman." Yet Justice F. Lewis Powell Jr. dissented in part because the lead opinion drew "a bright line between murder and all rapes—regardless of the degree of brutality of the rape or the effect upon the victim." As someone privy to the court's discussions, he presumably knew whether his colleagues deemed the victim's survival, or age, to be the crucial factor. Moreover, the plurality's stated view that "[s]hort of homicide," rape—presumably, of any kind—"is the 'ultimate violation of self'" corroborates his interpretation.

A DISPROPORTIONATE PENALTY

Apart from *Coker*, independent constitutional analysis supports the petitioner's bid to overturn his sentence. Under the governing "evolving standards of decency" test, the Eighth Amendment bars a penalty that is grossly out of proportion to the severity of the crime. For objective indicia of prevailing standards, the court looks mainly to legislative action; it also considers actual practice, as embodied in jury verdicts.

A mere five states have statutes that authorize execution for child rape, and all but Louisiana require a prior conviction of a sexual offense. While the court below cited a "trend" toward adoption of such laws since *Coker*, and recent Supreme Court cases outlawing death for juveniles and the mentally retarded take into account the direction of change, more significant is the fact that jurors have imposed that sentence in only two cases, in a sole jurisdiction. Indeed, Louisiana itself may have little interest in obtaining, as opposed to threatening, this sanction. An amicus brief filed by public defender offices notes that, "in the vast majority" of child rape cases, the prosecutor reduces the charge on the eve of trial. (This maneuver, typical of the gamesmanship pervasive in capital litigation, permits the state to prevail with a nonunanimous jury—after having forced these offices to expend the huge sums needed to prepare a defense against death.)

The Court also brings its own judgment to bear on a punishment's acceptability. Should the substantive excessiveness argument alone not persuade the justices, they should consider the practical realities that reinforce it. Child rape prosecutions pose too high a risk of convicting the innocent to comport with the heightened need for reliability in capital cases. Children are very susceptible to adult suggestion; their stories frequently change over time and in response to different questioners. Further, statutes often allow young witnesses to testify under conditions diluting the defendant's right to confront his accuser. In *Kennedy* itself, the victim recanted her initial account of an attack mounted by two teenagers, and the prosecution introduced critical evidence in the form of a videotaped interview with her.

Finally, even if constitutional—and despite the heinous nature of the crime—statutes like Louisiana's represent bad social policy. Child rape is generally committed by close family members or friends. By raising the stakes to life or death, such laws will likely augment the existing problem of underreporting. Moreover, protracted capital proceedings will worsen the youthful witness's trauma. For these reasons, even death penalty advocates should resist it in this context.

19

THE ARGUMENTS IN FAVOR OF, AND AGAINST, THE DEATH PENALTY FOR CHILD RAPE

Marci Hamilton

The argument in favor of the death penalty for child rape is simple justice. If capital punishment is appropriate for murder, applying it to child rape is not a large extension. The crime closest to murder is the rape of a child, whose childhood is essentially exterminated and whose future is forever changed. The whole culture suffers grievously, too, from the severe disabilities generated by child sex abuse.

Some argue that there should be simply a bright line at murder for the death penalty, but a crucial aspect of its internal logic—deterrence—is obviously very important in the context of child rape.

The argument against this punishment, though, is that the severity of the penalty is likely to lead legislators and others to think that they have accomplished more than they actually have by imposing it. The truth is that life in prison without parole is just as successful in serving society's need to keep child rapists away from children as the death penalty would be. There is no quantum increase in child safety that depends upon whether the perpetrator is alive and locked away, or dead and gone.

One can understand, though, the motivation behind imposing capital punishment for child rape. As it has become increasingly clear to policymakers that child predators are permanent recidivists, frustration has grown. Desperate to protect our children, we have thrown everything we can concoct at the predators to keep our children safe—sex offender registries, to track the ones who are now out of prison; GPS monitoring units on offenders during parole, to improve the quality of the tracking; and increasingly stiff sentences to achieve the greatest effect in deterrence and incapacitation that, as a society, we possibly can. (There is also the idea of pedophile-free zones, but as I discussed [elsewhere] . . . this much-touted solution is doomed to be ineffective and makes little sense.)

Of course, what we really want, as a society, is to rid the world of child sexual predators. The crime is so heinous and devastating that such offenders simply should not exist. Children should have childhoods filled with happiness and light—not terror and abuse that scars for a lifetime. But such predators do exist, our children remain at risk, and, worse, current data indicates that sex abuse is scarily prevalent, with at least 20 percent of boys sexually abused, and at least 25 percent of girls.

While the registries, GPS tracking, and longer sentences are all good ideas that make meaningful contributions to child safety, they do not get to the heart of the most serious problem we have: We don't know who most of the predators are.

There are two primary reasons we do not. First, we have engineered the statutes of limitations so that the vast majority of claims never get to court. The result of this appalling error is that we have an army of predators, currently grooming children to be victims, who operate under the anonymity of expired statutes of limitations.

Until we create opportunities for survivors to get into court, the current bells and whistles of predator treatment will remain irrelevant for a major class of predators. After all, you cannot put someone whose identity you do not know on a registry, attach a GPS monitor to his ankle, or increase his sentence. Thus, removing the statutes of limitations for child sex abuse is fundamentally necessary if we want to increase our knowledge of who the predators among us truly are— as I argue in more detail in my book . . . *Justice Denied: What America Must Do to Protect Its Children.*

Second, too often, known predators are permitted to plead to less serious charges, and thereby permitted to evade the registries that would otherwise list them, and the GPS monitoring and stiff sentences they would otherwise incur. More resources should be directed to prosecuting on the heaviest charges the evidence warrants.

There is an inherent difficulty with these cases, which involve child witnesses, and traumatized children at that. Prosecutors may hesitate to put children on the stand to be subjected to such a public process, not to mention cross-examination. But there is also a solvable difficulty here: Due to lack of resources and personnel, prosecutors cannot possibly keep up with the volume of sex abuse cases that exist. Here, more funding and more attorneys and staff dedicated to these crimes surely would help.

A recent case in Brooklyn of a rabbi who was credibly accused of sexually abusing two boys, but who was permitted to plead merely to "child endangerment," illustrates the problem: Because child endangerment is not a "sex crime," the perpetrator could not be added to a sex offender registry. In addition, the weaker charges led to probation rather than jail time.

When prosecutions in child abuse cases are watered down in this way, as they are far too often, the standard vicious cycle of child abuse continues: The predator avoids serious punishment, returns to ordinary life, and starts grooming the next victim, who is more than likely within the predator's own family or circle of friends.

ONE ARGUMENT AGAINST THE DEATH PENALTY FOR CHILD RAPE THAT IS QUITE UNPERSUASIVE: FEAR OF DETERRING REPORTING OF THE CRIME

Opponents of the death penalty for child rape have argued that it is a bad idea, because it will deter reporting of the crime, given the severity of the punishment. That seems far-fetched, however. To the contrary, you might get more reporting if the victim thinks that the predator, if convicted, truly will no longer be able to inflict abuse on them. The same result would follow, however, if the justice system reliably put away known child abusers instead of cycling them back into society. Thus, the death penalty and life sentences have the capacity to motivate victims to report in order to remove the predator from their lives. (To be sure, survivors of child sex abuse face many hurdles to reporting, which may not be affected in any way whatsoever by the potential penalty.)

In sum, whether or not the Court upholds the death penalty for child abusers this term, the entrenched barriers to identifying predators will not be eliminated, or even reduced. For that reason, from the perspective of the child being abused today or the survivor trying to cope in the wake of abuse decades ago, the case is a lot of hype—a paper battle that distracts from the far more essential battle for the reforms that are truly necessary if justice and decency are to be served.

20

ENGAGING CAPITAL EMOTIONS

Douglas A. Berman and Stephanos Bibas

Louisiana seeks to execute Patrick Kennedy for raping his eight-year-old stepdaughter. As the Supreme Court weighs the death penalty for this child rapist,[1] commentators are aghast. The *New York Times* and the *Los Angeles Times* editorial pages call child rape a heinous horror but dismiss this reality.[2] The death penalty, they claim, is inherently excessive for crimes short of homicide; visceral disgust at child rape, they assert, clouds reasoned reflection about proportional punishment. This position reflects long-standing criticisms of the death penalty as an expression of raw vengeance, a hot passion that clouds dispassionate justice. The march of justice seems to be in the other direction: away from emotion and toward reason, from Dr. McCoy to Mr. Spock, from the Furies to Athena in Aeschylus's *Eumenides.*

But the Furies will not die so easily, nor should we disdain them. Emotions and the passions they create are ever-present in our legal system. They bubble beneath any seemingly cool, detached analysis of crime and punishment. As astute observers highlight, debates over criminal law and practices turn not on neutral deterrence-speak, but rather on emotion-laden claims and concerns.[3] The undercurrents of emotion are especially salient in death-penalty debates. Those who deny or bemoan the benighted persistence of passion fail to appreciate its role.[4]

In this short essay, we suggest that the conventional attitude toward emotion in punishment is misguided. Part I begins by describing the existing legal terrain, and then part II evaluates it normatively. Descriptively, emotion is unavoidable in criminal justice and particularly in capital punishment. Indeed, recognizing emotion's role helps to explain many features of capital-punishment jurisprudence, from the debate over execution methods in *Baze* to the exemption of juvenile and mentally retarded defendants in *Roper* and *Atkins*.[5] Normatively, emotion is crucial to a criminal justice system that seeks both to educate citizens with its symbolism and to channel their justified outrage. Emotions deserve respect, especially when they reflect the public's moral perspective that certain crimes have profound emotional resonance.

In this vein, part III argues, the emotional case for the death penalty may be even stronger for child rape than for ordinary murders, for two reasons. The victim of a child rape ordinarily survives and has to deal with the emotions stirred up by victimization for the rest of her life. Moreover, the victim's parents and other members of the community may feel unique emotional harms from the rape of a child.

Finally, part IV considers how death-penalty opponents could better accept and harness emotional language. Emotional arguments are more promising strategies for abolitionists than simply questioning death penalty's cost and deterrent effects. The more successful foes of the death penalty speak the language of the emotions. Defense attorneys and reformers counter the emotional demands for justice with equally emotional pleas for mercy and for appreciating human fallibility. Rather than bemoaning emotional reactions, reformers should acknowledge emotion as the legitimate battlefield of criminal justice.

I. THE PREVALENCE OF EMOTIONS

The evolution of criminal law reflects the persistence of emotional threads. A sudden heat of passion mitigates a killing from murder to manslaughter.[6] The emotional fear of being battered, according to some feminist scholars and defense lawyers, justifies or excuses women who kill their abusers.[7] Hate crime laws target bigotry and disgust and combat hateful emotional messages.[8] Insanity defenses sometimes turn on emotional appreciation of a crime's wrongfulness or irresistible emotional impulses to act.[9]

The emotional topography is especially visible in enduring debates over capital punishment. For starters, why do communities persist in spending millions of dollars pursuing, defending, and seeking to carry out death sentences? Surely politicians and voters realize that years of litigation are not the most efficient way to incapacitate criminals, but efficiency is not the point. Legislatures continue to champion our society's ultimate punishment because elected officials and voters value the death penalty's unique symbolism, solemnity, and gravity.[10] Capital punishment expresses and educates our emotions, underscoring the solemnity of the community's judgment and condemnation.

Emotions undergird the Supreme Court's intricate modern regulation of capital punishment. The Framers wrote a seemingly emotional test into the Constitution: The ban on "cruel and unusual" punishments invites emotional reflection on which punishments are cruel and inhumane.[11] Moreover, the justices' extraordinary willingness to hear so many capital cases—and often to debate issues beyond the one at hand[12]—suggests that even the nation's top judges feel strongly about the death penalty.[13]

Consideration of criminals' emotional capacity helps to explain which kinds of defendants the Court has exempted from execution. When killers lack emotional capacity, society cannot justify blaming them fully. Killers who are mentally retarded are too irresponsible to earn our full emotional outrage.[14] For similar reasons, *Penry* invalidated jury instructions that limited juries' ability to take full account of a killer's mental disabilities.[15] And *Ford* and *Panetti* forbid executing someone who is now insane.[16] Executing an insane or mentally retarded person could further incapacitation or general deterrence, but cannot communicate to the uncomprehending criminal the emotional outrage and wrongness of his deed. The same reasoning helps to explain why *Roper* forbids executing those who killed as juveniles.[17] Juvenile killers are not fully developed adults and so arguably are not proper targets of full emotional blame, even though their execution may incapacitate or deter.

Notice the structure that emerges from these Eighth Amendment decisions. Judges assess offender characteristics to make sure that general classes of capital defendants have a constitutionally sufficient minimal level of emotional capacity, culpability, and comprehension. Offenders who fail to meet this threshold are not proper targets of society's emotional wrath.

But if offenders meet the judicial threshold of emotional capacity, other legal actors evaluate offenders and offenses more finely and emotionally. For example, jury discretion at sentencing gives emotions a legitimate, recognized role in capital punishment. Judges exemplify dispassionate reason; juries, emotional judgment. The populist jury, as the conscience of the community, is better able than a lone judge to sit in emotional and moral judgment of a fellow human. Legal intricacies must not unduly fetter jurors' ability to tailor punishments in light of their emotional instincts. Thus, *Woodson* invalidated mandatory death-penalty statutes that leave jurors no room to calibrate punishments to crimes.[18] *Lockett* and *Eddings* struck down laws that restricted jurors' consideration of mitigating factors.[19] *Ring* required that jurors, not judges, find defendants eligible to die.[20] *Penry* guaranteed that jurors have all the information and instructions they need to make moral evaluations.[21] And *Payne* stressed that juries can hear directly from victims in order to consider the complete "emotional impact" of the defender's crime.[22]

Research shows that juries attach great weight to offenders' emotional states. A significant predictor of a death sentence is whether a killer expresses remorse and seems sorry.[23] Is the killer someone with normal human emotions, who feels guilt and the pangs of regret at his awful misdeed? Or is he a stony-hearted monster who deserves outrage, not mercy? These classic jury questions drip with emotion. Tellingly, federal judges must now provide clear "statement[s] of reasons" for noncapital sentences,[24] but capital juries need not justify their sentences rationally.

Emotion is also relevant to the kinds of crimes that legislators have made eligible for capital punishment. One prominent aggravating circumstance asks whether a murder was heinous, atrocious, or cruel.[25] These terms, laden with emotion, pose quintessential jury questions that are not readily reducible to judicial doctrines. Another emotional extreme also serves as a common statutory aggravating factor: did the killer murder for hire?[26] Legislators and jurors are aghast at the willingness of a contract killer to extinguish a human life coldly just to make a buck.

For similar reasons, legislators allow, and jurors eagerly hear, victim testimony in capital cases. Many victims desperately want their day in court, to vent their emotions and perhaps find closure and healing. And jurors want to know how it felt to suffer, to empathize with one side and with the other before rendering their moral verdict. This lay morality is not a bloodless Kantian categorical imperative, but an emotional, affective judgment.

Finally, emotions have always played a role in parole and clemency determinations. Like jurors, parole boards and governors typically want to know if offenders have admitted guilt and expressed remorse. They also often want to hear from victims about whether they have been able to move on emotionally years after the crime or instead still seek and need community vindication through punishment. Failure to express remorse weighs heavily against parole or pardon, and victims' forgiveness can spur governors to grant clemency.[27]

In short, capital sentencing law and practice is suffused with emotion. Descriptively, the death decision is an emotional decision through and through.

II. JUSTIFYING EMOTIONAL JUSTICE

Emotions may in fact pervade the law, but does that make them right? Is our law just a jumble of backward, vengeful impulses, ones on which we as a civilized society should turn our backs? Are emotions— particularly punitive emotions—downright primitive and bestial?

On the contrary, punitive emotions deserve our respect, as a central part of what makes us human. When a wild animal threatens us, we do not judge or condemn it. We may incapacitate it or scare it off, but it is ludicrous to be angry at a shark or a tree for killing someone. Animals, plants, and objects are not moral agents. The same holds for very young children and truly insane adults.[28]

We are angry at moral agents because we acknowledge that they had the freedom to choose and chose wrongly. Anger recognizes and respects their freedom, holding them accountable for their choices. Our anger reflects our care for our victimized fellow man and our outrage at the criminal who should have known better. Anger underscores the moral community we share with victims and criminals.[29] Crimes have torn the social fabric and demand justice, payback to condemn the crime, vindicate the victim, and denounce the wrongdoer. Where there is no anger, there is no justice and no sense of community. Grave moral wrongs demand righteous indignation and action. Executing Adolf Eichmann was hardly necessary to incapacitate or deter him, but it was essential to condemn the Holocaust and vindicate its victims.

Given emotion's deep roots in the law, trying to uproot it may not only be futile, but dangerous. Punishment channels retributive anger, limiting it to proportional payback and tempering it with neutral adjudicators and punishers. If one squelches the impulse rather than channeling it, people may take the law into their own hands. That is the message, for example, of John Grisham's *A Time to Kill*: if the justice system does not offer a fair hope of justice, the victim's father may kill the perpetrator himself.[30]

Moreover, efforts to distance the death penalty from its emotional roots can produce a distorting cognitive dissonance. Modern litigation over lethal injection protocols reflects deep ambivalence about the emotions behind the death penalty.[31] The quest for painless execution methods is quixotic: states seek to inflict the ultimate violence while avoiding needless suffering. The offender deserves to suffer, yet we simultaneously want to see justice done and avert our eyes from it.

In recent decades, many psychologists have embraced the concept of emotional intelligence to help explain why traditional definitions of intelligence are lacking.[32] Legal scholars need to make a similar move when examining capital punishment. Only by raising our emotional IQ can we better understand the remarkable persistence of the death penalty in America.

III. EXECUTING CHILD RAPISTS?

Even if the death penalty is emotionally appropriate for the worst murders, that does not resolve Patrick Kennedy's case. Aren't murders qualitatively far worse than rapes? Shouldn't the worst penalty be reserved for the worst, most outrageous crime of all? But a strict ranking of murder as eclipsing all rapes, even child rapes, is emotionally tone deaf. In our view, child rape may present an even stronger emotional case for capital punishment than the ordinary murder, for at least two reasons.

First, the direct victim of a murder is dead. The victim of a rape almost always survives and must deal for the rest of her lifetime with the emotional scars this crime leaves behind.[33] Child rape in particular targets a defenseless victim, who often has been violated by a relative or trusted authority figure, as with Patrick Kennedy's stepdaughter. Observers understandably empathize with her wounded innocence and rage at his brutal breach of paternal trust.

Moreover, in the horrific universe of child rape, many survivors will bear grievous scars. A recent article highlighted the emotional scars of children who are raped and exploited by child pornographers.

> They are real children sometimes snatched from real streets in real neighborhoods both in the U.S. and abroad. . . . Sometimes, these children are being victimized by those they once held dear, Knoxville FBI Supervisory Agent Rob Root noted.
>
> "A lot of times it's familial relationships," Root said. "Sometimes it's neighbors. It's someone who has an ability to have contact with these children in private."
>
> US Attorney Russ Dedrick added, "A lot of these kids are just ruined for the rest of their lives."[34]

These child rape victims may have their horrifying treatment captured on film and then peddled around the world. They will spend their lives not only grappling with the anguish of rape, but fearing that any computer could replay their childhood horror. No punishment can erase that pain, but capital punishment is at least a fitting response because it is so solemn, severe, and final. The death penalty unequivocally proclaims society's empathy and outrage, that these victims bear no blame and need never fear that their abusers will repeat or keep exploiting their trauma.

Second, the innocent parents of the rape victim, and other parents, may feel unique emotional harm from the sexual violation of children. Precisely because children are innocent and defenseless, adults feel special affection and solicitude and responsibility toward them. We are to protect them, so any exploitation—especially sexual violation—outrages that trust. Denouncing and punishing that violation in the strongest possible terms repudiates the breach of trust and tries to repair it. It is all we can do to vindicate the wounded, suffering victim. Hence the father's natural impulse to kill the rapists of his ten-year-old daughter, and the jury's willingness to acquit him by reason of insanity, in *A Time to Kill.*

Disappointingly, much of the modern debate over capital child rape does not even acknowledge, let alone confront, the extraordinary emotional freight of every child rape. Of course, only the most heinous child rapes will deserve the death penalty, just as very few murders are thought to justify the ultimate punishment. But legislators, prosecutors, and juries are well equipped to decide which child rapes are so heinous as to call for the ultimate punishment. While judges should of course review these decisions, they should at the same time respect other actor's efforts to express society's outrage.

IV. EMOTIONALLY OPPOSING DEATH

Our argument is not that the modern administration of the death penalty is completely fine or that emotion always justifies society's ultimate sanction. Capital punishment in America has many short-comings, ranging from the evidentiary flaws exposed by innocence commissions to obvious race, sex, and wealth imbalances in its application. But those who oppose the death penalty need to stop simply reciting bloodless arguments about cost and deterrence in order to engage in rich emotional dialogue.

Indeed, the best capital defense attorneys already do this. When arguing to juries, they use mitigation experts to humanize defendants and get jurors to empathize with them and their often limited capacities. They work to evoke and highlight their clients' remorse and apologies. They counter the emotional language of justice with the equally emotional language of mercy.[35]

The most persuasive opponents of the death penalty neither deny the power of outrage nor demonize supporters as bloodthirsty animals. Rather, they persuade jurors who are open to the death penalty that the most authentic emotional response to this defendant is to feel at least a little pity, just enough to spare his life. This tactic works often enough with juries. Perhaps it is time to conduce more of the public-policy debates on this terrain as well.

Indeed, the modern political debate over the death penalty has been transformed not by new data about racial disparities or deterrence, but by concerns about convicting the innocent. Wrongful conviction is not unique to the death penalty, and evidentiary reforms attack the problem more directly than can punishment rules. Moreover, the actual percentage of wrongful executions is likely quite small. Nevertheless, because just the possibility of a wrongful execution has so much emotional resonance, that fear has fueled significant capital-punishment reforms.[36] Though costs and racial skews may animate criminal-justice reformers, emotional politicians and voters will be drawn to stories of individual capital cases gone wrong.

Reflecting again on the *Kennedy* case, the strongest policy argument against capital child-rape laws may be the particularly great worry about wrongful convictions. Rapes are often challenging to prosecute, and that is doubly true of cases depending on young child witnesses, who may have shaky memories and verbal skills. Hysteria over monsters in our midst can distract prosecutors and jurors from carefully judging guilt. Rather than resisting the emotional case for executing child rapists, opponents should develop their own emotional case for minimizing wrongful executions.

CONCLUSION

Emotions can evolve and be informed. Some opponents contend that capital-child-rape laws will harm child-rape victims and their families. If so, this harm will undercut the sympathy and empathy that drive these laws, leading legislators to pull back. As our discussion highlights, democratic processes engage capital emotions effectively in deciding which crimes are eligible for the death penalty. Thus, unelected judges should be wary of stifling a healthy, democratic national dialogue that can air and develop capital emotions.

Cool, somber courtrooms can seem hostile to emotional expression. But, especially in criminal justice, we must neither forget nor disdain seething passion. Especially where those passions are most intense, in capital cases, lawyers and scholars ought to combine doctrinal analysis with sensitivity to emotion.

21

CHILD RAPE, MORAL OUTRAGE, AND THE DEATH PENALTY

Susan A. Bandes

Is raping a child as heinous an act as taking a life? How should the comparative moral depravity of child rapists and murderers be measured? By what metric can the irrevocable harm murder inflicts on its victims be weighed against the long-term anguish inflicted on child rape victims? What is the judicial role in gauging the societal outrage and revulsion elicited by these two crimes, and in determining whether the death penalty is an appropriate response to those emotions?

In *Kennedy v. Louisiana*[1] the Supreme Court struggled with this daunting set of issues, which called for judgments that are inescapably moral and emotional. The Court also faced contentious questions about the nature and longevity of the psychological injuries to child rape victims and to their families,[2] about whether a capital prosecution would ameliorate or exacerbate those harms,[3] and about whether the strong emotions jurors feel in child rape cases are likely to overwhelm their capacity to decide fairly.[4] The *Kennedy* decision is a vivid illustration of the central point Douglas Berman and Stephanos Bibas make in *Engaging Capital Emotions*: that it is impossible to evaluate the legal issue raised by capital punishment without addressing the role of emotion.[5]

I've argued that once we acknowledge "the emotional wellsprings of the retributive calculus" we can have "a more clear-eyed debate about retribution's proper role in our capital punishment system."[6]

Berman and Bibas begin this debate.[7] They argue that child rape should be a capital crime, drawing support from the widely shared moral outrage the crime evokes, and from the crime's emotional toll on child rape victims and their families. Although I reach the opposite conclusion on the merits, their essay models precisely the sort of conversation we ought to be having.

Part I of this reply considers the role of emotion in capital jurisprudence. Section A discusses the importance of confronting emotion's role in capital punishment. Section B explores the difficulties with using moral outrage as a metric. Section C argues that the penal system should not merely reflect moral outrage, but channel and educate it. Part II focuses on the role of emotion in deciding whether child rape should be a capital crime. Section A considers the relevance of victim harm to the question facing the *Kennedy* court. Section B argues that there are three particular problems with allowing juries to sentence child rapists to death: the problematic role of anger and empathy, the problem of generic prejudice, and the issue of race.

I. Emotion and Capital Punishment

A. Why Emotion Must Be Part of the Conversation

As Berman and Bibas argue, it is important to bring emotion into the legal conversation for several reasons. First, emotions help explain why people hold the views they do about the death penalty.[8] When we engage in formulaic, affectless doctrinal discussions of deterrence, retribution, and incapacitation,[9] we talk past each other and grow increasingly polarized. These doctrinal categories have little to do with why people in fact support or oppose the death penalty.[10] The more we understand about why people take the positions they do, and why they adhere to them so vehemently, the more likely we are to persuade one another and move toward consensus.

Second, the capital system—like any legal institution—is premised on assumptions about human behavior. For example, it is built around assumptions about what motivates or deters criminal acts, about how judges and jurors decide, and about what victims need. As I mentioned above, the *Kennedy* opinions are rife with assumptions about human behavior, sometimes backed by empirical evidence, and sometimes not. When courts premise decisions on assumptions about human behavior, they ought to determine whether the available evidence supports those assumptions.

The third reason is the most challenging. Once we acknowledge that, as a descriptive matter, emotion pervades the law, we can proceed to the necessary normative discussion about *which* emotions should play roles in various legal contexts. There are many ways to approach this question. For example, there are philosophical debates about whether certain emotions are normatively desirable, such as the debate between Martha Nussbaum and Dan Kahan about the role of disgust in criminal law.[11] There are psychological, sociological, and neuroscientific arguments that certain emotions contribute to better decision making.[12] But it is often difficult to navigate around what the philosopher Hilary Kornbluth called "the very hazy borderline between epistemology and empirical psychology."[13] That is, what relevance does the way we *do* reason have for the question of how we *ought to* reason? Does the fact that we feel certain emotions itself demonstrate that they deserve respect?[14] Philosopher Anthony Appiah aptly describes the tension underlying many moral intuition analyses, observing that although we are right to "complain of normative systems that seem impossibly unmoored from human judgment," we ought not to perpetuate objectionable or outmoded intuitive assumptions on the theory that "whatever is, is right."[15]

Retributive theory tends to straddle this hazy borderline. Retributive arguments often draw support from the *fact* of the outrage engendered by crime, and the *fact* of the desire to act upon that outrage. When Berman and Bibas refer to retributive anger's "deep roots in the law,"[16] they are in part arguing that this retributive emotion deserves respect because it is such a basic and longstanding part of any punishment regime. Their argument is also, in part, empirical and pragmatic—an assertion that because the emotion is so entrenched, efforts to squelch it will fail, resulting in distortion, a loss of respect for the system, and even vigilante justice. And finally, their argument is explicitly normative. It is a contention that the legal system ought to reflect righteous anger and outrage, as a way of holding a moral agent accountable for his crime, expressing the community's condemnation, and vindicating the victim.

The relevant question for the legal system is what government actions should follow from the fact that certain crimes evoke widespread and intense moral outrage. Is the depth of the moral outrage a normative argument for a certain degree of punishment or a certain type of punishment? My response, in brief, is that emotions, and the actions that follow from them, must be evaluated in light of constitutional objectives. Moreover, as I will discuss below, the legal system should not simply reflect or evaluate emotional commitments. It must also channel, shape, and educate them.

Emotions are not inherently normative.[17] Whether they are desirable depends on what function they are meant to serve and what goals they are meant to attain. The question is not whether retribution ought to be encouraged, or victims ought to be helped to heal, as an abstract matter, but what role retribution or healing ought to play in the American system of capital punishment. Under current Eighth Amendment law, capital punishment is permitted to the extent it comports with "the evolving standards of decency that mark the progress of a maturing society,"[18] avoids wanton and unnecessary infliction of pain, is proportionate to the severity of the crime, and minimizes the risk of arbitrary and capricious action.[19] Of course, there is deep disagreement about the meaning and interpretation of the Eighth Amendment generally, and about the proper scope and application of these constitutional standards.[20] Nevertheless, these standards provide the framework within which interpretation must take place.

B. Taking the Measure of Moral Outrage

Does our understanding of the deep roots of the retributive emotions shed light on the questions of proportionality and evolving standards of decency the Court faced in *Kennedy*? Do the retributive emotions help us find a metric for determining what sorts of crimes, or what sorts of offenders, deserve the death penalty?

Retributivists "seek to punish an offender because she deserves to be punished in a manner commensurate with her legal wrongdoing and responsibility. . . . Not more, not less."[21] Although this principle has strong intuitive appeal,[22] it is in danger of being circular and indeterminate—an assertion that "we punish because it is the right thing to do, and we mete out the punishment that is right."[23] Paul Robinson and his coauthors have explored the notion of "empirical desert," arguing that people share robust intuitions about how serious punishment ought to be for a range of crimes. But Robinson notes that "modern notions of desert are ordinal rather than cardinal."[24] They tell us where on the continuum punishments should fall, but not what types of punishment should bracket the continuum. In short, people share strong intuitions about which crimes deserve the most serious punishments, but, at least thus far, the research has no implications for the question of what the most serious punishments ought to be.[25] As I will suggest shortly, it is plausible that the available punishments frame attitudes about appropriate punishment.

Another difficulty with gauging moral outrage as a measure of proper punishment is that people rarely feel one emotion in isolation. To get at the issue of what people want from punishment, it is necessary to examine a complex set of emotions. For example, it is important to disentangle moral outrage from fear. Studies show that when fear of returning the defendant to the community is taken out of the equation, and life without parole is offered as an option, support for the death penalty falls significantly.[26]

One final difficulty with measuring the retributive urge is that it is not static and does not always arise from the bottom up. The public's moral outrage not only influences penal policy, but is influenced by it, as I will discuss in the next section. The public's level of outrage is also influenced by media, political discourse, and all the other factors that routinely inform (or misinform) public opinion.

C. Channeling and Educating Moral Outrage

Berman and Bibas argue that "[g]rave moral wrongs demand righteous indignation and action," and that the death penalty is a way of "[d]enouncing and punishing [child rape] in the strongest possible terms."[27] They suggest that since child rape is as terrible a crime as capital murder, we ought to express our condemnation by punishing it the same way. This argument assumes that capital punishment is the proper expression of the strongest moral outrage.

My difficulty is with the authors' claim that the emotion of moral outrage provides support for the death penalty. It is one thing to say that the *emotion* deserves respect; it is quite another to say that the particular punishment does. I will first consider whether an understanding of the retributive emotions leads to a normative argument for capital punishment. In the next section, I will consider what guidance these emotions offer for the question of whether some child rapists should be executed.

Courts and other legal institutions play a role in guiding public reactions to crime and public expectations about punishment. The legal system is not a mere conduit for outrage. Rather, it channels outrage, ensuring that punishment is proportional and the product of deliberation. It separates the vengeful impulse from the legitimate retributive urge. Ideally, it ensures that serious decisions are not made in the initial stages of grief and fury that follow a heinous, high-profile crime[28] and that all relevant voices are heard—even those in danger of being overwhelmed by public outrage.

Moral outrage does not merely well up from the populace; it takes shape in a political and social context. When respected institutions send the insistent message that only the death penalty can truly express appropriate condemnation for the most heinous crimes, and that only the death penalty can honor the worth of the victims of these crimes, that message has consequences. It guides the public to feel moral outrage when it is *deprived* of the death penalty. It creates a set of emotional expectations. Once the death penalty is advertised as a sign of the highest respect for the victim, a prosecutor's failure to bring capital charges, a jury's failure to sentence the defendant to death, or the system's failure to execute the defendant are branded as signs of disrespect for the victim and inadequate moral condemnation.[29] If child rape is declared a capital crime because of the emotional devastation it causes, victims of other serious crimes might reasonably experience the decision as denigrating the nature and intensity of their suffering. They might come to feel that only a capital sentence can properly express society's condemnation.

There may be widely shared intuitions about which crimes are the most heinous, but the Court and other institutions play an important role in the debate about what punishments those heinous crimes deserve. Studies of "anchoring effects" suggest that those who define the initial outer boundaries for decision making exert significant influence.[30] If life without parole were the ultimate punishment, it might be viewed as an appropriate reflection of moral outrage at the crime and respect for the victim. The expressive function may be served by imposition of the most serious punishment *available*, rather than by imposition of the death penalty per se. This question deserves further study.

II. EMOTION, CHILD RAPE, AND THE DEATH PENALTY

In the next two sections, I will address the role of emotion in determining whether child rape should be a capital crime. This short Reply is meant primarily to address the Berman and Bibas essay, which was written prior to the Supreme Court's *Kennedy* decision. Therefore, I will address the authors' arguments in favor of making child rape a capital crime, with reference to the *Kennedy* opinion where relevant.

A. The Relevance of Harm to Victims

In the *Kennedy* case, Justice Kennedy acknowledges the anguish child rape victims suffer,[31] but despairs of "quantifying" this harm in the way one can "quantify" the harm caused by murder.[32] He rests his distinction between murder and child rape on the fact that only the former is irrevocable.[33] Justice Alito's dissent cites empirical evidence of the grievous and often long-term harm caused by child rape in support of his argument that Louisiana's legislative judgment was not unreasonable.[34] Berman and Bibas, too, cite the emotional devastation suffered by victims and their families as a compelling reason to treat the most heinous child rapes capitally. The focus on harm to victims poses some difficult issues for the criminal justice system. Most centrally, there is profound uncertainty about what role the emotional needs of victims ought to play in Eighth Amendment jurisprudence.

Berman and Bibas argue that the grievous harm suffered by child rape victims and their families makes child rape a crime worthy of capital punishment. In large part their argument is premised on the need for fitting retribution for this horrific crime. In taking the measure of a crime's heinousness and a criminal's depraved heart, it seems reasonable to ask whether it is the sort of crime that is likely to cause long-term harm. Nevertheless, the reliance on predictions of future harm poses some problems for the retributivist rationale.

Retributive rationales for punishment are generally backward-looking. They focus on the crime, or perhaps on the character of the defendant as inferred from the crime. As Mary Sigler said in explaining why "pickaxe murderer" Karla Faye Tucker did not deserve clemency despite her exemplary and remorseful conduct during her years on death row: "[from] the retributive perspective that provides the primary rationale for the death penalty,[35] . . . predictions about an offender's future conduct are irrelevant to determinations of desert."[36]

Berman and Bibas defend retributive punishments for child rapists because of what the future might hold—for both defendants and victims. They refer to the possibility of additional abusive acts by the defendant against the victim.[37] But an argument for capital punishment that relies on the future behavior of the defendant for support needs to encompass the possibility that the defendant's behavior will change in ways that could be helpful rather than harmful to the victim and her family. For example, as Justice Kennedy observed, the defendant might come to accept responsibility and express remorse for the harm he has caused.[38] Moreover, their prediction of future harm to victims requires speculation on what victims and their families will come to feel with the passage of time. It is difficult and dangerous enough to generalize about what victims need in the present.[39] Predicting how they will feel in the future is an even riskier endeavor.[40]

The discussion of victim harm contains some troubling ambiguities for the question facing the *Kennedy* court. Evidence of future harm might be offered as a general measure of the heinousness of child rape—an argument that this type of crime is worthy of the harshest form of retribution. But that argument flows almost imperceptibly into another: that the death penalty is needed to help individual victims heal. For example, Berman and Bibas argue that "[t]he death penalty unequivocally proclaims society's empathy and outrage, that these victims bear no blame and need never fear that their abusers will repeat or keep exploiting their trauma."[41] The question of whether society has a right to express its moral outrage by executing child rapists, however, is not the same as the question of what will help victims heal.

Justice Kennedy recognizes this distinction between the needs of society and the needs of the victim, suggesting that "[s]ociety's desire to inflict the death penalty for child rape by enlisting the child victim" in a lengthy and wrenching capital case might have the effect of inflicting additional harm on the child victim.[42] Justice Alito dismisses this argument as a policy concern irrelevant to the constitutional calculus, asserting that "the Eighth Amendment protects the right of an accused. It does not authorize this Court to strike down . . . laws on the ground that they are not in the best interests of crime victims or the broader society."[43] Yet if the future well-being of victims is at issue,[44] surely it is reasonable to seek evidence about whether the death penalty will contribute to that well-being or detract from it.

The move toward justifying capital punishment based on the emotional harm to individual victims creates an additional problem. It puts courts and juries in the position of passing judgment on that harm. Despite the Supreme Court's overconfident prediction to the contrary,[45] courts have consistently shown themselves unwilling and ill-equipped to regulate the admission of victim impact testimony by murder survivors in capital cases.[46] It is likely that courts would find evaluating child rape victims' testimony about emotional harm at least as unpalatable. But if capital charges and capital sentences are to be determined, in part, by the level of emotional devastation to victims, then prosecutors, judges, and juries will indeed need to evaluate claims of emotional harm, and defense attorneys will need to refute them.[47] This is a prospect that ought to give us pause.[48]

B. Jury Emotion and Child Rape

Thus far I have addressed the argument that moral outrage and other emotions lend support to making child rape a capital crime. I now turn my attention to the effect of these emotions on the trial process itself. Accusations of child rape evoke emotions in jurors, prosecutors, judges, and the public at large that may interfere with the ability to implement the death penalty in a constitutionally acceptable manner. There are three overlapping concerns: the problematic role of anger and empathy in this context; the problem of generic prejudice; and the issue of race.

The authors assert that "legislators, prosecutors, and juries are well equipped to decide which child rapes are so heinous as to call for the ultimate punishment."[49] There is substantial evidence casting doubt on this claim. As Berman and Bibas observe, accusations of child rape evoke understandable empathy for the victim and rage against the perpetrator. The law needs to make a difficult distinction between taking account of what people understandably feel and taking steps to ensure that those feelings don't adversely affect the fairness of the legal process.

Empathy and anger are both emotions that can have deleterious effects on the operation of the criminal justice system when not properly channeled. Both of these strong emotions evoke the desire to act. There is evidence that anger interferes with sound judgment by causing misattributions of blame,[50] and some evidence that it translates into harsher sentences.[51] In child sexual abuse prosecutions, this anger is coupled with intense empathy for the victim, and this empathy may drive jurors to want to alleviate the victim's suffering.[52] This combination of emotions renders child sexual abuse prosecutions particularly vulnerable to distortion and miscarriages of justice.

The concept of "generic prejudice" is useful in understanding one source of the concern. As Neil Vidmar explains, although any case may trigger prejudices that interfere with fairness, in some types of cases, the nature of the crime charged evokes prejudice against *any* person accused of committing that crime.[53] Generic prejudice implicates the jury's ability to decide whether a crime occurred or, if it occurred, whether the defendant was the perpetrator. As Vidmar found, generic prejudice is a significant problem in child sexual assault cases.[54]

> The issue was not mere disapprobation or abhorrence of sex abuse but rather attitudes and beliefs that bear on the presumption of innocence when a defendant is accused of sexual abuse. Simply upon hearing the nature of the charges against the defendant, substantial numbers of jurors swore under oath that they could not be impartial in deciding guilt or innocence and were found partial by the triers.[55]

Capital sentencing hearings, which focus on the more subjective question of whether a defendant deserves to die, raise particular problems in this regard. Jurors may want to ensure that the ultimate punishment available is meted out, and that desire may override their ability to determine whether the particular defendant deserves to die. The life-and-death decision is inherently moral and emotional, but it must also be particularized. There is no mandatory death penalty for any type of crime, no matter how repugnant. The decision must focus on the question of *which* child rapists deserve to die, and there is reason to seriously question the ability of juries to make this decision based on constitutionally acceptable criteria.[56]

Finally, there is substantial evidence that race can play a distorting role in capital murder cases. As sociologist Craig Haney explains, jurors must cross an "empathic divide" in capital cases, and "in the case of African American capital defendants, the empathic divide" is especially wide.[57] In the context of capital murder, a defendant accused of killing a white victim is significantly more likely to be capitally charged and sentenced to death than one who is accused of killing a black victim.[58] As to what would occur if capital rape were reinstituted, the evidence about the role of race in capital rape cases prior to 1977 (when the Court held in *Coker v. Georgia* that the death penalty is a disproportionate sentence for the rape of an adult woman)[59] is not encouraging. Whatever one might think about the *Coker* decision—and I tend to agree with Berman and Bibas that it is emotionally tone deaf on the devastation caused by rape—the Court was facing a particular problem concerning race, rape, and the empathic divide. Consider these statistics from the defendant's brief in *Kennedy v. Louisiana*.

> The practice [of executing rapists] originated in the antebellum South, where blacks were hanged (and often lynched) for raping white women; "[n]o white rapists are known to have been hanged." Even during the mid-twentieth century period ending with the last execution in this country for rape in 1964, over 89% of those executed for rape were black, while blacks and whites were executed for murder in almost identical numbers. All fourteen rapists Louisiana executed during the 1940's and 1950's were black.[60]

CONCLUSION

There is ample reason to believe that the legal system should not simply place its imprimatur on the emotions evoked by child rape. The better path is the one Berman and Bibas recommend (though I would follow it to a different destination). We need to take those emotions very seriously. We also need far more empirical evidence on how a wide range of emotions operate and can be effectively channeled. Most important, we need to continue to evaluate the retributive emotions and debate their place in the legal system. Justice Stevens recently protested that our current death penalty jurisprudence is the "product of habit and inattention rather than an acceptable deliberative process."[61] A broadly acceptable process will be one that both respects and evaluates the moral and emotional concerns animating the debate about capital punishment.

PART FIVE

CAPITAL PUNISHMENT AND DNA

22

THE KIRK BLOODSWORTH STORY

The Justice Project

In June 1993, Kirk Bloodsworth's case became the first capital conviction in the United States to be overturned as a result of DNA testing. On July 25, 1984, a nine-year-old girl was found dead in a wooded area. She had been beaten with a rock, sexually assaulted, and strangled. An honorably discharged former Marine and Maryland resident, Bloodsworth was convicted of sexual assault, rape, and first-degree premeditated murder. He was convicted and sentenced to death on March 8, 1985. The ruling was appealed a year later on the grounds that evidence was withheld at trial, and Bloodsworth received a new trial. He was found guilty again and sentenced to two consecutive life terms.

After years of fighting for a DNA test, evidence from the crime scene was sent to a lab for testing. Final reports from state and federal labs concluded that Bloodsworth's DNA did not match any of the evidence received for testing. On June 28, 1993, a Baltimore County circuit judge ordered Bloodsworth released from prison due to the results of his DNA test, and in December 1993, Maryland's governor pardoned Bloodsworth.

By the time of his release, Bloodsworth served almost nine years in prison, including two on death row for a crime he did not commit.

On September 5, 2003, almost a decade later, Bloodsworth heard the news he had been waiting to hear for twenty years: the state of

Maryland finally charged someone with the rape and murder of young Dawn Hamilton after matching DNA evidence with information from state and federal databases. The evidence matched the DNA of a man named Kimberly Shay Ruffner, who had been arrested on charges of robbery and attempted rape and murder a few weeks after Bloodsworth's arrest in 1984. He pled guilty on May 20, 2004, to the murder for which Bloodsworth had been wrongfully convicted.

Today, Bloodsworth is a program officer for the Justice Project's Campaign for Criminal Justice Reform and the Justice Project Education Fund, and he has been an ardent supporter of the Innocence Protection Act (IPA). The IPA, which was signed into law by President George W. Bush on October 30, 2004, as part of the larger Justice for All Act of 2004, established the Kirk Bloodsworth Post-Conviction DNA Testing Program, which will help states defray the costs of post-conviction DNA testing.

Over the years, Bloodsworth has been a national spokesman educating the public on issues surrounding wrongful convictions and innocence and helping other wrongfully convicted death row exonerees readjust to society. He has also spoken about the terrible injustices of the capital punishment system on numerous television shows, including *Oprah*, and his story has been featured in national publications, including the *New York Times Magazine*.

In September 2004, Bloodsworth took part in the release of a book that chronicles his twenty-year journey, *Bloodsworth: The True Story of the First Death Row Inmate Exonerated by DNA* by Tim Junkin. . . .

PROSECUTOR'S EVIDENCE AT TRIAL

The prosecution based its case on several points.

An anonymous caller tipped police that Bloodsworth had been seen with the girl earlier in the day.

A witness identified Bloodsworth from a police sketch compiled by five witnesses.

The five witnesses testified that they had seen Bloodsworth with the little girl.

Bloodsworth had told acquaintances he had done something "terrible" that day that would affect his marriage.

In his first police interrogation, Bloodsworth mentioned a "bloody rock," even though no weapons were known of at the time.

Testimony was given that a shoe impression found near the victim's body was made by a shoe that matched Bloodsworth's size.

POSTCONVICTION CHALLENGES

In 1986 Bloodsworth's attorney filed an appeal contending the following:

Bloodsworth mentioned the bloody rock because the police had one on the table next to him while they interrogated him.

The "terrible" thing mentioned to acquaintances was that he had failed to buy his wife dinner as he had promised.

Police withheld information from defense attorneys relating to the possibility of another suspect.

The Maryland Court of Appeals overturned Bloodsworth's conviction in July 1986 because of the withheld information. He was retried, and a jury convicted him a second time. This time, Bloodsworth was sentenced to two consecutive life terms.

After an appeal of the second conviction was denied, Bloodsworth's lawyer moved to have the evidence released for more sophisticated testing than was available at the time of trial. The prosecution agreed. In April 1992, the victim's panties and shorts, a stick found near the murder scene, reference blood samples from Bloodsworth and the victim, and an autopsy slide were sent to Forensic Science Associates (FSA) for polymerase chain reaction (PCR) testing.

DNA RESULTS

The FSA report, issued on May 17, 1993, stated that semen on the autopsy slide was insufficient for testing. It also stated that a small semen stain had been found on the panties.

The report indicated that the majority of DNA associated with the epithelial fraction had the same genotype as the semen due to the low level of epithelial cells present in the stain. It was an expected result, according to the report. Finally, the report concluded that Bloodsworth's DNA did not match any of the evidence received for testing. FSA did, however, request a fresh sample of Bloodsworth's blood for retesting in accord with questions about proper labeling on the original sample.

On June 3, 1993, FSA issued a second report that stated its findings regarding Bloodsworth's DNA were replicated and that he could not be responsible.

On June 25, 1993, the FBI conducted its own test of the evidence and discovered the same results as FSA. In Maryland, new evidence can be presented no later than one year after the final appeal. Prosecutors joined a petition with Bloodsworth's attorneys to grant Bloodsworth a pardon. A Baltimore County circuit judge ordered Bloodsworth released from prison on June 28, 1993. Maryland's governor pardoned Bloodsworth in December 1993. Bloodsworth served almost nine years of the second sentence, including two years on death row.

23

LIFE AFTER DNA EXONERATION

Megan Feldman

Before Charles Chatman walked out of prison [in January 2008], before he was reunited with his family, before his story graced the pages of the *New York Times* and he was invited onto *Dr. Phil* as a heroic symbol of broken justice, he was just another convicted sex offender who swore he was innocent.

Chatman was twenty-one years old in 1981 when he was wrongly convicted of rape and sentenced to ninety-nine years in prison. In the time that followed, he moved between hope that his case would be reopened and anger at the prolonged injustice he felt powerless to stop.

He spent his early years in prison trying to keep his supposed crime a secret, ready to defend himself from inmates who called him out for being a rapist. As time dragged on, his anger turned to hate and he picked fights, mostly with white inmates, who for him personified a racist system that allowed a mostly white jury to sentence a black man to prison solely on the word of a white woman.

"I believe I was accused and tried and convicted because of my race," he says. "That thought, in that place, had time to fester, build up. There were times it was so bad it was consuming me. I couldn't be around people of other races."

Things got so bad that he couldn't sleep, couldn't function; he stopped returning his family's letters and pulled away from them. He preferred the quiet of solitary confinement to human contact, particularly dreading visits from the women in his family. He sensed lingering doubt in their eyes. Was he a rapist or not?

Then, in the spring of 2001, everything changed. He was tossed into solitary at the Mark Michael Unit just outside of Tennessee Colony for nine days after spouting a homosexual slur at a guard. Chatman, five foot nine, shy, and built like a block, filled the silence by reading his Bible, the only book allowed in solitary. His favorite verse was from Psalms 27. "Wait on the Lord," it read. "Be of good courage, and he shall strengthen thine heart: Wait, I say, on the Lord."

But Chatman was tired of waiting. He'd waited twenty years, and lately he thought the waiting might break him. Months before, he had learned of a bill working its way through the Texas legislature that would give convicts who met certain statutory requirements access to DNA testing. He had gotten a copy of the legislation and began filing motions requesting testing, even before the bill became law.

Chatman settled onto the cot in his cell, the only sound the thin mattress shifting under his weight. He tried to focus on his tattered Bible. And then he heard it. A voice. "Get up, Charles," the voice said. "You're going to succeed." Chatman sat up and looked around, figuring it was God. But what was he supposed to do? All he could think of was to walk over to the desk, sit down and with slow, deliberate strokes, pen yet another motion to the Dallas district court that twenty years earlier had convicted him of a rape he didn't commit.

A few days later, a letter arrived—the first good news he had received since getting arrested in 1981: Judge John Creuzot had determined his request for DNA testing had merit and appointed an attorney to his case to begin the process.

Another six and a half years would elapse before Chatman became the fifteenth man in Dallas County to be freed by DNA evidence. Chatman's twenty-seven years behind bars is the longest term of wrongful imprisonment for any DNA exoneree in Texas, and one of the longest in the nation.

His case is representative of two of the most prevalent causes of wrongful convictions—eyewitness misidentification and reliance on forensic evidence of limited value. Chatman himself is emblematic of those who are most often unjustly imprisoned: black men accused of raping white women. And with Dallas County having more DNA exonerations than any other county in the country, as well as a district attorney who has made national headlines for his commitment to justice for the wrongly convicted, a steady flow of innocent prisoners may yet follow in Chatman's footsteps.

Walking out of prison in January, after decades of being told what to do and when to do it, Chatman, at forty-seven, finds himself facing a new challenge. Imagine being frozen in time, while outside everything changed—cars, clothes, culture. But he stayed the same, trapped in a 1981 version of himself, while anger and resentment ate away at him. He kept a form letter describing his plight, sending it to lawyers and judges, reporters and politicians and talk show hosts. But for the most part, no one believed him. Until one day, they did.

And suddenly, like an astronaut returning to earth, he reenters this changed world, which seems to be spinning faster. There is so much to learn—cell phones, ATMs and computers, new highways, new buildings, and new family members. There is a local network of social service agencies—nonprofits and faith-based institutions—that can help ease Chatman's transition back into the community. And the state of Texas has a compensation system that can provide Chatman with $50,000 for each year he was imprisoned. But what amount of money can fairly compensate him for the years he has lost and the damage he has endured by living behind bars for twenty-seven years as an innocent man?

On January 14, 1981, Madalaine Magin, fifty-two, arrived home from her nursing duties at Dallas's Methodist Hospital around 5:30 p.m. After her mother and sister died, leaving her alone in the Oak Cliff house they shared, she became the sole white resident on the block. As she usually did after work, she read the paper, made dinner, and watched the news. She went to bed around 10:30 p.m.

According to court records, at some point during the night, she awoke and bolted upright in bed. There was a man standing in the doorway. She wasn't wearing her glasses but would later testify that from the dim light of an adjoining room she could make out he was black and wore a dark cap pulled down over his head. Standing with the light behind him, however, his face was shadowed.

Magin grew shocked, scared, asking him who he was, how he got in. But he said nothing. She pulled a sheet up to her chin, which he pulled back down before he removed his pants and shoes. As she lay there motionless, he pulled off her pajama pants and proceeded to rape her. Keeping her eyes tightly shut, Magin pleaded with him to leave her alone. Instead he made conversation, asking when she'd last had sex. She didn't say, but the truth was never. She had never married and was a virgin. Some time elapsed, and she begged the man to let her go to the bathroom. He did but followed, standing next to the mirror while she sat on the toilet. Then he raped her again.

Afterward, she told him she would give him all of her money, anything, if he would just please leave. Naked from the waist down, she walked into the dining room and handed him the fifteen dollars in her purse. He demanded jewelry and a gun. She told him she had neither. Angry, he ordered her to lie on the floor, face-down, and put her hands behind her back. He used two scarves from her bedroom to tie her wrists and ankles, and while she lay there bound, he walked through the house opening drawers, looking into cupboards and searching closets. After all the banging and shuffling subsided, she heard him leaving the house, hauling his plunder with him. Only after she heard a car driving away did she manage to untie her wrists, crawl to the phone and dial the police.

A few days later at around 9:30 a.m., Charles Chatman was walking to a bus stop in a neighborhood a few miles away from Magin's house. Since his mother died several years before and he'd never had a relationship with his father, Chatman lived with one of his older sisters, Claudette Smith, who had two children of her own. Chatman had dropped out of Roseville High School in tenth grade and was serving a four-year probated sentence for burglarizing a house. He worked part-time helping his sister clean restaurants at night, but he'd left the house that morning determined to find another job, hopefully as a forklift operator.

As he and his friends neared the bus stop, a police cruiser approached and an officer got out and asked for identification. Seconds later, Chatman was handcuffed and on his way to jail. He assumed it had something to do with his probation. He learned later that a woman had picked his photograph out of a lineup and accused him of raping her. It seemed so preposterous, so untrue, that he figured he'd be out within days. But on January 29, several days after his arrest, he found himself standing in a live lineup with a group of twenty-something black men. When he saw the middle-aged white woman on the other side of the glass, he recognized her. He'd seen her in the neighborhood he used to live in, before he moved in with his sister.

"I knew who she was, and I knew I hadn't done anything to her, so I wasn't worried about it," Chatman would say later. "I had no front teeth—I got them knocked out playing football—she should have been able to see that."

But when Magin picked Chatman's photo out of a lineup, she said she recognized him from the neighborhood. And, looking at him in the live lineup, she told investigators she was certain he was the man who raped her. Chatman was charged with aggravated rape and spent the next seven months in the county jail awaiting trial. He recalls seeing his defense attorney once during that time. At one point, in late summer of 1981, he became so frustrated that he called the attorney, Pat Robertson, collect. "I'm glad you called," Chatman recalls the lawyer saying. "Because the trial is tomorrow."

Robertson doesn't remember that conversation, but he does recall the case. "Could I have done anything else other than what I did? I don't know," he says. "Back in those days, a white lady takes the stand and points a finger and says, 'That's the guy,' he's dead meat."

Chatman also phoned his sister, who knew that he had worked in her cleaning business on the night of the rape and would swear to as much in court. He couldn't reach anyone else in the family, and besides, most of them would be working.

When the trial began on August 12, the state called Magin as its first witness. After she described the sordid details of her rape, the prosecutor turned to the final line of questioning. "I would like for you to look around the courtroom today and if you see the individual who did these things to you, will you point him out for the court?"

"Yes," she replied, staring at Chatman. "He's the black man sitting at the table wearing the cream-colored pullover sweater."

Chatman felt as though he was trapped in some hellish nightmare. He couldn't believe all these people thought he did this. He had a girlfriend, Cynthia—they had met in high school—what would she think? Even worse, what about his sister, aunts, and nieces? "It was really degrading," he would say later. "The prosecutor made me seem like I was the most horrible person on earth."

Smith testified that her brother worked for her cleaning company the night of the rape. She thought there was a log book somewhere that would bear his signature for picking up his pay, but she hadn't been able to find it.

The alibi that Smith had provided was no match for the certainty of Magin's eyewitness testimony, which was corroborated somewhat by a forensic serologist who testified that she had determined from sperm removed from the victim's bed sheets and vagina that Chatman's blood type—type O—matched the blood type of the perpetrator. The fact that 40 percent of the black male population possessed the same blood type was of little moment to the jury. On August 13, it returned a verdict of guilty. Eight days later, Judge John Mead sentenced Chatman to ninety-nine years in prison.

Chatman was stunned. "I didn't understand the system," he would say later. "I trusted the system, and I trusted it too much, I guess. I thought someone, somebody in there—the judge, the lawyer, the jury—would do the right thing."

But the right thing wasn't done—not until Chatman, through his court-appointed lawyer, filed a motion for DNA testing. And even then, the state contested the motion, arguing in its response that the "unequivocal" testimony of Magin "alone is sufficient to support Chatman's conviction." Creuzot disagreed and in 2002 granted Chatman's request.

But it took two more years and a new lawyer—public defender Michelle Moore—before the Orchid Cellmark Laboratory in Dallas determined that it had testable evidence that could contain DNA. And it wasn't until June 2004 that the lab reported a new obstacle: There wasn't enough biological evidence remaining to extract a complete DNA profile, and if they tested it, they ran the risk of destroying it.

When Moore broke the news, she remembers Chatman's shoulders slumping, a defeated look on his face.

"He just had this look in his eye, like, 'How can this be happening?'" she recalls. It could have been the end of Chatman's efforts if not for an idea that came from talks between the attorneys and the judge. Why not send the biological evidence back to the Southwest Institute of Forensic Science to be preserved until testing technology improved? Creuzot signed the order for storage of the evidence.

There was nothing for Chatman to do but wait. "At first I kept going to the prison law library, but I couldn't find anything that would speed up the process," he recalls. "I was down about it, frustrated." One thing that helped was praying with a Christian prison ministry. Its sessions were some of the few times he didn't notice friction between inmates of different races or gangs, and most important, they helped alleviate his rage.

Amarillo attorney Jeff Blackburn, chief counsel for the Innocence Project of Texas, a consortium of university students and volunteer lawyers dedicated to assisting the wrongly convicted, says many of the exonerees he has worked with were able to maintain their resolve in prison by committing themselves to religion, whether Islam, Judaism, or Christianity. "The guys that develop some spiritual mechanism to get outside themselves have done a lot better," he says.

Whether it was religion or what Chatman calls his natural "hardheadedness," he had a tireless tenacity that helped him through his ordeal. He shocked fellow inmates when he refused to take parole in 2001 and again in 2004. The parole board asked him to recount his crime, and he refused. To him, it would have been an admission of guilt, and he didn't want to walk back into the world as a convicted sex offender. "Life in prison for a sex crime is hell," he would say later. "I believed it would be worse on the outside—trying to get a place to live, find a job, face my family."

After three years of waiting, in January 2007, he got a call from his lawyer. Moore had spoken with lab technicians at Orchid Cellmark who told her that they now had the technology to test the sperm sample. There was still a risk the entire sample could be consumed without obtaining a complete profile, but Chatman insisted they proceed, figuring it was his only chance.

Creuzot, amicable and street smart, with a history of championing community reentry programs, offered to pay for the testing out of his courtroom budget. "Usually the parties would pay for it," the judge says. "But when the question of who would pay came up, I said I would. There was something about him; I can't say what it was . . . I wanted this man's test to happen."

By mid-December, the lab managed to extract a complete DNA profile. "There was a glimmer of hope for the first time," Moore recalls. "Suddenly, he could think about being outside."

To make the DNA comparison, Creuzot had ordered Chatman returned to the Dallas County jail, and on the morning of January 2, jail guards escorted him into the holding cell adjoining Creuzot's chambers. Seated in a chair outside the cell, Chatman held his breath, steeling himself for yet another disappointment. The slight, bespectacled judge walked in and wished him a Happy New Year. Then Creuzot embraced him, tears in his eyes. "It wasn't you," the judge told him.

Chatman had long imagined what he'd do when his moment of freedom came, but he was so stunned, so dazed, that all he could do was sit down and try to breathe. Creuzot asked if Chatman had any family he wanted to call. Yes, Chatman replied, his aunt, Ethel Bradley, but he hadn't dialed her number in twenty-seven years; he'd grown distant from nearly all of his family.

Creuzot held out his cell phone, but Chatman stared at it, his face blank. "What's that?" he asked. The judge showed him how to dial, and when Chatman's aunt answered, she couldn't believe it. "Oh, my God!" was about all she could say.

It was a powerful moment for Creuzot, as well. His seven-year-old, Ethan, happened to be at the courthouse that day, and after telling Chatman the news, Creuzot spoke with his son. "It's very likely that Mr. Chatman has served the longest period of time in prison for something he didn't do," he told him. "Your daddy has really worked hard on this. You were just a little baby when we started talking about it."

Ethan seemed impressed, so when Creuzot ordered a Texas Land and Cattle T-bone to be delivered for Chatman, he ordered a hamburger for his son. A short time later, the burly, soft-spoken Chatman ate his first meal as a free man with the judge's son.

The next day, before the hearing for his release, Chatman grew nervous as he prepared to face the media, and Ethan agreed to stand by his side. "I drew a little strength from Ethan," Chatman says.

※※※

Attempts to reach Madalaine Magin about Chatman's exoneration proved unsuccessful.

Upon his release from the county jail, a small group of relatives surrounded him. His aunt had begun a chain of phone calls the day before, and while not everyone in their large family could get off work to meet him, he recognized a few familiar faces. There was Larry Crayton, his nephew, who had visited him several times in prison.

Chatman's sister, Claudette Smith, couldn't get off work to be there, but her daughter, Chatman's niece LaFreda Williams, stood there waiting. She was ten when he was convicted and was now a full-faced woman with two children of her own.

That moment felt like a dream. Family with whom he had cut ties, whom he hadn't heard from or seen in years, were celebrating his release. Part of him was even afraid it wasn't real, that he would awake back in prison to realize that none of this was really happening.

Only it was.

For twenty-seven years he was more of a number than a name—32559, the number that identified him in prison. Now, on a cold, overcast day in mid-January, he goes about the business of building a new identity, starting with the Texas Department of Public Safety in Plano. Others waiting to take their driving test queue up inside the building, but Chatman has been on the inside too long.

"It's cold, but I'm getting some fresh air," he says. A single white flake floats down from the sky. He grins. "It's snowing!"

For the past week, his niece and nephew have taken turns shepherding him between government offices to help him establish his official existence in the outside world. The task required a trip to the Dallas Independent School District offices to retrieve copies of his school records and multiple visits to the Social Security Administration and various Department of Public Safety offices. Days of standing in line finally netted him a Social Security card, and now all he has to do is pass the driving test to get his license.

He's concerned, shifting his weight while he stands in the parking lot. It's not like he has logged in much time on the road recently. Even before going to prison, he had never learned to drive. "I've been practicing the last couple days," he says. "I'm most nervous about parallel parking." He will drive Williams's pink Mary Kay Cadillac for the test. A few minutes later, an officer approaches. It's time to get behind the wheel.

Williams sits in the waiting area, fielding a call from the Carrollton apartment complex she hopes will rent to Chatman. It doesn't sound good.

"So we'll pick up the deposit check and keep looking," she says, exasperated, into her pink phone. Then she hangs up and sighs heavily. The manager told her that anyone who doesn't have a job must find someone to guarantee the rent in the event of nonpayment. And that person, in this case Williams, has to have a monthly income of at least six times the rent of around $700. Williams just doesn't make that kind of money with Mary Kay Cosmetics. "This is a nightmare," she says. "I hate to tell him this just isn't gonna work. He is going to be so disappointed. We looked at ten apartments on Saturday."

For most exonerees, finding a place to live is their first challenge in the outside world. Until the legal matter of their compensation for wrongful imprisonment is resolved, their lawyers don't want to risk expunging their records and wiping out evidence of their convictions. But with their conviction remaining on their records, exonerees will find landlords reluctant to rent to them and employers hesitant to hire them.

Chatman is more fortunate than some: He has a stack of news articles documenting his release and the backing of a Lubbock law firm, Glasheen, Valles & DeHoyos, that works closely with the Innocence Project of Texas to help exonerees get settled and bring federal civil rights suits against those who may be responsible for their wrongful conviction, including municipal governments, police, and prosecutors.

Williams calls Kris Moore (no relation to Michelle Moore), one of the Lubbock attorneys who represents Chatman and five other exonerees in their civil rights litigation. She tells Moore about Chatman's housing dilemma. The firm would later agree to help pay his rent for six months and has similar arrangements with the other exonerees it represents.

"I went from one property management company to another saying, 'I'm willing to guarantee their rent,'" Moore would later say of his efforts to find housing for exonerees. "Time and again, they wanted me to indemnify them for any crime committed on the property. That's the kind of mentality they have—they don't care that the guy was innocent; all they care is he was in jail."

Minutes after his niece spoke with Moore about the apartment problems, Chatman walks into the waiting room with bad news. "I didn't pass, baby," he tells her. "I gotta come back and do it again tomorrow." He passed parallel parking, but his right-hand turns swung out too wide.

"OK, you need more practice," Williams says. "Hell, you only drove one time before you came up here."

Driving is just one of the mechanical challenges Chatman must master. Since his bewilderment with Creuzot's cell phone, he has learned to use his own, a new Razr, complete with Bluetooth.

At one point, he dials Joyce Ann Brown, founder and director of Mothers/Fathers for the Advancement of Social Systems (MASS), a local nonprofit that helps prisoners readjust to society through counseling and job training. Chatman plans to meet with Brown, who before starting the group spent nine years incarcerated for a crime she didn't commit. "Can I talk to Ms. Brown, please?" he says into his new phone. Then he turns to Williams, amazed. "He knows who I am!"

She nods, a bit weary. "Most offices have caller ID now, Charles." He leaves a message.

Earlier, Williams helped him open a checking account and taught him how to use an ATM card. He'd never banked before going to prison, accustomed instead to stashing cash in his pockets or underneath the carpet at his sister's house.

Even something as simple as shopping for groceries is no easy matter. "I went to the one where you had to check and sack yourself," Chatman says, laughing at his childlike innocence. "The lady had to come help me do it."

For many freed by DNA evidence, perhaps the biggest challenge is making the transition from the rigid structure of an institution to the unlimited choice of the free world. "All of them seem very hopeful," says Kris Moore. "Just getting out is such a wonder. I hope it stays that way for Charles, but I know he has the hardest part ahead of him."

The same road has been traveled by more than two hundred people across the country who since 1989 have been exonerated by DNA. Last fall, the *New York Times* interviewed 115 exonerees and found that most had struggled to keep jobs, pay for health care, rebuild family ties, and shed the psychological effects of years of false imprisonment. A third of them were now living stable lives of work, family, and homeownership, but one-sixth had landed back in prison or gotten mired in drug or alcohol addiction. About half fell somewhere between those two extremes, drifting between jobs and leaning heavily on loved ones or lawyers. For most, the justice system had failed to make amends. Nearly 40 percent received no money from the government to compensate them for their time in prison; half had lawsuits pending to receive that compensation; and most had received no government services since their release.

In Dallas County, the wrongfully convicted have access to less state support than parolees. "The irony is someone who did it and is out on parole has more access to those kinds of resources than someone who never did it in the first place," says Michael Ware, a former criminal defense attorney hired last year by the Dallas County District Attorney's office to review some four hundred requests for postconviction DNA testing. "Parolees at least have a parole officer who's a supervisor—someone who's providing some guidance." For instance, parole officers make sure that former inmates have housing upon their release and connect them with community services

While Texas law provides for up to $50,000 of compensation per year of wrongful imprisonment, as well as one year of counseling, if an exoneree decides to take the statutory compensation, he must forego any civil rights claims he might have.

"It's such a ridiculously low amount to give someone for what they've missed, and it doesn't hold anyone accountable for putting an innocent man in prison," Kris Moore says. But the litigation can go on for years, and in some cases may be unwinnable because the government can assert claims of sovereign immunity.

Chatman is receiving some financial assistance from the law firm, which in addition to helping him pay his rent, has paid for new furniture and arranged financing for his new GMC Sierra pickup. But it can't go on helping him indefinitely. "We'd like to see more programs, more grants that would help these guys transition back to life," Kris Moore says.

On top of their physical needs, exonerees have suffered psychological wounds from years of being locked up without cause. "These guys are a lot different from the regular guys coming out," attorney Blackburn says. "It's a lot harder for them to swallow going back to regular existence because of what regular society has done to them. They have a deeper grudge."

There is a sense of powerlessness, betrayal, and fear that is difficult to shake. Michelle Moore, the Dallas County public defender who represented Chatman, recalls another exoneree who was terrified to take the bus. "A lady sat down next to him, and he thought, 'What if she yells "rape"? They'll come and get me.'"

For Chatman, the swirl of emotions, memories, and spiraling thoughts tends to come when he lies down at the end of the day. He's been sleeping only a few hours each night, watching television until he drifts off. "My family, they don't understand why I stay up," he says. "I'll lay there and all that stuff comes back—what happened to me, the things I did, prison life. . . . My family tries to help me, but they don't know what I need. I don't know what I need."

On a crisp morning in late January, Chatman stands in the parking lot of his new apartment complex, a brick-and-wood development on a wide road in Carrollton. The uniform units, pool, and manicured landscaping couldn't be more different from his childhood neighborhood in Oak Cliff, which he recently drove through. He was surprised to see so many boarded-up houses. He climbs into the driver's seat of his black pickup wearing jeans, a buttoned-up shirt, and a black do-rag. A few days before, he passed the driving test on the second try.

"I'm scared to get on the freeway—I just followed LaFreda here," he says. His family made certain his truck was hooked up to OnStar, the directional assistance service, and he's testing it out. Tentatively, he pushes a button on the rearview mirror and a voice comes over the speaker. "Welcome to OnStar," it says. "How can I assist you, Mr. Chatman?"

Doing his best to act nonchalant, as if he has always been able to do this, he asks directions to the nearest Wachovia bank.

He has a busy day ahead of him. He declined a request from the city of Carrollton to participate in the Martin Luther King Jr. march that morning because he needed time to himself and has an apartment full of furniture to arrange. Later he plans to get together with his old girlfriend, Cynthia, and her family. He was close to her mother and sister growing up. "I'm not looking to rekindle anything," he is careful to say. "She has kids, and I think she's married."

A few minutes later, he directs two men who haul his dining room table, chair, and two couches up the stairs and into his one-bedroom apartment. "This is nice, huh?" he says, looking around. "'Course, I don't have anything to compare it to since it's my first apartment."

Then his niece arrives with his sister, who gets her first glimpse of his apartment. Smith eyes the beige-and-black color scheme with approval. "I'm gonna spend lots of time here—till you get a girl-friend—when you get a girlfriend I'll stay home." She and her brother have a lot of time to make up for.

In the twenty-seven years after she testified in her brother's case, she didn't visit him once. When she recalls this, she tears up. "At first, we thought we could get him out," she says. "But then we realized it was way beyond our control—we didn't have money for lawyers. It was devastating. I feel like I let him down—like we should have kept in better contact."

But Chatman, as he has several times in recent weeks, explains that if anyone's responsible for the deterioration of their relationship, it's him. His niece and other women in his family sent him letters, but he withdrew from them and stopped responding.

"I always had this nagging thought—do they believe me?" he says. "Every time I saw them or talked to them, I'd try to read what they said, what was in their eyes. It's a real battle. Did they believe me? I don't know."

What he does know is that he is loved, which may help him through the difficult times that lie ahead. He says he wants to take auto mechanic classes and help the Innocence Project vet the claims of other convicts. Who better than him to detect when someone is lying or shading the truth?

He says he still has hard days, days when he thinks about all he has gone through and tries to make sense out of why it happened. But then he looks at his new apartment and his new furniture, and he steps outdoors, because he can. "I tell my family that I don't want to dwell on the past because they have been through a lot too—and God blessed us. So why should we rain on our own parade?"

24

DEATH AND INNOCENCE

Capital Punishment Is on the Decline, Largely Because of DNA Testing and Its Ramifications for the Legal System

Gregg Sangillo

At first glance, the decline of the death penalty in the United States is somewhat surprising.

In the 1990s, death sentences and executions reached peak levels in the wake of the Supreme Court's 1976 reinstatement of capital punishment, after a four-year gap. Public support for the death penalty has declined since 1994, according to the Gallup poll, but still stood at 67 percent [in 2006].

Most Republican candidates and officeholders are strong supporters of the death penalty, and even Democratic candidates have generally embraced capital punishment ever since Michael Dukakis lost his presidential bid in 1988 partly because his opposition to the death penalty opened him to the "soft on crime" label.

Notwithstanding the politics of capital punishment, however, the number of executions in the United States dropped to fifty-three in 2006 from a peak of ninety-eight in 1999. An even more telling figure, many experts say, is the decline in death sentences, just 128 nationwide in 2005 after hitting 317 in 1996. And when Sen. John Kerry (D-MA) ran for president in 2004, his opposition to capital punishment was not a big issue.

What changed? The biggest factor, according to many experts, is that the introduction of DNA testing in criminal cases in the early 1990s has cast a shadow over the legal system. DNA testing can provide exact matches between suspects and crime-scene evidence such as blood, semen, and hair, even years after a murder, and it can also prove that a suspect—or a convict—did not commit the crime in question. The New York City–based Innocence Project, cofounded by Barry Scheck and Peter Neufeld, lists 200 postconviction exonerations in the United States stemming from DNA testing. Fourteen of those cases involved death sentences. In light of such findings, and after a rash of wrongful convictions, Illinois governor George Ryan, a conservative Republican, commuted the sentences of 171 condemned men in 2003.

"In the early days, it was assumed that we just didn't make mistakes with any regularity in serious felony convictions, and the emergence of all these DNA exonerations has, I think, slowed down enthusiasm for the death penalty," says Daniel Givelber, a law professor at Northeastern University in Boston. "It has sort of made people question their certainty."

The advent of DNA tests has had widespread ramifications, experts say. The prospect of wrongfully convicting a defendant has made prosecutors more cautious in seeking the death penalty and made judges more inclined to overturn death sentences. The newfound skepticism has lengthened legal processes and increased the expense of carrying a death sentence through to conclusion.

"There's been a shift in the way we discuss the death penalty— away from morality toward what we call the concept of innocence, which is basically whether a bureaucratic machine the size of the US criminal-justice system can work without any mistakes," says Frank Baumgartner, a political science professor at Pennsylvania State University. "And when you pose the question that way, there's obviously only one answer."

Such obsession with perfection and "innocence" is overblown, supporters of capital punishment argue. Dudley Sharp, who heads an organization called Justice Matters based in Houston, says that almost all postconviction exonerations turn on legal points, not actual evidence such as DNA tests. The justice system—including the long appeals process—is designed to weed out mistakes, and it does, he contends. "I don't think anybody could imagine anything that accurate," he says.

Samuel Millsap, a former district attorney in Bexar County,

Texas, lost his certainty about the infallibility of the justice system in dramatic fashion. He was elected as a strong supporter of capital punishment, and his San Antonio office tried and executed half a dozen people in the 1980s. But after the *Houston Chronicle* published a story in 2005 questioning Ruben Cantu's 1993 conviction and execution, Millsap gave in to his mounting doubts and became an active opponent of the death penalty. "I think the system is absolutely broken," he says. "I believe that it's probable that we have executed innocent people in Texas."

WORRYING ABOUT INNOCENCE

Publicity over DNA tests that have exonerated condemned men has been reflected in popular culture in the past decade, producing a rash of books, TV shows, and movies. Best-selling crime novelist John Grisham's latest book, *The Innocent Man*, is based on a true story about a wrongful conviction.

Concern that innocent people could be executed has breathed new life into an anti-capital-punishment movement that had its first US victory in 1847, when Michigan abolished the death penalty for all crimes except treason. Opponents mostly still wage a limited crusade, however, focused on the legal system.

"There's no broad social movement—it's not like the civil-rights movement or something," Baumgartner explains. "It's very oriented toward university based projects." In a forthcoming book, Baumgartner and a coauthor trace the drive to reexamine capital cases to projects at several law and journalism schools in the early 1980s, including Northwestern University in Illinois. In addition to academics, some journalists and lawyers have also pursued the cause. California, Connecticut, Illinois, North Carolina, and Wisconsin have formed government-sponsored innocence commissions.

The focus on innocence remains controversial in criminal justice circles, however. Death-penalty advocates accuse abolitionists of obscuring the fact that most of the people exonerated are not actually "innocent" at all but have merely found legal loopholes through which to squirm. Sharp has examined claims made by groups like the Death Penalty Information Center, whose Web site lists 123 people who have been "released from death row with evidence of their innocence." In reading through case files, in combination with other studies, Sharp found only seventeen cases in which freed capital convicts were likely to have been truly innocent.

Sharp attributes the decline in death sentences to a commensurate drop in crime levels over the past two decades. But Baumgartner contends that factoring in the reduction in crime doesn't explain the decrease in executions and death sentences: Murder rates fell throughout the 1990s, but executions increased until 1999.

Although DNA evidence is rarely a factor in capital cases, Richard Dieter, executive director of the Death Penalty Information Center, says that its mere existence raises questions about the entire criminal-justice system. "Everybody is aware that mistakes have been made," he says. "If we had DNA, we'd expose even more, but not every case has it." And Baumgartner argues that DNA testing has had a huge psychological effect on the public. "When it's presented as the accused criminal or the convicted criminal himself saying that he's innocent, it's not that credible. The DNA makes it way more credible, because there's some guy in a white lab coat who's done the study."

Some supporters of capital punishment say that, eventually, DNA testing will make the application of death sentences much more accurate. Arguing for a defendant's right to postconviction DNA testing, former FBI director William Sessions wrote in a 2003 *Washington Post* op-ed, "As DNA technology continues to improve, so does its ability to identify the true perpetrators of crimes and exclude those who are wrongly suspected or charged." In 2004, President George W. Bush, a strong backer of capital punishment, signed the Justice for All Act, which offered federal grants to states to conduct DNA testing and to increase compensation for those wrongfully convicted.

Dieter partially agrees with Sessions's analysis. "Our organization, the Death Penalty Information Center, probably would go out of existence if all of those [structural] problems were eliminated," he says. "We don't try to raise [capital punishment's] rightness or wrongness as a theory. And I think, in a democracy, if people absolutely want the death penalty, it's better that we have one that's fair, that's accurate, that doesn't capture innocent people." But he hastens to add, "It's somewhat hypothetical to think that we can eliminate all of these problems in a human institution."

POLITICAL DEVELOPMENTS

The watershed event in the innocence movement came in Illinois, where Governor Ryan ordered a moratorium on executions in 2000 after research by a professor and his journalism students at Northwestern exonerated Anthony Porter, who had been convicted of a double murder in 1982, shortly before his execution date. Evidence subsequently emerged that police had tortured other death-row inmates into confessing to crimes they didn't commit. Shortly before Ryan left office in 2003, he commuted the sentences of all 171 people on the state's death row. "Anthony Porter was 48 hours away from being wheeled into the execution chamber where the state would kill him," Ryan said in his announcement. "It would be all so antiseptic that most of us wouldn't have even paused for a second, except that Anthony Porter was innocent."

In 2004, state supreme courts in Kansas and New York declared their states' death-penalty statutes unconstitutional, although the US Supreme Court later overturned the Kansas ruling. [In 2006], acting on the advice of a state-sponsored commission, the New Jersey legislature imposed a moratorium on capital punishment. After gruesome accounts of botched executions, several state courts have reopened the question of whether lethal injections might run afoul of the Constitution's ban on "cruel and unusual punishment."

[In 2007], measures to halt executions in several states have gone further than any in recent memory. In February, the Montana Senate gave preliminary approval to a bill abolishing the death penalty. In March, legislation to repeal the death penalty in Nebraska failed in the state's judiciary committee by one vote; a measure to reform capital punishment is tied up in the legislature. Also in March, a bill repealing the death penalty in Maryland failed on a tie vote in committee.

Capital punishment has been a powerful issue in political campaigns, although there are signs that it is weakening. In 1992, then governor Bill Clinton made a point of leaving the presidential campaign trail to preside over the execution of Ricky Ray Rector, whose case raised questions of severe brain damage. In 1994, New York governor Mario Cuomo, a death-penalty foe, lost reelection to Republican George Pataki in a campaign that focused on the issue.

In the 2000 presidential campaign, George W. Bush, who had

presided over more executions than any other Texas governor, got no argument from Vice President Gore, also a supporter of capital punishment. In fact, Gore's only criticism of Bush's death-penalty record was that Bush wasn't tough enough. During the second presidential debate, Gore attacked Bush for not supporting a hate-crimes law that could have been attached to the conviction of the men who dragged James Byrd, an African American, to his death behind a pickup truck in Jasper. In response, Bush questioned whether an extra law was needed. "Guess what's going to happen to them?" he asked eagerly. "They're going to be put to death." (Two of the three men convicted of the crime were sentenced to death.)

In 2004, however, Senator Kerry said he opposed capital punishment on moral grounds and because he believes it is unfairly applied, although he did make an exception for terrorists. Peter Loge, a former aide to Senator Edward Kennedy, D-MA, and to Congressman Brad Sherman, D-CA, points out that Kerry's stance never became a campaign issue. "The last presidential campaign was just mean and vicious, with both sides accusing the other of making stuff up. [But] the death penalty never came up," says Loge, whose public-affairs firm represents families of violent crime victims who nevertheless oppose capital punishment. "To me, that says [GOP] pollsters look at all the data and say, 'You know what? Just don't talk about it. Nobody cares.'" Loge also notes that Senator Jon Corzine's opposition to capital punishment was not an issue in a bitter gubernatorial campaign in New Jersey.

Democratic governor Jim Doyle of Wisconsin, a death-penalty opponent, was reelected in 2006. Newly elected Maryland governor Martin O'Malley, another Democrat, has stridently opposed capital punishment. In perhaps the most noteworthy case, Democratic Virginia governor Tim Kaine has steadfastly maintained his opposition, even though his state trails only Texas in the number of people it has executed since 1976.

CLOGS IN THE WHEEL

The potential impact of DNA evidence has made the process of trying a death-penalty case even more cumbersome and expensive. That, in turn, has had the effect of delaying executions and buying more time for appeals. "What we know about the appeals process is that, on average, among those offenders who get executed after a death sentence, there's a lapse of usually between ten to twelve years," says James Acker, a criminal-justice professor at the State University of New York (Albany). More convicts are being exonerated (or having their death sentences commuted), in part, because errors in the process are bound to surface as the cases undergo so much scrutiny at the trial, appellate, and habeas corpus stages.

The truth is, lengthy appeals most often center on legal and administrative issues. Basic questions of guilt and innocence are not much debated after the trial. "When it gets down to appeal, they're talking about, 'Were the jury instructions appropriate? Was the jury seated correctly?'" Givelber says. "Although [trials are] reviewed again and again and again, they're never reviewed on the basic question of whether the defendant did it."

One relatively new issue under debate is the adequacy of legal representation. In 2003 the Supreme Court ruled in *Wiggins v. Smith* that defendants in capital cases must receive adequate counsel. Amid rising questions about innocence, defense attorneys are spending more money on capital cases across the country, and courts are setting higher standards for public defenders and other lawyers who handle these cases. With more money flowing to defense attorneys, prosecutors are likewise spending more, in an arms race that makes counties think twice about bringing such cases in the first place. A death-penalty case "costs $1 million, and [a county's] whole budget could be $2 million," Dieter says. "And some of these are retrials—they already did this case once."

JUDICIAL REVIEW

Throughout the 1990s, the Supreme Court issued rulings intended to speed the seemingly endless process of appeals in capital cases. But in this decade, the Court has chipped away at states' ability to carry out executions. In *Atkins v. Virginia*, the justices ruled in 2002 that executing mentally retarded defendants violates the Eighth Amendment ban on cruel and unusual punishment. In the 2005 decision in *Roper v. Simmons*, the Court barred states from executing people who were under the age of eighteen when they committed their crimes. [In 2006], in the *Hill v. McDonough* case dealing with lethal injections, the high court ruled that death-row inmates may challenge their convictions under expansive civil-rights laws as well as under narrow habeas corpus arguments.

"It's hard for the Supreme Court to affect what juries decide about guilt or innocence," Dieter says. "But they can make restrictions, or just give the death penalty a second look. And I think that's what they've done in requiring better quality of counsel, checking on the prosecutors' use of jury strikes, eliminating the death penalty for some offenders, and looking at the mental illness problems. All of these things are happening in a climate in which the death penalty is a little bit more on the defensive."

Ultimately, Baumgartner says, the Supreme Court may one day declare capital punishment unconstitutional—as it did in 1972—on grounds that it has come to be applied too unevenly and unpredictably. According to the Death Penalty Information Center, 83 percent of all executions in 2006 took place in the South; [in 2007], twelve out of fourteen executions have occurred in Texas. "It's possible that as it becomes more and more rare, the Supreme Court will say that if it's unusual, it's unconstitutional," Baumgartner says. "How they define 'unusual' could mean that it's only used in five states, and forty-five other states virtually never use it. We're not at that point yet, but we're moving in that direction."

Robert Blecker, who teaches constitutional history at New York Law School, derides that idea. "It is not at all difficult for me to stomach the fact that some states execute and others do not, in terms of federalism," he says. "The essential trade we made in 1788 [in writing the Constitution] was one that acknowledged that it is primarily a state function to define, detect, prosecute, and punish crime."

THEORY VERSUS PRACTICE

Despite the drop in death sentences, public support for capital punishment remains fairly high. In an October 2006 Gallup poll, 67 percent of those surveyed said that they favor capital punishment. But that's well below the 80 percent support recorded in 1994. When pollsters probe beneath the surface, moreover, they find indications that support is lessening. When respondents are given the option of backing an alternative sentence of life without parole, support for the death penalty drops to 47 percent, according to a May 2006 Gallup poll. Likewise, Baumgartner says, jurors' theoretical support for the concept of capital punishment weakens when they have to make real-world decisions in capital cases.

Millsap changed his mind on the death penalty because of personal experience. When he was the Bexar County district attorney, the main criticism he faced from his constituents was that his office did not use the death penalty enough, he says. But he started to have doubts after reading news reports on the issue. After the controversial June 2000 execution of Gary Graham, a Texas man who was convicted on the testimony of a single eyewitness, "I came out in favor of a moratorium," he says. "I took the position that there ought not to be any more executions until we had a system that we were confident was doing what it was supposed to do—mainly, to protect the innocent." His wife accused him of being disingenuous on the matter, he says, and encouraged him to oppose the death penalty in all cases.

When a *Houston Chronicle* story called one of his own cases into question, he turned into an unequivocal opponent of capital punishment. In November 2005, the *Chronicle* reported that Ruben Cantu, a man whom Millsap's office tried and executed, may very well have been innocent. Juan Moreno, the victim of the shooting who survived, and the lone eyewitness to the crime, told the paper that Cantu was innocent and that he had fingered Cantu only because of pressure from the police. "I acknowledged at that point, publicly, responsibility for not simply the decision to prosecute the case, but I [also] assumed responsibility for the execution," Millsap recalls. "And with the understanding that while his innocence had not been established, it was clear to me that the case should not have been prosecuted as a death-penalty case."

Since then Millsap has worked to get the death penalty abolished in Montana, New Jersey, New Mexico, and other states. He still believes that in the vast majority of cases, states execute only the guilty. But he adds, "There's just lots of ways that the system can break down, and I think does break down. Fortunately, I believe it doesn't happen often. But if it happens once, that's too often."

DEATH AND HARMLESS ERROR

A Rhetorical Response to Judging Innocence

Colin Starger

Professor [Brandon L.] Garrett's impressive empirical analysis of the first two hundred postconviction DNA exonerations in the United States ("Garrett Study") has the potential to affect contemporary debates surrounding our nation's criminal justice system. This response explores this potential by harnessing the study's data in support of arguments for and against a contested doctrinal proposition—that guilt-based harmless error rules should never apply in death penalty appeals.

My analysis starts with the premise that the study's real-world impact will necessarily depend on how jurists, politicians, and scholars extrapolate the explanatory power of the data beyond the two hundred cases themselves. While critics of contemporary criminal justice policies will likely see Professor Garrett's data as revealing the tip of an iceberg of deeper structural flaws, defenders of the status quo will predictably resist generalizations from this closed data set to any larger picture of criminal justice administration. Much therefore rides on the perceived inductive reach of these two hundred cases.

Perhaps wisely, Professor Garrett declines to engage in a specific evaluation of his study's implications in terms of the number of innocents still in prison, except to assert cautiously that known innocence cases "represent the tip of an iceberg."[1] Curious readers might nonetheless persist in asking: just how much larger is the phenomenon that these cases represent? I suggest that this line of inquiry is not a particularly useful one because the empirical question it asks is essentially unanswerable. Given that conclusive forensic proof of guilt or innocence remains unavailable in the overwhelming majority of convictions, any attempt to precisely quantify the data's representativeness inevitably will rest on guesses (educated or not) concerning either overall system error rates or the raw numbers of undiscovered wrongful convictions.

Rather than attempt such quasi-empirical triangulations, I propose instead to test the explanatory power of the Garrett Study via a rhetorical experiment. Specifically, I hope to gauge the practical reach of the study by examining its persuasive impact when called into service to support a particular and contested proposition—that guilt-based harmless error rules should never apply in death penalty appeals.[2] The experiment is designed to test what persuasive "truths" might emerge from the study when it is subjected to the crucible of an imagined adversarial process. Though the actual proposition chosen for debate matters, the assumption animating the experiment is that dialectical process and rhetorical dynamics would cause similar "truths" to emerge even when contesting different propositions.

The crux of the rhetorical experiment has three stages, mirroring the stages in a typical litigation briefing. Reasoning from the Garrett Study, I first advance imagined prima facie arguments in support of the proposition that guilt-based harmless error rules should never apply in death penalty appeals. Second, I respond to the prima facie case with counterarguments focusing on potential and perceived weaknesses in the study. Third, I offer a reply to rehabilitate the original proposition and the relevance of the study. After the arguments are submitted, I conclude the experiment by attempting to assume a neutral stance and analyzing the broader rhetorical and practical implications of the imagined exchange.

PRIMA FACIE CASE: GUILT-BASED HARMLESS ERROR RULES SHOULD NEVER APPLY IN DEATH PENALTY APPEALS

Guilt-based harmless error rules empower courts to deny relief to criminal appellants despite finding legal error in the proceedings that led to conviction. As Professor Garrett observes, these guilt-based rules surface in various doctrinal inquiries such as the *Chapman* test (which excuses constitutional error at trial if the state shows beyond a reasonable doubt that the error did not contribute to the guilty verdict) or the *Strickland* test (which precludes a finding of constitutional error when ineffective assistance of counsel failed to prejudice the outcome due to the evidence of the client's guilt).[3] Harmless error rules exist to limit or prevent reversals of otherwise reliable convictions or sentences on technicalities.

A critical assumption that must underlie the creation and application of guilt-based harmless error rules is that reviewing courts can effectively judge the reliability of a conviction independent of any legal error that may have occurred in the proceedings below. By definition, harmless error rules only come into play when a fairness-implicating error has occurred. Ultimately, then, a conclusion that a conviction is reliable represents a judgment on the substantive correctness of the guilty verdict or guilty plea. It then follows that guilt-based harmless error rules must assume that courts can effectively judge the guilt or innocence of an appellant.

Professor Garrett's study of the first two hundred postconviction DNA exonerations in the United States undermines this assumption. At the most basic level, all two hundred cases represent discrete instances where the courts failed to detect innocence. Every one of these two hundred individuals had his or her conviction sustained on appeal and was not exonerated until after postconviction DNA testing yielded exculpatory results and/or a "hit" to a third party in a DNA database. Without question, courts have confidently but mistakenly judged actually innocent appellants to be guilty.

The Garrett Study further allows for a nuanced analysis of the precise manner in which the courts went astray. In 133 of 200 cases, courts issued nonsummary written opinions explaining their reasons for granting or denying relief. A key finding of the study is that in 18 of these 133 cases—14 percent—courts actually did reverse and vacate the innocent person's conviction. Although these 18 reversals were all sustained on appeal, they do not represent exoneration by the courts. In 12 of these 18 cases, the person was retried and reconvicted, and only later exonerated by DNA testing. In the remaining 6 cases, exculpatory DNA results were obtained while the person awaited his retrial.[4] Nonetheless, the 14 percent reversal rate represents a baseline in the data set where the court system "got it right" at least once.

Obviously, this 14 percent success rate pales in comparison to its complimentary 86 percent failure rate. Even more revealing, however, is that in 43 of the 133 cases with written decisions—32 percent—courts made adverse guilt-based harmless error rulings in the course of denying relief.[5] Looking more closely, Professor Garrett reveals that in 23 of these 43 harmless error cases, the court actually found an underlying legal or constitutional error, but then denied relief on harmlessness or lack-of-prejudice grounds.[6] In other words, application of guilt-based rules caused 23 innocent individuals (17 percent of the 133 cases) to languish in prison despite judicial recognition that the proceedings that led to their conviction were in fact flawed and unfair.

These findings should give pause to even the most ardent supporters of the death penalty. Guilt-based harmless error rules permit the state to execute an individual in the face of legal error. This represents a judgment that the evidence of guilt is so strong that it outweighs or excuses admitted unfairness or technical deficiency and therefore permits taking the life of the condemned. Yet Professor Garrett has shown that courts demonstrate a guilt-confirming bias even when reviewing cases of actually innocent defendants. More courts identified reversible error but excused the failing on (incorrect) harmlessness grounds than identified error and permitted reversal—even if reconviction ultimately ensued.

While it may be unrealistic (though not unreasonable) to demand zero errors and execution of only the guilty, it seems entirely reasonable to require that no execution proceed if a court has identified reversible error. After all, "technical" procedural protections exist only because of their presumed role in enhancing the truth-seeking process of trial and in preventing wrongful conviction. Professor Garrett has demonstrated that courts can be seriously wrong when they ignore the legal recognition of errors in the truth-seeking process and substitute their own subjective assessment of guilt.

RESPONSE: JURIES REAL SOURCE OF ERROR;
CAPITAL REVIEW ADEQUATE

Harmless error rules cannot be strictly equated with an affirmative appellate judgment of guilt or innocence. Rather, harmless error analysis recognizes that fact finders' verdicts should not be disturbed for any or all procedural defects. In this way, harmless error rules actually represent deference to the judgment of juries more than confidence in the record-reviewing power of appellate courts. The real problem identified by Professor Garrett's study is that juries can make mistakes. However, this problem cannot be solved by tinkering with guilt-based harmless error rules.

Although Professor Garrett devotes much attention to the path of eventually exonerated defendants' appeals, the bottom line is that 191 of the 200 wrongful convictions in his study—96 percent—resulted from a fact finder's verdict after trial; a mere 9 cases resulted from guilty pleas.[7] In 18 of the 200 cases, appellate courts judged legal error to be serious enough to disturb the jury's judgment. However, as already cited, in 12 of these reversals the innocent defendant was again convicted at trial. In other words, even when appellate courts get it right, the case will likely be returned to a jury for another chance to get it wrong. Professor Garrett's study thus underscores a simple truth—juries are human and therefore fallible. Nonetheless, the reality remains that juries are a constitutionally required centerpiece of our criminal justice system.

With respect to the specific question of harmless error in the death penalty context, Professor Garrett's study supports the proposition that appellate courts currently give capital cases the additional scrutiny they deserve. Although a 14 percent overall reversal rate has already been cited, Professor Garrett himself is careful to distinguish between innocent appellants' reversal rates in capital versus noncapital cases. As it turns out, 12 of the 133 cases with written decisions in the data set were capital cases, and 7 of the 18 reversals with written decisions were also in capital cases, resulting in a capital reversal rate of 58 percent.[8] This 58 percent attrition rate is similar to the 68 percent capital attrition rate found in all capital appeals from 1973 through 1995 in the landmark Liebman, Fagan, and West study.[9] This high reversal rate therefore seems reliable and generalizable beyond Professor Garrett's own narrow data set to the capital system at large.

For present purposes, the germane bottom line from these two studies is that one can reasonably expect approximately 58–68 percent of all capital convictions to be reversed. The logical counterpart of this conclusion is that guilt-based harmless error rules will ultimately be ignored or overcome in a comfortable majority of all capital cases. Indeed, it is not clear in the study how many capital cases, if any, were among the 23 cases where harmless error applied to defeat a meritorious claim. In short, the issue of guilt-based harmless error rules blocking relief for innocent appellants does not seem to be a significant problem in the capital context.

Finally, the harmless error question needs to be understood in the context of courts granting relief for the actually guilty. In addition to a 58 percent capital reversal rate, Professor Garrett found a 9 percent reversal rate for noncapital cases in the data set.[10] Of course, nothing in Professor Garrett's study directly suggests that a higher percentage of capital defendants are actually innocent than noncapital defendants. And nothing in the study suggests that anywhere near 58 percent–68 percent of people on death row are actually innocent, or that 9 percent of convicted rape, murder, and rape-murder defendants in our system are actually innocent. Thus, it seems apparent that more defendants will obtain relief than are actually innocent. Put another way, despite the presence of the contested harmless error system, it appears that significant numbers of actually guilty defendants will obtain reversals. This suggests that harmless error rules may in fact be too lenient, and that the problem of actually guilty people unjustifiably earning relief is far more pronounced in the capital context.

In sum, it appears that courts may already be disturbing jury judgments too frequently and that harmless error rules should not be cast aside.

REPLY: PROCESS MATTERS; DEATH IS DIFFERENT

Regardless of whether guilt-based harmless error rules are characterized as affirmative judgments or deference-based judgments, they still focus the court's attention on the reliability of the verdict instead of the fairness of the process. While it may be true that juries bear the most responsibility for wrongful convictions, this cannot be a reason to defer to jury judgment in the face of procedural error. The point is that courts can competently judge process, and that fair process has an underappreciated instrumental value in truth seeking. Abolishing guilt-based error rules in capital appeals may not solve the problem of jury mistake, but it would prevent courts from potentially compounding such mistakes.

It may well be that the unreliable application of harmless error rules is a more pronounced problem outside the capital context than within it. But this does not mean that the capital system is working properly. Indeed, a 58–68 percent reversal rate suggests that capital trials frequently suffer from intense flaws, and that appellate confidence in the system as a whole is not great.[11] Moreover, a higher reversal rate in capital cases does not challenge Professor Garrett's basic finding that appellate courts frequently mistook innocent appellants for guilty ones. All 133 cases with written decisions in the study were serious crimes—rapes, murders, and rape-murders—and in 67 of those cases (50 percent), courts (incorrectly) referred to appellant's guilt.[12] Disturbingly, in 13 of these cases (10 percent), the court actually characterized the evidence of guilt as "overwhelming."[13] This suggests a powerful guilt-confirming bias.

Regardless of how many capital defendants had adverse harmless error rulings made against them, the fact remains that at least fourteen innocent men have walked off death row only because postconviction DNA testing proved innocence that juries and courts failed to detect. This raw number is significant as it represents fourteen concrete instances where the state came close to killing the wrong man. While it may be possible that truly guilty individuals have earned some kind of relief because their trials were unfair, Professor Garrett's study should put an end to the horribly naive conception that our death penalty system could never shed innocent blood. Since executing an innocent can never be harmless, guilt-based harmless error rules should never apply in death penalty appeals.

CONCLUSION: EXPERIMENTAL OBSERVATIONS

Although the particular arguments advanced for and against the proposition might easily have varied, this exchange evidences many rhetorical characteristics one would expect when the proposition debated calls upon empirical support for a question that is not strictly empirical. Doctrinal or moral premises behind guilt-based harmless error rules immediately become contested, and empirical interpretations of innocence data vary depending on prior doctrinal perspective. A 58 percent capital reversal rate can mean the system is catching errors or it can mean the system is constantly breaking, depending on whether one views the system as broken or functioning.

A particular and revealing characteristic of the debate regarding this data set is the unknown (and unknowable) rate of wrongful conviction. Whether more actually guilty defendants win release than actually innocent people suffer incarceration or execution cannot be answered. The inability to answer this question naturally does not deter the use of statistics to buttress an argument that the rate is likely acceptably low or unacceptably high. Yet a rhetorical void is created without an empirical answer to the rate of wrongful conviction question, and this void leaves a more fundamental question unasked: What is an acceptable error rate in the administration of the death penalty? As a society, can we agree that it is acceptable that one innocent be killed for every hundred guilty men executed? Can we agree on one for one thousand?

With the question reframed this way, it seems clear that the argument against harmless error rules in death penalty cases best rests on a nonempirical appeal to the value of an individual life and thus predicts the reply's closing focus on the fourteen men released from death row.[14] Conversely, this reframing suggests that the argument in support of harmless error rules derives its greatest strength from an appeal to the specter of guilty individuals escaping just punishment. In the end, this experiment suggests that the illuminating power of Professor Garrett's study will depend on our ability to honestly struggle with the ultimate nonempirical questions it raises.

26

TESTIMONY OF BARRY C. SCHECK BEFORE THE MARYLAND COMMISSION ON CAPITAL PUNISHMENT

September 5, 2008

. . . I am cofounder and codirector of the Innocence Project. I appreciate the opportunity to testify and ask that my written statement and materials be included in the record.

The Innocence Project assists persons in proving their innocence through postconviction DNA testing. To date there have been 220 men and women exonerated by postconviction DNA testing nationwide. The Innocence Project has, in the vast majority of these cases, either represented or assisted in the representation of these innocents. Of particular relevance to this commission's work, seventeen of the people proven innocent by DNA evidence had been sentenced to death. One of these seventeen men was exonerated just two weeks ago.

Today I will address those elements of the commission's mandate relating to an examination of the risk of executing an innocent and the impact of DNA evidence in assuring fairness and accuracy in capital cases.

Every time an innocent is convicted the person who really committed the crime escapes justice and may commit other crimes. The Innocence Project works on reforms that go to the root causes of wrongful convictions—mistaken identification, false confessions, unreliable forensic science, law enforcement misconduct, and ineffective defense counsel. Our policy agenda is a pro-law enforcement agenda, win-win reforms that protect the innocent and help identify the guilty. It is precisely because of the dual nature of our work—both the efforts to exonerate the innocent and the constructive efforts to strengthen the capacity of the criminal justice system to make more accurate guilt/innocence determinations—that we may be able to provide a somewhat unique and hopefully helpful perspective on the complicated risk/benefit question you asked us to address.

In the most serious crimes, criminalists believe that more than 85 percent do not involve biological evidence susceptible to DNA testing, perhaps our best tool for producing highly reliable—but certainly not infallible—evidence of guilt or innocence. Most homicide cases turn on eyewitness testimony, confessions, the credibility of witnesses, or circumstantial evidence, not DNA testing. Therefore DNA testing is not a panacea that can prevent wrongful executions. Although DNA has helped us to shed light on the existence of wrongful convictions across the nation, it simply does not have the capacity to ensure either a fair or accurate application of this irreversible sentence.

Having worked in this field for thirty years, perhaps the most significant lesson I have learned is that in matters of crime and justice humility is important because even the most experienced among us are often wrong. My partner Peter Neufeld and I have reviewed hundreds of cases. In some cases, after I have pored over reams of court transcripts, scrutinized piles of police reports, dissected crime lab analyses, sifted through evidence and property logs, and studied scores of witness statements, I have strongly suspected some men's guilt, only later to discover I was wrong. No less often, someone I strongly suspect is innocent turns out to be guilty. Indeed, because every one of us is human and all of us are actors in a fact-finding mission, if just one of us makes an error, jumps to a conclusion, or acts on a false assumption, an innocent man can be condemned to a guilty man's fate.

THE RISK OF EXECUTING AN INNOCENT

What Can Be Learned from DNA Exonerations

Postconviction DNA testing has demonstrated that the risk of convicting an innocent is much greater than even the most cynical expected, and it naturally follows that the risk of executing an innocent is greater than previously believed. No one can responsibly or sensibly quantify the risk of executing an innocent; there are simply too many sources of error that occur at unknowable rates at every stage of the criminal process to make that kind of judgment.

DNA testing has, on the other hand, provided some very sobering data about the frequency of error in different parts of the system that are very compelling in trying to assess, with necessarily incomplete information, the fallibility of the system as a whole:

FBI Exclusion Data. The National Institute of Justice has performed the only known survey of DNA exclusions of defendants in criminal cases. In that study the FBI reported that since it began conducting such DNA testing in 1989, it found that in at least 24 percent of the cases where it gets results—ordinarily matters where a suspect has been arrested or indicted based on non-DNA evidence—the defendant was excluded.[1] This robust finding is also conservative because if four suspects in a case are excluded for purposes of this statistic the FBI will count it as just one "primary" suspect being excluded. Surveys by the National Institute of Justice corroborate that private laboratories, as well as state and local laboratories, report similar exclusion rates, or even higher exclusion rates.

Preconviction/Postindictment Exclusions. Although unfortunately no one is keeping systematic track of the data, law enforcement officials across the country acknowledge that thousands of cases, including many homicides, arrests, and indictments based on seemingly compelling proof like a detailed confession or multiple eyewitnesses, have been vacated and the real assailant identified before conviction based upon DNA testing.

Governor Warner's Virginia Experiment. In 2001, the Innocence Project asked officials in Virginia to search the state's archives for a former lab analyst's old notebooks, since DNA testing on vaginal swabs she had remarkably stapled into her notebook had led to the exoneration of one of our clients, Marvin Anderson. Officials subsequently discovered notebooks with biological evidence from over 330 old cases, most of them collected before DNA testing was available. Two more people were exonerated after DNA testing on samples from the notebooks. Recognizing that this evidence could shed light on the propriety of the convictions in those cases, Virginia Governor Warner declared that, "A look back at these retained case files is the only morally acceptable course," and agreed to test all of them. He started out, however, with a small random sample of these convicted felons. Out of the first twenty-nine of these randomly selected cases, there were two exonerations (and in one case the real assailant was identified), which is close to a 7 percent exoneration rate. ["Follow the DNA to find the truth," *Roanoke Times*, December 16, 2005.] It is worth emphasizing that Virginia is second only to Texas in executions.

SOME CASE HISTORIES OF DNA EXONERATIONS: FALSE GUILTY PLEAS TO CAPITAL OFFENSES

There are seventeen cases where innocent men were sentenced to death and subsequently exonerated by DNA testing. The cases are all documented on our website. One of those men, Kirk Bloodsworth, a former United States Marine, sits on this very commission. Kirk was the first man in the United States whose capital conviction was overturned by postconviction DNA testing. Kirk was convicted based on the mistaken identification of five eyewitnesses of having raped and murdered a little girl in Baltimore County, Maryland. Even after DNA testing forced a prosecutor to vacate his conviction and dismiss the case against him, the prosecutor still wouldn't concede Kirk was innocent. It wasn't until, after years of prodding her to do so, a DNA profile from semen found in the girl's underwear was run in the CODIS system and came up with a "hit" to the real assailant who, astonishingly, had actually lived on the same cellblock with Kirk. For those of you who haven't, I urge you to read his wonderful book, written with Tim Junkin, entitled *Bloodsworth*, to get a true sense of how an innocent, a Marine with no criminal record, could come so close to execution.

Similarly, last fall, John Grisham . . . [came] out with his first nonfiction book about the case of Ron Williamson, one of our clients who came within five days of execution in Oklahoma.[2] That case is also chronicled in *Actual Innocence*,[3] a book Jim Dwyer, Peter Neufeld, and I wrote about DNA exoneration cases and the lessons that can be learned from them.

Each of the seventeen DNA exonerations of men sentenced to death is a chilling reminder of how the innocent can be executed, as are the more than thirty homicide cases where innocents were convicted, but not sentenced to death before DNA exonerated them. Many of these men—Eddie Joe Lloyd in Detroit, Michigan; John Restivo, John Kogut, and Dennis Halstead in Nassau County, New York—I know very well and feel certain they would have been sentenced to death and possibly executed if Michigan or New York had capital punishment when they were convicted.

But I would like to bring to your attention some case histories not generally known, but that are very instructive about the risk of error generated peculiarly by capital punishment and the extreme difficulty of ever finding out about such grievous errors: the false guilty plea and/or false confession cases. The very fact that someone might plead guilty and/or give a false confession in a capital case to avoid execution might seem unlikely or preposterous to some, but DNA testing shows this does happen, and one must assume that in cases where DNA testing is not available, or would not be probative, discovering a false confession would be close to impossible.

Anthony Gray, who was convicted in Prince George's County, Maryland, was sentenced to two concurrent life sentences after pleading guilty to rape and murder charges in order to avoid the death penalty. Police officers had coaxed a confession out of Gray, who is borderline retarded, by telling him that two other men arrested in connection with the case had told police that Gray was involved. DNA results generated before Gray entered his plea excluded him and the two other men as the source of the sperm recovered from the victim.

Some years later, the conviction came under intense scrutiny when a man arrested in connection with a burglary reported unpublicized details about the rape and murder for which Mr. Gray had been convicted. While DNA testing of semen recovered from the crime scene had excluded Mr. Gray and the other two men originally arrested for the crime, it did produce a match to the burglary suspect, who eventually pled guilty to the crime for which Mr. Gray had been imprisoned for seven years.

David Vasquez was arrested for the murder of a woman in Arlington, Virginia, who had been sexually assaulted and then hung. Vasquez, who is mentally impaired, confessed to the crime and provided details that were not released to the public. Mr. Vasquez could not provide an alibi and was placed near the scene of the crime by two eyewitnesses. Additionally, investigators found two pubic hairs at the crime scene that resembled those of Vasquez.

Faced with what appeared to be a collection of evidence that pointed to his guilt, Mr. Vasquez entered a guilty plea. DNA testing later proved that the murder was committed by another man, Timothy Spencer. Prosecutors joined with defense attorneys to secure the eventual pardon of Mr. Vasquez.

Christopher Ochoa pled guilty to the rape and murder of an Austin, Texas, woman. He confessed to the crime and implicated another man, Richard Danziger. The state offered to give him a life sentence if he agreed to plead guilty and testify against Danziger at trial. Under threat of receiving the death penalty and by the advice of his attorney, Ochoa agreed to their terms.

At trial, however, Mr. Ochoa changed his story and claimed that he, and not Mr. Danziger, had shot the victim. Consequently, prosecutors charged Mr. Danziger with rape instead of the murder. Mr. Danziger could not provide a reason as to why Mr. Ochoa, his friend, might have testified against him.

Both men received life sentences and years later, the police, then-governor Bush's office, and the District Attorney's Office received letters from a man named Achim Marino, claiming that he was solely responsible for the crime for which Ochoa and Danziger had been convicted. His letter told investigators precisely where to locate items that were stolen from the scene of the crime, which police were able to obtain. Thirteen years after the commission of the crime, Ochoa and Danziger were exonerated and released from prison. Ochoa, who recently graduated law school and wishes to become a prosecutor, now states that his confession and implication of Danziger were the results of police pressure and fear of the death penalty.

Jerry Frank Townsend, a mentally retarded man in Florida, was convicted of six murders and one rape and sentenced to seven concurrent life sentences. This began when, in 1979, Townsend was arrested for raping a pregnant woman in Miami, Florida. During the investigation, he confessed to other murders. The confessions were largely the consequence of Townsend wanting to please authority figures, a common adaptive practice by someone with his limited mental capacities.

Eventually, Townsend was cleared by DNA evidence following actions in 1998, when a victim's mother asked a Ft. Lauderdale police detective to review the Townsend cases. In 2000, DNA testing of preserved evidence implicated another man, Eddie Lee Mosley, and also cleared Townsend for two of the six murders. This cast substantial doubt on the accuracy of all of Townsend's confessions. In April 2001, further DNA testing cleared Townsend of two additional killings to which he had previously confessed, and ultimately, two months later, he was cleared of all charges and released from prison—after having served twenty-two years for crimes he did not commit.

Each of these cases demonstrates an unfortunate ripple effect caused by the presence of the death penalty. Because each of the men featured in the aforementioned case studies feared being sentenced to death, they pled guilty to crimes they did not commit in order to secure a lesser sentence. Some have expressed concern that repealing the death penalty will weaken the ability of prosecutors to get life without parole pleas. Whatever the merits of that argument, it must be acknowledged that fear of the death penalty has often resulted in innocents falsely pleading guilty to life without parole.

RECENT NON-DNA CASES WHERE THERE IS STRONG PROOF INNOCENTS WERE EXECUTED

Wrongful convictions and executions have happened and will continue to happen. This occurrence is not an urban myth or a fantasy drummed up by any particular advocacy group. Let me provide you with compelling examples of possible innocents who were executed that have come to light in the past year alone:

Cameron Willingham of Corsicana, Texas, was executed in February 2004 for murder by arson. Later that year, an investigation proved and newspaper accounts published new scientific evidence that it was impossible to determine arson after all. A panel comprised of national arson experts concurred in March 2006 that the science underlying Willingham's conviction was invalid. The panel also looked at the case of Ernest Willis, another Texan, who was convicted of murder by arson and concluded that in his case as well, the science was unsupportable. Although Willis and Willingham were on death row in Texas at the same time, Willis was exonerated—and later compensated by the state—when his conviction was undermined and only through a retrial could he have remained on death row. There is no evidence demonstrating that the facts in the Willingham case, however, were ever revisited until now. Just last month, the Texas Forensic Science Commission announced its intention to investigate possible professional negligence or misconduct connected to the arson analysis in the Willingham case.

Ruben Cantu of San Antonio, Texas, was executed in August 1993 for a robbery-murder. The *Houston Chronicle* investigated claims that Cantu was innocent and that the identification made by a survivor of the robbery was coerced by law enforcement. A codefendant subsequently signed an affidavit stating that Cantu was not present and had no role in the commission of the robbery or murder.[4]

Carlos DeLuna of Corpus Christi, Texas, was executed in December 1989 for the stabbing death of a convenience store clerk. Although DeLuna identified another man as the perpetrator, his claims were dismissed. In June of 2006, the *Chicago Tribune* discovered that the person DeLuna named, Carlos Hernandez, was no stranger to law enforcement and had a history of knife-related violence. Hernandez reportedly also told friends and family that he committed the crime. Hernandez died in jail in 1999.[5]

THE CAUSES OF WRONGFUL CONVICTION

Fundamental Flaws in the Criminal Justice System

Each of the aforementioned cases is instructive because they reveal not only how easily mistakes can happen, but also how many miscarriages of justice cannot be proven in the absence of a definitive test like DNA. Indeed, only a narrow percentage of criminal cases involve biological evidence that can be subjected to DNA testing, and in many instances that evidence has been contaminated, degraded, lost, or destroyed when a case is revisited years later in the postconviction context.

The nation's 220 DNA exonerations have taught us that any number of factors—sometimes many functioning at once—can yield a wrongful conviction and that the appeals process does not provide the needed protections to detect them. The public benefit of DNA exonerations, however, lies in their opportunity to understand how the criminal justice system—from eyewitness to police to prosecutor to judge to jury to appellate courts to the Supreme Court—can find a person guilty beyond a reasonable doubt when the accused is simply innocent.

The Innocence Project has examined these 220 wrongful convictions proven through DNA testing, and identified those factors that confound the criminal justice system, sometimes at the earliest stages. These include, but are not limited to mistaken eyewitness identifications; faulty forensic work—predicated on improper crime scene collection, contamination, drylabbing, falsified results, the use of unvalidated assays, and statistical exaggerations about their rigor; false or coerced confessions; reliance on jailhouse informants; poor defense; and prosecutorial misconduct.

RECENT MARYLAND DEBACLES AFFECTING THE QUALITY OF FORENSIC RESULTS

These problems happen across the nation and do not stop at state borders. Indeed, despite its efforts to implement some of the reforms intended to curb the production of wrongful convictions, lingering questions about guilt and innocence have not been put to rest in Maryland.

In 2003, the Baltimore County Police Department was forced to evaluate nearly five hundred cases when it came to light that Concepcion Bacasnot, an incompetent serologist, provided false testimony that contributed to the conviction of Bernard Webster, another Maryland man proven innocent through DNA testing. Mr. Webster spent twenty years in prison for a rape that he did not commit while the actual rapist went on to attack at least one other woman in her home in Baltimore. The discovery of Ms. Bacasnot's faulty testimony led Bill

Toohey, a police spokesman, to state the following: "The very first thing we did was to make sure there is no one on death row because of her work." Ms. Bacasnot had previously resigned in 1987, after she demonstrated a lack of basic knowledge of serology in the pretrial hearing of Robert Bedford's capital case.

Just last month, the *Baltimore Sun* reported on the dismissal of a city crime lab director following revelations of DNA contamination and "other operational issues." Police disclosed that a partial review of twenty-five hundred cases found twelve instances in which a previously unknown genetic profile was linked to a laboratory employee. A supervisor in the crime lab's DNA unit conceded last week that a full accounting of the scope of the problem would present a challenge for them. Further, the director of the national crime lab accreditation board—which accredited the lab in December of 2006—expressed astonishment that the lab had failed to take steps to catalogue the DNA profiles of its own employees.

And in February of last year, an audit of the Maryland State Police by the legislature's Joint Audit Committee found lapses in the agency's use of DNA evidence. According to the audit, more than twenty-five thousand samples were neither analyzed nor entered into the DNA database over a three-year period. . . .

As these cases demonstrate, Maryland has a troubled history with forensic error and misconduct, extending into even recent headlines.

STATUS OF MARYLAND REFORMS AIMED AT SOLVING CRIME AND CURBING THE RISK OF EXECUTING AN INNOCENT

There are a number of measures that Maryland could but to date has not taken to more proactively solve crimes and curb the risk of convicting or executing innocents. While Maryland has implemented a number of forward-thinking reforms in some areas, much more could and should be done to assure the fair administration of justice, including—

Oversight Authority of Maryland's Crime Laboratories

Regardless of the relative weight one believes should be given to evidence of forensic error or misconduct in their assessment of a particular case, there is no question that Maryland has a disturbing history in this regard. Without an honest accounting of the state of forensic analysis in Maryland, it is simply irresponsible to allow forensic results to influence matters of life and death.

In recognition of this reality, efforts have been made to address the problem, but they remain insufficient. In April of last year, Maryland passed a groundbreaking law establishing oversight of the state's crime laboratories by an independent board—the state's Department of Health and Mental Hygiene—with experience in clinical laboratory practices. While this law recognizes the incredible pressures experienced by state crime labs, including a lack of qualified and trained staff, as well as inadequate resources and equipment, the governor has not committed to funding the necessary positions so that it may be implemented. Therefore, this innovative law is only symbolic and is not positioned to address some of the lingering crime laboratory problems in Maryland already described.

Elimination of DNA Backlog

In July of last year, perhaps in anticipation of first-time legislation in Maryland requiring the collection of DNA from individuals upon arrest, the governor announced the clearance of a backlog of more than twenty-four thousand untested samples in the possession of the Maryland State Police. Unfortunately, this laudable progress did not address the backlog in metropolitan labs in jurisdictions such as Baltimore City or Prince Georges County. Neither county-funded nor locally funded crime labs, therefore, were provided with the resources they needed to clear their backlogs since they did not receive the state money needed to accomplish these goals.

Perhaps even more troubling, however, is that Maryland has prioritized database expansion of offender profiles over crime scene evidence processing, failing to take into consideration that without crime scene profiles, offender profiles will lay dormant and crimes will go unsolved. After all, any DNA database is only as good as the matches it can generate.

According to Gene Watch UK, a British organization that monitors DNA usage in the United Kingdom, the collection of DNA from crime scenes increases the chance of identifying a crime's suspect by 14 percent as compared with cases when DNA is not collected.[6] An influx of crime scene evidence also has borne dividends within the United States. A federal grant gave the Detroit Police Department resources to forward significant collections of crime scene evidence to the Michigan State Police for comparison with the existing profiles in its DNA database. Of 171 genetic profiles generated from of the crime scene evidence in those cases, 72 linked to known offenders in the state's databank, for a 43 percent success rate.[7]

The prompt collection and processing of crime scene evidence also will prevent innocent individuals from languishing behind bars, thereby protecting their basic liberties. Delays in DNA analysis can prompt defendants to take unfounded guilty pleas, rather than remain indefinitely in jail. Moreover, the slow turnaround times surely have delayed trials across Maryland.

Two reforms needed to improve Maryland's criminal justice system are to ensure that (1) the processing of actual crime scene DNA evidence takes priority over the processing of offender samples and that (2) additional resources are provided to city and county-funded crime labs to reduce their existing backlogs. Of course, the recent mandated addition of arrestee profiles to Maryland's databases will place additional resource burdens upon crime laboratories, exacerbating a situation that was not fully addressed by the governor's prioritization of backlog reduction at the state level.

Proper Preservation of Biological Evidence

Modern DNA technology, coupled with today's comprehensive information and communications technology, has exponentially increased the power of preserved evidence. Preserved evidence can not only prove (or disprove) claims of innocence in ways unimaginable just a generation ago, but it can also solve old cases. In July of [2008], for instance, cold-case detectives in Montgomery County located a sample of bodily fluids associated with a 1982 murder in their files and subsequent DNA testing identified the culprit and provided long-awaited answers to the victim's family.[8]

As technology improves, even evidence currently viewed as insignificant may have probative value. Unfortunately, though, evidence preservation policies in Maryland have proven insufficient to keep up with technology's promise. Although DNA testing is the gold standard of forensic technology, when properly performed on untainted evidence, efforts to locate that very evidence in Maryland continue to fall short. Just last year, Maryland's highest court held that greater efforts had to be made to find evidence connected to a 1974 murder case, arguing that searching the police department's evidence room was insufficient.[9] City prosecutors and police told the judge in this case that a thorough search for the evidence would require an inventory with a $50,000 price tag.[10]

Those who litigate innocence claims in Baltimore argue that this case is not anomalous, indicating that pre-1990 cases are difficult to track by complaint number. In order to realize the probative value of biological evidence, statewide efforts must be undertaken to assure that old evidence is catalogued and can be located.

Eyewitness Identification Reform

Two of the three DNA exonerations in Maryland were plagued by mistaken eyewitness identifications. Indeed, mistaken eyewitness identifications were a contributing factor in more than 75 percent of the nation's wrongful convictions proven by DNA testing. Despite solid and growing proof of the inaccuracy of traditional eyewitness identification procedures—and the availability of simple measures to reform them—eyewitness identifications obtained through time-honored but flawed protocols remain among the most commonly used and compelling evidence brought against criminal defendants.

Last year, the Maryland legislature passed a law requiring each law enforcement agency in the state to adopt written policies that comply with standards issued by the Department of Justice. Those DOJ standards, established nearly a decade ago, do not include the use of a blind administrator, the single best reform available to minimize the possibility of the lineup administrator from providing inadvertent or intentional verbal or nonverbal cues to influence the eyewitness to pick the suspect.

Despite the rather restrained requirements placed upon law

enforcement agencies across the state, there has been partial compliance at best. Many law enforcement agencies did not—as they were required to by law—file copies of their policies with the Department of State Police. Of those agencies that did comply with the requirement that they submit their policies, not all drafted policies that comply with the moderate standards promulgated by the DOJ.

The Electronic Recording of Custodial Interrogations in All Jurisdictions

Earlier this year, the Maryland legislature passed a criminal procedure law establishing as public policy that certain law enforcement agencies should make reasonable efforts to record custodial interrogations in connection with murder, rape, and certain sexual offense cases. It also called upon the Governor's Office of Crime Control and Prevention (GOCCP) to report on the progress of jurisdictions in establishing interrogation rooms capable of creating audiovisual recordings of custodial interrogations. While $2 million has been committed by GOCCP to this effort over a two-year period, these monies cannot be used for interrogation rooms in Maryland State Police barracks, which investigate all homicide investigations for all the Division of Correction and all outlying jurisdictions. And despite the commitment of funds to this endeavor, many jurisdictions have not been outfitted with interrogation rooms. To date, the Baltimore Police Department does not have a single interrogation room.

Increased Resources for Indigent Defense and Prosecution

The United States and Maryland constitutions assure the provision of counsel for those accused of crimes, regardless of the ability to pay.[11] Despite these constitutional protections, indigent defense remains sorely underfunded across the nation. Because capital cases are such an extraordinary drain on defender resources, given the stakes involved, the presence of a death penalty can force the diversion of resources away from many of the other important, noncapital cases that office handles.

Indeed, it is incumbent upon defender agencies, through thorough investigations, to identify the very causes of wrongful conviction, from faulty forensic testimony to mistaken eyewitness identification.

When defender agencies are forced to make difficult decisions in the face of limited resources, inevitably the administration of justice suffers. A Standing Committee of the American Bar Association on Legal Aid and Indigent Defendants has recommended that each state government establish oversight entities charged with ensuring uniform, quality indigent defense in all criminal proceedings.[12] As well, prosecutorial agencies must also juggle resources in order to prepare for capital cases. In recent years, State's Attorney Patricia Jessamy has asserted that her agency has been "hobbled by lack of funds," pointing to an inability to hire investigators to monitor witnesses.

Maryland should establish a commission charged with identifying the current resource shortfalls for both defense and prosecutorial agencies, in light of representations from both that funding shortages are affecting the delivery of their services.

THE IMPACT OF DNA EVIDENCE IN ASSURING THE FAIRNESS AND ACCURACY OF CAPITAL CASES

The question I have come here to address is the impact of DNA on ensuring fairness and accuracy in capital cases. When it comes to fairness, DNA has no impact on ensuring the death penalty is administered fairly and uniformly. I understand that racial, geographic, and socioeconomic disparities have already been discussed at previous hearings, so I will not discuss them here except to say that if you seek to reduce arbitrariness in the death penalty, DNA cannot help you.

With respect to accuracy, some have proposed the notion that if the death penalty was restricted to only cases where DNA could prove guilt, the risk of executing an innocent person would be eliminated. This is simply untrue. Maryland has experienced its share of crime lab difficulties, which, on its face should demonstrate the potential fallibilities of forensic evidence. Crime lab difficulties aside, we have come to learn that it is the precision of DNA databases that underpins the reliability of DNA evidence. Specifically, questions are being raised— even in very recent headlines—about the probability of a match between a DNA profile, or partial profile, derived from crime scene evidence entered in CODIS (the FBI's national DNA database) and a convicted offender's profile.

A DNA profile is considered complete when it identifies genetic characteristics at various locations, or markers, on the human genome. When a DNA profile derived from crime scene evidence fails to match the DNA profile of a particular individual, even at one marker, this is considered an "exclusion." Exclusions are absolute. Therefore, at the Innocence Project, we are always certain of a petitioner's innocence when a match between his profile and the crime scene evidence cannot be made. On the other hand, inclusions—when a DNA profile derived from crime scene evidence matches the DNA profile of a particular individual—are subject to greater interpretation. There are several reasons for this, not least of which is the possibility of the cross-contamination of samples.

Indeed, a death penalty based upon DNA evidence would actually *increase* the arbitrariness of the death penalty system, as the capital punishment system would be reserved for those who left DNA behind at the crime scene, and not necessarily the "worst of the worst." Is the murder of one person involving a struggle really more death-worthy than someone who shoots ten people from a distance and thus leaves no DNA behind?

CONCLUSION

Public opinion remains ambiguous about the question of whether capital punishment ought to be an available sentencing option, but support for the death penalty, regardless of country or region, is greatest when no other sentencing options are presented to respondents.[13] The same is true for Maryland.[14] Reasonable people, however, can differ as to whether the death penalty is a morally appropriate punishment for the most heinous of murders committed by the worst of the worst offenders.

I also assume that reasonable people agree—and this is a moral question—that since "death is different," an irreversible punishment, all necessary resources must be provided to ensure that every aspect of the capital punishment system—investigation, defense, prosecution, trial, appeal, and postconviction—is as fair and accurate a result as possible.

As the nation's wrongful convictions have revealed, errors can occur at every turn, and it is only DNA testing—when properly performed—that can topple a house of cards built upon just one imperfect element. Since DNA exists in relatively so few cases, an individual's life can hinge on a sloppy report, an inadvertent cue, or the work of an overburdened practitioner. And even though its reach is limited with respect to its ability to shed light on every case, DNA has helped us to expose a range of systemic problems, including:

- Juries relying on incorrect, misleading or partial information;
- Public and private defenders providing ineffective assistance of counsel;
- Crime lab mishandling and contamination of evidence; the falsification of results; the misrepresentation of forensic findings on the stand; and the provision of statistical exaggerations about the results of testing;
- Witnesses misidentifying innocent people as the actual perpetrators;
- Innocent people confessing to crimes that they did not commit;
- Innocent people pleading to crimes they did not commit, particularly when they fear the administration of the death penalty; and
- Unreliable informants acting on the basis of real or perceived incentives.

If steps are taken to address those problems, that will also help to reduce wrongful convictions. But note that I say "reduce" wrongful convictions—because when human beings are involved, you can never completely eliminate them. Can we state with certainty that Maryland's criminal justice system, as currently operated, will always uncover actual innocence in capital cases? Given the range of potential error, even an excellent judicial case review process simply cannot fairly be expected to, without fail, identify every miscarriage of justice.

It is precisely these error-prone areas that require and deserve attention, as well as the dedication of resources. Rather than focusing limited resources on the administration of the death penalty, we should shift our attention and resources to the prevention of wrongful conviction and the implementation of policies that will help us solve more crimes. In doing so, we will meet the dual goal of making our streets safer and enhancing public confidence in the criminal justice system.

With a current death row population of five individuals, Maryland's death penalty system appears, in large part, a symbolic exercise, yet the risk of executing an innocent—particularly in light of proven wrongful convictions associated with heinous crimes—still exists. We have to ask ourselves how much risk is acceptable when a life is at stake and an execution cannot be reversed, particularly when other aspects of the criminal justice system deserving our attention remain unaddressed.

Maryland must recognize and reform the various systemic weaknesses that can cause wrongful convictions—and therefore, wrongful executions. It is only after having implemented those reforms, assessed their effectiveness, and soberly recognized the remaining threat of wrongful conviction presented by systemic and human error, that Maryland can fairly assess whether a capital punishment system should persist. At this time, however, the risk of executing an innocent person is too great, and therefore unacceptable. . . .

ADDENDUM

Chairman Benjamin Civiletti
Maryland Commission on Capital Punishment
Governor's Office of Crime Control and Prevention

Dear Chairman Civiletti and Commission Members:

Thank you again for the opportunity to speak before the Commission on September 5, 2008. I ask that the attached written testimony, along with this letter and supplemental materials—intended to respond to the particular questions raised by your members—be included in the record.

Commissioner Schellenberger asked for documentation of the percentage range I cited where DNA testing will be dispositive of guilt in capital cases. This figure is based upon frequent representations from our nation's leading criminologists. Barry A. J. Fisher, past president of the American Academy of Forensic Sciences, past president of the International Association of Forensic Sciences, past president of the American Society of Crime Laboratory Directors and a past chairman of the American Society of Crime Laboratory Directors–Laboratory

Accreditation Board, recently testified before the California Commission on the Fair Administration of Justice and stated that DNA testing constitutes approximately 5 percent of the work of crime labs. Michael M. Baden, MD, director of the Medicological Investigations Unit of the New York State Police, in testimony before the US Senate Committee on the Judiciary indicated that "in less than 10 percent of murders, the criminal leaves DNA evidence behind." James Christy, director of the Future Explorations Unit of the Department of Defense's Cyber Crime Unit was quoted as saying that "only about 1 percent of criminal cases introduce DNA evidence." Nonetheless, there is no rigorous study I know of that establishes whether there is a higher percentage in capital cases.

While Commissioner Schellenberger agreed in response to my question that no more than half of capital cases likely contain testable biological evidence, I just picked that number for purposes of advancing the discussion. As reflected in my testimony, the 10 percent estimate given by Dr. Baden and the observations of Barry Fisher are consistent with my own experience. So I think it's safe to say that an estimate that 50 percent of homicide cases contain biological evidence susceptible to dispositive, or even very informative DNA testing, would be a substantial overestimate of the actual rate. But even granting such an estimate, the mere presence of biological evidence that might have come from the assailant must be considered in the context of several other factors.

First, the presence of testable biological evidence from a crime scene does not mean that once the evidence is tested, it is always dispositive or material evidence of guilt. For instance, matching DNA-tested fingernail scrapings from a murder victim to a suspect where there is evidence of a struggle, or matching semen to a suspect in a rape murder, is likely to be dispositive of guilt, but matching DNA tests of a hair recovered from a crime scene from a suspect may not, in some cases, be equally powerful proof unless the hair was found in a probative location, such as under a fingernail or in the hand of the victim after a struggle.

Second, despite the fact that DNA is the gold standard of forensic assays, DNA tests are only as good as the humans charged with performing them—an old saw in forensic circles is "DNA testing is, in theory, foolproof but any fool can do it." Evidence from across the nation of cross-contamination, mislabeling of evidence, mistakes, forensic misconduct and other quality assurance problems demonstrates the fallibility of even this most robust of forensic tests. Of course, as I mentioned in my oral testimony, just last month, such a problem occurred in Maryland's backyard when Baltimore City's Crime Lab director of ten years was fired following revelations that employees at the lab had tainted evidence with their own DNA. This is the kind of problem that can lead to false exclusions of guilty parties, and false inclusions of innocents, particularly in situations where there are mixed samples.

Third, and perhaps most importantly, even if half of all capital cases contained testable biological evidence, which could be directly tied to the crime, and that evidence was subjected to reliable DNA testing, it would only provide highly probative evidence about guilt or innocence in half of all capital cases. As I point out in the attached testimony, under a framework in which DNA is used as a sentencing tool, a person who committed a single stabbing where DNA evidence was available for testing would receive the death penalty, while an individual who shot ten men, where there was an absence of biological evidence, would not. In light of this, it is inconceivable to me that this commission would conclude that DNA testing alone could eliminate the risk of error or be the basis for assuring the fairness of the capital punishment system.

Commissioner Campbell asked whether recent advances in forensic technology assure us that the risk of executing an innocent has diminished. Actually, the opposite is true. DNA testing has exposed serious scientific problems in many other forensic disciplines that have not been seriously examined for years. I raised the Cameron Todd Willingham arson murder case during my testimony not because I believe that Marylanders should wrestle with a possible wrongful execution in Texas, but because it is exemplary of an instance where science that was largely thought to be sound was later determined to be unsound. Who's to say that in twenty or thirty years there won't be further advances that reveal our current methods to be based on false assumptions? Science never stops advancing, and there is always the potential for another breakthrough to raise new questions about old methods. Simply because we are only now beginning to understand the scope of issues affecting the quality of forensic results does not mean that we can be assured that the risk of executing a wrong-fully convicted person is now minimized.

Chicago Tribune reporters in 2004 conducted an exhaustive investigation on state-funded crime laboratories and determined that more than a quarter of 200 DNA and death row exonerations since 1986 involved "faulty crime lab work or testimony."[15] After their review of DNA exonerations, professors Michael Saks and Jonathan J. Koehler concluded that 63 percent involved forensic science testing errors and 27 percent involved false or misleading testimony by forensic experts.[16] Professor Samuel Gross and his University of Michigan colleagues examined 340 DNA and non-DNA exonerations, and found that 24 involved forensic scientists who committed perjury.[17] Finally, after studying the first 200 DNA exonerations, University of Virginia Law Professor Brandon Garrett concluded that missteps involving forensic evidence were present in 57 percent of the wrongful convictions.[18]

These findings, combined with the exposure of crime lab scandals and instances of misleading forensic testimony, led Congress to call upon the National Academy of Sciences (NAS) to study the validity of forensic techniques currently in use. I have attached the agendas from each of the seven meetings to provide the Commission with a sense of the breadth and scope of this inquiry. For instance, NAS recently received oral and written submissions from the United States Secret Service, in which that entity calls for a "strategic plan for research and development throughout the forensic disciplines to include statistical studies which are needed to provide stronger scientific foundations in various disciplines."

Indeed, the NAS is investigating a host of forensic disciplines currently employed, ranging from forensic odontology, ballistics, arson, hair microscopy to fingerprints. (And to provide the Commission with a more immediate sense of some of the problems with fingerprints, a traditionally well-regarded forensic discipline, I am including two reports on the Brandon Mayfield case—one from the FBI and the other from the Office of the Inspector General, which I began to describe to you during my oral testimony.) Based upon the testimony provided to date, I am confident that NAS will conclude in its final report that sweeping changes must be made in a great number of disciplines.

Considering the epic scale of the NAS inquiry and history of problems in all forensic disciplines, DNA cannot be looked upon as the silver bullet that lends fairness to a death penalty; DNA is only dispositive of guilt in a small universe of cases. DNA cases can, however, allow us to shed light on issues plaguing the criminal justice system. It is critically important that policymakers closely track these cases, for while DNA is only probative in a fraction of all criminal cases, the practices leading to wrongful convictions are fundamental to the vast majority of criminal investigations. Reforming those practices will help us not only free the innocent, but identify the guilty.

Commissioner Jones specifically asked about one of these necessary reforms, namely, eyewitness identification. Indeed, more than 75 percent of the nation's DNA exonerations contained at least one eyewitness misidentification. To address Commissioner Jones's question, I have included the Innocence Project's model legislation and best model practices, informed by more than twenty-five years of social science research, a resource guide that describes each of the model practices and the specific scientific research that informs them, copies of model practices being employed in other jurisdictions (i.e., New Jersey and Wisconsin), and some information about the laptop computer technology that Maryland might consider employing statewide.

In short, before deciding whether to continue to expend energy and resources on the administration of capital punishment—which cannot eliminate the risk of executing an innocent no matter how much you tinker, narrow, or modify it—Maryland would do well to take stock of serious problems faced by the system and implement the simple and readily available reforms demonstrated to address them, including those highlighted in my submitted testimony.

If there are any questions that I did not address in this letter or my testimony, please feel free to call upon me at any stage in your work.

Sincerely,

Barry C. Scheck
Codirector

PART SIX

CAPITAL PUNISHMENT AND RACISM

27

OF THE COMING OF JOHN

W. E. B. Du Bois

What bring they 'neath the midnight,
Beside the River-sea?
They bring the human heart wherein
No nightly calm can be;
That droppeth never with the wind,
Nor drieth with the dew;
O calm it, God; thy calm is broad
To cover spirits too.
The river floweth on.

—MRS. BROWNING

CARLISLE Street runs westward from the centre of Johnstown, across a great black bridge, down a hill and up again, by little shops and meat-markets, past single-storied homes, until suddenly it stops against a wide green lawn. It is a broad, restful place, with two large buildings outlined against the west. When at evening the winds come swelling from the east, and the great pall of the city's smoke hangs wearily above the valley, then the red west glows like a dreamland down Carlisle Street, and, at the tolling of the supper-bell, throws the passing forms of students in dark silhouette against the sky. Tall and black, they move slowly by, and seem in the sinister light to flit before the city like dim warning ghosts. Perhaps they are; for this is Wells

Institute, and these black students have few dealings with the white city below.

And if you will notice, night after night, there is one dark form that ever hurries last and late toward the twinkling lights of Swain Hall,—for Jones is never on time. A long, straggling fellow he is, brown and hard-haired, who seems to be growing straight out of his clothes, and walks with a half-apologetic roll. He used perpetually to set the quiet dining-room into waves of merriment, as he stole to his place after the bell had tapped for prayers; he seemed so perfectly awkward. And yet one glance at his face made one forgive him much,—that broad, good-natured smile in which lay no bit of art or artifice, but seemed just bubbling good-nature and genuine satisfaction with the world.

He came to us from Altamaha, away down there beneath the gnarled oaks of Southeastern Georgia, where the sea croons to the sands and the sands listen till they sink half drowned beneath the waters, rising only here and there in long, low islands. The white folk of Altamaha voted John a good boy,—fine plough-hand, good in the rice-fields, handy everywhere, and always good-natured and respectful. But they shook their heads when his mother wanted to send him off to school. "It'll spoil him,—ruin him," they said; and they talked as though they knew. But full half the black folk followed him proudly to the station, and carried his queer little trunk and many bundles. And there they shook and shook hands, and the girls kissed him shyly and the boys clapped him on the back. So the train came, and he pinched his little sister lovingly, and put his great arms about his mother's neck, and then was away with a puff and a roar into the great yellow world that flamed and flared about the doubtful pilgrim. Up the coast they hurried, past the squares and palmettos of Savannah, through the cotton-fields and through the weary night, to Millville, and came with the morning to the noise and bustle of Johnstown.

And they that stood behind, that morning in Altamaha, and watched the train as it noisily bore playmate and brother and son away to the world, had thereafter one ever-recurring word,—"When John comes." Then what parties were to be, and what speakings in the churches; what new furniture in the front room,—perhaps even a new front room; and there would be a new schoolhouse, with John as teacher; and then perhaps a big wedding; all this and more—when John comes. But the white people shook their heads.

At first he was coming at Christmas-time,—but the vacation proved too short; and then, the next summer,—but times were hard and schooling costly, and so, instead, he worked in Johnstown. And so it drifted to the next summer, and the next,—till playmates scattered, and mother grew gray, and sister went up to the Judge's kitchen to work. And still the legend lingered,—"When John comes."

Up at the Judge's they rather liked this refrain; for they too had a John—a fair-haired, smooth-faced boy, who had played many a long summer's day to its close with his darker namesake. "Yes, sir! John is at Princeton, sir," said the broad-shouldered gray-haired Judge every morning as he marched down to the post-office. "Showing the Yankees what a Southern gentleman can do," he added; and strode home again with his letters and papers. Up at the great pillared house they lingered long over the Princeton letter,—the Judge and his frail wife, his sister and growing daughters. "It'll make a man of him," said the Judge, "college is the place." And then he asked the shy little waitress, "Well, Jennie, how's your John?" and added reflectively, "Too bad, too bad your mother sent him off,—it will spoil him." And the waitress wondered.

Thus in the far-away Southern village the world lay waiting, half consciously, the coming of two young men, and dreamed in an inarticulate way of new things that would be done and new thoughts that all would think. And yet it was singular that few thought of two Johns,— for the black folk thought of one John, and he was black; and the white folk thought of another John, and he was white. And neither world thought the other world's thought, save with a vague unrest.

Up in Johnstown, at the Institute, we were long puzzled at the case of John Jones. For a long time the clay seemed unfit for any sort of moulding. He was loud and boisterous, always laughing and singing, and never able to work consecutively at anything. He did not know how to study; he had no idea of thoroughness; and with his tardiness, carelessness, and appalling good-humor, we were sore perplexed. One night we sat in faculty-meeting, worried and serious; for Jones was in trouble again. This last escapade was too much, and so we solemnly voted "that Jones, on account of repeated disorder and inattention to work, be suspended for the rest of the term."

It seemed to us that the first time life ever struck Jones as a really serious thing was when the Dean told him he must leave school. He stared at the gray-haired man blankly, with great eyes. "Why,—why," he faltered, "but—I haven't graduated!" Then the Dean slowly and clearly explained, reminding him of the tardiness and the carelessness, of the poor lessons and neglected work, of the noise and disorder, until the fellow hung his head in confusion. Then he said quickly, "But you won't tell mammy and sister,—you won't write mammy, now will you? For if you won't I'll go out into the city and work, and come back next term and show you something." So the Dean promised faithfully, and John shouldered his little trunk, giving neither word nor look to the giggling boys, and walked down Carlisle Street to the great city, with sober eyes and a set and serious face.

Perhaps we imagined it, but someway it seemed to us that the serious look that crept over his boyish face that afternoon never left it again. When he came back to us he went to work with all his rugged strength. It was a hard struggle, for things did not come easily to him,—few crowding memories of early life and teaching came to help him on his new way; but all the world toward which he strove was of his own building, and he builded slow and hard. As the light dawned lingeringly on his new creations, he sat rapt and silent before the vision, or wandered alone over the green campus peering through and beyond the world of men into a world of thought. And the thoughts at times puzzled him sorely; he could not see just why the circle was not square, and carried it out fifty-six decimal places one midnight,—would have gone further, indeed, had not the matron rapped for lights out. He caught terrible colds lying on his back in the meadows of nights, trying to think out the solar system; he had grave doubts as to the ethics of the Fall of Rome, and strongly suspected the Germans of being thieves and rascals, despite his text-books; he pondered long over every new Greek word, and wondered why this meant that and why it couldn't mean something else, and how it must have felt to think all things in Greek. So he thought and puzzled along for himself,—pausing perplexed where others skipped merrily, and walking steadily through the difficulties where the rest stopped and surrendered.

Thus he grew in body and soul, and with him his clothes seemed to grow and arrange themselves; coat sleeves got longer, cuffs appeared, and collars got less soiled. Now and then his boots shone, and a new dignity crept into his walk. And we who saw daily a new thoughtfulness growing in his eyes began to expect something of this plodding boy. Thus he passed out of the preparatory school into college, and we who watched him felt four more years of change, which almost transformed the tall, grave man who bowed to us commencement morning. He had left his queer thought-world and come back to a world of motion and of men. He looked now for the first time sharply about him, and wondered he had seen so little before. He grew slowly to feel almost for the first time the Veil that lay between him and the white world; he first noticed now the oppression that had not seemed oppression before, differences that erstwhile seemed natural, restraints and slights that in his boyhood days had gone unnoticed or been greeted with a laugh. He felt angry now when men did not call him "Mister," he clenched his hands at the "Jim Crow" cars, and chafed at the color-line that hemmed in him and his. A tinge of sarcasm crept into his speech, and a vague bitterness into his life; and he sat long hours wondering and planning a way around these crooked things. Daily he found himself shrinking from the choked and narrow life of his native town. And yet he always planned to go back to Altamaha,—always planned to work there. Still, more and more as the day approached he hesitated with a nameless dread; and even the day after graduation he seized with eagerness the offer of the Dean to send him North with the quartette during the summer vacation, to sing for the Institute. A breath of air before the plunge, he said to himself in half apology.

It was a bright September afternoon, and the streets of New York were brilliant with moving men. They reminded John of the sea, as he sat in the square and watched them, so changelessly changing, so bright and dark, so grave and gay. He scanned their rich and faultless clothes, the way they carried their hands, the shape of their hats; he peered into the hurrying carriages. Then, leaning back with a sigh, he said, "This is the World." The notion suddenly seized him to see where the world was going; since many of the richer and brighter seemed hurrying all one way. So when a tall, light-haired young man and a little talkative lady came by, he rose half hesitatingly and followed them. Up the street they went, past stores and gay shops, across a broad square, until with a hundred others they entered the high portal of a great building.

He was pushed toward the ticket-office with the others, and felt in his pocket for the new five-dollar bill he had hoarded. There seemed really no time for hesitation, so he drew it bravely out, passed it to the busy clerk, and received simply a ticket but no change. When at last he realized that he had paid five dollars to enter he knew not what, he stood stock-still amazed. "Be careful," said a low voice behind him; "you must not lynch the colored gentleman simply because he's in your way," and a girl looked up roguishly into the eyes of her fair-haired escort. A shade of annoyance passed over the escort's face. "You *will* not understand us at the South," he said half impatiently, as if continuing an argument. "With all your professions, one never sees in the North so cordial and intimate relations between white and black as are everyday occurrences with us. Why, I remember my closest playfellow in boyhood was a little Negro named after me, and surely no two,—*well!*" The man stopped short and flushed to the roots of his hair, for there directly beside his reserved orchestra chairs sat the Negro he had stumbled over in the hallway. He hesitated and grew pale with anger, called the usher and gave him his card, with a few peremptory words, and slowly sat down. The lady deftly changed the subject.

All this John did not see, for he sat in a half-maze minding the scene about him; the delicate beauty of the hall, the faint perfume, the moving myriad of men, the rich clothing and low hum of talking seemed all a part of a world so different from his, so strangely more beautiful than anything he had known, that he sat in dreamland, and started when, after a hush, rose high and clear the music of Lohengrin's swan. The infinite beauty of the wail lingered and swept through every muscle of his frame, and put it all a-tune. He closed his eyes and grasped the elbows of the chair, touching unwittingly the lady's arm. And the lady drew away. A deep longing swelled in all his heart to rise with that clear music out of the dirt and dust of that low life that held him prisoned and befouled. If he could only live up in the free air where birds sang and setting suns had no touch of blood! Who had called him to be the slave and butt of all? And if he had called, what right had he to call when a world like this lay open before men?

Then the movement changed, and fuller, mightier harmony swelled away. He looked thoughtfully across the hall, and wondered why the beautiful gray-haired woman looked so listless, and what the little man could be whispering about. He would not like to be listless and idle, he thought, for he felt with the music the movement of power within him. If he but had some master-work, some life-service, hard,—aye, bitter hard, but without the cringing and sickening servility, without the cruel hurt that hardened his heart and soul. When at last a soft sorrow crept across the violins, there came to him the vision of a far-off home,—the great eyes of his sister, and the dark drawn face of his mother. And his heart sank below the waters, even as the sea-sand sinks by the shores of Altamaha, only to be lifted aloft again with that last ethereal wail of the swan that quivered and faded away into the sky.

It left John sitting so silent and rapt that he did not for some time notice the usher tapping him lightly on the shoulder and saying politely, "Will you step this way, please, sir?" A little surprised, he arose quickly at the last tap, and, turning to leave his seat, looked full into the face of the fair-haired young man. For the first time the young man recognized his dark boyhood playmate, and John knew that it was the Judge's son. The white John started, lifted his hand, and then froze into his chair; the black John smiled lightly, then grimly, and followed the usher down the aisle. The manager was sorry, very, very sorry,—but he explained that some mistake had been made in selling the gentleman a seat already disposed of; he would refund the money, of course,—and indeed felt the matter keenly, and so forth, and—before he had finished John was gone, walking hurriedly across the square and down the broad streets, and as he passed the park he buttoned his coat and said, "John Jones, you're a natural-born fool." Then he went to his lodgings and wrote a letter, and tore it up; he wrote another, and threw it in the fire. Then he seized a scrap of paper and wrote: "Dear Mother and Sister—I am coming—John."

"Perhaps," said John, as he settled himself on the train, "perhaps I am to blame myself in struggling against my manifest destiny simply because it looks hard and unpleasant. Here is my duty to Altamaha plain before me; perhaps they'll let me help settle the Negro problems there,—perhaps they won't. 'I will go in to the King, which is not according to the law; and if I perish, I perish.'" And then he mused and dreamed, and planned a life-work; and the train flew south.

Down in Altamaha, after seven long years, all the world knew John was coming. The homes were scrubbed and scoured,—above all, one; the gardens and yards had an unwonted trimness, and Jennie bought a new gingham. With some finesse and negotiation, all the dark Methodists and Presbyterians were induced to join in a monster welcome at the Baptist Church; and as the day drew near, warm discussions arose on every corner as to the exact extent and nature of John's accomplishments. It was noontide on a gray and cloudy day when he came. The black town flocked to the depot, with a little of the white at the edges,—a happy throng, with "Good-mawnings" and "Howdys" and laughing and joking and jostling. Mother sat yonder in the window watching; but sister Jennie stood on the platform, nervously fingering her dress,—tall and lithe, with soft brown skin and loving eyes peering from out a tangled wilderness of hair. John rose gloomily as the train stopped, for he was thinking of the "Jim Crow" car; he stepped to the platform, and paused: a little dingy station, a black crowd gaudy and dirty, a half-mile of dilapidated shanties along a straggling ditch of mud. An overwhelming sense of the sordidness and narrowness of it all seized him; he looked in vain for his mother, kissed coldly the tall, strange girl who called him brother, spoke a short, dry word here and there; then, lingering neither for handshaking nor gossip, started silently up the street, raising his hat merely to the last eager old aunty, to her open-mouthed astonishment. The people were distinctly bewildered. This silent, cold man,—was this John? Where was his smile and hearty hand-grasp? "Peared kind o' down in the mouf," said the Methodist preacher thoughtfully. "Seemed monstus stuck up," complained a Baptist sister. But the white postmaster from the edge of the crowd expressed the opinion of his folks plainly. "That damn Nigger," said he, as he shouldered the mail and arranged his tobacco, "has gone North and got plum full o' fool notions; but they won't work in Altamaha." And the crowd melted away.

The meeting of welcome at the Baptist Church was a failure. Rain spoiled the barbecue, and thunder turned the milk in the ice-cream. When the speaking came at night, the house was crowded to overflowing. The three preachers had especially prepared themselves, but somehow John's manner seemed to throw a blanket over everything,—he seemed so cold and preoccupied, and had so strange an air of restraint that the Methodist brother could not warm up to his theme and elicited not a single "Amen"; the Presbyterian prayer was but feebly responded to, and even the Baptist preacher, though he wakened faint enthusiasm, got so mixed up in his favorite sentence that he had to close it by stopping fully fifteen minutes sooner than he meant. The people moved uneasily in their seats as John rose to reply. He spoke slowly and methodically. The age, he said, demanded new ideas; we were far different from those men of the seventeenth and eighteenth centuries,—with broader ideas of human brotherhood and destiny. Then he spoke of the rise of charity and popular education, and particularly of the spread of wealth and work. The question was, then, he added reflectively, looking at the low discolored ceiling, what part the Negroes of this land would take in the striving of the new century. He sketched in vague outline the new Industrial School that might rise among these pines, he spoke in detail of the charitable and philanthropic work that might be organized, of money that might be saved for banks and business. Finally he urged unity, and deprecated especially religious and denominational bickering. "To-day," he said, with a smile, "the world cares little whether a man be Baptist or Methodist, or indeed a churchman at all, so long as he is good and true. What difference does it make whether a man be baptized in river or wash-bowl, or not at all? Let's leave all that littleness, and look higher." Then, thinking of nothing else, he slowly sat down. A painful hush seized that crowded mass. Little had they understood of what he said, for he spoke an unknown tongue, save the last word about baptism; that they knew, and they sat very still while the clock ticked. Then at last a low suppressed snarl came from the Amen corner, and an old bent man arose, walked over the seats, and climbed straight up into the pulpit. He was wrinkled and black, with scant gray and tufted hair; his voice and hands shook as with palsy; but on his face lay the intense rapt look of the religious fanatic. He seized the Bible with his rough, huge hands; twice he raised it inarticulate, and then fairly burst into the words, with rude and awful eloquence. He quivered, swayed, and bent; then rose aloft in perfect majesty, till the people moaned and wept, wailed and shouted, and a wild shrieking arose from the corners where all the pent-up feeling of the hour gathered itself and rushed into the air. John never knew clearly what the old man said; he only felt himself held up to scorn and scathing denunciation for trampling on the true Religion, and he realized with amazement that all unknowingly he had put rough, rude hands on something this little world held sacred. He arose silently, and passed out into the night. Down toward the sea he went, in the fitful starlight, half conscious of the girl who followed timidly after him. When at last he stood upon the bluff, he turned to his little sister and looked upon her sorrowfully, remembering with sudden pain how little thought he had given her. He put his arm about her and let her passion of tears spend itself on his shoulder.

Long they stood together, peering over the gray unresting water.

"John," she said, "does it make every one—unhappy when they study and learn lots of things?"

He paused and smiled. "I am afraid it does," he said.

"And, John, are you glad you studied?"

"Yes," came the answer, slowly but positively.

She watched the flickering lights upon the sea, and said thoughtfully, "I wish I was unhappy,—and—and," putting both arms about his neck, "I think I am, a little, John."

It was several days later that John walked up to the Judge's house to ask for the privilege of teaching the Negro school. The Judge himself met him at the front door, stared a little hard at him, and said brusquely, "Go 'round to the kitchen door, John, and wait." Sitting on the kitchen steps, John stared at the corn, thoroughly perplexed. What on earth had come over him? Every step he made offended some one. He had come to save his people, and before he left the depot he had hurt them. He sought to teach them at the church, and had outraged their deepest feelings. He had schooled himself to be respectful to the Judge, and then blundered into his front door. And all the time he had meant right,—and yet, and yet, somehow he found it so hard and strange to fit his old surroundings again, to find his place in the world about him. He could not remember that he used to have any difficulty in the past, when life was glad and gay. The world seemed smooth and easy then. Perhaps,—but his sister came to the kitchen door just then and said the Judge awaited him.

The Judge sat in the dining-room amid his morning's mail, and he did not ask John to sit down. He plunged squarely into the business. "You've come for the school, I suppose. Well, John, I want to speak to you plainly. You know I'm a friend to your people. I've helped you and your family, and would have done more if you hadn't got the notion of going off. Now I like the colored people, and sympathize with all their reasonable aspirations; but you and I both know, John, that in this country the Negro must remain subordinate, and can never expect to be the equal of white men. In their place, your people can be honest and respectful; and God knows, I'll do what I can to help them. But when they want to reverse nature, and rule white men, and marry white women, and sit in my parlor, then, by God! we'll hold them under if we have to lynch every Nigger in the land. Now, John, the question is, are you, with your education and Northern notions, going to accept the situation and teach the darkies to be faithful servants and laborers as your fathers were,—I knew your father, John, he belonged to my brother, and he was a good Nigger. Well—well, are you going to be like him, or are you going to try to put fool ideas of rising and equality into these folks' heads, and make them discontented and unhappy?"

"I am going to accept the situation, Judge Henderson," answered John, with a brevity that did not escape the keen old man. He hesitated a moment, and then said shortly, "Very well,—we'll try you awhile. Good-morning."

It was a full month after the opening of the Negro school that the other John came home, tall, gay, and headstrong. The mother wept, the sisters sang. The whole white town was glad. A proud man was the Judge, and it was a goodly sight to see the two swinging down Main Street together. And yet all did not go smoothly between them, for the younger man could not and did not veil his contempt for the little town, and plainly had his heart set on New York. Now the one cherished ambition of the Judge was to see his son mayor of Altamaha, representative to the legislature, and—who could say?— governor of Georgia. So the argument often waxed hot between them. "Good heavens, father," the younger man would say after dinner, as he lighted a cigar and stood by the fireplace, "you surely don't expect a young fellow like me to settle down permanently in this—this God-forgotten town with nothing but mud and Negroes?" "I did," the Judge would answer laconically; and on this particular day it seemed from the gathering scowl that he was about to add something more emphatic, but neighbors had already begun to drop in to admire his son, and the conversation drifted.

"Heah that John is livenin' things up at the darky school," volunteered the postmaster, after a pause.

"What now?" asked the Judge, sharply.

"Oh, nothin' in particulah,—just his almighty air and uppish ways.

B'lieve I did heah somethin' about his givin' talks on the French Revolution, equality, and such like. He's what I call a dangerous Nigger."

"Have you heard him say anything out of the way?"

"Why, no,—but Sally, our girl, told my wife a lot of rot. Then,
too, I don't need to heah: a Nigger what won't say 'sir' to a white
man, or—"

"Who is this John?" interrupted the son.

"Why, it's little black John, Peggy's son,—your old playfellow."

The young man's face flushed angrily, and then he laughed.

"Oh," said he, "it's the darky that tried to force himself into a seat
beside the lady I was escorting—"

But Judge Henderson waited to hear no more. He had been net-
tled all day, and now at this he rose with a half-smothered oath, took
his hat and cane, and walked straight to the schoolhouse.

For John, it had been a long, hard pull to get things started in the
rickety old shanty that sheltered his school. The Negroes were rent
into factions for and against him, the parents were careless, the children irregular and dirty, and books, pencils, and slates largely missing.
Nevertheless, he struggled hopefully on, and seemed to see at last
some glimmering of dawn. The attendance was larger and the children were a shade cleaner this week. Even the booby class in reading
showed a little comforting progress. So John settled himself with
renewed patience this afternoon.

"Now, Mandy," he said cheerfully, "that's better; but you mustn't
chop your words up so: 'If—the—man—goes.' Why, your little
brother even wouldn't tell a story that way, now would he?"

"Naw, suh, he cain't talk."

"All right; now let's try again: 'If the man—'"

"John!"

The whole school started in surprise, and the teacher half arose,
as the red, angry face of the Judge appeared in the open doorway.

"John, this school is closed. You children can go home and get to
work. The white people of Altamaha are not spending their money on
black folks to have their heads crammed with impudence and lies.
Clear out! I'll lock the door myself."

Up at the great pillared house the tall young son wandered aim-
lessly about after his father's abrupt departure. In the house there was
little to interest him; the books were old and stale, the local news-

paper flat, and the women had retired with headaches and sewing. He tried a nap, but it was too warm. So he sauntered out into the fields, complaining disconsolately, "Good Lord! how long will this imprisonment last!" He was not a bad fellow,—just a little spoiled and self-indulgent, and as headstrong as his proud father. He seemed a young man pleasant to look upon, as he sat on the great black stump at the edge of the pines idly swinging his legs and smoking. "Why, there isn't even a girl worth getting up a respectable flirtation with," he growled. Just then his eye caught a tall, willowy figure hurrying toward him on the narrow path. He looked with interest at first, and then burst into a laugh as he said, "Well, I declare, if it isn't Jennie, the little brown kitchen-maid! Why, I never noticed before what a trim little body she is. Hello, Jennie! Why, you haven't kissed me since I came home," he said gaily. The young girl stared at him in surprise and confusion,— faltered something inarticulate, and attempted to pass. But a willful mood had seized the young idler, and he caught at her arm. Frightened, she slipped by; and half mischievously he turned and ran after her through the tall pines.

Yonder, toward the sea, at the end of the path, came John slowly, with his head down. He had turned wearily homeward from the schoolhouse; then, thinking to shield his mother from the blow, started to meet his sister as she came from work and break the news of his dismissal to her. "I'll go away," he said slowly; "I'll go away and find work, and send for them. I cannot live here longer." And then the fierce, buried anger surged up into his throat. He waved his arms and hurried wildly up the path.

The great brown sea lay silent. The air scarce breathed. The dying day bathed the twisted oaks and mighty pines in black and gold. There came from the wind no warning, not a whisper from the cloudless sky. There was only a black man hurrying on with an ache in his heart, seeing neither sun nor sea, but starting as from a dream at the frightened cry that woke the pines, to see his dark sister struggling in the arms of a tall and fair-haired man.

He said not a word, but, seizing a fallen limb, struck him with all the pent-up hatred of his great black arm; and the body lay white and still beneath the pines, all bathed in sunshine and in blood. John looked at it dreamily, then walked back to the house briskly, and said in a soft voice, "Mammy, I'm going away,—I'm going to be free."

She gazed at him dimly and faltered, "No'th, honey, is yo' gwine No'th agin?"

He looked out where the North Star glistened pale above the waters, and said, "Yes, mammy, I'm going—North."

Then, without another word, he went out into the narrow lane, up by the straight pines, to the same winding path, and seated himself on the great black stump, looking at the blood where the body had lain. Yonder in the gray past he had played with that dead boy, romping together under the solemn trees. The night deepened; he thought of the boys at Johnstown. He wondered how Brown had turned out, and Carey? And Jones,—Jones? Why, *he* was Jones, and he wondered what they would all say when they knew, when they knew, in that great long dining-room with its hundreds of merry eyes. Then as the sheen of the starlight stole over him, he thought of the gilded ceiling of that vast concert hall, and heard stealing toward him the faint sweet music of the swan. Hark! was it music, or the hurry and shouting of men? Yes, surely! Clear and high the faint sweet melody rose and fluttered like a living thing, so that the very earth trembled as with the tramp of horses and murmur of angry men.

He leaned back and smiled toward the sea, whence rose the strange melody, away from the dark shadows where lay the noise of horses galloping, galloping on. With an effort he roused himself, bent forward, and looked steadily down the pathway, softly humming the "Song of the Bride,"—

"Freudig geführt, ziehet dahin."

Amid the trees in the dim morning twilight he watched their shadows dancing and heard their horses thundering toward him, until at last they came sweeping like a storm, and he saw in front that haggard white-haired man, whose eyes flashed red with fury. Oh, how he pitied him,—pitied him,—and wondered if he had the coiling twisted rope. Then, as the storm burst round him, he rose slowly to his feet and turned his closed eyes toward the Sea.

And the world whistled in his ears.

28

THE PERSISTENT PROBLEM OF RACIAL DISPARITIES IN THE FEDERAL DEATH PENALTY

A Report of the American Civil Liberties Union

INTRODUCTION

In 1991, in the first federal death penalty prosecution post-*Furman*,[1] the federal government obtained a death sentence against David Ronald Chandler. Although Chandler's death sentence ultimately was commuted, apparently because of serious questions about his guilt,[2] the government has proceeded with federal death prosecutions at an ever-accelerating pace.[3] This paper details the profoundly troubling evidence that racial disparities continue to plague the modern federal death penalty. Of the next six federal inmates scheduled for execution, all are African American defendants. [Editors' note: as of publication, none of these individuals has been executed.] Defendants of color make up the majority of federal death row and the majority of modern federal executions. Furthermore, modern attorneys general seek the death penalty at far higher rates if the victim is white, and white federal defendants are far more likely to have their death charges reduced to life sentences through plea-bargaining. Given this evidence, Congress should take four steps: (1) implement an immediate moratorium on federal executions and prosecutions; (2) fund a thorough study of the federal death penalty and its racial disparities; (3) enact a federal Racial Justice Act permitting capital defendants to use statistical evidence as proof of racial bias; and (4) enact legislation requiring the Department of Justice to provide regularly information about implementation of the federal death penalty, including statistical data about the race of victims and defendants in cases submitted and recommended for capital prosecutions.

THE EVIDENCE

1. *All six of the next scheduled federal executions*
   are African American inmates.

Six African American federal death row inmates—Richard Tipton, Cory Johnson, James H. Roane Jr., Bruce Webster, Orlando Hall, and Anthony Battle—all face impending execution. Three defendants, Richard Tipton, Cory Johnson, and James H. Roane Jr., were sentenced to death in February 1993 in Richmond, Virginia. Their executions were scheduled in May 2006, but the executions have been stayed because of litigation challenging the constitutionality of the government's lethal injection protocol.[4] Bruce Webster was sentenced to death in November 1995 in Fort Worth, Texas. His execution date was scheduled for April 16, 2007, but it is currently stayed.[5] Orlando Hall was sentenced to death in June 1996, also in Forth Worth, Texas. Anthony Battle was sentenced to death in March 1997 in Atlanta, Georgia. Scheduling of execution dates for Hall and Battle are also stayed pending the lethal injection litigation.[6]

2. *Two of the three men executed in the modern federal*
   death penalty era were men of color.

The United States federal government has executed three individuals since 1976: Timothy McVeigh, a white defendant executed in 2001; Juan Garza, a Latino defendant executed in 2001; and Louis Jones, an African American defendant executed in 2003.[7]

3. *The death penalty has been reduced to life sentences through*
   plea bargains for white defendants at almost twice the rate
   as for defendants of color.

A 2000 US Department of Justice study of the federal death penalty found that a far greater percentage of white defendants were able to avoid the death penalty through plea bargains than black defendants or Hispanic defendants.[8] According to the study, 48 percent of white defendants received a sentence less than death through plea bargains while only 25 percent of black defendants and 28 percent of Hispanic defendants pled to life sentences. Rory Little, a former federal prosecutor and member of the Department of Justice Capital Case Review Committee,[9] attributed these "racially disparate capital punishment statistics" to the exercise of federal prosecutorial discretion and "the exercise of leniency."[10]

A follow-up report in 2001 by the Department of Justice nonetheless asserted that it is "unwarranted" to suspect racial discrimination played a role in generating these sharp racial disparities in plea-bargaining because "it takes two to make a plea agreement."[11] The clear implication of this statement is that black and Hispanic defendants have rejected plea offers at a greater rate than white defendants. The Department of Justice, however, did not come forth with any evidence in either its initial 2000 report or its follow-up 2001 report showing that black and Hispanic defendants have been offered life pleas at the same rate as white defendants, but have rejected them at a greater rate.[12] Thus, there is no reason to believe that the "racially disparate capital punishment statistics" regarding plea bargains is the result of black and Hispanic defendants rejecting plea bargains at a greater rate than white defendants.

4. *US attorneys general have been far more likely to seek the death penalty in cases involving white victims, and the problem is getting worse.*

Like the overwhelming majority of state death penalty systems,[13] there is strong evidence that the federal death penalty discriminates on the basis of the race of the victim, with the US Attorney General far more likely to seek a death sentence in white victim cases than in cases with victims of color. Federal regulations require that United States Attorneys submit for the attorney general's review all cases indicted for federal crimes that could qualify for the federal death penalty.[14] The attorney general then authorizes[15] death penalty prosecutions in cases from this group of death-eligible cases.[16] Data about authorization rates is available for Attorneys General Reno, Ashcroft, and Gonzales. Each was substantially more likely to seek the death penalty in white victim cases, defined as a case with one or more white victims.[17]

Attorney General Reno authorized the death penalty in one out of every five cases if no victim was white, but she authorized the death penalty in more than one out of every three cases if at least one victim was white.[18] In other words, a federal defendant's odds of facing the death penalty went from one out of five to one out of three if a victim was white.[19] Attorney General Ashcroft also authorized the death penalty in a greater percentage of cases with white victims than victims of color. He authorized the Department of Justice to seek the death penalty in roughly the same proportions as Attorney General Reno.[20]

The statistics from Attorney General Gonzales are even more troubling. To date, he has authorized the death penalty in only one out of every six cases with no white victim, but almost one out of every two cases with a white victim.[21]

Across all three attorneys general, the AG death penalty seek rate was 35 percent (146/416) in white victim cases, compared with 19 percent (212/1090) in all other cases.[22] This represents a statistically significant 16-percentage point disparity between the two rates. It means that the risk of a death penalty authorization is 1.8 times higher (35/19) in white victim cases than in other cases. It also means that the risk of a death penalty authorization is 84 percent higher (16/19) in white victim cases than in other cases.

By continuing to authorize the death penalty disproportionately for cases with white victims, the federal government is sending the intolerable message that it values the life of a white person more than the life of a person of color.

5. *The majority of defendants sentenced to death in the modern era of the federal death penalty are persons of color.*

As noted above, fifty-four individuals[23] have been sentenced to death in the modern federal death penalty era: of these, thirty-three defendants—more than half[24]—are persons of color. Twenty-seven African American defendants, twenty-one white defendants, five Latino defendants and one Native American defendant have been sentenced to death under the federal death penalty laws.[25] These percentages reflect larger disparities than those observed on many state death rows.[26] Furthermore, the disparities also represent a significant shift from the pre-*Furman* death penalty era. Before Furman, the federal government executed thirty-four individuals between August 17, 1927, and March 15, 1963.[27] Of those executed, twenty-eight were white, two were Native American and three were African American.[28] While these disparities alone do not prove bias in the federal system, they raise serious questions about it.

RECOMMENDATIONS

This evidence of racial disparities in the implementation of the federal death penalty fundamentally challenges its legitimacy and requires immediate action. First, Congress should implement a moratorium on federal death penalty prosecutions and executions. A moratorium is necessary until it is clear that the federal death penalty can be implemented without racial bias.

Second, Congress should fund a federal study to examine racial disparities and the implementation of the federal death penalty. The study should examine, among other issues, why cases are selected for the death penalty and why cases are selected for federal prosecution instead of state prosecution.[29]

Third, Congress should enact a federal Racial Justice Act, similar to the statute adopted by the state of Kentucky.[30] This legislation would allow capital defendants to use statistical evidence as proof of racial bias.[31] Under current federal law, although an employee can use statistical evidence in civil rights litigation as evidence of discrimination, a capital defendant cannot challenge his capital charge, conviction or death sentence with persuasive statistical proof of racial bias.[32] The Racial Justice Act is necessary to ensure that the question of life or death for federal defendants does not turn on the race of the defendant or the victim.

Fourth, Congress should enact reporting legislation that would require the Department of Justice to provide annually information about the implementation of the federal death penalty. This information should include statistical data relevant to studying racial disparities, including: (1) for each United States Attorney's office, the number of homicide cases reviewed by the office, broken down by race of defendant and race of victim, the number of cases indicted with capital-eligible crimes by race of defendant and race of victim, and the number of cases submitted to the Attorney General's Review Committee on Capital Cases by race of defendant and race of victim; (2) information about cases approved and rejected by the attorney general for capital prosecution, broken down by race of defendant and race of victim; and (3) information about plea bargaining, including the numbers of plea offers extended and entered, by race of defendant and race of victim. The reporting legislation should also require the Department of Justice to provide financial information, including the cost of prosecuting federal capital and non-capital homicide cases. Transparency about the implementation of the federal death penalty is a critical step toward ensuring that the death penalty is not administered in an arbitrary or discriminatory manner.

APPENDIX A

All Federal Defendants Sentenced to Death in the Modern Death Penalty Era (Post-*Furman*)

Last Name	First Name	D-Race	Year	Executed
Agofsky	Shannon	W	2004	
Allen	Billie	B	1998	
Barrett	Kenneth	W	2005	
Basham	Branden	W	2004	
Battle	Anthony	B	1997	
Bernard	Brandon	B	2000	
Bolden	Robert	B	2006	
Bourgeois	Alfred	B	2004	
Brown	Meier	B	2003	
Caro	Carlos	L	2007	
Corley	Odell	B	2004	
Davis	Len	B	1996	
Fell	Donald	W	2005	

Fields	Edward	W	2005	
Fields	Sherman	B	2001	
Fulks	Chadrick	W	2004	
Gabrion	Marvin	W	2002	
Garza	Juan	L	1993	Y (2001)
Hall	Orlando	B	1995	
Hammer	David	W	1998	
Hardy	Paul	B	1996	
Higgs	Dustin	B	2000	
Holder	Norris	B	1998	
Honken	Dustin	W	2004	
Jackson	David	B	2006	
Jackson	Richard	W	2001	
Johnson	Angela	W	2004	
Johnson	Cory	B	1993	
Johnson	Darryl	B	1997	
Jones	Louis	B	1995	Y (2003)
Kadamovas	Jurijus	W	2007	
Lawrence	Daryl	B	2006	
LeCroy	William	W	2001	
Lee	Daniel	W	1999	
Lighty	Kenneth	B	2005	
McVeigh	Timothy	W	1997	Y (2001)
Mikhel	Iouri	W	2007	
Mikos	Ronald	W	2005	
Mitchell	Lezmond	N	2003	
Nelson	Keith	W	2001	
Ortiz	Arboleda	L	2000	
Paul	Jeffrey	W	1997	
Purkey	Wesley	W	1998	
Roane	James	B	1993	
Robinson	Julius	B	2002	
Rodriguez	Alfonso	L	2006	
Sampson	Gary	W	2003	
Sinisterra	German	L	2000	
Stitt	Richard	B	1998	
Tipton	Richard	B	1993	
Vialva	Christopher	B	2000	

Webster	Bruce	B	1996
Wilson	Ronell	B	2007

Total 54, white 21, black 27, Asian 0, Native American 1, Latino 5

Resentenced/Commuted to Life Sentence

Last Name	First Name	D-Race	Year
Chandler	David	W	1991
Chanthadara	Boutaem	A	1995
McCullah	John	W	1993

APPENDIX B

Seek Rates by Attorney General and Race of the Victim

	Considered (N)	Authorized (N)	Seek Rates	Seek Rate Difference
Janet Reno (1995–2000)[33]				
All Cases	600	149	24.83%	
Cases ≥1 white victim	185	66	35.68%	15.68%
Cases with no white victim	415	83	20.00%	
John Ashcroft (2001–2005)[34]				
All Cases	623	138	22.15%	
Cases ≥1 white victim	164	52	31.71%	12.97%
Cases with no white victim	458	86	18.74%	
Alberto Gonzales (2005–present)[35]				
All Cases	328	71	21.65%	
Cases ≥1 white victim	67	28	41.79%	25.31%
Cases with no white victim	261	42	16.48%	

29

GEORGIA'S RACIST DEATH PENALTY

Heather Gray

Thinking back on 2007, one of the major victories for human rights was the end of the death penalty in New Jersey. On December 13, 2007, the New Jersey legislature repealed the cruel practice, and we are told that Governor Jon S. Corzine will sign the bill. New Jersey is the first state to ban the death penalty since executions began again after the US Supreme Court's *Gregg v. Georgia* decision in 1976. We in Georgia feature considerably in the recent efforts to end the death penalty in the United States. This is probably because Georgia has an outrageously cruel history of executing minors, mentally retarded, mentally ill, and particularly black males who have been accused of killing whites. Our notorious racist history is prime grounds for resistance.

The US record on capital punishment overall, however, is dismal. With New Jersey's decision, there are now thirty-seven states with the death penalty and thirteen without. Compared to the rest of the industrialized world, the United States stands as one of the most backward regarding capital punishment—all of Western Europe, most of Eastern Europe, Russia, Australia, Canada, and South Africa have all abandoned the death penalty. In fact, according to sociologist Michael Radelet in his article "Thirty Years after Gregg," "In 2005, 94 percent of all known judicial executions (those imposed by courts of law) were carried out in just four countries: China, Iran, Saudi Arabia, and the United States."

Radelet says further that the US "Supreme Court decisions can be reflective of standards of decency, albeit belatedly, (as) in March 2005 the Court finally banned the death penalty for prisoners who committed their crimes prior to their eighteenth birthdays." The age of eighteen is the international standard. He tells us that between 1990 and December 2005 Amnesty International documented forty-six executions of child offenders in eight countries (the Democratic Republic of the Congo, Iran, Nigeria, Pakistan, Saudi Arabia, the United States, China, and Yemen). In that time period, there were nineteen executions of child offenders in the United States, giving it the world record for this barbaric procedure.

Capital punishment in the United States is also extremely racist in nature, and the excellent work by Iowa University law professor David Baldus and his colleagues clearly demonstrates this reality. Baldus reports in 1990 that in Georgia "the death sentence was four times more likely to be applied when the victim was white rather than black and that blacks who kill whites are 11 times more likely to receive the death penalty than whites who kill blacks" (Georgia Moratorium Campaign).

Racist traditions in criminal justice are definitely maintained in Georgia's courtrooms. Georgia attorney Stephen Bright notes in the *Santa Clara Law Review*, "At least five men who were sentenced to death in Georgia had lawyers who referred to them in court as 'niggers.'"

This also demonstrates another major problem with death penalty convictions, which is that they are generally reserved for the poor who cannot afford other than court-appointed attorneys who are renowned for not pursuing justice for their clients or have no resources for adequate defense.

Here's some background on critical Georgia cases regarding challenges to the death penalty.

In 1972 the *Furman v. Georgia* case was decided by the US Supreme Court. The argument under *Furman* was of the capricious and racist nature of the death penalty in the United States. In a 5–4 decision, the court overruled the use of the death penalty. The justices expressed concern about the "standardless discretion" of death penalty convictions.

After *Furman*, the implementation of capital punishment was suspended and the states went back to the drawing board to develop procedures they hoped would pass muster with the court. They needed to prove to the Supreme Court that they had a standardized process that would eliminate the capricious application of the death penalty. Florida led the way in this, but by 1976, Radelet notes that thirty-five states had passed new death penalty laws. Georgia was one of them.

By 1975 *Gregg v. Georgia* was before the Supreme Court along with cases from other southern states—North Carolina, Louisiana, Florida, and Texas—saying that they had resolved the problem. The court agreed that the statutes presented by the states with "guided discretion" for juries in death penalty convictions likely resolved the problems referred to in the *Furman* case. After the Court's *Gregg* decision announcement in 1976, the states once again resumed killing their death-row inmates. Radelet makes convincing arguments in his 2006 article, however, that since *Gregg* the new statutes did not resolve the random and capricious nature of death penalty convictions!

The third and critical case presented before the court by Georgia was *McClesky v. Kemp* in 1987 (Kemp being the superintendent of the Georgia Diagnostic and Classification Center in Jackson, Georgia, where death-row inmates are housed and executed). The Baldus study was presented to the Supreme Court stating that McClesky, a black male accused of killing a white male, was given the death penalty under racially biased conditions relating to the race of the victim. The Court ruled that McClesky's equal protection had not been violated.

The Supreme Court did not allow for McClesky to demonstrate the glaring institutional racism in America as his defense; rather, he had to prove that there had been a deliberate attempt by Georgia authorities to violate his "individual" rights. McClesky was executed by the state of Georgia on September 25, 1991.

On September 24, 1991, the day before McClesky was executed, I interviewed attorney Stephen Bright on my radio program. There was still hope that the Court would stop the procedure. Activists in Georgia quickly transcribed the interview as McClesky wanted to read it. Later in the week, I went to McClesky's funeral in Atlanta.

The history of the death penalty in Georgia demonstrates the egregious ongoing racist nature of the punishment as demonstrated in a fascinating article by the *Athens Observer* in 1994 titled "Sentenced to Death." The paper states, "Racism is the vilest and most notorious aspect of the unfairness that has infected Georgia's death penalty throughout its history. It is a tragic fact that traditionally capital pun-

ishment in Georgia has been used to perpetuate white supremacy."
This continues today, of course!

What is interesting about the *Athens Observer* article, however,
are the criteria for crimes that were given the death penalty in
Georgia. Clearly, as indicated by the so-called crimes, there was significant resistance by African slaves to their oppression and efforts by
abolitionists attempting to free the slaves, none of which was appre-
ciated by Georgia's white elite.

Here's a summary on how, historically, one could be given a death
penalty conviction in Georgia.

In 1775 capital crimes involved "any slave who killed a white
person, grievously wounded, maimed or bruised a white person, was
convicted for a third time of striking a white person, raised or
attempted an insurrection, or endeavored to entice a slave to run
away and leave the colony." The 1755 law also made it a capital
crime for a slave to steal slaves, to administer poison to anyone, to
burn or destroy stacks of crops, to set fire to tar or turpentine barrels,
or to attempt to run away from his master.

In 1816, "Georgia statute made the following acts capital crimes,
but only if committed by a slave or a 'free person of color': poisoning
or attempted poisoning; insurrection or attempted insurrection; rape
or attempted rape of a white female; assaulting a white person with a
deadly weapon or with intent to murder; maiming a white person;
and burglary."

To maintain slavery, in 1829 Georgia decided to punish white
abolitionists. In 1829, "whites could be executed for introducing into
Georgia, or circulating in Georgia, any publication for the purpose of
inciting a revolt among the slaves." This statute was again repeated in
1863 in the midst of the Civil War.

The racist nature of the death penalty in Georgia, and throughout
America itself, is appalling. When Georgia began executing death-row
inmates with a vengeance after the 1976 *Gregg* decision, the first one
was in 1983 and fourteen in total throughout the 1980s. Many of us
involved with the Georgia Committee against the Death Penalty
would make the trek to the Jackson Diagnostic Center, about forty-
five miles south of Atlanta, to be outside the prison when the executions took place. Invariably the Ku Klux Klan was there to celebrate
the death of yet another black inmate.

The ritual surrounding the executions at Jackson is always surreal. When you enter the grounds of the prison, the guards will search your car, ask if you are for or against the execution, and then point you in the appropriate direction. Invariably we would form a circle and sing protest or peace songs, while the Klan in the opposite area chanted their vicious racial slurs. Ultimately, the guards will inform us when the inmate, who has been strapped to the electric chair with currents coursing through his body, has been killed. The state of Georgia will also have jets flying over the Jackson prison as the inmate is being executed which is rather like some sort of decadent ritual demonstrating the state's power over life. In some ways, the inmate is a blood sacrifice to the all-powerful state.

Then I would make my way back to Atlanta on Interstate 75 as if life was somehow normal after that experience. It never is! It's been said that if Jesus were alive today and executed, people would walk around wearing an electric chair or maybe a lethal injection needle rather than a cross.

As Supreme Court Justice William Brennan said in his dissent on the *McClesky* case:

> Warren McClesky doubtless asked his lawyer whether a jury was likely to sentence him to die. A candid reply to this question would have been disturbing. First, counsel would have to tell McClesky that few of the details of the crime or of McClesky's past criminal conduct were more important than the fact that his victim was white. Furthermore, counsel would feel bound to tell McClesky that defendants charged with killing white victims in Georgia are 4.3 times as likely to be sentenced to death as defendants charged with killing blacks. In addition, frankness would compel the disclosure that it was more likely than not that the race of McCleskey's victim would determine whether he received the death sentence. Finally, the assessment would not be complete without the information that cases involving black defendants and white victims are more likely to result in a death sentence than cases featuring any other combination of defendant and victim. The story could be told in a variety of ways, but McClesky could not fail to grasp its essential narrative line: there was a significant chance that race would play a prominent role in determining if he lived or died.

Anyone who thinks that racism and the maintenance of white supremacy is not a leading reason for implementing the capital punishment in the United States must be kidding himself. As Supreme Court Justice Harry Blackmun ultimately conceded, "Even under the most sophisticated death penalty statutes, race continues to play a major role in determining who shall live and who shall die." Hopefully, the wise decision by the New Jersey legislature to end the death penalty bodes well for an America that might sometime rid itself of the scourge of capital punishment.

30

LOOKING DEATHWORTHY

Perceived Stereotypicality of Black Defendants Predicts Capital-Sentencing Outcomes

Jennifer L. Eberhardt, Paul G. Davies, Valerie J. Purdie-Vaughns, and Sheri Lynn Johnson

Race matters in capital punishment. Even when statistically controlling for a wide variety of nonracial factors that may influence sentencing, numerous researchers have found that murderers of white victims are more likely than murderers of black victims to be sentenced to death.[1] The US GAO has described this race-of-victim effect as "remarkably consistent across data sets, states, data collection methods, and analytic techniques."[2]

In one of the most comprehensive studies to date, the race of the victim and the race of the defendant each were found to influence sentencing.[3] Not only did killing a white person rather than a black person increase the likelihood of being sentenced to death, but also black defendants were more likely than white defendants to be sentenced to death.

In the current research, we used the data set from this study by Baldus and his colleagues to investigate whether the probability of receiving the death penalty is significantly influenced by the degree to which the defendant is perceived to have a stereotypically black appearance (e.g., broad nose, thick lips, dark skin).[4] In particular, we considered the effect of a black defendant's perceived stereotypicality for those cases in which race is most salient—when a black defendant is charged with murdering a white victim. Although systematic studies of death sentencing have been conducted for decades, no prior studies have examined this potential influence of physical appearance on death-sentencing decisions.

A growing body of research demonstrates that people more readily apply racial stereotypes to blacks who are thought to look more stereotypically black, compared with blacks who are thought to look less stereotypically black.[5] People associate black physical traits with criminality in particular. The more stereotypically black a person's physical traits appear to be, the more criminal that person is perceived to be.[6] A recent study found that perceived stereotypicality correlated with the actual sentencing decisions of judges.[7] Even with differences in defendants' criminal histories statistically controlled, those defendants who possessed the most stereotypically black facial features served up to eight months longer in prison for felonies than defendants who possessed the least stereotypically black features. The present study examined the extent to which perceived stereotypicality of black defendants influenced jurors' death-sentencing decisions in cases with both white and black victims. We argue that only in death-eligible cases involving white victims—cases in which race is most salient—will black defendants' physical traits function as a significant determinant of deathworthiness.

Phase I: Black Defendant, White Victim

Method

We used an extensive database[8] containing more than 600 death-eligible cases from Philadelphia, Pennsylvania, that advanced to penalty phase between 1979 and 1999. Forty-four of these cases involved black male defendants who were convicted of murdering white victims. We obtained the photographs of these black defendants and presented all 44 of them (in a slide-show format) to naive raters who did not know that the photographs depicted convicted murderers. Raters were asked to rate the stereotypicality of each black defendant's appearance and were told they could use any number of features (e.g., lips, nose, hair texture, skin tone) to arrive at their judgments (fig. 1).

Stanford undergraduates served as the raters. To control for potential order effects, we presented the photographs in a different

Fig. 1. Examples of variation in stereotypicality of black faces. These images are the faces of people with no criminal history and are shown here for illustrative purposes only. The face on the right would be considered more stereotypically black than the face on the left.

random order in each of two sessions. Thirty-two raters (twenty-six white, four Asian, and two of other ethnicities) participated in one session, and nineteen raters (six white, eleven Asian, and two of other ethnicities) participated in the second session. The raters were shown a black-and-white photograph of each defendant's face. The photographs were edited such that the backgrounds and image sizes were standardized, and only the face and a portion of the neck were visible. Raters were told that all the faces they would be viewing were of black males. The defendants' faces were projected one at a time onto a screen at the front of the room for four seconds each as participants recorded stereotypicality ratings using a scale from 1 (not at all stereotypical) to 11 (extremely stereotypical). In both sessions, raters were kept blind to the purpose of the study and the identity of the men in the photographs. The data were analyzed for effects of order and rater's race, but none emerged.

Results

We computed an analysis of covariance (ANCOVA) using stereo-typicality (low-high median split) as the independent variable, the percentage of death sentences imposed as the dependent variable, and six nonracial factors known to influence sentencing[9] as covariates: (a) aggravating circumstances, (b) mitigating circumstances, (c) severity of the murder (as determined by blind ratings of the cases once purged of racial information), (d) the defendant's socioeconomic status, (e) the victim's socioeconomic status, and (f) the defendant's attractiveness.[10] As per Pennsylvania statute (Judiciary and Judicial Procedure, 2005), aggravating circumstances included factors such as the victim's status as a police officer, prosecution witness, or drug-trafficking competitor; the defendant's prior convictions for voluntary manslaughter or violent felonies; and characteristics of the crime, such as torture, kidnapping, or payment for the murder. Mitigating circumstances included factors such as the defendant's youth or advanced age, extreme mental or emotional disturbance, lack of prior criminal convictions, minor or coerced role in the crime, and impaired ability to appreciate the criminality of his conduct. The Baldus database of death-eligible defendants is arguably one of the most comprehensive to date; using it allowed us to control for the key variables known to influence sentencing outcomes.

The results confirmed that, above and beyond the effects of the covariates, defendants whose appearance was perceived as more stereotypically black were more likely to receive a death sentence than defendants whose appearance was perceived as less stereotypically black, $F(1, 36)= 4.11$, $p < .05$, $\eta_p^2 = .10$ (fig. 2a). In fact, 24.4 percent of those black defendants who fell in the lower half of the stereotypicality distribution received a death sentence, whereas 57.5 percent of those black defendants who fell in the upper half received a death sentence.

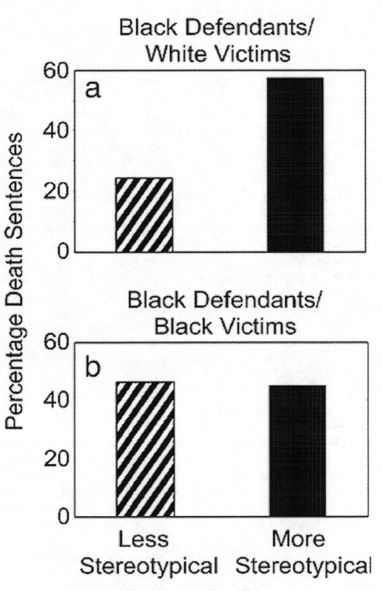

Fig. 2. Percentage of death sentences imposed in (a) cases involving white victims and (b) cases involving black victims as a function of the perceived stereotypicality of black defendants' appearance.

PHASE II: BLACK DEFENDANT, BLACK VICTIM

Method

Using the same database and procedures described earlier, we examined whether this stereotypicality effect extended to cases in which the victims were black. Of all cases that advanced to penalty phase, 308 involved black male defendants who were convicted of murdering black victims. The photographs for all of these defendants were obtained. The death-sentencing rate for these 308 defendants, however, was only 27 percent (as compared with 41percent for the cases with white victims). Given both the low death-sentencing rate and the large number of cases involving black defendants and black victims, we selected 118 of these 308 cases randomly from the database with the stipulation that those defendants receiving the death sentence be oversampled. This oversampling yielded a subset of cases in which the death-sentencing rate (46%) was not significantly different from that for the cases with white victims (41%; F=1). Using this subset provided a conservative test of our hypothesis. We then presented this subset of black defendants who murdered black victims to eighteen raters (twelve white and six Asian), who rated the faces on stereotypicality.[11]

Results

Employing the same analyses as we did for the cases with white victims, we found that the perceived stereotypicality of black defendants convicted of murdering black victims did not predict death sentencing, $F (1,110) < 1$ (fig. 2b). Black defendants who fell in the upper and lower halves of the stereotypicality distribution were sentenced to death at almost identical rates (45% vs. 46.6%, respectively). Thus, defendants who were perceived to be more stereotypically black were more likely to be sentenced to death only when their victims were white.

Although the two phases of this experiment were designed and conducted separately, readers may be interested in knowing whether combining the data from the two phases would produce a significant interactive effect of victims' race and defendants' stereotypicality on death-sentencing outcomes. Analysis confirmed that the interaction of victims race (black vs. white) and victims' stereotypicality (low vs. high) was indeed significant, $F(1,158) = 4.97$, $p < .05$, $\eta_p^2 = .03$.

DISCUSSION

Why might a defendant's perceived stereotypicality matter for black murderers of white victims, but not for black murderers of black victims? One possibility is that the interracial character of cases involving a black defendant and a white victim renders race especially salient. Such crimes could be interpreted or treated as matters of intergroup conflict.[12] The salience of race may incline jurors to think about race as a relevant and useful heuristic for determining the blameworthiness of the defendant and the perniciousness of the crime. According to this racial-salience hypothesis, defendants' perceived stereotypicality should not influence death-sentencing outcomes in cases involving a black defendant and a black victim. In those cases, the intraracial character of the crime may lead jurors to view the crime as a matter of interpersonal rather than intergroup conflict.[13]

These research findings augment and complicate the current body of evidence regarding the role of race in capital sentencing. Whereas previous studies examined intergroup differences in death-sentencing outcomes, our results suggest that racial discrimination may also operate through intragroup distinctions based on perceived racial stereotypicality

Our findings suggest that in cases involving a black defendant and a white victim—cases in which the likelihood of the death penalty is already high—jurors are influenced not simply by the knowledge that the defendant is black, but also by the extent to which the defendant appears stereotypically black. In fact, for those defendants who fell in the top half as opposed to the bottom half of the stereotypicality distribution, the chance of receiving a death sentence more than doubled. Previous laboratory research has already shown that people associate black physical traits with criminality.[14] The present research demonstrates that in actual sentencing decisions, jurors may treat these traits as powerful cues to deathworthiness.

Notes

Introduction

1. Stuart Banner, *The Death Penalty: An American History* (Cambridge, MA: Harvard University Press, 2002), p. 1. This book is an invaluable resource for anybody interested in the death penalty as a moral, social, or political issue.

2. For a narrative history of the founding of Rhode Island and its founder, Roger Williams, see Linda Krager and Joe Barnhart, *Trust and Treachery* (Macon, GA: Mercer University Press, 2003). See also the selection "History of the Death Penalty" from the Death Penalty Information Center, included in this volume.

3. Ted Nugent, "Of Life, Liberty and NRA," *Waco Tribune Herald*, May 17, 2009.

4. Banner, *Death Penalty*, p. 275.

5. Ibid., p. 263.

6. For an account of greater historical accuracy, see relevant portions of Banner, *Death Penalty*.

7. Stuart Taylor Jr., "Court, 5–4, Rejects Racial Challenge to Death Penalty," *New York Times*, April 23, 1987.

8. Brandon Barrett, "Judging Innocence," *Columbia Law Review* 108, no. 1 (January 2008).

9. David Grann, "Trial by Fire: Did Texas Execute an Innocent Man?" *New Yorker*, September 7, 2009.

CHAPTER 1: HISTORY OF THE DEATH PENALTY

1. L. Randa, ed., *Society's Final Solution: A History and Discussion of the Death Penalty* (Lanham, MD: University Press of America, 1997).

2. Ibid.

3. W. Schabas, *The Abolition of the Death Penalty in International Law*, 2nd ed. (Cambridge, MA: Cambridge University Press, 1997).

4. R. Bohm, *Deathquest: An Introduction to the Theory and Practice of Capital Punishment in the United States* (Cincinnati, OH: Anderson Publishing, 1999); Randa, *Society's Final Solution*; Schabas, *Abolition of the Death Penalty in International Law*.

5. Bohm, *Deathquest*; Schabas, *Abolition of the Death Penalty in International Law*.

6. Bohm, *Deathquest*.

7. Randa, *Society's Final Solution*.

8. H. Bedau, ed., *The Death Penalty in America: Current Controversies* (Oxford: Oxford University Press, 1997); Bohm, *Deathquest*.

9. Bohm, *Deathquest*.

10. Ibid.; Schabas, *Abolition of the Death Penalty in International Law*.

11. Bohm, *Deathquest*.

12. Ibid.

13. Schabas, *Abolition of the Death Penalty in International Law*.

14. Gallup Poll News Service, June 2, 2004. See also Death Penalty Information Center's report, "Sentencing for Life: Americans Embrace Alternatives to the Death Penalty," April 1993.

15. Bedau, *Death Penalty in America*.

16. K. O'Shea, *Women and the Death Penalty in the United States, 1900–1998* (Westport, CT: Praeger, 1999), with updates by the Death Penalty Information Center.

17. Bohm, *Deathquest*; Schabas, *Abolition of the Death Penalty in International Law*.

18. Amnesty International, "List of Abolitionist and Retentionist Countries," Report ACT 50/01/99, updated June 2004; Schabas, *Abolition of the Death Penalty in International Law*.

19. *New York Times*, April 29, 1999.

20. Amnesty International, "List of Abolitionist and Retentionist Countries."

21. Ibid.

CHAPTER 8: *BAZE-D* AND CONFUSED: WHAT'S THE DEAL WITH LETHAL INJECTION? A DEBATE

1. Deborah W. Denno, "The Lethal Injection Quandary: How Medicine Has Dismantled the Death Penalty," *Fordham Law Review* 76 (2007): 49, 66.
2. *Lightbourne v. McCollum* (Fla. November 1, 2007).
3. *Taylor v. Crawford* (W.D. Mo. September 12, 2006).
4. Denno, " The Lethal Injection Quandary," p. 73.

CHAPTER 9: *BAZE V. REES,* SUPREME COURT OF THE UNITED STATES

1. Most footnotes and internal notes omitted.
2. Petitioners did allude to an "alternative chemical or combination of chemicals" that could replace Kentucky's three-drug protocol in their post-trial brief, but based on the arguments presented there, it is clear they intended to refer only to other, allegedly less painful drugs that could substitute for potassium chloride as a heart-stopping agent. Likewise, the only alternatives to the three-drug protocol presented to the Kentucky Supreme Court were those that replaced potassium chloride with other drugs for inducing cardiac arrest, or that omitted pancuronium bromide, or that added an analgesic to relieve pain.

CHAPTER 10: *BAZE V. REES:* JUSTICE RUTH GINSBURG, DISSENTING; JUSTICE DAVID SOUTER, JOINING

1. Most footnotes and internal notes omitted.
2. Petitioners' expert testified that a layperson could not tell from visual observation if a paralyzed inmate was conscious and that doing so would be difficult even for a professional. Kentucky's warden candidly admitted: "I honestly don't know what you'd look for."
3. The length of the tubing contributes to the risk that the inmate will receive an inadequate dose of sodium thiopental. The warden and deputy warden watch for obvious leaks in the execution chamber, but the line also snakes into the neighboring control room through a small hole in the wall.

CHAPTER 11: *BAZE V. REES:*
JUSTICE JOHN PAUL STEVENS, CONCURRING

1. Most footnotes and internal notes omitted.
2. Retribution is the most common basis of support for the death penalty. A recent study found that 37 percent of death penalty supporters cited "an eye for an eye/they took a life/fits the crime" as their reason for supporting capital punishment. Another 13 percent cited "They deserve it." The next most common reasons—"sav[ing] taxpayers money/cost associated with prison" and deterrence—were each cited by 11 percent of supporters. See Department of Justice, Bureau of Justice Statistics, *Sourcebook of Criminal Justice Statistics* 147 (2003): table 2.55; online at http://www.albany.edu/sourcebook/pdf/t255.pdf.
3. For example, family members of victims of the Oklahoma City bombing called for the government to "put [Timothy McVeigh] inside a bomb and blow it up." Edward Walsh, "One Arraigned, Two Undergo Questioning," *Washington Post*, April 22, 1995, pp. A1, A13. Commentators at the time noted that an overwhelming percentage of Americans felt that executing McVeigh was not enough. Linder, "A Political Verdict: McVeigh: When Death Is Not Enough," *L.A. Times*, June 8, 1997, p. M1.
4. See L. S. Salinas, "Is It Time to Kill the Death Penalty?" *American Journal of Criminal Law* 34 (2006): 39.

CHAPTER 12: *BAZE V. REES:*
JUSTICE ANTONIN SCALIA, CONCURRING; JUSTICE CLARENCE THOMAS, JOINING

1. Most footnotes and internal notes omitted.
2. Cass R. Sunstein and Adrian Vermeule, "Is Capital Punishment Morally Required? Acts, Omissions, and Life-Life Tradeoffs," *Stanford Law Review* 58 (2006) (listing the approximately half a dozen studies supporting this conclusion).

CHAPTER 13: *BAZE V. REES:*
JUSTICE STEPHEN BREYER, CONCURRING

1. Most internal notes omitted.

2. See Deborarh W. Denno, "When Legislatures Delegate Death: The Troubling Paradox behind State Uses of Electrocution and Lethal Injection and What It Says about Us," *Ohio State Law Journal* 63 (2002): 63.

CHAPTER 14: *BAZE V. REES*: JUSTICE CLARENCE THOMAS, CONCURRING; JUSTICE ANTONIN SCALIA, JOINING

1. Internal notes omitted.

CHAPTER 15: *KENNEDY V. LOUISIANA*, SUPREME COURT OF THE UNITED STATES

1. Internal notes omitted.

CHAPTER 16: *KENNEDY V. LOUISIANA*, JUSTICE SAMUEL ALITO, DISSENTING

1. Most endnotes and internal citations omitted.

2. Those states are Arizona, California, Connecticut, the District of Columbia, Florida, Illinois, Iowa, Kansas, Kentucky, Massachusetts, Minnesota, Missouri, Nebraska, New Jersey, North Dakota, Oregon, Pennsylvania, South Carolina, Texas, Virginia, Washington, and Wisconsin. §71.09.010 (West 1992 and Supp. 2002); Wis. Stat. §980.01–13 (2005).

3. Of course, the other five capital child rape statutes are too recent for any individual to have been sentenced to death under them.

4. Melissa Meister, "Murdering Innocence: The Constitutionality of Capital Child Rape Statutes," *Arizona Law Review* 45 (2003): 197, 208–209.

5. C. Bagley and K. King, *Child Sexual Abuse: The Search for Healing* (London: Tavistock Routledge, 1990).

CHAPTER 17: THE SUPREME COURT IS WRONG ON THE DEATH PENALTY

1. Editors' note. By a vote of 7–2, the Court refused to reconsider the decision, but did add a footnote to the original decision acknowledging the updated Military Code, but adding: "We find that the military penalty does not affect our reasoning or our conclusions."

CHAPTER 20: ENGAGING CAPITAL EMOTIONS

1. Editors' note: the US Supreme Court in *Kennedy v. Louisiana* (see the first selection in this section) ruled that the death penalty for rape of a child would constitute "cruel and unusual punishment," violating the Eighth Amendment to the Constitution.

2. Editorial, "Not Justice: Louisiana Wants to Execute a Child Rapist. The Crime Is Heinous, but the Death Penalty Is Too Harsh," *L.A. Times*, April 16, 2008, p. A16; Editorial, "The Limits of the Death Penalty," *New York Times*, April 16, 2008, p. A24.

3. See, e.g., Dan M. Kahan, "The Secret Ambition of Deterrence," *Harvard Law Review* 113 (1999): 436–51 (noting that while death-penalty debates invoke deterrence statistics, what really influences supporters and opponents is not deterrence but expressive judgments rooted in values, emotions, and sympathies).

4. The leading anthology on the role of emotions in the law is Susan A. Bandes, ed., *The Passions of Law* (New York: NYU Press, 1999). For a more recent exploration of the role of emotion in the death penalty generally, see Susan A. Bandes, "The Heart Has Its Reasons: Examining the Strange Persistence of the American Death Penalty," *Studies in Law, Politics, and Society* 42.

5. *Baze v. Rees*, 128 S. Ct. 1520, 1533–37 (2008) (plurality opinion) (holding that three-drug method of lethal injection was not inherently cruel and unusual punishment); *Roper v. Simmons*, 543 U.S. 551, 569–75 (2005) (forbidding execution for crime committed while under age eighteen); *Atkins v. Virginia*, 536 U.S. 304, 317-22 (2002) (forbidding execution of mentally retarded criminals).

6. See, e.g. *Mullaney v. Wilbur*, 421 U.S. 684, 692–96 (1975).

7. See, e.g., *Bechtel v. State*, 840 P.2d 1, 8, 11 (Okla. Crim. App. 1992) (quoting Lenore Walker, *The Battered Woman Syndrome* [1979]) (excising reasonableness requirement from jury instructions, to allow self-defense to

women who kill abusers during a lull); *State v. Norman*, 378 S.E.2d 8 (N.C. 1989); Cathryn Jo Rosen, "The Excuse of Self-Defense: Correcting a Historical Accident on Behalf of Battered Women Who Kill," *American University Law Review* 36 (1986): 11, 56 (advocating self-defense excuse for battered women who kill abusers).

8. See, e.g., Dan M. Kahan, "The Progressive Appropriation of Disgust," in *The Passions of the Law*, pp. 63, 69–71 (suggesting that hate crimes are useful tools to express disgust at bigotry).

9. See Model Penal Code§ 4.01, explanatory note (2001) (noting that the term "appreciate" in Model Penal Code's insanity test is broad enough to encompass apprehending the deeper significance of one's acts).

10. See *Gregg v. Georgia*, 428 U.S. 153, 183 (1976) (plurality opinion) (discussing the death penalty as, in part, an expression of society's moral outrage at particularly offensive conduct).

11. US Const. amend. VIII.

12. In *Kansas v. Marsh*, 126 S. Ct. 2516, 2531–39, 2544–46 (2006), which evaluated capital jury instructions, Justices David Souter and Antonin Scalia wrote extended separate opinions to debate the frequency of wrongful capital convictions. In *Baze v. Rees*, 128 S. Ct. 1520, 1542–56 (2008), which evaluated Kentucky's lethal-injection protocol, Justices John Paul Stevens and Antonin Scalia wrote extended separate opinions to debate the basic constitutionality of the death penalty.

13. See generally Douglas A. Berman, "A Capital Waste of Time? Examining the Supreme Court's 'Culture of Death,'" *Ohio Northern University Law Review* 34 (2008): 861–82 (noting and criticizing the Supreme Court's tendency to devote a large part of its limited docket to death penalty cases).

14. See *Atkins v. Virginia*, 536 U.S. 304, 318–19 (2002). *Atkins* itself emphasized that mental retardation impairs understanding, reasoning, communication, and impulse control. The Court may have used the clinical, scientific language of mental capacity in part because it felt that courts should not speak the language of emotion. But one could just as easily understand this scientific reasoning in lay emotional terms. Mentally retarded killers have difficulty appreciating how badly their crimes hurt others and educating and controlling their emotional impulses. To that extent at least, mentally retarded defendants have impaired emotional capacities, and partly for that reason society is less justified in levying *its* full emotional outrage upon them.

15. *Penry v. Lynaugh*, 492 U.S. 302, 322 (1989) (requiring that jury instructions inform the jury that it can consider and give effect to evidence of defendant's mental retardation and abuse, so that the jury may offer "reasoned moral response" to mitigating evidence), *abrogated on other grounds by Atkins v. Virginia*, 536 U.S. 304 (2002) (banning execution of mentally

retarded defendants, but not affecting *Penry*'s guarantee of jury consideration of other mental disabilities).

16. *Ford v. Wainwright*, 477 U.S. 399, 406–10 (1986); *Panetti v. Quar-
terman*, 127 S. Ct. 2842, 2859–63 (2007) (holding that a death-row inmate
may not be executed if he lacks mental capacity to understand that he is about
to be executed and that this execution will be punishment for his crime).

17. *Roper v. Simmons*, 543 U.S. 551, 570–71 (2005).

18. *Woodson v. North Carolina*, 428 U.S. 280, 303–05 (1976) (plurality
opinion) (forbidding mandatory death penalty for all first-degree murders).

19. *Eddings v. Oklahoma*, 455 U.S. 104, 113–16 (1982) (requiring
courts to consider offender's unhappy upbringing, emotional disturbance,
turbulent family history, and beatings by his father as mitigating evidence in
capital case); *Lockett v. Ohio*, 438 U.S. 586, 604 (1978) (plurality opinion)
(holding that death-penalty statute must permit jury to consider all mitigating evidence relating to the defendant's character, record, or offense).

20. *Ring v. Arizona*, 536 U.S. 584, 609 (2002).

21. *Penry v. Lynaugh*, 492 U.S. 302, 322 (1989) (requiring that a jury
be permitted to consider and give mitigating effects to evidence of defendant's
mental retardation and abuse), *abrogated on other grounds by Atkins v. Virginia*, 536 U.S. 304 (2002) (banning execution of mentally retarded defendants, but not affecting *Penry*'s guarantee of jury consideration of other
mental disabilities).

22. *Payne v. Tennessee*, 501 U.S. 808, 817 (1991) (overruling prior
holdings that limited the presentation of "'victim impact' evidence relating to
the personal characteristics of the victim and the emotional impact of the
crimes on the victim's family").

23. Theodore Eisenberg, Stephen P. Garvey, and Martin T. Wells, "But
Was He Sorry? The Role of Remorse in Capital Sentencing," *Cornel Law
Review* 83 (1998): 1600. Where jurors consider a murder to have been especially heinous, however, a perpetrator's remorse likely will not influence his
sentence.

24. *Rita v. United States*, 127 S. Ct. 2456, 2468 (2007).

25. Model Penal Code § 210.6(3)(h) (2001) (specifying capital aggravating circumstance for murders that were "especially heinous, atrocious or
cruel, manifesting exceptional depravity").

26. See ibid. § 210.6(3)(g) (specifying capital aggravating circumstance
for murders committed "for pecuniary gain").

27. See 2001 Guidance to United States Attorneys in Clemency Matters
§ 1–2.112(3), reprinted in *Federal Sentencing Reporter* 13 (2001): 195 (suggesting, however, that absence of remorse should not entirely preclude
clemency).

28. Here we are discussing moral agency in the context of free will, blame, and responsibility for one's actions. Broader considerations of human dignity protect children, the mentally ill, and others from being victimized, even though they are not fully responsible for their actions.

29. Walter Berns, "For Capital Punishment: The Morality of Anger," *Harper's*, April 1979, p. 15.

30. Cf. John Grisham, *A Time to Kill* (New York: Dell, 2004). Note that in the book, the father killed his daughter's assailants because he feared they would not be punished. Of course, outside of fiction child rapists normally receive some punishment, though perhaps not as much as the populace would like. Thus, the fear of vigilantism is not as great in modern America as it is in fiction.

31. See *Baze v. Rees*, 128 S. Ct. 1520 (2008) (note the fractured Supreme Court opinions, reflecting the Court's own ambivalence about pain in executions).

32. See, e.g., Daniel Goleman, *Emotional Intelligence: Why It Can Matter More Than IQ* (New York: Bantam, 2006).

33. The Supreme Court emphasized this point in the course of banning capital punishment for the rape of an adult in *Coker v. Georgia*, 433 U.S. 584, 598 (1977): "Life is over for the victim of the murderer; for the rape victim, life may not be nearly so happy as it was, but it is not over and normally is not beyond repair." To our modern ears, this sentence seems quite emotionally insensitive; it fails to recognize how badly rape can scar its victims. It is especially dated in light of modern research on the social and personal impact of sexual violations. See, e.g., National Center for Victims of Crime & Crime Victims Research & Treatment Center, "Rape in America: A Report to the Nation" (1992), pp. 7–8.

34. Jamie Satterfield, "Hunting Predators," *Knoxville News*, May 18, 2008, p. A14, available at http://www.knoxnews.com/news/2008/may/18/hunting-predators/.

35. See Anthony V. Alfieri, "Mitigation, Mercy, and Delay: The Moral Politics of Death Penalty Abolitionists," *Harvard Civil Rights–Civil Liberties Law Review* 31(1996): 331–33 (noting, however, that this strategy does not always succeed).

36. See generally Lawrence C. Marshall, "The Innocence Revolution and the Death Penalty," *Ohio State Journal of Criminal Law* 1 (2004): 573.

CHAPTER 21: CHILD RAPE, MORAL OUTRAGE, AND THE DEATH PENALTY

1. No. 07-343 (U.S. June 25, 2008).

2. See ibid., slip opinion, p. 24 (majority opinion); see also ibid., slip opinion, pp. 21–23 (Justice Alito, dissenting).

3. See ibid., slip opinion, p. 32 (majority opinion); see also ibid., slip opinion, 16 (Alito, J., dissenting).

4. See ibid., slip opinion, p. 29 (majority opinion); see also ibid., slip opinion, pp. 18–19 (Alito, J., dissenting).

5. Douglas A. Berman and Stephanos Bibas, "Engaging Capital Emotions," *Northwestern University Law Review Colloquy* 102 (2008): 355.

6. Susan A. Bandes, "The Heart Has Its Reasons: Examining the Strange Persistence of the American Death Penalty," *Studies in Law, Politics, and Society* 42 (2008): 28 [hereinafter Bandes, "The Heart Has Its Reasons"].

7. Robert Blecker has also prominently argued in favor of the death penalty based on what he calls "emotive retributivism." See, e.g., Robert Blecker, "But Did They Listen? The New Jersey Death Penalty Commission's Exercise in Abolitionism: A Reply" (July 24, 2007) (unpublished manuscript), available at http://works.bepress.com/cgi/viewcontent.cgi?article=1000&context=robertblecker.

8. Bandes, "The Heart Has Its Reasons," pp. 22–23.

9. Ibid.

10. Ibid.

11. See Martha C. Nussbaum, "'Secret Sewers of Vice': Disgust, Bodies and the Law," in *The Passions of Law*, ed. Susan Bandes (New York: New York University Press, 2000), pp. 19–62; Dan M. Kahan, "The Progressive Appropriation of Disgust," in *The Passions of Law*, pp. 63–79.

12. See generally Antonio R. Damasio, *Descartes' Error: Emotion, Reason, and the Human Brain* (Quill/Harper/Collins 1994).

13. Hilary Kornblith, "The Laws of Thought," *Philosophy & Phenomenological Research* 52 (1992): 896.

14. For a discussion of the relevance of emotion in decision-making processes, see Susan A. Bandes, "Emotions, Values and the Construction of Risk," *PENNumbra–University of Pennsylvania Law Review* 156 (2008): 421, http://www.pennumbra.com/responses/03-2008/Bandes.pdf [hereinafter Bandes, "Emotions, Values, and the Construction of Risk"] (commenting on Dan M. Kahan, "Two Conceptions of Emotion in Risk Regulation," *PENNumbra–University of Pennsylvania law Review* 156).

15. Kwame Anthony Appiah, *Experiments in Ethics* (Cambridge, MA: Harvard University Press, 2008), pp. 76–77.

Notes   357

16. Berman and Bibas, "Engaging Capital Emotions," p. 360.

17. See Susan A. Bandes, "Empathy, Narrative and Victim Impact Statements," *University of Chicago Law Review* 63(1996): 405.

18. *Kennedy v. Louisiana*, No. 07-343, slip opinion, p. 8 (U.S. June 25, 2008) (quoting *Trop v. Dulles*, 356 U.S. 86, 101 [1958]).

19. See generally *Gregg v. Georgia*, 428 U.S. 153 (1976).

20. Compare Justice Stevens's concurrence in *Baze v. Rees*, 128 S. Ct. 1520, 1551–52 (2008) (Justice Stevens, concurring in the judgment), which draws on his own experience implementing the death penalty to buttress his conclusion that capital punishment is unconstitutional, to Justice Scalia's concurrence, and 128 S. Ct. at 1552–53 (Justice Scalia, concurring in the judgment), in which he argues that Justice Stevens's conclusion is insupportable as a matter of constitutional interpretation and that the legitimacy of capital punishment is a legislative question.

21. Dan Markel, "Against Mercy," *Minnesota Law Review* 88 (2004): 1441.

22. See Mary Sigler, "Mercy, Clemency, and the Case of Karla Faye Tucker," *Ohio Supreme Court Journal of Criminal Law* 4 (2007): 464.

23. Bandes, "The Heart Has Its Reasons," p. 27.

24. Paul Robinson and Robert Kurzban, "Concordance and Conflict in Intuitions of Justice," *Minnesota Law Review* 91 (2007): 1835, available at http://local.law.umn.edu/uploads/images/6298/Robinson_Kurzban_Final.

25. See ibid.

26. See *Baze v. Rees*, 128 S.Ct. 1520, 1546 (2008) (Justice Stevens concurring in the judgment).

27. Berman and Bibas, "Engaging Capital Emotions," pp. 360, 362.

28. See Susan A. Bandes, "The Lessons of *Capturing the Friedmans*: Moral Panic, Institutional Denial, and Due Process," *Law, Culture, and the Humanities* 3 (2007): 293 [hereinafter Bandes, "The Lessons of *Capturing the Friedmans*"] (discussing high-profile child sexual abuse prosecutions in which legal institutions exacerbate rather than channel public outrage).

29. See Susan A. Bandes, "Victims, 'Closure,' and the Sociology of Emotion," *Law and Contemporary Problems* 72, n. 1 (2009) (hereinafter Bandes, "The Sociology of Emotion"), available at http://papers.ssrn.com/sol3/papers.cfm?abstract_id=1112140 (discussing the deleterious consequences of this message).

30. See J. J. Prescott and Sonja Starr, "Improving Criminal Jury Decision Making After the *Blakely* Revolution," *University of Illinois Law Review* (2006): 325–26 (discussing the importance of providing the jury with a well-chosen "base anchor" to guide sentencing discretion, given the strong influence that the anchor will exert on deliberation); see also Stephanos Bibas, "Plea Bargaining Outside the Shadow of Trial," *Harvard Law Review*

117 (2004): 2516–18 (discussing the strong "anchoring" influence of a prosecutor's initial charge on subsequent plea negotiations).

31. See *Kennedy v. Louisiana*, No. 07-343, slip opinion, p. 24 (U.S. June 25, 2008).

32. See ibid., slip opinion, p. 29.

33. See ibid., slip opinion, p. 27.

34. See ibid., slip opinion, p. 22 (Justice Alito dissenting).

35. Sigler, "Mercy, Clemency, and the Case of Karla Faye Tucker," p. 477.

36. Ibid., p. 473.

37. The authors raise the possibility that the victims "may have their horrifying treatment captured on film and then peddled around the world" and will "spend their lives not only grappling with the anguish of rape, but fearing that any computer could replay their childhood horror." This scenario seems to encompass additional abuse by both the defendant and unknown third parties. Berman and Bibas, "Engaging Capital Emotions," p. 362.

38. See *Kennedy*, No. 07-343, slip opinion, p. 36 (majority opinion) ("In most cases justice is not better served by terminating the life of the perpetrator rather than confining him and preserving the possibility that he and the system will find ways to allow him to understand the enormity of his offense."); see also Stephanos Bibas and Richard A. Bierschbach, "Integrating Remorse and Apology into Criminal Procedure," *Yale Law Journal* 114 (2004): 85, (arguing for the importance of remorse in the criminal justice system).

39. Bandes, "Empathy, Narrative and Victim Impact Statements," p. 405.

40. Lynne Henderson, "The Wrongs of Victims' Rights," *Stanford law Review* 37 (1985): 964.

41. Berman and Bibas, "Engaging Capital Emotions," p. 362.

42. *Kennedy*, No. 07-343, slip opinion, p. 32.

43. Ibid., slip opinion, p. 16 (Justice Alito dissenting).

44. Later in his dissent, Justice Alito argues at length that the harm to child rape victims is severe and long-lasting, and that the "problems that afflict child-rape victims often become society's problems as well." Ibid., slip opinion, pp. 20–23.

45. See *Payne v. Tennessee*, 501 U.S. 808, 836 (1991) (Justice Souter concurring) (expressing confidence in the "traditional guard against the inflammatory risk, in the trial judge's authority and responsibility to control the proceedings consistently with due process, on which ground defendants may object and, if necessary, appeal").

46. See John H. Blume, "Ten Years of *Payne*: Victim Impact Evidence in Capital Cases," *Cornell Law Review* 88 (2003): 270–73; Wayne A. Logan, "Through the Past Darkly: A Survey of the Uses and Abuses of Victim Impact Evidence in Capital Trials," *Arizona Law Review* 41 (1999): 145.

47. See Bandes, "Empathy, Narrative and Victim Impact Statements," p. 407, n.235; Vivian Berger, "*Payne* and Suffering—A Personal Reflection and a Victim-Centered Critique," *Florida State University Law Review* 20 (1992): 50–51 (discussing the specter of "mini-trials" on the victim's character).

48. One dramatic example of this dynamic came in the oral argument in the *Kennedy* case, in which counsel for the state began her oral argument with an agonizing description of the injuries to the victim, and Justice Stevens inquired whether the injuries were permanent. Counsel responded that, after surgery, the physical injuries had healed. Transcript of Oral argument, pp. 28–29, *Kennedy*, No. 07-343.

49. Berman and Bibas, "Engaging Capital Emotions," p. 362.

50. Bandes, "The Sociology of Emotion," p. 21.

51. See Janice Nadler and Mary R. Rose, "Victim Impact Testimony and the Psychology of Punishment," *Cornell Law Review* 88 (2003): 445–46.

52. See, e.g., Daniel Goleman, *Social Intelligence: The New Science of Human Relationships* (New York: Random House, 2006), p. 96 (discussing the neural dynamics of empathy and compassion).

53. Neil Vidmar, "Generic Prejudice and the Presumption of Guilt in Sex Abuse Trials," *Law and Human Behavior* 21 (1997): 6.

54. Ibid. The well-known "moral panics" that led to child sexual abuse allegations against hundreds of daycare workers in the 1980s are a painful illustration of the results of this dynamic. See generally Bandes, "The Lessons of *Capturing the Friedmans.*"

55. Vidmar, "Generic Prejudice and the Presumption of Guilt in Sex Abuse Trials," p. 18.

56. Justice Kennedy's majority opinion expresses this very concern. See *Kennedy v. Louisiana*, No. 07-343, slip opinion, p. 29 (U.S. June 25, 2008) (stating that when dealing with "a crime [such as child rape] that in many cases will overwhelm a decent person's judgment, we have no confidence that the imposition of the death penalty would not be so arbitrary as to be 'freakish'") (quoting *Furman v. Georgia*, 408 U.S. 238, 310 [1972]). There is also reason to question the ability of prosecutors and judges to withstand the substantial pressures that arise in cases involving child rape and capital punishment. See, e.g., Stephen B. Bright and Patrick J. Keenan, "Judges and the Politics of Death: Deciding between the Bill of Rights and the Next Election in Capital Cases," *Boston University Law Review* 75 (1995): 759 (discussing political pressure on judges in capital cases); James S. Liebman, et al., "A Broken System, Part II: Why There Is So Much Error in Capital Cases, and What Can Be Done about It" (2002), pp. 169–70, available at http://www2 .law.columbia.edu/brokensystem2/report.pdf (discussing factors interfering

with fair verdicts, including effects of political pressure on prosecutors and judges).

57. Craig Haney, *Death by Design: Capital Punishment as a Social Psychological System* (Oxford: Oxford University Press, 2005), p. 203.

58. See David C. Baldus, George Woodworth, Charles A. Pulaski Jr., *Equal Justice and the Death Penalty* (Lebanon, NH: Northeastern University Press, 1990), p. 316

59. *Coker v. Georgia*, 433 U.S. 584, 598–99 (1977).

60. Brief for Petitioner, p. 43, n.16, *Kennedy v. Louisiana*, No. 07-343 (U.S. June 25, 2008) (citations omitted).

61. *Baze v. Rees*, 128 S.Ct. 1520, 1546 (2008) (Justice Stevens concurring in judgment).

CHAPTER 25: DEATH AND HARMLESS ERROR: A RHETORICAL RESPONSE TO JUDGING INNOCENCE

1. Brandon L. Garrett, "Judging Innocence," *Columbia Law Review* 108 (2008): 62.

2. My choice of proposition was inspired by recent remarks of Judge Carolyn Engel Temin, a senior judge in the Court of Common Pleas in Philadelphia. I participated in a panel with Judge Temin at a Constitution Project sponsored conference on the legacy of *Strickland v. Washington* held at the Library of Congress. At one point in her presentation, Judge Temin declared that she wanted to go "on the record" as believing that there can be no harmless error in the penalty phase of death penalty cases. Webcast of Judge Temin's remarks is available at http://www.loc.gov/law/news/webcasts.html. I chose to raise the stakes by shifting focus to the guilt phase and the implied question of innocence. Of course, the idea that different harmless error rules might apply in the capital context has previously received scholarly attention. See, e.g., David McCord, "Is Death 'Different' for Purposes of Harmless Error Analysis? Should It Be? An Assessment of United States and Louisiana Supreme Court Case Law," *Louisiana Law Review* 59 (1999): 1105.

3. See Garrett, "Judging Innocence," pp. 107–109.

4. See ibid., pp. 98–99.

5. See ibid., p. 108, table 8.

6. Ibid.

7. See ibid., p. 74.

8. Ibid., pp. 99–100. The six reversals without written decisions resulted from DNA exonerations prior to retrial.

9. See James S. Liebman et al., "Capital Attrition: Error Rates in Capital Cases 1973–1995," *Texas Law Review* 78 (2000): 1854. Professor Garrett also notes that his "reversal" rate is calculated slightly differently from the "attrition" rate calculation by Liebman et al. See Garrett, "Judging Innocence," p. 100, nn. 167–68.

10. This reversal rate also seems plausibly representative as it is statistically indistinguishable from the 8 percent reversal rate found in the professor's own randomly matched comparison group of 121 noncapital cases. See Garrett, "Judging Innocence," p. 99. Of course, this reversal rate would presumably describe a reversal rate for all rape, murder, and rape-murder convictions combined (the crimes comprising the data sets) rather that describe a more general noncapital reversal rate.

11. Furthermore, it needs to be pointed out that the high 58–68 percent capital reversal rate may well be lower since the passage of the Antiterrorism and Effective Death Penalty Act (AEDPA) in 2000. Professor Garrett acknowledges that AEDPA had little effect on his data set since almost all the habeas petitions in the innocence group were filed before AEDPA's 1996 effective date. See Garrett, "Judging Innocence," p. 101. Similarly, the Liebman, Fagan, and West study concerned only pre-AEDPA appeals. See Liebman et al., "Capital Attrition." However, at least one recent study concludes that significantly fewer habeas writs are being granted post-AEDPA. See Nancy J. King et al., "Final Technical Report: Habeas Litigation in US District Courts" (2007), pp. 60–62, National Center for State Courts, available at http://law.vanderbilt.edu/article-search/article-detail/download.aspx?id=1639.

12. See Garrett, "Judging Innocence," p. 108.

13. Ibid.

14. As of January 26, 2008, there have been fifteen men released from death row because of postconviction DNA testing. On May 11, 2007, Curtis Edward McCarty was exonerated after serving over twenty-one years—including sixteen on Oklahoma's death row—for a crime he did not commit. See Cheryl Camp, "Convicted Murderer Is Freed in Wake of Tainted Evidence," *New York Times*, May 22, 2007, p. A16. I had the honor of representing Mr. McCarty, along with a talented team of lawyers from Oklahoma, during his exoneration.

CHAPTER 26: TESTIMONY OF BARRY C. SCHECK BEFORE THE MARYLAND COMMISSION ON CAPITAL PUNISHMENT

1. Department of Justice, Office of Justice Programs, National Institute of Justice, NCJ 161258, "Convicted by Juries, Exonerated by Science: Case Studies in the Use of DNA Evidence to Establish Innocence After Trial," June 1996, p. 20.

2. John Grisham, *The Innocent* (New York: Doubleday, 2006).

3. Barry Scheck, Peter Neufeld, and Jim Dwyer, *Actual Innocence* (New York: Doubleday, 2000).

4. See http://www.chron.com/disp/story.mpl/front/3472872.html.

5. See http://www.chicagotribune.com/services/newspaper/printedition/friday/friday/chi-tx-1-story,0,4226884.htmlstory.

6. See GeneWatch UK, "Police Retention of DNA: A briefing for Members of the Scottish Parliament," Feb. 2006 (available at www.genewatch.org/uploads/f03c6d66a9b354535738483c1c3d49e4/MSPbriefpolicendnadfinal.rtf) (offering that matches to suspects rise from 26 percent to 40 percent when crime scene DNA is collected).

7. Mike Martindale, "DNA Used to Crack 72 Metro Cold Cases," *Detroit News*, June 19, 2007.

8. Patrick Dunne, "DNA Test Helps Solve 26-Year-Old Case," Gazette.net, 23 July 23, 2008.

9. *Douglas S. Arey v. State*, CA No. 82, Sept. term 2006. Reported. Opinion by J. Raker. Filed August 1, 2007.

10. Melisa Harris, "DNA Search Delayed," *Baltimore Sun*, April 18, 2008.

11. *Gideon v. Wainwright*, 372 U.S. 335 (1963).

12. ABA Standing Committee on Legal Aid and Indigent Defendants, *Gideon's Broken Promise: America's Continuing Quest for Equal Justice* (2004).

13. Franklin E. Zimring, *The Contradictions of American Capital Punishment* (New York: Oxford University Press, 2003).

14. Maryland poll regarding the death penalty, conducted by Gonzalez Research & Marketing Strategies (March 2007).

15. Maurice Possley et al., "Scandal Touches Even Elite Labs: Flawed Work, Resistance to Scrutiny Seen Across U.S.," *Chicago Tribune*, October 21, 2004, p. 1.

16. See Michael J. Saks and Jonathan J. Koehler, "The Coming Paradigm Shift in Forensic Identification Science," *Science* 309 (2005): fig. 1, 892 (reviewing 86 DNA exoneration cases and noting "Percentages exceed 100% because more than one factor was found in many cases").

17. Samuel R. Gross et al., "Exonerations in the United States: 1989 through 2003," *Journal of Criminal Law and Criminology* 95 (2005): 543.

18. For example, in a comprehensive review of the first 200 convictions overturned with DNA evidence, 113 cases (57%) involved introduction of forensic evidence at trial, with serological analysis of blood or semen the most common (79 cases), followed by expert comparison of hair evidence (43 cases), soil comparison (5 cases), DNA tests (3 cases), bite mark evidence (3 cases), fingerprint evidence (2 cases), dog scent identification (2 cases), spectrographic voice evidence (1 case), shoe prints (1 case), and fiber comparison (1 case). Brandon L. Garrett, "Judging Innocence," *Columbia Law Review* 108 (2008): 81.

CHAPTER 28: THE PERSISTENT PROBLEM OF RACIAL DISPARITIES IN THE FEDERAL DEATH PENALTY

1. In *Furman v. Georgia*, 408 U.S. 238, 241 (1972), the Supreme Court held the Georgia statutory death penalty unconstitutional. Four years later, in 1976, the Court upheld the constitutionality of Georgia's substantially revised statute. *Gregg v. Georgia*, 428 U.S. 153, 187 (1976). The "modern death penalty era" is used throughout this paper to refer to those cases prosecuted after Furman under revised death penalty statutes.

2. See *United States v. Quinones*, 205 F. Supp. 2d 256, 266 n.13 (S.D.N.Y. 2002), reversed on other grounds, 313 F.3d 49 (2d Cir. 2002) ("[A]s the government concedes, at least one of the 31 federal death row inmates, David Ronald Chandler, had a colorable claim of actual innocence, but his sentence was commuted by President Clinton . . . [and] seemingly prompted by serious doubts about Chandler's guilt").

3. See Marcia Coyle, "Federal Death Penalty Stalls," *National Law Journal* (April 30, 2007). ("There is no question that the Bush administration has been more aggressive than prior administrations in pursuing federal death sentences. And there is no question that the federal death row has been growing because of that effort even as state death rows decline.")

4. See Death Penalty Information Center (DPIC), Federal Death Row Prisoners (April 11, 2007), available at http://www.deathpenaltyinfo.org/article.php?scid=29&did=193 [hereinafter DPIC]; see also, *Roane v. Gonzales*, No. 1:05-CV-2337 (RWR) (D.D.C. Feb. 27, 2006) (order granting motion for preliminary injunction barring execution of James Roane Jr., Richard Tipton, and Cory Johnson).

5. See DPIC; *Roane v. Gonzales*, Case No. 1:05-CV-2337 (RWR) (D.D.C. Feb. 21, 2007) (order granting motion for preliminary injection barring execution of Bruce Webster).

6. *Roane v. Gonzales*, No. 1:05-CV-2337 (RWR) (D.D.C. June 11, 2007) (order granting motion for preliminary injunction barring scheduling of execution dates for Anthony Battle and Orlando Hall).

7. See DPIC.

8. See US Department of Justice, "The Federal Death Penalty System, A Statistical Survey" (September 12, 2000), pp. 34–35, available at http://www.usdoj.gov/dag/pubdoc/dpsurvey.html.

9. Attorney General Janet Reno established the Death Penalty Review Committee in 1995. See Rory K. Little, "The Federal Death Penalty: History and Some Thoughts about the Department of Justice's Role," *Fordham Urban Law Journal* 26 (1999): 409–10. US Attorneys submit cases that they have charged as capital-eligible crimes to the Review Committee, which in turn makes advisory recommendations to the attorney general about whether the government should seek the death penalty. The attorney general appoints the committee members, usually senior attorneys within the Department of Justice.

10. See ibid., p. 487 (quoting Kenneth Culp Davis, "the power to be lenient is the power to discriminate").

11. See US Department of Justice, "The Federal Death Penalty System: Supplementary Data, Analysis and Revised Protocols for Capital Case Review" (June 6, 2001), pp. 14–15 (hereinafter DOJ 2001 report) available at http://www.usdoj.gov/dag/pubdoc/deathpenaltystudy.htm.

12. Ibid.

13. See, e.g., Stephanie Hindson, Hillary Potter, and Michael Radelet, "Race, Gender, Region and Death Sentencing in Colorado, 1980–1999," *University of Colorado Law Review* 77: 549 (finding that the death penalty is sought at significantly higher rates for white victims than black victims); Michael J. Songer, Isaac Unah, "The Effect of Race, Gender, and Location on Prosecutorial Decisions to Seek the Death Penalty in South Carolina," *South Carolina Law Review* 58 (2006): 288 (finding that prosecutors in South Carolina were 3.5 times more likely to seek the death penalty if the victim was white and the defendant black than in any other combination, a statistically significant finding); Isaac Unah and John Charles Boger, "Preliminary Report of the Findings of the North Carolina Death Penalty Study 2001" (2001), available at http://www.unc.edu/~iunah/prelim_rpt_nc_dpp.pdf (concluding that the race of the victim was statistically significant in predicting who will receive the death sentence in North Carolina); US General Accounting Office, "Death Penalty Sentencing: Research Indicates Pattern of Racial Disparateness" (1990) (GAO report concluding that race of the victim was "found to

influence the likelihood of being charged with capital murder or receiving the death penalty" and noting that this "finding was remarkably consistent across data sets, states, data collection methods, and analytic techniques."); see also David C. Baldus and George Woodworth, "Race Discrimination in the Administration of the Death Penalty: An Overview of the Empirical Evidence with Special Emphasis on the Post-1990 Research," *Criminal Law Bulletin* 41, no. 2 (April 2005): 6 (reviewing studies, including the Baldus study of Georgia discussed in *McKleskey v. Kemp*, 481 U.S. 279 [1987]).

14. Failure to submit cases for consideration may mask additional racial disparities by removing from scrutiny the potentially discriminatory decisions by United States Attorneys whether to charge a particular case with a federal, death-eligible crime.

15. The Attorney General's Review Committee first reviews submitted cases, but its recommendations are not binding on the attorney general's decision. See Little, "The Federal Death Penalty: History and Some Thoughts about the Department of Justice's Role," pp. 409–10.

16. Scholars sometimes refer to the rate at which the attorney general authorizes cases as the "seek rate." For example, if an attorney general reviewed 100 cases and authorized 50 cases, that would constitute a 50 percent seek rate.

17. See appendix B.

18. Attorney General Reno authorized the death penalty in 66 of the 185 cases with white victims, a seek rate of 36 percent, compared with 83 of the 415 cases with no white victim, a seek rate of 20 percent. This difference in the seek rates is 16 percent and is statistically significant. See appendix B.

19. In 2006, the RAND Corporation released a study of the federal death penalty in which it concluded that the observed racial disparities disappear after adjusting for case characteristics, including aggravating factors. See Stephen Klein, Richard Berk, and Laura Hickman, "Race and the Decision to Seek the Death Penalty in Federal Cases" (2006), pp. iii, xvii, available at www.ncjrs.gov/pdffiles1/nij/grants/214730.pdf. This study was limited to cases during Attorney General Janet Reno's term, and its methodology has been heavily criticized. See, e.g., Professor David Baldus, "Review of 'Race and the Decision to Seek the Death Penalty in Federal Cases,'" submitted February 19, 2006 (criticizing, inter alia, the study's methodology for analyzing race). See also Stephen B. Bright et al., "The Death Penalty in the Twenty-First Century," *American University Law Review* 45 (1995): 341 (GAO statistician Dr. Harriet Ganson explaining that the conclusion by lead researcher Steven Klein that no disparities were observed in a similar study of California's death row was inconsistent with the data).

20. Attorney General Ashcroft authorized the death penalty in 52 of the

164 cases with white victims, a seek rate of 32 percent, compared with 86 of the 459 cases with no white victim, a seek rate of 19 percent. The difference in the seek rates based on the race of the victim is 13 percent and is statistically significant. See appendix B.

21. Attorney General Gonzales authorized the death penalty in 28 of the 67 cases with white victims, a seek rate of 42 percent, compared with 43 out of the 261 cases with no white victim, a seek rate of 16 percent. The difference in these seek rates is 25 percent and is statistically significant. The seek rate difference for Attorney General Gonzales between cases with white victims and cases with no white victims is significantly higher than the seek rate differences for Attorneys General Reno and Ashcroft.

22. See appendix B.

23. An additional three individuals initially received sentences of death but subsequently received life sentences, either through new sentencing hearings or commutation. Two of these individuals are white and one is Asian American. See DPIC, Federal Death Row Prisoners (April 11, 2007); appendix A.

24. Sixty-one percent of all individuals sentenced to death under the modern federal death penalty have been people of color. See appendix A, compiled with information from DPIC, Federal Death Row Prisoners (April 11, 2007).

25. Ibid.

26. See US Department of Justice, "The Federal Death Penalty System, A Statistical Survey," p. 36 n. 28 (reporting the percentages of state defendants awaiting execution in 1998 by race: white, 55 percent; black, 43 percent; other, 2 percent). See also DPIC (2007), available at http://www.death penaltyinfo.org/article.php?scid=5&did=184#inmaterace (reporting the percentage of state defendants awaiting execution as of 2007 by race: white, 45 percent; black, 42 percent; Latino, 11 percent; other, 2 percent). Compare appendix A (reporting the percentage of federal death row defendants as of 2007 by race: white, 39 percent; black, 50 percent; Latino, 9 percent; Native Americans, 2 percent).

27. See Kevin McNally, "Race and the Federal Death Penalty: A Nonexistent Problem Gets Worse," *DePaul Law Review* 53 (2004): 1615.

28. Ibid.

29. See, e.g., National Institute of Justice, "Strategic Planning Meeting on Research Involving the Federal Death Penalty System, Summary of Proceedings" (January 10, 2001), pp. 2–3 ("[Participant researchers] noted that research focusing on cases within Federal jurisdiction should draw upon all potential capital cases coming to Federal prosecutors, not just those submitted for death penalty review. . . . [A]n ideal study would include decision making at every juncture in the case process leading to a death sentence [and]

. . . all State and Federal capital-eligible cases should be combined for analysis in order to more fully understand whether race/ethnicity is a neutral factor"). These issues were not addressed by the 2006 RAND study. Congress should also request the release of the RAND data so that it may be examined by outside statisticians.

30. Ky. Rev. Stat. Ann. § 532.300 (West 2006).

31. Ibid.

32. See Erwin Chemerinsky, "Eliminating Discrimination in Administering the Death Penalty: The Need for the Racial Justice Act," *Santa Clara Law Review* 35 (1995): 519–20, 525–27 (comparing the goals and methods of proof in the proposed federal Racial Justice Act with those in the 1964 Civil Rights Act); but cf. *McCleskey v. Kemp*, 481 U.S. 279, 306, 313 (1987) (holding that statistical proof is inadequate to prove a constitutional violation of race discrimination in capital cases).

33. This data is from the RAND study. See "Race and the Decision to Seek the Death Penalty in Federal Cases."

34. The data for this section of the data is from information collected by the Federal Death Penalty Resource Counsel.

35. Ibid. This information includes all cases through May 10, 2007.

CHAPTER 30: LOOKING DEATHWORTHY: PERCEIVED STEREOTYPICALITY OF BLACK DEFENDANTS PREDICTS CAPITAL-SENTENCING OUTCOMES

1. D. C. Baldus, C. A. Pulaski, and G. Woodworth, "Comparative Review of Death Sentences: An Empirical Study of the Georgia Experience," *Journal of Criminal Law and Criminology* 74 (1983): 661–753; D. C. Baldus, G. Woodworth, and C. A. Pulaski, "Monitoring and Evaluating Contemporary Death Sentencing Systems: Lessons from Georgia" *U.C. Davis Law Review* 18 (1985): 1375–1407; D. C. Baldus, G. Woodworth, and C. A. Pulaski, *Equal Justice and the Death Penalty: A Legal and Empirical Analysis* (Boston: Northeastern University Press, 1990); D. C. Baldus, G. Woodworth, and C. A. Pulaski, "Reflections on the 'Inevitability' of Racial Discrimination in Capital Sentencing and the 'Impossibility' of Its Prevention, Detection, and Correction," *Washington and Lee Law Review* 51 (1994): 359–419; D. C. Baldus, G. Woodworth, D. Zuckerman, N. A. Weiner, and B. Broffitt, "Racial Discrimination and the Death Penalty in the Post-Furman Era: An Empirical and Legal Overview, with Recent Findings

from Philadelphia," *Cornell Law Review* 83 (1998): 1638–770; W. J. Bowers, G. L. Pierce, and J. F. McDevitt, *Legal Homicide: Death as Punishment in America, 1864–1982* (Boston: Northeastern University Press, 1984); S. R. Gross and R. Mauro, *Death and Discrimination: Racial Disparities in Capital Sentencing* (Boston: Northeastern University Press, 1989); M. L. Radelet, "Racial Characteristics and the Imposition of the Death Penalty," *American Sociological Review* 46 (1981): 918–27; US General Accounting Office (GAO), *Death Penalty Sentencing: Research Indicates Pattern of Racial Disparities* (Washington, DC: Author, 1990).

2. US GAO, *Death Penalty Sentencing*, p. 5.

3. D. C. Baldus et al., "Racial Discrimination and the Death Penalty in the Post-Furman Era."

4. Ibid.

5. I. V. Blair, C. M. Judd, and J. L. Fallman, 2004. "The Automaticity of Race and Afrocentric Facial Features in Social Judgments," *Journal of Personality and Social Psychology* 87 (2004): 763–78; I. V. Blair, C. M. Judd, M. S. Sadler, and C. Jenkins, "The Role of Afrocentric Features in Person Perception: Judging by Features and Categories," *Journal of Personality and Social Psychology* 83 (2002): 5–25; J. L. Eberhardt, P. A. Goff, V. J. Purdie, and P. G. Davies, "Seeing Black: Race, Crime, and Visual Processing," *Journal of Personality and Social Psychology* 87 (2004): 876–93; K. B. Maddox, "Perspectives on Racial Phenotypicality Bias," *Personality and Social Psychology Review* 8 (2004): 383–401; K. B. Maddox and S. A. Gray, "Cognitive Representations of Black Americans: Reexploring the Role of Skin Tone," *Personality and Social Psychology Bulletin* 28 (2002): 250–59; K. B. Maddox and S. A. Gray, "Manipulating Subcategory Salience: Exploring the Link between Skin Tone and Social Perception of Blacks," *European Journal of Social Psychology* 34 (2004): 533–46.

6. Eberhardt et al., "Seeing Black."

7. I. V. Blair, C. M. Judd, and K. M. Chapleau, "The Influence of Afrocentric Facial Features in Criminal Sentencing," *Psychological Science* 15 (2004): 674–79.

8. Compiled by Baldus et al., "Racial Discrimination and the Death Penalty in the Post-Furman Era."

9. Baldus et al., "Racial Discrimination and the Death Penalty in the Post-Furman Era"; D. Landy and E. Aronson, "The Influence of the Character of the Criminal and His Victim on the Decisions of Simulated Jurors," *Journal of Experimental Social Psychology* 5 (1969): 141–52; J. E. Stewart, "Defendant's Attractiveness as a Factor in the Outcome of Criminal Trials: An Observational Study," *Journal of Applied Social Psychology* 10 (1980): 348–61.

10. With the exception of defendant's attractiveness, all of the covariates employed here were included in the Baldus database and have been described in detail elsewhere (e.g., see Baldus et al., "Racial Discrimination and the Death Penalty in the Post-Furman Era"). We added defendant's attractiveness, basing this variable on forty-two naive participants' ratings of the defendants' faces using a scale from 1 (not at all attractive) to 11 (extremely attractive).

11. Faces of fifteen of the black defendants who murdered white victims were repeated in this session. Analysis of the ratings confirmed interrater reliability.

12. D. A. Prentice and D. T. Miller, eds., *Cultural Divides: Understanding and Overcoming Group Conflict* (New York: Russell Sage Foundation, 1999).

13. Ibid.

14. Eberhardt et al., "Seeing Black."

CONTRIBUTORS

SAMUEL ALITO, associate justice, United States Supreme Court.

SUSAN A. BANDES, Distinguished Research Professor, DePaul University College of Law.

VINCE BEISER is an award-winning journalist based in Los Angeles.

VIVIAN BERGER, Nash Professor of Law Emerita, Columbia University School of Law.

DOUGLAS A. BERMAN, William B. Saxbe Designated Professor of Law, Moritz College of Law, Ohio State University.

WALTER BERNS, professor emeritus, Georgetown University.

STEPHANOS BIBAS, professor, University of Pennsylvania Law School.

STEPHEN BREYER, associate justice, United States Supreme Court.

MAHUA DAS, a practicing attorney in Calcutta, India, and a commentator on human rights and women's issues.

PAUL G. DAVIES, assistant professor of social psychology, University of British Columbia.

W. E. B. DU BOIS (1868–1963), American civil rights activist and author.

JENNIFER L. EBERHARDT, associate professor of psychology, Stanford University.

MEGAN FELDMAN, staff writer, *Dallas Observer*.

RUTH GINSBURG, associate justice, United States Supreme Court.

DAVID GRANN, author and staff writer at the *New Yorker*.

HEATHER GRAY, producer of "Just Peace" on WRFG-Atlanta 89.3 FM, covering local, regional, national, and international news.

MARCI HAMILTON, Crane Senior Research Fellow, Program in Law and Public Affairs, Princeton University.

SHERI LYNN JOHNSON, professor, Cornell School of Law, and assistant director of the Cornell Death Penalty Project.

ANTHONY KENNEDY, associate justice, United States Supreme Court.

ALISON J. NATHAN, Alexander Fellow, New York University School of Law.

VALERIE J. PURDIE-VAUGHNS, assistant professor of psychology, Yale University.

JOHN ROBERTS, chief justice, United States Supreme Court.

GREGG SANGILLO, reporter for the *National Journal* and *CongressDaily*.

ANTONIN SCALIA, associate justice, United States Supreme Court.

BARRY C. SCHECK, attorney and cofounder and director of the Innocence Project.

DAVID SOUTER, associate justice, United States Supreme Court.

COLIN STARGER, acting assistant professor of lawyering, New York University School of Law.

JOHN PAUL STEVENS, associate justice, United States Supreme Court.

CLARENCE THOMAS, associate justice, United States Supreme Court.

LAWRENCE H. TRIBE, professor of constitutional law, and Carl M. Loeb University Professor, Harvard Law School.

SOURCES AND PERMISSIONS

Minor style changes and corrections of inadvertent grammatical slips have been made in the reprinted text of the original sources.

I. HISTORY OF THE DEATH PENALTY

© 2009. Death Penalty Information Center. Reprinted courtesy of the Death Penalty Information Center.

2. DEATH SENTENCES AND EXECUTIONS IN 2008: SUMMARY REPORT

Reprinted courtesy of Amnesty International USA from a March 23, 2009, Amnesty International press release.

3. NUMBER OF EXECUTIONS AS OF MAY 20, 2011, BY STATE SINCE 1976

From http://www.deathpenaltyinfo.org/number-executions-state-and-region-1976. Reprinted courtesy of the Death Penalty Information Center.

4. THE MORALITY OF ANGER

Originally published in *For Capital Punishment: Crime and the Morality of the Death Penalty* (Lanham, MD: University Press of America, 1991).
    Reprinted by permission of the University Press of America.

5. EXECUTION IS INHERENTLY INHUMANE, UNFAIRLY APPLIED, AND INEFFECTIVE IN DETERRING CRIME

From *Hinduism Today*, October/November/December 2006. Reprinted courtesy of *Hinduism Today*.

6. TRIAL BY FIRE: DID TEXAS EXECUTE AN INNOCENT MAN?

© 2002 by David Grann. Originally published in the *New Yorker*, September 7, 2009. Reprinted by permission of the author.

7. A GUILTY MAN [AND THE HISTORY OF LETHAL INJECTION]

Originally appeared in *Mother Jones*, September/October 2005. Reprinted courtesy of the author.

8. *BAZE*-D AND CONFUSED: WHAT'S THE DEAL WITH LETHAL INJECTION? A DEBATE

Originally published in the *University of Pennsylvania Law Review PENNumbra* 156 (2008): 312, 315–16, http://pennumbra.com/debates/pdfs/lethalinjection.pdf. Reprinted by permission of the *University of Pennsylvania Law Review*.

17. THE SUPREME COURT IS WRONG ON THE DEATH PENALTY

Originally published in the *Wall Street Journal*, July 31, 2008. Reprinted courtesy of the author.

18. THE DEATH PENALTY: UNWISE FOR CHILD RAPE

Reprinted with permission from the *National Law Journal*, January 21, 2008.

19. THE ARGUMENTS IN FAVOR OF, AND AGAINST, THE DEATH PENALTY FOR CHILD RAPE

This column first appeared on www.findlaw.com as one of Professor Hamilton's bimonthly columns. It is reprinted by kind permission of Professor Marci Hamilton.

20. ENGAGING CAPITAL EMOTIONS

Originally published in the *Northwestern University Law Review* 102 (2008): 355–64. Reprinted by special permission of Northwestern School of Law, *Northwestern University Law Review.*

21. CHILD RAPE, MORAL OUTRAGE, AND THE DEATH PENALTY

Originally published in the *Northwestern University Law Review* 103 (2008): 17–28. Reprinted by special permission of Northwestern School of Law, *Northwestern University Law Review.*

22. THE KIRK BLOODSWORTH STORY

Reprinted with permission of the Justice Project.

23. LIFE AFTER DNA EXONERATION

Originally published in the *Dallas Observer*, February 6, 2008. Reprinted with permission of the author and the *Dallas Observer*.

24. DEATH AND INNOCENCE: CAPITAL PUNISHMENT IS ON THE DECLINE, LARGELY BECAUSE OF DNA TESTING AND ITS RAMIFICATIONS FOR THE LEGAL SYSTEM

Reprinted with permission from the *National Journal*, April 28, 2007. Copyright 2010 by National Journal Group, Inc. All rights reserved.

25. DEATH AND HARMLESS ERROR: A RHETORICAL RESPONSE TO JUDGING INNOCENCE

Originally published in the *Columbia Law Review*, February 2008. Reprinted by permission of the *Columbia Law Review*.

26. TESTIMONY OF BARRY C. SCHECK BEFORE THE MARYLAND COMMISSION ON CAPITAL PUNISHMENT

Testimony given before the Maryland Commission on Capital Punishment, September 5, 2008.

27. OF THE COMING OF JOHN

Originally published as chapter 13 of *The Souls of Black Folk* by DuBois (1903).

28. THE PERSISTENT PROBLEM OF RACIAL DISPARITIES IN THE FEDERAL DEATH PENALTY

A report of the American Civil Liberties Union, June 25, 2007. Copyright American Civil Liberties Union Foundation. Reprinted with permission.

29. GEORGIA'S RACIST DEATH PENALTY

© *CounterPunch*, January 2, 2008. All rights reserved. Reprinted with permission.

30. LOOKING DEATHWORTHY: PERCEIVED STEREOTYPICALITY OF BLACK DEFENDANTS PREDICTS CAPITAL-SENTENCING OUTCOMES

Reprinted with permission from Cornell Law Faculty Publications. Paper 41. http://scholarship.law.cornell.edu/lsrp_papers/41.